THE
APOSTOLIC
FATHERS

THE
APOSTOLIC
FATHERS

·· *Second Edition* ··

Translated by
J. B. Lightfoot *and* J. R. Harmer

· · ·

Edited and Revised by
Michael W. Holmes

BAKER BOOK HOUSE
Grand Rapids, Michigan 49516

Copyright 1989 by
Baker Book House Company

First edition published in London
by Macmillan and Company in 1891,
reprinted by Baker Book House in 1956.

Library of Congress Cataloging-in-Publication Data

Apostolic Fathers (Early Christian collection). English.
    The apostolic Fathers / J.B. Lightfoot and J.R. Harmer,
translators ; edited and revised by Michael W. Holmes.—2nd ed.
        p.   cm.
    Translation from the Greek.
    Includes indexes.
    ISBN 0-8010-5655-1
    1. Christian literature, Early—Greek authors.   I. Lightfoot,
Joseph Barber, 1828–1889. II. Harmer, J. R. (John Reginald), b.
1857.   III. Holmes, Michael William.   IV. Title.
BR60.A62   1989
270.1—dc20   89-35173
                                                            CIP

Contents

Preface

Joseph Barber Lightfoot (1828–1889), sometime Hulsean and Lady Margaret Professor of Divinity at the University of Cambridge and later Bishop of Durham, is widely recognized as one of the greatest New Testament and patristic scholars England has ever produced. He was a scholar of unrivaled erudition, clarity of insight, and sobriety of judgment (an assessment with which on the Continent no less a scholar than Adolf von Harnack concurred). As renowned as he is for his biblical commentaries, whose luster the passing of a century has scarcely diminished, it is his work on the apostolic fathers which must be reckoned as his most enduring contribution. His treatment of Ignatius, for example, continues to represent, in the estimation of William R. Schoedel (a distinguished commentator in his own right), an inescapable point of departure for all work on the Antiochian bishop.

With regard to the apostolic fathers, it is his massive, learned, and lucid five-volume magnum opus on Clement of Rome, Ignatius of Antioch, and Polycarp of Smyrna for which he is best known: *The Apostolic Fathers, Part I: S. Clement of Rome*[1] and *Part II: S. Ignatius. S. Polycarp.*[2] Two years after his death J. R. Harmer, a younger colleague, edited and published the Greek and Latin texts of the apostolic fathers together with an English translation in one volume.[3] The translations were taken from notes found among Lightfoot's papers or from the larger edition. The texts of Clement, Ignatius, Polycarp, and the *Didache* were also taken from the larger edition, while Harmer contributed the

1. 2 vols. (London: Macmillan, 1869; 2d ed., 1890).
2. 3 vols. (London: Macmillan, 1885; 2d ed., 1889).
3. J. B. Lightfoot and J. R. Harmer, eds., *The Apostolic Fathers. Revised Greek Texts with Introductions and English Translations* (London: Macmillan, 1891; repr. Grand Rapids: Baker, 1984).

vii

texts of the *Epistle of Barnabas,* the *Shepherd of Hermas,* and the *Epistle to Diognetus.* In 1956 another one-volume work[4] containing English translations with brief introductions by Lightfoot appeared.

The latter volume is the basis for the following revised translation of the *Apostolic Fathers.* Of all Lightfoot's work, it is the translation which has suffered most severely from the passage of time, not the least reason being changes in English style and usage, particularly during the last half-century. As a consequence, while the underlying basis of the translation remains sound, not a few readers have found the translation itself more difficult and off-putting than helpful. Thus a revision of the translation is needed if it is to continue to serve the future as well as it has the past. Moreover, the task of revision afforded an opportunity to take into account new discoveries and insights that have enhanced our understanding of Hellenistic Greek and Greco-Roman culture during the last century.

In revising Lightfoot's translation changes generally have been made only as they seemed to be required by considerations of clarity, readability, and contemporary (American) English usage. Occasionally the revised translation reflects an interpretation of the underlying text that differs significantly from Lightfoot's, in which case his is retained in a note. In addition new introductions have been supplied for each of the individual documents, as well as a general introduction to the collection as a whole. The biblical references have for the most part been taken from Lightfoot's other works, and all have been checked against the sources. All other notes have been newly composed for this revision.

The textual basis of this revision is the collection of texts edited by Lightfoot and Harmer in their one-volume Greek-English edition. Here too changes have been made as the evidence seemed to require, particularly in those instances where new witnesses to the text have come to light. Whenever a different reading than that followed by Lightfoot or Harmer has been adopted, his will be found in a note, together with a list of

---

4. J. B. Lightfoot, *The Apostolic Fathers.* Edited and completed by J. R. Harmer (Grand Rapids: Baker, 1956).

the supporting witnesses.[5] The chapter and verse divisions follow the usage of the standard editions.

A number of obligations have been incurred in the course of revision, and it is gratifying to have an opportunity to acknowledge them. I would like to thank first of all the regents and administration of Bethel College and Seminary for granting a sabbatical leave of absence during which I was able to complete the revision. I would also like to express my appreciation to Luther Northwestern Theological Seminary, where I spent the sabbatical, for granting visiting scholar status and providing not only congenial accommodations but also a lively and stimulating atmosphere in which to work. The library staffs at Bethel College, particularly Mrs. Judy Schwarze in the interlibrary loan department, and Luther Northwestern were very helpful in obtaining otherwise inaccessible materials. The purchase of some needed reference tools was facilitated by grants from the Professional Development Committee at the college. Dr. Joseph Alexanian of Trinity College (Deerfield, Ill.) kindly reviewed the translation of the Armenian fragments of Papias (he bears, however, no responsibility for the final form in which they appear). A series of departmental secretaries, including Mrs. Elsie Hoffman, Mrs. Sherry Borstad, and Mrs. Mary Duffee, worked on various parts of the manuscript with admirable skill and patience. Then there have been the students in my "After the Apostles" course, especially the class of 1987, which was the first to read some of these translations in draft form; their interest and curiosity have been a source of continuing encouragement.

Finally, I would like to acknowledge a debt of a different order and magnitude by dedicating this volume to my teachers, especially Bruce M. Metzger of Princeton Theological Seminary, Walter L. Liefeld and Murray J. Harris of Trinity Evangelical Divinity School, and R. J. "Quince" Adams, formerly of the University of California at Santa Barbara. Their instruction and example extended far beyond the classroom, and for that I will always be grateful.

MICHAEL W. HOLMES
January 1989

5. Textual notes are also provided in certain other specific instances as well; see below, p. xv.

List of Abbreviations
and Short Titles

BIBLICAL BOOKS

Gen.

Exod.

Lev.

Num.

Deut.

Josh.

Judg.

Ruth

1–2 Sam.

1–2 Kings

1–2 Chron.

Ezra

Neh.

Esther

Job

Ps(s).

Prov.

Eccles.

Song of Sol.

Isa.

Jer.

Lam.

Ezek.

Dan.

Hos.

Joel

Amos

Obad.

Jon.

Mic.

Nah.

Hab.

Zeph.

Hag.

Zech.

Mal.

Matt.

Mark

Luke

John

Acts

Rom.

1–2 Cor.

Gal.

Eph.

Phil.

Col.

1–2 Thess.

1–2 Tim.

Titus

Philem.

Heb.

James

1–2 Pet.

1–2–3 John

Jude

Rev.

APOSTOLIC FATHERS

1 Clem. *1 Clement*

2 Clem. *2 Clement*

Ign. *Eph.* Ignatius, *to the Ephesians*

Magn. *Magnesians*

Trall. *Trallians*

Rom.	*Romans*
Phld.	*Philadelphians*
Smyrn.	*Smyrnaeans*
Pol.	*Polycarp*
Pol. Phil.	Polycarp, *to the Philippians*
Mart. Pol.	*Martyrdom of Polycarp*
Did.	*Didache*
Barn.	*Epistle of Barnabas*
Herm. Man.	*Shepherd of Hermas, Mandate*
Sim.	*Similitude*
Vis.	*Vision*
Diogn.	*Epistle to Diognetus*
Pap. Frag.	*Fragments of Papias*

SHORT TITLES AND OTHER ABBREVIATIONS

BAGD	W. Bauer, W. F. Arndt, F. W. Gingrich, and F. W. Danker. *A Greek-English Lexicon of the New Testament and Other Early Christian Literature.* 2d ed. Chicago: University of Chicago Press, 1979.
ca.	about
cf.	compare
Kraft, *Barnabas and the Didache*	R. A. Kraft. *Barnabas and the Didache.* The Apostolic Fathers, vol. 3. New York: Nelson, 1965.
Lightfoot, *AF*	J. B. Lightfoot. *The Apostolic Fathers, Part I: S. Clement of Rome.* 2d ed., 2 vols.; *Part II: S. Ignatius. S. Polycarp.* 2d ed., 3 vols. London: Macmillan, 1890, 1889; repr. Grand Rapids: Baker, 1981.
Lightfoot, *Apostolic Fathers*	J. B. Lightfoot. *The Apostolic Fathers.* Edited and completed by J. R. Harmer. London: Macmillan, 1891; repr. Grand Rapids: Baker, 1956. [Eng. trans. only]
Lightfoot, *Essays*	J. B. Lightfoot. *Essays on the Work Entitled Supernatural Religion.* London: Macmillan, 1889.
LXX	The Septuagint, the oldest Greek translation of the Hebrew Bible (the Old Testament).

Richardson,
Fathers

C. C. Richardson, ed. *Early Christian Fathers.* Philadelphia: Westminster, 1953; repr. New York: Macmillan, 1970.

Schoedel,
Ignatius

W. R. Schoedel. *Ignatius of Antioch. A Commentary on the Letters of Ignatius of Antioch.* Philadelphia: Fortress, 1985.

Schoedel,
Polycarp

W. R. Schoedel. *Polycarp, Martyrdom of Polycarp, Papias.* The Apostolic Fathers, vol. 5. Camden, N.J.: Nelson, 1967.

Note to the Reader

The reader's attention is directed to two distinctive features of this translation of the *Apostolic Fathers*.

First, contrary to common practice, outlines and chapter, section, and/or paragraph headings have not been provided. The former tend to be either ignored or plagiarized, while the latter too often create a misleading impression of a document's character, purpose, and even genre. In addition, from a pedagogical perspective it is well known that one who reads with pen or pencil in hand generally understands more of what is read than one who reads more passively. These seemed to be good and sufficient grounds, therefore, for omitting outlines and headings and instead encouraging readers to provide their own.

Second, those readers who utilize or consult more than one translation will soon note that the various English translations often differ, sometimes considerably, from one another. There are basically two reasons for these differences: either the translators are offering different renderings or interpretations of the same text, or they are translating different texts. Since not a few theologically or historically significant passages in the *Apostolic Fathers* remain the subject of intense discussion (see e.g., *1 Clem.* 44.2–3), some readers may wish to know if differences at a particular point are interpretive or textual in origin.

To accommodate these readers, textual notes have been given whenever one or more of a select group of English translations[1] followed a different textual reading than that adopted by the present revision. This means that the absence of a textual note signals that a difference between translations is interpretive in nature rather than textual. Exceptions to this guideline are the final chapters (107–14) of the *Shepherd of Hermas*,

---

1. Those by Lightfoot, Lake, Glimm et al., Goodspeed, Richardson et al., and Grant et al; see the bibliography at the end of the introduction for details.

where it proved to be impractical to note all the variations, which in any case are relatively inconsequential, and the *Fragments of Papias*, which are all derived from the texts of other authors and thus have no independent textual basis.

Introduction

The term *apostolic fathers* is traditionally used to designate the collection of the earliest extant Christian writings outside the New Testament. These documents are a primary resource for the study of early Christianity, especially the postapostolic period (ca. A.D. 70–135). They provide significant and often unparalleled glimpses of and insights into the life of Christians and the Christian movement during a critical transitional stage in its history.

It was a time, for example, when problems could no longer be solved by seeking an authoritative answer from an apostle. As a consequence, the church had to begin to deal with the question of sources of authority and authoritative tradition at a time when new challenges and pressures, both internal and external, were confronting the new religious movement in increasingly forceful terms. Moreover, key developments in the process leading to the formation of catholic Christianity, such as the emergence of the monepiscopal or "single bishop" system of church governance and the *regula fidei*, or "rule of faith," have their roots in this period. Thus this is clearly a crucial moment in the history of a movement that would in the space of barely two centuries conquer the Roman Empire, and the apostolic fathers are crucial witnesses to it.

The writers of these documents—many of whom unfortunately remain anonymous—constitute a diverse and fascinating group. Too often, however, they have been treated unjustly by those who have studied them. It is true that they are not particularly distinguished as writers.[1] But beyond this they

---

1. Cf. Lightfoot's estimation: "Their style is loose; there is a want of arrangement in their topics and an absence of system in their teaching. On the one hand they present a marked contrast to the depth and clearness of conception with which the several Apostolic writers place before us different aspects

have frequently been severely criticized, for example, for falling away from the purity or high level of the apostolic faith, or for institutionalizing or otherwise restricting the freedom of the gospel. Leaving aside the unwarranted tone of moralizing superiority evident in such criticism, it may, in view of the history of scholarship, be seriously doubted whether those making such criticisms are any more free of these faults than those whom they are criticizing. In any case, it is often a matter of unfairly censuring the writers for not doing or being something they never intended to do or to be in the first place.

Taken on their own terms and in the context of their own times, these writers prove to be engaging characters. They are real people struggling to deal with various opportunities, problems, and crises as best they can. There is, as Lightfoot observes, the "gentleness and serenity of Clement," whose spirit, "absorbed in contemplating the harmonies of nature and of grace," overflows with pastoral concern; the "fiery zeal" of Ignatius, in whom the passionate desire for martyrdom overwhelms all other concerns; the enduring faithfulness of Polycarp, whose entire eighty-six-year life "is spent in maintaining the faith once delivered to the saints"; the "moral earnestness and the simple fervour" of the *Shepherd of Hermas* and the *Didache;* and the "intensity of conviction" and righteous indignation of the *Epistle to Diognetus,* which "contrasts the helpless isolation and the universal sovereignty of the Christian."[2] Even in the *Epistle of Barnabas,* which Lightfoot thought was "overlaid by a rigid and extravagant" allegorical interpretation of Scripture, one "cannot fail to recognise a very genuine underlying faith," and the same must surely be said of Papias, in spite of the fact that the surviving fragments of his work "do not leave a favourable impression of his theological depth."[3] In short, for all their differences and disagreements, they share a deep and genuine devotion to Jesus. As Lightfoot aptly puts it:

---

of the Gospel. . . . On the other they lack the scientific spirit which distinguished the fathers of the fourth and fifth centuries, and enabled them to formulate the doctrines of the faith as a bulwark against lawless speculation" (*AF* 1.1.7).

2. Ibid. 1.1.7–8.

3. Ibid. 1.1.8.

There is a breadth of moral sympathy, an earnest sense of personal responsibility, a fervour of Christian devotion, which are the noblest testimony to the influence of the Gospel on characters obviously very diverse, and will always command for their writings a respect wholly disproportionate to their literary merits.[4]

THE COLLECTION

Although the term *apostolic fathers* seems to have been used as early as the sixth century by Severus, the Monophysite patriarch of Antioch, its modern significance dates to 1672, when French scholar J. B. Cotelier published two volumes entitled *SS. Patrum qui temporibus apostolicis floruerunt . . . opera . . . vera et suppositicia.* He included among the works he attributed to these "holy fathers who were active in apostolic times" the recently (re)discovered writings of Barnabas, Clement of Rome, Hermas, Ignatius of Antioch, and Polycarp of Smyrna. A. Gallandi expanded the collection to include the *Epistle to Diognetus*, the *Fragments of Papias*, and Quadratus in 1765. The last widely accepted addition was the *Didache*, following its discovery in 1873. Despite occasional calls either to enlarge or reduce[5] the bounds of the collection, the preceding list of works has become the de facto canon of apostolic fathers. The present edition differs from it only in that it does not give separate treatment to Quadratus.[6]

The form of the collection as it exists today, therefore, is largely a matter of tradition and somewhat arbitrary. It pos-

---

4. Ibid. 1.1.7.

5. E. J. Goodspeed (*The Apostolic Fathers: An American Translation* [New York: Harper and Bros., 1950]) included the *Doctrina*, now known only in a Latin form, which he believed to be the source of the "Two Ways" document now incorporated into both the *Didache* (chaps. 1–5) and the *Epistle of Barnabas* (chaps. 18–20). R. M. Grant, on the other hand, excluded the *Epistle to Diognetus* from the series he edited (*The Apostolic Fathers. A New Translation and Commentary*, 6 vols. [New York and Camden: Nelson, 1964–1968]) because it belongs more appropriately with the apologetic literature of the later second century.

6. The extant fragment of his work is given in full, however, in the introduction to the *Epistle to Diognetus*; see pp. 291–94 below.

sesses no particular unity or coherence with regard to chronology, theological orientation, or literary genre. Rather than attempting to impose an extrinsic or artificial unity upon the collection, it is preferable to accept the lack of coherence for what it is: eloquent testimony to the vigorous diversity characteristic of early Christianity at this time in history. In this way the documents can be appreciated for what they are—evidence of the actual issues and concerns with which early Christian believers struggled in their efforts to integrate faith and life—rather than devalued for something they are not.

THE HISTORICAL SETTING

In order to understand the apostolic fathers it is helpful to have some sense of the historical context within which the documents were written. The following brief sketch outlines the main trends and developments during the postapostolic period and beyond.

Christianity at the End of the Apostolic Period

By the end of Nero's reign (A.D. 68) Christianity had spread throughout much of the eastern Mediterranean region, largely as a consequence of ongoing evangelistic efforts on the part of the faithful. The church at Antioch, where some of the first Gentile evangelization occurred, was a leader in this respect, and teams commissioned by the congregation there had by A.D. 55 established daughter congregations throughout Galatia, western Asia Minor, and several key cities in Greece, including Philippi, Thessalonica, and Corinth. It is quite improbable that Antioch was the only congregation involved in this type of activity, and it appears that by 55 to 65 other teams of itinerant merchants and travelers had penetrated Cappadocia, Bithynia, and Pontus to the north and were working eastward through Syria toward Edessa. To the south the excellent communication, travel, and trade between Alexandria and the rest of Egypt make it unlikely that Christianity was still unknown in the

Nile Valley outside of Alexandria. What had begun in Jerusalem as just another Jewish sect among many was by around A.D. 65 a common part of the urban scene in many Greek cities.

New converts were increasingly pagan and Gentile in background, although Jewish Christians apparently continued to have access to the synagogues which were to be found in nearly every city. The Roman government generally exhibited a relatively benign attitude toward the church, largely because of its Jewish roots, though it was just beginning to differentiate between Judaism and its offspring.

Along with growth came new needs and problems, and these in turn gave rise to new answers and solutions. Different forms of internal organization (congregational, presbyterian, and episcopal) were being tried, and channels of communication between congregations, which facilitated the exchange of aid and advice, were coming into existence. Congregations enjoyed the benefits (and sometimes the tensions) of being ministered to by both resident pastors and itinerant apostles and prophets. Hymns and spiritual songs took their place alongside the Scriptures (especially the Psalms) in worship, for which Sunday had become the firmly established day, and rudimentary liturgical forms and creeds (the earliest of which was "Jesus is Lord") were being written. These hymns, forms, and creeds contributed to and in turn became a part of the church's still developing and steadily clearer sense of self-identity and understanding. In addition, the church now possessed several documents explicating the substance and implications of its beliefs, largely because of the efforts of Paul of Tarsus and his predecessors and colleagues. In sum, to borrow a phrase from the author of the Acts of the Apostles, it could still be said that "so the churches were strengthened in the faith, and increased in numbers daily" (Acts 16:5).

This happy scene was not to last, however. Between A.D. 64 and 70 the consequences of two events (the fire in Rome and the fall of Jerusalem) and the culmination of a trend (the dying off of the apostles and other key leaders of the early church) would interact to confront a new generation of leaders with a quite different set of challenges and circumstances from those faced by their predecessors.

Jewish-Christian Relations (70–135)

The boundaries of this period are provided by two important dates in Jewish history: the repeated destruction of Jerusalem during the first (66–74) and second (132–135) Jewish revolts against Rome. Though Christians participated in neither, both (the first more directly than the second) affected the church and its future, and therefore merit a closer look.

Though the first revolt lasted until the fall of Masada in A.D. 74, the key event was the destruction of the temple in 70 by the Roman general Titus. He put down the rebellion hoping that the loss of the temple would contribute to the extermination of both Jews and Christians. While his hope went unrealized, his impact was in some respects greater than he might have anticipated.

In response to the loss of the temple, Judaism underwent a major reformulation. The temple as a focal point for the faith was replaced by the synagogue and an academy at Jamnia (Yavneh), and scholarly rabbis like Johanan ben Zakkai and Akiba eventually replaced the priests as key leaders of the people. Of all the various strands and varieties of Judaism that existed before the revolt, only the Pharisaic branch appears to have survived the ensuing turmoil, and it did so largely by transforming itself into rabbinic Judaism. The reformulation included a purge of sectarian tendencies, especially those thought to be responsible for starting the war. Further, the dividing line between Jew and non-Jew was more sharply defined; for example, the twelfth of the "Eighteen Benedictions," the oldest part of the synagogue service, was reworded to exclude sectarians and heretics, including Christians: "For the renegades let there be no hope, and may . . . the Nazarenes and heretics perish as in a moment; may they be blotted out of the book of life and not enrolled with the righteous. . . . "[7] At the same time evangelistic efforts directed toward outsiders continued apace; Josephus, the Jewish historian, wrote at least in part to commend the Jewish faith to his fellow Roman citizens.

---

7. The full text can be found in C. K. Barrett, *The New Testament Background: Selected Documents* (New York: Macmillan, 1957), 167; rev. ed. (San Francisco: Harper and Row, 1989), 211.

The eventual effect of the reworded Twelfth Benediction on the church was gradually to close off access to the synagogue on the part of Jewish Christians, which increased the distance and sharpened the distinction—and the hostility—between the synagogue and the church. Each thought that it was the true Israel, and consequently that the other had fallen away from God. Classic statements of this perspective from the Christian side include Justin Martyr's *Dialogue with Trypho*, a Jewish rabbi, and the anonymous *Epistle of Barnabas*, likely written from Alexandria between 70 and 130. Among other things the latter writer collects a number of scriptural prophecies that allegedly prove that the Jews missed their opportunity due to ignorance and disobedience and were rejected and replaced as God's people by the Christians. The bitterness of this intramural fight, however, goes beyond theological differences; anti-Semitism, a not uncommon feature of Greco-Roman culture, was on occasion to be found within the church as well.

The second revolt of 132–135, led by messianic aspirant Simon Bar Kochba, marks the beginning of the end of this overtly hostile phase of Jewish-Christian relations. After Hadrian succeeded in putting down the revolt he leveled and rebuilt Jerusalem (now called Aelia Capitolina) and forbade Jews from entering. One consequence was that many Jews increasingly isolated themselves from non-Jewish people and culture and heightened the social barriers between themselves and the rest of society. Thus there arose a sense of increasing distance between the two movements at a time when each was being more and more distracted by other pressing concerns, and the open hostility began to fade. The levels of suspicion and hostility remained high, however, and though individuals from each side might establish contact (Origen and Jerome would learn Hebrew from rabbinic instructors), Judaism and Christianity would not be on good terms for centuries to come.

Though less noticed at the time, the gradual closure of the synagogue to Christians also meant the loss of an important source of learned converts for the church. From this point on the intellectual focus of the church would shift increasingly toward the Greek philosophical tradition from which a growing percentage of the more intellectually inclined converts was being drawn. This laid the basis for a Jewish reform movement to eventually express its most fundamental tenets in terms drawn primarily from Greek philosophy.

Internal Developments (70–135)

The fall of Jerusalem roughly coincided with the acceleration of another trend: the death of first-generation Christian leaders. Together this meant for the church at large the loss of its stabilizing center or foundation. Whereas it had once been possible to settle disagreements by calling an apostolic council in Jerusalem or seeking the guidance of a recognized figure such as James or Paul, the church now experienced the loss of authority figures of sufficient stature to arbitrate disputes or establish points of doctrine or practice.

One consequence of this was the flourishing of diversity within the church. We may imagine a spectrum ranging from those who still considered Christianity to be a reform group within Judaism to others who regarded it as some sort of new mystery cult, with nearly every imaginable position in between occupied by various groups, all of whom considered themselves to be legitimate expressions of authentic Christianity. And who was to say they were not? For while there was emerging an increasingly clear sense of an essential center or core of beliefs, and certain extremes like docetism and extreme libertinism were, when recognized, rejected, beyond this the boundaries between "authentic" and "inauthentic" expressions of the faith were still being explored and drawn. The concept of a normative Christianity was only beginning to emerge during this time, and when it did, it did so in terms that reflect the motto on the great seal of the United States, *e pluribus unum*: "out of many, one." The apostles, as it were, had defined the center; it fell to later generations to attempt to define the boundaries.

Signs of an emerging normative Christianity and indications that the vacuum left by the death of the apostles would not remain empty for long may be seen in subsequent developments regarding written sources of authority and in church structure. To replace the oral testimony of eyewitnesses of the life and resurrection of Jesus there came into existence within a decade or so on either side of A.D. 70 written accounts, or gospels, recounting his life and ministry. In addition there began to be formed partial collections of apostolic letters as churches exchanged copies of whatever documents happened to be available to them, and a history of the early church (the Acts of the Apostles) was composed. Because these writings were considered to be authoritative witnesses to Jesus, to whom also the Scriptures (i.e., what came to be known as the Old Testament) testified, the new writings were soon put on the same level as the others; we find references at this time to the "Scriptures, the Gospel, and the Apostle" (i.e., the Old Testament, Gospels, and Epistles) being used in worship services. In short, the apostles and other leaders were in some respects replaced by collections of written documents derived from them, though there was as yet no concern to determine the contents or boundaries of these varying collections.

There was also during this time a trend toward centralization and standardization of church structures. The surviving sources are not clear as to the precise rate and scope of the change, but the initial steps in that direction are evident during this period, particularly in the letters of Ignatius. Whereas most Pauline churches were supervised by a twofold structure consisting of elders/overseers ("bishops") and deacons, we find in the Ignatian churches a threefold structure consisting of one bishop under whom served elders and deacons. For Ignatius, the bishop was constitutive of the church; no valid eucharist or baptism could be held in his absence, and he was to be obeyed as though he were God himself. Clearly there is a move here toward a structure in which the bishop at least partially fills the vacuum left by the apostles. (Claims that these bishops and their predecessors could be traced back in an unbroken chain to the apostles themselves apparently represent later after-the-fact efforts to justify the new development in church organization that these monarchical bishops represent.) The change was not everywhere welcomed, and old ways died hard; the fact that the *Didache* warns against despising the residential leaders (bishops and deacons) in favor of the more prestigious traveling apostles and prophets reveals a certain resistance to this new organizational model. It was, however, the wave of the future.

The *Didache* itself, a manual providing guidance on how to conduct various church activities such as baptism (the preferred mode was immersion, although pouring water over the head was also acceptable in a pinch) or the Lord's Supper (appropriate prayers for the bread and the cup are provided), is an example of another way the church grappled, usually successfully, with the challenges presented by the new circumstances in which it found itself.

Expansion, both internal and geographical, continued throughout this time, though occasional warnings against "lukewarmness" hint that it was not always at the same intense pace or with the same enthusiasm as earlier (see the *Shepherd of Hermas*). Christianity was strongest in Asia; much of the work there and in Bithynia and Cappadocia appears to have concentrated on filling in the gaps between earlier missionary efforts. Further to the east the faith followed the caravan routes past Edessa into Adiabene, beyond the Euphrates, where it was established by about 100. In Egypt some form of Christianity had likely spread beyond the Fayyum, perhaps as far as Oxyrhynchus. Congregations could also be found at Nicopolis, on the western side of Greece, and in and around Rome and Puteoli in Italy; if others existed west or north at this time they have left no certain trace of their existence.

Lack of evidence frustrates efforts to ascertain much about the social or economic circumstances and outlook of these congregations, beyond the observation that Christianity remained overwhelmingly urban in its make-up. The conversion of philosophers such as Justin Martyr indicates the faith's growing attractiveness to intellectuals; the popularity of various apocryphal gospels and acts testifies to another quite different level of intellectual interest or attainment. Beyond this little is known.

Church and State (70–160)

As Christianity emerged from the shadow of the synagogue it became increasingly visible to the rest of Greco-Roman society, which in general was not impressed with what it saw. Indeed, the earliest documented instance in which the Roman government distinguished between Jew and Christian is quite a bloody one. Nero, needing a scapegoat for the disastrous fire in Rome in

64, which he was widely rumored to have set, blamed the Christians, members of an "extremely pernicious superstition," in the words of a later Roman historian who recounted the event.[8] Many were put to death in the arena, while others were burned to provide illumination for the shows. Tradition has it that Peter and Paul were among Nero's victims at this time.

This outbreak of persecution did not establish an absolute precedent for dealing with Christians (persecution would remain local and sporadic, rather than empirewide and systematic, until 250), but Nero's action and the attitude toward the new religion reflected in the historian's remarks did set a tone for relations between church, state, and society that would continue for over two centuries. Pliny, the governor of Bithynia in 112, for example, found it necessary to write to the emperor Trajan for advice on how to deal with some believers who had been brought to his attention. While the surviving correspondence reveals no evidence of laws directed specifically against Christians, Pliny nonetheless knew without asking that Christians meant trouble.

For their part the Christians tried to follow the guidance of 1 Peter 2 and Romans 13 and live as good citizens. This advice is echoed in *1 Clement*, which, among other matters, exhorts believers to fulfill their social obligations according to a standard that is little different from the accepted mores of Greco-Roman society and includes an extensive prayer on behalf of the Roman government.

When this proved insufficient, however, and the government demanded of the church an allegiance it could give only to its Lord, the church for the most part refused to cooperate. To the Romans, who viewed religion as essentially a public matter whose primary function was to serve and protect the interests of the state and the empire, the refusal to acknowledge the emperor as lord and offer a sacrifice to him was treason, and the Christians were atheists who deserved the death penalty. The *Martyrdom of Polycarp* sets forth the issues and consequences

8. Tacitus, *Annals* 15.44, in C. K. Barrett, *The New Testament Background: Selected Documents* (New York: Macmillan, 1957), 15–16; rev. ed. (San Francisco: Harper and Row, 1989), 15–16.

in classic form: asked to "swear by the Genius of Caesar," Polycarp refused and was executed. He was only one of the first of many believers to whom martyrdom for the sake of their Lord was preferable to apostasy.

Throughout the postapostolic period, then, we find the emerging Christian movement struggling to define itself vis-à-vis its Jewish roots and, increasingly, vis-à-vis the Greco-Roman culture and society into which it was expanding. Moreover, a central aspect of this struggle involved the tension between continuity and change: how to maintain and propagate the tradition received from Jesus and his followers in the midst of rapidly changing circumstances and in the face of new and often unanticipated challenges. When read in light of this particular historical context, it is possible to appreciate the writings of the apostolic fathers for what they are: the stories and records of real people trying to "keep the faith" to the best of their abilities and gifts. In this respect surely they have something in common with believers and the church throughout history.

THE IMPACT OF THE APOSTOLIC FATHERS
ON THE STUDY OF THE EARLY CHURCH

Prior to the nineteenth century the apostolic fathers had almost no impact upon the study of the early church. Eusebius, an early church historian, made good use of many of them, but his was an isolated example. Very rarely are any of them (primarily Ignatius) mentioned in the doctrinal controversies of the fourth and fifth centuries.[9] From about the fifth to the sixteenth centuries these documents were virtually unknown, especially in the West.[10] The rediscovery and publication between 1633 and 1645 of *1* and *2 Clement*, the *Epistle of Barnabas*, and the letters of Polycarp and Ignatius (in their genuine form) meant that they were once again the common property of

9. Lightfoot, *AF* 1.1.11.

10. Cf. R. M. Grant, "The Apostolic Fathers' First Thousand Years," *Church History* 31 (1962):421–29; repr. *Church History* supp. (1988):20–28.

theologians and historians. This was a time, however, of intense doctrinal controversy, usually carried out along denominational lines, and the use of these documents was largely restricted to the buttressing of positions already arrived at on other grounds. Moreover, there remained some question as to their authenticity, since they were still closely associated with a large number of spurious documents bearing similar titles or claiming the same authorship.

The mid-nineteenth century witnessed a fundamental change in this state of affairs. In Germany D. F. Strauss, F. C. Baur,[11] and a small group of associates known as the "Tübingen School"[12] developed a fundamentally different paradigm for understanding the history of early Christianity. Utilizing a Hegelian dialectic and taking his cue from 1 Corinthians 1 and the disagreement between Peter and Paul recorded in Galatians 2, Baur argued that the history of the early church is best understood in terms of a struggle or conflict between the Petrine (Jewish) and Pauline (Gentile) factions within the church. Furthermore, in his opinion this conflict continued unabated well into the middle of the second century, and the synthesis or resolution of the struggle, out of which arose the Catholic Church, was achieved only at the very end of that century. Having constructed this chronological framework, Baur then used it to date the New Testament and other early Christian writings. Those which betrayed some evidence of the struggle, such as 1 and 2 Corinthians, Romans, and Galatians, were obviously very early, while those which showed no trace of the conflict (such as John, Mark, or the Pastorals) or portrayed Peter and Paul as cooperating, as the Book of Acts does, must be late and inauthentic. Since *1 Clement* and the letters of Ignatius fall into this second category, Baur argued that they were forgeries composed during the time of Pope Victor (189–198).

It was in this context that Theodor Zahn and J. B. Lightfoot published their ground-breaking studies of Ignatius and Clem-

---

11. Professor at Tübingen from 1826 until his death in 1860.

12. For a history of this influential group, see H. Harris, *The Tübingen School* (Oxford: Clarendon, 1975).

ent.[13] Like Baur, Lightfoot was convinced of the necessity of dealing with the New Testament, not in isolation as was the usual practice, but in relation to the entire corpus of early Christian writings. The most important works were those alleged to be by Clement of Rome and Ignatius of Antioch, representing two of the four major centers of Christianity at the time; as Baur himself recognized, his entire reconstruction was built upon the inauthenticity of these documents. By establishing the authenticity and dates of *1 Clement* and Ignatius's letters, almost beyond questioning,[14] Zahn and especially Lightfoot demolished the foundation upon which Baur's chronology rested and put in its place a set of reference points which continue to serve as the fundamental framework for the study of this period. In short, it is the apostolic fathers who have provided an Archimedean point for the study of early Christian literature, especially the New Testament.[15]

In the twentieth century Walter Bauer, the renowned lexicographer, published a ground-breaking study that devoted extensive attention to the apostolic fathers.[16] Surveying the early church region by region, he argued that in many places the earliest discernible form of Christianity was often a form that later came to be labeled as heresy. As he developed his thesis he relied extensively upon evidence drawn from the apostolic fathers, offering thought-provoking and occasionally original interpretations of points long viewed as settled. Overall it has been an extremely influential book. Although at many points

13. T. Zahn, *Ignatius von Antiochien* (Gotha: Perthes, 1873), to which Lightfoot assigned "a distinct place in the train of influences which led to my change of opinion" (*AF* 2.1.x; his own exegetical notes, however, had already been written some years before); J. B. Lightfoot, *The Apostolic Fathers, Part I: S. Clement of Rome* (London: Macmillan, 1869; 2d ed., 1890); *Part II: S. Ignatius. S. Polycarp* (London: Macmillan, 1885; 2d ed., 1889).

14. For recent challenges, see the introductions to each below.

15. An excellent account of Strauss, Baur, and Lightfoot, told with considerable verve, wit, and insight, is given by Stephen Neill and Tom Wright, *The Interpretation of the New Testament 1861–1986* (Oxford and New York: Oxford University Press, 1988), 1–64.

16. W. Bauer, *Rechtgläubigkeit und Ketzerei in ältesten Christentum* (Tübingen: Mohr/Siebeck, 1934; 2d ed., with additions by G. Strecker, 1964); Eng. trans.: *Orthodoxy and Heresy in Earliest Christianity* (Philadelphia: Fortress, 1971).

his conclusions have required modification or even rejection in light of further research and new evidence, especially archaeological discoveries,[17] he nevertheless succeeded in raising what are still fundamental questions for any historian of the early church and has forcefully reminded New Testament scholars, as Lightfoot did in his day, of the fundamental significance of the apostolic fathers for the study of the New Testament.

Recent years have witnessed an upsurge of interest in the writings of the apostolic fathers, not only in terms of books devoted specifically to them, but also in terms of books that deal with early Christian literature and history as a whole rather than limiting attention only to the canonical writings and the apostolic period. Noteworthy examples of the latter category include *Antioch and Rome: New Testament Cradles of Catholic Christianity*,[18] which seeks to survey the history of two key Christian communities through the time of Ignatius and Clement of Rome, and *The Churches the Apostles Left Behind*.[19] H. Koester, who devotes the second volume of his *Introduction to the New Testament*[20] to the history and literature of early Christianity, places the New Testament writings in the larger context of the apostolic fathers as well as Gnostic and apocryphal documents. In addition to an increasing number of monographs and technical studies devoted to the apostolic fathers, at least two major English New Testament commentary series[21] are also devoting volumes to these important writings.[22]

17. See, for a recent example, Tom Robinson, *The Bauer Thesis Examined: The Geography of Heresy in the Early Christian Church* (Lewiston, N.Y.: Edwin Mellen, 1988).

18. R. E. Brown and J. P. Meier, *Antioch and Rome: New Testament Cradles of Catholic Christianity* (Mahwah, N.J.: Paulist, 1983).

19. R. E. Brown, *The Churches the Apostles Left Behind* (Mahwah, N.J.: Paulist, 1984).

20. H. Koester, *Introduction to the New Testament*, 2 vols. (Berlin and New York/Philadelphia: De Gruyter/Fortress, 1982).

21. The Hermenia series plans to publish individual volumes on each of the major writers, of which W. R. Schoedel's *Ignatius of Antioch* (Philadelphia: Fortress, 1985) was the first to appear. It is reported that the *New International Greek New Testament Commentary* plans to issue two volumes covering the apostolic fathers.

22. In this they are following a precedent firmly established by Hans Lietzmann in his *Handbuch zum Neuen Testament*.

SELECT BIBLIOGRAPHY

In addition to the items mentioned in the bibliographies at the end of the introductions to the individual writings, the following works may be consulted.

TEXTS AND TRANSLATIONS

Texts

Bihlmeyer, Karl. *Die Apostolischen Väter: Neubearbeitung der Funkschen Ausgabe.* Erster teil: *Didache, Barnabas, Klemens I und II, Ignatius, Polykarp, Papias, Quadratus, Diognetbrief.* 3d ed. by Wilhelm Schneemelcher. Tübingen: Mohr/Siebeck, 1970.

Whittaker, Molly. *Der Hirt des Hermas.* 2d ed. Berlin: Akademie-Verlag, 1967.

Texts with Translations

Lake, Kirsopp. *The Apostolic Fathers.* Loeb Classical Library. 2 vols. London/Cambridge, Mass.: Heinemann/Harvard University Press, 1912–1913.

Lightfoot, J. B., and J. R. Harmer. *The Apostolic Fathers. Revised Greek Texts with Introductions and English Translations.* London: Macmillan, 1891; repr. Grand Rapids: Baker, 1984.

English Translations

Glimm, F. X., J. M. F. Marique, and G. G. Walsh. *The Apostolic Fathers.* The Fathers of the Church, vol. 1. Washington, D.C.: Catholic University of America Press, 1947.

Goodspeed, E. J. *The Apostolic Fathers. An American Translation.* New York: Harper and Bros., 1950.

Richardson, Cyril C., E. R. Fairweather, E. R. Hardy, and M. H. Shepherd. *Early Christian Fathers.* Philadelphia: Westminster, 1953; repr. Macmillan, 1970. [Does not include the *Epistle of Barnabas,* the *Shepherd of Hermas,* or the *Fragments of Papias.*]

Sparks, Jack. *The Apostolic Fathers.* Nashville/New York: Nelson, 1978.

Staniforth, Maxwell. *Early Christian Writings.* Rev. ed. New York: Penguin, 1987. [Includes only *1 Clement,* the letters of Ignatius and Polycarp, the *Martyrdom of Polycarp,* the *Epistle to Diognetus,* the *Epistle of Barnabas,* and the *Didache.*]

Translation with Commentary

Grant, R. M., ed. *The Apostolic Fathers. A New Translation and Commentary*. 6 vols. New York/Camden, N.J.: Nelson, 1964–1968.

GUIDES TO EARLY CHRISTIAN LITERATURE

Altaner, B. *Patrology*. Translated by H. C. Graef. New York: Herder and Herder, 1961.

Altaner, B., and A. Stuiber. *Patrologie*. 9th ed. Freiburg: Herder and Herder, 1980.

Goodspeed, E. J. *A History of Early Christian Literature*. Rev. ed. Chicago: University of Chicago Press, 1966.

Quasten, J. *Patrology*. 3 vols. Westminster, Md.: Newman, 1951–1960.

COLLECTIONS OF OTHER EARLY CHRISTIAN LITERATURE

New Testament Apocrypha

Hennecke, E., and W. Schneemelcher, eds. *New Testament Apocrypha*. 2 vols. Philadelphia: Westminster, 1963, 1965.

James, M. R. *The Apocryphal New Testament*. Oxford: Clarendon, 1924.

Gnostic Writings

Layton, Bentley. *The Gnostic Scriptures: A New Translation with Annotations and Introductions*. Garden City, N.Y.: Doubleday, 1987.

Robinson, James M., ed. *The Nag Hammadi Library*. Rev. ed. San Francisco: Harper and Row, 1988.

Odes of Solomon

Charlesworth, J. H., trans. and ed. "Odes of Solomon." In *The Old Testament Pseudepigrapha*, edited by J. H. Charlesworth, 2:725–71. 2 vols. Garden City, N.Y.: Doubleday, 1983, 1985.

HISTORY OF THE JEWS AND JUDAISM

Cohen, Shaye J. D. *From the Maccabees to the Mishnah*. Philadelphia: Westminster, 1987.

Nickelsburg, G. W. E., and M. E. Stone. *Faith and Piety in Early Judaism. Texts and Documents.* Philadelphia: Fortress, 1983.

Stone, M. E. *Scriptures, Sects, and Visions: A Profile of Judaism from Ezra to the Jewish Revolts.* Philadelphia: Fortress, 1980.

History of the Early Church

Chadwick, Henry. *The Early Church.* Baltimore: Penguin, 1967.

Davies, J. G. *The Early Christian Church.* London: Weidenfeld and Nicolson, 1965. Repr. Grand Rapids: Baker, 1980.

Frend, W. H. C. *The Early Church.* London: SCM, 1982.

———. *The Rise of Christianity.* Philadelphia: Fortress, 1984.

Eusebius. *Ecclesiastical History.* Translated by Roy J. Deferrari. 2 vols. New York: Fathers of the Church, 1953, 1955.

Grant, R. M. *Augustus to Constantine. The Thrust of the Christian Movement into the Roman World.* New York: Harper and Row, 1970.

Harnack, A. *The Mission and Expansion of Christianity in the First Three Centuries.* Translated and edited by J. Moffat. 2d rev. ed. London/New York: Williams and Norgate/Putnam, 1908.

Jedin, H., and J. Dolan, eds. *History of the Church.* Vol. 1, *From the Apostolic Community to Constantine,* by K. Baus. New York: Herder and Herder, 1965.

Walsh, Michael. *The Triumph of the Meek. Why Early Christianity Succeeded.* San Francisco: Harper and Row, 1986.

Early Christian Archaeology

Snyder, Graydon F. *Ante Pacem. Archaeological Evidence of Church Life Before Constantine.* Macon, Ga.: Mercer University Press, 1985.

Early Christian Doctrine and Practice

Daniélou, J. *A History of Early Christian Doctrine Before the Council of Nicaea.* Translated by J. A. Baker and D. Smith. 3 vols. London/

Philadelphia: Darton, Longman, and Todd/Westminster, 1964, 1973, 1977.

Davies, J. G. *Daily Life in the Early Church*. London: Lutterworth, 1952. [= *Daily Life of Early Christians*. New York: Duell, Sloan and Pearce, 1953]

Ferguson, E. *Early Christians Speak. Faith and Life in the First Three Centuries*. Austin, Tex.: Sweet, 1971.

González, J. L. *A History of Christian Thought*. Vol. 1, *From the Beginnings to the Council of Chalcedon*. Nashville: Abingdon, 1970.

Kelly, J. N. D. *Early Christian Creeds*. 3d ed. London: Longman, 1972.

———. *Early Christian Doctrines*. 5th ed. London: A. and C. Black, 1977.

GENERAL WORKS ON THE APOSTOLIC FATHERS AND RELATED TOPICS

Barnard, L. W. *Studies in the Apostolic Fathers and Their Background*. New York: Schocken, 1966.

Bauer, W. *Orthodoxy and Heresy in Earliest Christianity*. Edited by R. A. Kraft and G. Krodel. Philadelphia: Fortress, 1971.

Benko, Stephen. *Pagan Rome and the Early Christians*. Bloomington, Ind.: Indiana University Press, 1984.

Brown, R. E. *The Churches the Apostles Left Behind*. Mahwah, N.J.: Paulist, 1984.

Brown, R. E., and J. P. Meier. *Antioch and Rome*. Mahwah, N.J.: Paulist, 1983.

Campenhausen, H. von. *Ecclesiastical Authority and Spiritual Power in the Church of the First Three Centuries*. Translated by J. A. Baker. Stanford, Calif.: Stanford University Press, 1969.

———. *The Formation of the Christian Bible*. Translated by J. A. Baker. Philadelphia: Fortress, 1972.

———. *Tradition and Life in the Church: Essays and Lectures in Church History*. Translated by A. V. Littledale. Philadelphia: Fortress, 1968.

Ehrhardt, A. A. T. *The Apostolic Succession in the First Two Centuries of the Church*. London: Lutterworth, 1953.

Ferguson, Everett. *Backgrounds of Early Christianity*. Grand Rapids: Eerdmans, 1987.

Fox, Robin Lane. *Pagans and Christians*. New York: Alfred A. Knopf, 1987.

Frend, W. H. C. *Martyrdom and Persecution in the Early Church: A Study of a Conflict from the Maccabees to Donatus*. Garden City, N.Y.: Doubleday, 1967.

Grant, R. M. *After the New Testament*. Philadelphia: Fortress, 1967.

———. *The Apostolic Fathers. A New Translation and Commentary*. Vol. 1, *An Introduction*. New York: Nelson, 1964.

———. *Early Christianity and Society*. New York: Harper and Row, 1977.

Koester, H. *Introduction to the New Testament*. Vol. 1, *History, Culture, and Religion of the Hellenistic Age*. Vol. 2, *History and Literature of Early Christianity*. Philadelphia: Fortress, 1982.

Lawson, John. *A Theological and Historical Introduction to the Apostolic Fathers*. New York: Macmillan, 1961.

MacMullen, R. *Christianizing the Roman Empire*. New Haven: Yale University Press, 1984.

Nock, A. D. *Conversion: The Old and New in Religion from Alexander the Great to Augustine of Hippo*. New York/London: Oxford, 1933.

Perkins, P. *The Gnostic Dialogue: The Early Church and the Crisis of Gnosticism*. Mahwah, N.J.: Paulist, 1980.

Roberts, C. H. *Manuscript, Society and Belief in Early Christian Egypt*. New York/London: Oxford, 1979.

Sanders, E. P., ed. *Jewish and Christian Self-Definition*. Vol. 1, *The Shaping of Christianity in the Second and Third Centuries*. Philadelphia: Fortress, 1980.

Turner, H. E. W. *The Pattern of Christian Truth: A Study in the Relations Between Orthodoxy and Heresy in the Early Church*. London: Mowbray, 1954.

Bibliographic Guides

Collins, J. J., et al., eds. *New Testament Abstracts*, vols. 1ff. Cambridge, Mass.: Weston School of Theology, 1956–

Geerard, M., ed. *Clavis Patrum Graecorum*. Vol. 1, *Patres Antenicaeni*. Turnhout: Brepols, 1983.

Halton, T. P., and R. D. Sider. "A Decade of Patristic Scholarship 1970–1979." *Classical World* 76 (Nov.–Dec. 1982): 65–93.

Nober, P., and R. North, eds. *Elenchus Bibliographicus Biblicus*, vol. 49ff. Rome: Biblical Institute Press, 1968–   .

Schneemelcher, W., et al., eds. *Bibliographia Patristica. Internationale Patristische Bibliographie*, vol. 1 (1956) ff. Berlin/New York: De Gruyter, 1959–   .

Schoedel, William R. "The Apostolic Fathers." In *The New Testament and Its Modern Interpreters*, edited by E. J. Epp and G. W. MacRae, 457–98. Atlanta: Scholars, 1989.

The Letter of the Romans
to the Corinthians
(1 Clement)

INTRODUCTION

The letter from the Christians in Rome to their fellow believers in Corinth known as *1 Clement* is one of the earliest—if not the earliest—extant Christian documents outside the New Testament. Written in Rome around the time that John was composing the Book of Revelation on the island of Patmos, it reveals something of both the circumstances and attitudes of the Roman Christians, circumstances and attitudes that differ dramatically from those of their Christian sisters and brothers in Asia Minor to whom Revelation was addressed. Whereas in Revelation Rome is presented as the great harlot whose attacks upon the church must be resisted (to the point of death, if necessary), in *1 Clement* one finds a much more positive view of the Roman government (cf. the prayer in 60.4–61), and the elements of peace, harmony, and order that are so important to the author(s) of this letter reflect some of the fundamental values of Roman society. Thus it provides important evidence of the diverse and creative ways in which Christians sought to come to terms with the Greco-Roman culture and society within which the church was so rapidly expanding.

Occasion

The same kind of factiousness that Paul had earlier encountered in Corinth apparently flared up once again in that congregation near the end of the first century. Though details regarding the exact cause or motivation are not clear, it appears that

23

some of the younger men in the congregation had provoked a revolt (this is the Roman point of view; the younger men no doubt defended their action in more positive terms) and succeeded in deposing the established leadership of the church (3.3; 44.6; 47.6). When news of this reached Rome (47.7), the leaders of the congregation there were sufficiently distressed by this breach of proper conduct and order and the damage it inflicted upon the good name of the Corinthian congregation (1.1; cf. 39.1), that they wrote this long letter and even dispatched mediators (63.3; 65.1) in an effort to restore peace and order to the Corinthian congregation.

Authorship

While the letter, which was sent on behalf of the whole church (see the subscription), does not name its writer, well-attested ancient tradition identifies it as the work of Clement,[1] though precisely who he is is not clear. Tradition also identifies him as the third bishop of Rome after Peter, but this is unlikely because the office of monarchical bishop, in the sense intended by this later tradition, does not appear to have existed in Rome at this time. Leadership seems to have been entrusted to a group of presbyters or bishops (the two appear to be synonymous in *1 Clement*; see 44.1–6), among whom Clement almost certainly was a (if not the) leading figure. It is possible that the *Shepherd of Hermas* (Vis. 2.4.3) speaks of this same person, in which case Clement would have served as the corresponding secretary for the Roman church. Lightfoot[2] offers the attractive hypothesis that Clement was a freedman of the household of the emperor's cousin, the consul Titus Flavius Clemens, who according to one ancient historian was executed on the charge of atheism—a frequent accusation made against Christians. The attempt by Origen[3] to identify him with the Clement mentioned in Philippians 4:3 is an unlikely conjecture at best.

---

1. Cf. Eusebius, *Church History* 4.23.11.
2. *AF* 1.1.25–61.
3. Origen, *Commentary on John* 6.36; cf. Eusebius, *Church History* 3.15.1.

Date

There is widespread agreement in dating this letter about A.D. 95 or 96, in the last year of the emperor Domitian or the first of his successor, Nerva.[4] Several considerations support this conclusion.

At the time of writing, the church in Rome appears to be facing some sort of persecution; in fact, the letter to Corinth has been delayed because of it (1.1; cf. 7.1). Based on what is known of the course of early persecutions, this suggests either the last years of Nero (A.D. 64–68) or the date given above. The former date, however, appears to be ruled out by two points: (1) in chapters 5 and 6 the Neronian persecution, which according to tradition included Peter and Paul among its victims, is an event of the past; and (2) the reference to those "who from youth to old age have lived blameless lives among us" (63.3) would seem to require a date subsequent to the late 60s. At the same time, the observation that some of the leaders appointed by the apostles are still living (44.3–5) rules out any date much beyond the turn of the century. Finally, what external evidence there is (chiefly references in Hegesippus and Irenaeus) is consistent with a date of 95 or 96.

Reception of the Letter

Although it is not known how the Corinthians reacted to this letter,[5] later Christian writers held it in high regard. It was quoted frequently, and Clement of Alexandria cites it as Scripture. It was even made part of some copies of the New Testament. In the important biblical manuscript known as Codex Alexandrinus (copied in the fifth c.) *1 Clement* (together with *2 Clement*) stands immediately after Revelation, and in a Syrian manuscript of the New Testament dating from the twelfth century the two letters are found right after the catholic Epistles

4. Dissenting opinions have been registered by J. A. T. Robinson (*Redating the New Testament* [Philadelphia: Westminster, 1976], 327–35), who argues for A.D 70; A. E. Wilhelm-Hooijbergh ("A Different View of Clemens Romanus," *Heythrop Journal* 16 [1975]: 266–88), who dates it a year earlier; and L. L. Welborn, "On the Date of First Clement," *Biblical Research* 29 (1984): 35–54.

5. Cf., however, the introduction to 2 *Clement* below.

(which is how *1 Clement* is explicitly described) and before the Pauline letters.[6] The late fourth-century Syrian work, the *Apostolic Canons*, lists both *1* and *2 Clement* as part of the New Testament,[7] and at about the same time in Alexandria Didymus the Blind appears to have counted *1 Clement* as part of his canon.[8]

The Text

Despite the popularity of this document in antiquity, relatively few manuscripts of the letter have survived. It was not until 1873 that a complete copy of the text was discovered by Bryennios in a manuscript (= C below) that includes, among other items, *1 Clement, 2 Clement, Barnabas,* and the *Didache*. The sources for the text (and the symbols used to represent them) are as follows:

A = Codex Alexandrinus (fifth c.; lacks 57.7–63.4)

C = Codex Hierosolymitanus (A.D. 1056)

L = the Latin translation of the letter (probably made in the second or third c.; now preserved in a single eleventh-c. MS

S = the Syriac translation (preserved in a New Testament MS dated A.D. 1169–70)

Co = the Coptic translation (incompletely preserved in two MSS from the fourth and seventh c., respectively)

In addition, Clement of Alexandria and Jerome occasionally preserve quotations from Clement.

BIBLIOGRAPHY

Bowe, Barbara Ellen. *A Church in Crisis: Ecclesiology and Paraenesis in Clement of Rome.* Minneapolis: Fortress, 1988.

Clarke, W. K. L. *The First Epistle of Clement to the Corinthians.* London: SPCK, 1937.

6. Cf. Lightfoot, *AF* 1.1.129–35.

7. Text in B. M. Metzger, *The Canon of the New Testament* (Oxford: Clarendon, 1987), 313.

8. B. D. Ehrman, "The New Testament Canon of Didymus the Blind," *Vigiliae Christianae* 37 (1983):1–21.

Fuellenbach, J. *Ecclesiastical Office and the Primacy of Rome: An Evaluation of Recent Theological Discussion of First Clement.* Washington: Catholic University of America Press, 1980.

Grant, R. M., and H. H. Graham. *First and Second Clement.* The Apostolic Fathers, vol. 2. New York: Nelson, 1965.

Hagner, D. A. *The Use of the Old and New Testaments in Clement of Rome.* Leiden: E. J. Brill, 1973.

Harnack, A. *Das Schreiben der römischen Kirche an die korinthische aus der Zeit Domitians.* Leipzig: Hinrichs, 1929.

Jaubert, A. *Clément de Rome: Epître aux Corinthiens.* Paris: Cerf, 1971.

Kleist, J. A. *The Epistles of St. Clement of Rome and St. Ignatius of Antioch.* Ancient Christian Writers, vol. 1. Westminster, Md.: Newman, 1946.

Knopf, R. *Die Lehre der zwölf Apostel. Die zwei Clemensbriefe.* Tübingen: Mohr, 1920.

Lightfoot, J. B. *The Apostolic Fathers, Part I: S. Clement of Rome.* 2d ed. 2 vols. London: Macmillan, 1890.

Richardson, C. C. "The Letter of the Church of Rome to the Church of Corinth, Commonly Called Clement's First Letter." In *Early Christian Fathers,* edited by C. C. Richardson, 33–73. Philadelphia: Westminster, 1953. Repr. Macmillan, 1970.

The Letter of the Romans
to the Corinthians
commonly known as First Clement

The church of God which sojourns in Rome to the church of God which sojourns in Corinth, to those who are called and sanctified by the will of God through our Lord Jesus Christ. May grace and peace from almighty God through Jesus Christ be yours in abundance.

1. Because of the sudden and repeated misfortunes and reverses which have happened to us, brothers, we acknowledge that we have been somewhat slow in giving attention to the matters in dispute among you, dear friends, especially the detestable and unholy schism, so alien and strange to those chosen by God, which a few reckless and arrogant persons have kindled to such a pitch of insanity that your good name, once so renowned and loved by all, has been greatly reviled. (2) For has anyone ever visited you who did not approve your most excellent and steadfast faith? Who did not admire your sober and magnanimous Christian piety? Who did not proclaim the magnificent character of your hospitality? Who did not congratulate you on your complete and sound knowledge? (3) For you did everything without partiality, and you lived in accordance with the laws of God, submitting yourselves to your leaders and giving to the older men among you the honor due them. You instructed the young to think temperate and proper thoughts; you charged the women to perform all their duties with a blameless, reverent,[1] and pure conscience, cherishing their own husbands, as is right; and you taught them to abide

---

1. *reverent*: so AC; LSCo omit.

by the rule of obedience, and to manage the affairs of their household with dignity and all discretion.

2. Moreover, you were all humble and free from arrogance, submitting rather than demanding submission, "more glad to give than to receive,"[2] and content with the provisions which God[3] supplies. And giving heed to his words, you stored them up diligently in your hearts, and kept his sufferings before your eyes. (2) Thus a profound and rich peace was given to all, together with an insatiable desire to do good, and an abundant outpouring of the Holy Spirit fell upon everyone as well. (3) Being full of holy counsel, with excellent zeal and a devout confidence you stretched out your hands to almighty God, imploring him to be merciful, if inadvertently you had committed any sin. (4) You struggled day and night on behalf of all the brotherhood, that through fear[4] and conscientiousness the number of his elect might be saved. (5) You were sincere and innocent and free from malice one toward another. (6) Every faction and every schism were abominable to you. You mourned for the transgressions of your neighbors: you considered their shortcomings to be your own. (7) You never once regretted doing good, but were "ready for every good work."[5] (8) Being adorned with a virtuous and honorable manner of life, you performed all your duties in the fear of him. The commandments and the ordinances of the Lord were "written on the tablets of your hearts."[6]

3. All glory and growth were given to you, and then that which is written was fulfilled: "My beloved ate and drank and was enlarged and grew fat and kicked."[7] (2) From this came jealousy and envy, strife and sedition, persecution and anarchy, war and captivity. (3) So men were stirred up: "Those without honor against the honored," those of no repute against the highly reputed, the foolish against the wise, "the young against

---

2. Cf. Acts 20:35.

3. *God*: so Lightfoot and Harnack, following A; most recent editors read *Christ*, following CLSCo.

4. *fear*: so C; ALSCo read *compassion*.

5. Titus 3:1.

6. Cf. Prov. 7:3.

7. Deut. 32:15.

the elders."[8] (4) For this reason "righteousness" and peace "stand at a distance,"[9] while each one has abandoned the fear of God and become nearly blind with respect to faith in Him, neither walking according to the laws of His commandments nor living in accordance with his duty toward Christ. Instead, each follows the lusts of his evil heart, inasmuch as they have assumed that attitude of unrighteous and ungodly jealousy through which, in fact, "death entered into the world."[10]

4. For thus it is written: "And it came to pass after certain days that Cain offered from the fruits of the earth a sacrifice to God, and Abel also offered a sacrifice from the first-born of the sheep and from their fat. (2) And God looked with favor upon Abel and upon his gifts, but to Cain and his sacrifices he gave no heed. (3) And Cain was greatly distressed and his face was downcast. (4) And God said to Cain, 'Why are you so distressed and why is your face downcast? If you have offered correctly but not divided correctly, did you not sin? (5) Be quiet; he shall turn to you, and you shall rule over him.' (6) And Cain said to Abel his brother, 'Let us go out to the field.' And it came to pass, while they were in the field, that Cain rose up against Abel his brother and killed him."[11] (7) You see, brothers, jealousy and envy brought about a brother's murder. (8) Because of jealousy our father Jacob ran away from the presence of Esau his brother. (9) Jealousy caused Joseph to be persecuted nearly to death, and to be sold into slavery. (10) Jealousy compelled Moses to flee from the presence of Pharaoh, king of Egypt, when he was asked by his own countryman, "Who made you a judge or a ruler over us? Do you want to kill me, just as you killed the Egyptian yesterday?"[12] (11) Because of jealousy Aaron and Miriam were excluded from the camp. (12) Jealousy brought Dathan and Abiram down alive into Hades, because they revolted against Moses, the servant of God. (13) Because of jealousy David not only was envied by the Philistines, but also was persecuted by Saul, king of Israel.[13]

8. Isa. 3:5.
9. Cf. Isa. 59:14.
10. Wisd. of Sol. 2:24.
11. Gen. 4:3–8.
12. Exod. 2:14.
13. *king of Israel*: so ALSCo [Lightfoot]; C omits.

5. But to pass from the examples of ancient times, let us come to those champions who lived nearest to our time. Let us set before us the noble examples which belong to our own generation. (2) Because of jealousy and envy the greatest and most righteous pillars[14] were persecuted, and fought to the death. (3) Let us set before our eyes the good apostles. (4) There was Peter, who, because of unrighteous jealousy, endured not one or two but many trials, and thus having given his testimony went to his appointed place of glory. (5) Because of jealousy and strife Paul by his example pointed out the way to the prize for patient endurance. (6) After he had been seven times in chains, had been driven into exile, had been stoned, and had preached in the East and in the West, he won the genuine glory for his faith, (7) having taught righteousness to the whole world and having reached the farthest limits of the West.[15] Finally, when he had given his testimony before the rulers, he thus departed from the world and went to the holy place, having become an outstanding example of patient endurance.

6. To these men who lived holy lives there was joined a vast multitude of the elect who, having suffered many torments and tortures because of jealousy, set an illustrious example among us. (2) Because of jealousy women were persecuted as Danaids and Dircae,[16] suffering in this way terrible and unholy tortures, but they safely reached the goal in the race of faith, and received a noble reward, their physical weakness notwithstanding. (3) Jealousy has estranged wives from their husbands and annulled the saying of our father Adam, "This is now bone of my bones and flesh of my flesh."[17] (4) Jealousy and strife have overthrown great cities and uprooted great nations.

7. We write these things, dear friends, not only to admonish

14. *pillars*: i.e., of the church; cf. Gal. 2:9.

15. *farthest . . . West*: i.e., the Straits of Gibraltar.

16. *women . . . Dircae*: in ancient mythology, the daughters of Danaüs were given as prizes to the winners of a race; thus it is likely that this is a reference to Christian women being raped prior to being martyred. Dirce was tied to the horns of a bull and then dragged to death. Lightfoot suspects that all the extant witnesses are corrupt at this point, and is disposed to adopt, in place of *Danaïds* and *Dircae*, a conjectural emendation: *women, tender maidens, even slave girls, were persecuted.*

17. Gen. 2:23.

you, but also to remind ourselves. For we are in the same arena, and the same contest awaits us. (2) Therefore let us abandon empty and futile thoughts, and let us conform to the glorious and holy rule of our tradition; (3) indeed, let us note what is good and what is pleasing and what is acceptable in the sight of him who made us. (4) Let us fix our eyes on the blood of Christ and understand how precious it is to his Father, because, being poured out for our salvation, it won for the whole world the grace of repentance. (5) Let us review all the generations in turn, and learn that from generation to generation the Master has given an opportunity for repentance to those who desire to turn to him. (6) Noah preached repentance, and those who obeyed were saved. (7) Jonah preached destruction to the people of Nineveh; but they, repenting of their sins, made atonement to God by their prayers and received salvation, even though they were alienated from God.

8. The ministers of the grace of God spoke about repentance through the Holy Spirit; (2) indeed, the Master of the universe himself spoke about repentance with an oath: "For as I live, says the Lord, I do not desire the death of the sinner, so much as his repentance."[18] He also added this merciful declaration: (3) "Repent, O house of Israel, of your iniquity; say to the sons of my people, Though your sins reach from the earth to heaven, and though they be redder than scarlet and blacker than sackcloth, yet if you turn to me with your whole heart and say 'Father,' I will listen to you as a holy people."[19] (4) And in another place he says this: "Wash and be clean; remove the wickedness from your souls out of my sight. Put an end to your wickedness; learn to do good; seek out justice; deliver the one who is wronged: give judgment on behalf of the orphan, and grant justice to the widow. And come, let us reason together, he says:[20] even though your sins be as crimson, I will make them white as snow; and though they be as scarlet, I will make them white as wool. And if you are willing and listen to me, you shall eat the good things of the earth; but if you are not willing

18. Cf. Ezek. 33:11.

19. Possibly a loose paraphrase of Ezek. 33, or from an apocryphal work attributed to Ezekiel.

20. *he says*: so A; CS read *the Lord says*.

and do not listen to me, a sword shall devour you, for the mouth of the Lord has spoken these things."[21] (5) Seeing, then, that he desires all his beloved to participate in repentance, he confirmed it by an act of his almighty will.

9. Therefore let us be obedient to his magnificent and glorious will, and presenting ourselves as suppliants of his mercy and goodness, let us fall down before him and return to his compassions, laying aside the fruitless toil and the strife and the jealousy that leads to death. (2) Let us fix our eyes on those who perfectly served his magnificent glory. (3) Let us take Enoch, for example, who was found righteous in obedience and so was taken up and did not experience death. (4) Noah, being found faithful, proclaimed a second birth to the world by his ministry, and through him the Master saved the living creatures that entered into the ark in harmony.

10. Abraham, who was called "the Friend," was found faithful in that he became obedient to the words of God. (2) He obediently went forth from his country, from his people, and from his father's house, leaving a small country, a weak people, and an insignificant house in order that he might inherit the promises of God. (3) For He says to him: "Go forth from your country and from your people and from your father's house to the land which I will show you, and I will make you into a great nation, and I will bless you and will make your name great, and you will be blessed. And I will bless those who bless you, and I will curse those who curse you, and in you all the tribes of the earth will be blessed."[22] (4) And again, when he separated from Lot, God said to him: "Lift up your eyes, and look from the place where you now are to the north and the south and the sunrise and the sea; for all the land that you see I will give to you and your seed forever. (5) Furthermore, I will make your seed like the dust of the earth. If anyone can count the dust of the earth, then your seed will be counted."[23] (6) And again he says: "God led Abraham forth and said to him, 'Look up to heaven and count the stars, if you are able to count them; so shall your seed be!' And Abraham believed God, and it was

21. Isa. 1:16–20.
22. Gen. 12:1–3.
23. Gen. 13:14–16.

reckoned to him as righteousness."[24] (7) Because of his faith and hospitality a son was given to him in his old age, and for the sake of obedience he offered him as a sacrifice to God on one of the mountains which He showed him.

11. Because of his hospitality and godliness Lot was saved from Sodom, when the entire region was judged by fire and brimstone.[25] In this way the Master clearly demonstrated that he does not forsake those who hope in him, but destines to punishment and torment those who turn aside. (2) Of this his wife was destined to be a sign, for after leaving with him she changed her mind and no longer agreed, and as a result she became a pillar of salt to this day, that it might be known to all that those who are double-minded and those who question the power of God fall under judgment and become a warning to all generations.

12. Because of her faith and hospitality Rahab the harlot was saved.[26] (2) For when the spies were sent to Jericho by Joshua the son of Nun, the king of the land realized that they had come to spy out his country, and so he sent out men to capture them, intending to put them to death as soon as they were caught. (3) The hospitable Rahab, however, took them in and hid them in an upstairs room under some flax-stalks. (4) And when the king's men arrived and said, "The men spying on our land came to you; bring them out, for so the king commands," she answered, "Yes, the men whom you seek came to me, but they left immediately and are already on their way," and she pointed them in the opposite direction. (5) Then she said to the men: "I am absolutely convinced that the Lord your God is handing this country over to you, for fear and terror of you have fallen upon all the inhabitants. Therefore, when you do take it, save me and my father's house." (6) And they said to her: "It shall be exactly as you have said. Therefore, when you learn that we are coming, gather together all your family under your roof, and they will be saved. But anybody found outside the house will perish." (7) And in addition they gave her a sign, that she should hang from her house something scarlet—

24. Gen. 15:5–6.
25. Gen. 19.
26. Josh. 2.

making it clear that through the blood of the Lord redemption will come to all who believe and hope in God. (8) You see, dear friends, not only faith but prophecy is found in this woman.

13. Let us therefore be humble, brothers, laying aside all arrogance and conceit and foolishness and anger, and let us do what is written. For the Holy Spirit says: "Let not the wise man boast about his wisdom, nor the strong about his strength, nor the rich about his wealth; but let him who boasts boast in the Lord, that he may seek him out, and do justice and righteousness."[27] Most of all, let us remember the words of the Lord Jesus, which he spoke as he taught gentleness and patience. (2) For he said this: "Show mercy, that you may receive mercy; forgive, that you may be forgiven. As you do, so shall it be done to you. As you give, so shall it be given to you. As you judge, so shall you be judged. As you show kindness, so shall kindness be shown to you. With the measure you use, it will be measured to you."[28] (3) With this commandment and these precepts let us strengthen ourselves, that we may humbly walk in obedience to his holy words. For the Holy Word says, (4) "Upon whom shall I look, except upon the one who is gentle and quiet and who trembles at my words?"[29]

14. Therefore it is right and holy, brothers, that we should be obedient to God rather than follow those who in arrogance and unruliness have set themselves up as leaders in abominable jealousy. (2) For we shall bring upon ourselves no ordinary harm, but rather great danger, if we recklessly surrender ourselves to the purposes of men who launch out into strife and dissension in order to alienate us from what is right. (3) Let us be kind to them,[30] in accordance with the compassion and tenderness of him who made us. (4) For it is written: "The kind

27. Jer. 9:23–24; 1 Sam. 2:10; 1 Cor. 1:31; 2 Cor. 10:17.

28. Cf. Matt. 5:7; 6:14; 7:1–2; Luke 6:31, 36–38. Because of the differences between these citations and the canonical texts, it is widely thought that Clement is here (and in 46.8 as well) dependent on an extracanonical source, either written or oral. This is certainly possible, but as Lightfoot observes, "As Clement's quotations are often very loose, we need not go beyond the Canonical Gospels for the source of this passage" (*AF* 1.2.52).

29. Isa. 66:2.

30. *to them*: i.e., the leaders of the schism (so Lightfoot, following A; CSLCo read *to one another*).

shall inhabit the land, and the innocent shall be left on it; but
those who transgress shall be utterly destroyed from it."[31] (5)
And again he says: "I saw the ungodly lifted up on high and
exalted as the cedars of Lebanon. But I passed by, and behold, he
was no more; I searched for his place, but I could not find it.
Guard innocence and observe righteousness, for there is a remnant[32] for the peaceful man."[33]

15. Therefore let us unite with those who devoutly practice
peace, and not with those who hypocritically wish for peace. (2)
For somewhere he says, "This people honors me with their
lips, but their heart is far from me";[34] (3) and again, "They
blessed with their mouth, but they cursed with their heart."[35]
(4) And again he says, "They loved him with their mouth, but
with their tongue they lied to him; their heart was not right
with him, nor were they faithful to his covenant."[36] (5) Therefore, "let the deceitful lips that speak evil against the righteous
be struck dumb."[37] And again: "May the Lord utterly destroy
all the deceitful lips, the boastful tongue, and those who say,
'Let us praise[38] our tongue; our lips are our own. Who is lord
over us?' (6) Because of the misery of the needy and because of
the groaning of the poor I will now arise, says the Lord. I will
place him in safety; (7) I will deal boldly with him."[39]

16. For Christ is with those who are humble, not with those
who exalt themselves over his flock. (2) The majestic[40] scepter
of God, our Lord Christ Jesus,[41] did not come with the pomp of
arrogance or pride (though he could have done so), but in humility, just as the Holy Spirit spoke concerning him. (3) For he
says: "Lord, who believed our report? And to whom was the
arm of the Lord revealed? In his presence we announced that he

---

31. Prov. 2:21–22; cf. Ps. 37 (LXX 36):9, 38.
32. *remnant*: i.e., posterity or descendants.
33. Ps. 37 (LXX 36):35–37.
34. Mark 7:6; Matt. 15:8; Isa. 29:13.
35. Ps. 62:4 (LXX 61:5).
36. Ps. 78 (LXX 77):36–37.
37. Ps. 31:18 (LXX 30:19).
38. *praise*: or possibly *magnify*.
39. Ps. 12:4–6 (LXX 11:3–5).
40. *majestic*: so ACL [Lightfoot]; SCo Jerome omit.
41. *our . . . Jesus*: so A(Co); CLS read *the Lord Jesus Christ*.

was like a child, like a root in thirsty ground. He has no attractiveness or glory. We saw him, and he had no attractiveness or beauty; instead his 'attractiveness' was despised, inferior to that of men. He was a man of stripes and of toil, knowing how to endure weakness, for his face is turned away; he was dishonored and not blessed. (4) This is he who bears our sins and suffers pain for our sakes, and we regarded him as subject to toil and stripes and affliction. (5) But he was wounded because of our sins and has been afflicted because of our transgressions. The chastisement that resulted in our peace fell upon him; by his wounds we were healed. (6) We all went astray like sheep, each one went astray in his own way; (7) and the Lord delivered him up for our sins. And he does not open his mouth, because he is afflicted; like a sheep he was led to slaughter, and like a lamb before his shearer is dumb, so he does not open his mouth. In his humiliation justice was denied him. (8) Who shall tell about his descendants? For his life was taken away from the earth. (9) For the transgressions of my people he came to his death. (10) But I will sacrifice the wicked for his burial, and the rich for his death; for he committed no sin, and no deceit was found in his mouth. And the Lord desires to cleanse him of his stripes. (11) If you make an offering for sin, your soul will see a long-lived posterity. (12) And the Lord desires to take away the torment of his soul, to show him light and to form him with understanding, to justify a Just One who is a good servant to many. And he will bear their sins. (13) Therefore he will inherit many, and will share the spoils of the strong, because his soul was delivered to death and he was reckoned as one of the transgressors; (14) and he bore the sins of many, and because of their sins he was delivered up."[42] (15) And again he himself says: "But I am a worm and not a man, a reproach among men and an object of contempt to the people. (16) All those who saw me mocked me; they 'spoke with their lips'; they shook their heads, saying, 'He hoped in the Lord; let him deliver him, let him save him, because he takes pleasure in him' "[43] (17) You see, dear friends, the kind of pattern that has been given to us; for if the Lord so humbled himself, what

42. Isa. 53:1–12.
43. Ps. 22:6–8 (LXX 21:7–9).

should we do, who through him have come under the yoke of his grace?

17. Let us be imitators also of those who went about "in goatskins and sheepskins,"[44] preaching the coming of Christ. We mean Elijah and Elisha, and likewise Ezekiel, the prophets, and alongside them those ancient men of renown as well. (2) Abraham was greatly renowned and was called the "Friend of God"; yet when he looked intently at the glory of God, he said humbly, "I am only dust and ashes."[45] (3) Moreover, concerning Job it is thus written: "And Job was righteous and blameless, one who was true and who honored God and avoided all evil."[46] (4) Yet he accuses himself, saying: "No one is clean from stain; no, not even if his life lasts but for a day."[47] (5) Moses was called "faithful in all his house,"[48] and through his ministry God judged Egypt with their plagues and the torments. But even he, though greatly glorified, did not boast but said, when an oracle was given to him at the bush, "Who am I, that you should send me? I have a feeble voice and a slow tongue."[49] (6) And again he says, "I am only steam from a pot."[50]

18. And what shall we say about the illustrious David, to whom God said: "I have found a man after my own heart, David the son of Jesse; I have anointed him with eternal mercy."[51] (2) Yet he too says to God: "Have mercy upon me, O God, according to your great mercy; and according to the abundance of your compassions, blot out my iniquity. (3) Wash me thoroughly from my transgression, and cleanse me from my sin. For I acknowledge my transgression, and my sin is always before me. (4) Against you only have I sinned, and I have done evil in your sight, that you may be justified in your words, and may conquer when you contend. (5) For in transgressions I was brought forth, and in sins my mother conceived me. (6) For you have loved truth; the unseen and hidden things of your wisdom

44. Cf. Heb. 11:37.
45. Gen. 18:27.
46. Job 1:1.
47. Cf. Job 14:4–5.
48. Num. 12:7; Heb. 3:2.
49. Exod. 3:11; 4:10.
50. Source unknown.
51. Ps. 89:20 (LXX 88:21); Acts 13:22 (cf. 1 Sam. 13:14).

you have shown to me. (7) You will sprinkle me with hyssop, and I will be cleansed; you will wash me, and I will become whiter than snow. (8) You will make me hear joy and gladness; the bones which have been humbled will rejoice. (9) Hide your face from my sins, and blot out all my transgressions. (10) Create a clean heart within me, O God, and renew a right spirit within me. (11) Do not cast me away from your presence, and do not take your Holy Spirit from me. (12) Restore to me the joy of your salvation, and strengthen me with a guiding spirit. (13) I will teach sinners your ways, and the godless will turn back to you. (14) Deliver me from bloodguiltiness, O God, the God of my salvation. (15) My tongue will rejoice in your righteousness. Lord, you will open my mouth, and my lips will proclaim your praise. (16) For if you had desired sacrifice, I would have given it; but in whole burnt offerings you will take no pleasure. (17) The sacrifice for God is a broken spirit; a broken and humbled heart God will not despise."[52]

19. Accordingly, the humility and subordination of so many and such great men of renown have, through their obedience, improved not only us but also the generations before us, and likewise those who have received his oracles in fear and truth. (2) Seeing, then, that we have a share in many great and glorious deeds, let us hasten on to the goal of peace, which has been handed down to us from the beginning; let us fix our eyes upon the Father and Maker of the whole world, and hold fast to his magnificent and excellent gifts and benefits of peace. (3) Let us see him in our mind, and let us look with the eyes of the soul on his patient will. Let us note how free from anger he is toward all his creation.

20. The heavens move at his direction and obey him in peace. (2) Day and night complete the course assigned by him, neither hindering the other. (3) The sun and the moon and the choirs of stars circle in harmony within the courses assigned to them, according to his direction, without any deviation at all. (4) The earth, bearing fruit in the proper seasons in fulfillment of his will, brings forth food in full abundance for both men and beasts and all living things which are upon it, without dissension or altering anything he has decreed. (5) Moreover, the in-

52. Ps. 51:1–17 (LXX 50:1–19).

comprehensible depths of the abysses and the indescribable judgments[53] of the underworld are constrained by the same ordinances. (6) The basin of the boundless sea, gathered together by his creative action "into its reservoirs,"[54] does not flow beyond the barriers surrounding it; instead it behaves just as he ordered it. (7) For he said: "Thus far shall you come, and your waves shall break within you."[55] (8) The ocean—impassable by men—and the worlds beyond it are directed by the same ordinances of the Master. (9) The seasons, spring and summer and autumn and winter, give way in succession, one to the other, in peace. (10) The winds from the different quarters fulfill their ministry in the proper season without disturbance; the everflowing springs, created for enjoyment and health, give without fail their life-sustaining breasts to mankind. Even the smallest living things come together in harmony and peace. (11) All these things the great Creator and Master of the universe ordered to exist in peace and harmony, thus doing good to all things, but especially abundantly to us who have taken refuge in his compassionate mercies through our Lord Jesus Christ, (12) to whom be the glory and the majesty for ever and ever. Amen.

21. Take care, dear friends, lest his many benefits turn into a judgment upon all of us,[56] as will happen if we fail to live worthily of him, and to do harmoniously those things which are good and well-pleasing in his sight. (2) For he says somewhere, "The Spirit of the Lord is a lamp searching the depths of the heart."[57] (3) Let us realize how near he is, and that nothing escapes him, either of our thoughts or the plans which we make. (4) It is right, therefore, that we should not be deserters from his will. (5) Let us offend foolish and senseless men who

53. *judgments*: reading *krimata* ("judgments," "decisions") with ACLSCo. But this is felt by many to be very awkward. Lightfoot prefers to strike out the word (poss. trans.: "indescribable *things* of the underworld"); others emend *krimata* to *klimata* ("regions"). Neither suggestion seems necessary, however, especially as all the textual witnesses are united at this point. Perhaps *krimata* should be translated as "punishments;" so BAGD, p. 450; and cf. *1 Clem.* 28.1.

54. Gen. 1:9 (LXX only).

55. Job 38:11.

56. *all of us*: so A(C); LSCo read *us*.

57. Prov. 20:27.

exalt themselves and boast in the arrogance of their words, rather than God. (6) Let us fear the Lord Jesus Christ,[58] whose blood was given for us. Let us respect our leaders; let us honor our elders; let us instruct our young with instruction that leads to the fear of God. Let us guide our women toward that which is good: (7) let them reveal a disposition to purity worthy of admiration; let them exhibit a sincere desire to be gentle; let them demonstrate by their silence the moderation of their tongue; let them show their love, without partiality and in holiness, equally toward all those who fear God. (8) Let our children receive the instruction which is in Christ: let them learn how strong humility is before God, what pure love is able to accomplish before God, how the fear of him is good and great and saves all those who live in it in holiness with a pure mind. (9) For he is the searcher of thoughts and desires; his breath is in us, and when he so desires, he will take it away.

22. Now faith in Christ confirms all these things, for he himself through the Holy Spirit thus calls us: "Come, my children, listen to me; I will teach you the fear of the Lord. (2) Who is the man who desires life, who loves to see good days? (3) Keep your tongue from evil, and your lips from speaking deceit. (4) Turn aside from evil and do good. (5) Seek peace and pursue it. (6) The eyes of the Lord are upon the righteous, and his ears are turned to their prayers. But the face of the Lord is against those who do evil, to destroy any remembrance of them from the earth. (7) The righteous cried out, and the Lord heard him, and delivered him from all his troubles. Many are the troubles of the righteous, but the Lord shall deliver him from them all."[59] (8) Furthermore,[60] "many are the afflictions of the sinner, but mercy will surround those who set their hope on the Lord."[61]

23. The Father, who is merciful in all things, and ready to do good, has compassion on those who fear him, and gently and lovingly bestows his favors on those who draw near to him

---

58. *Christ*: so AL [Lightfoot]; CSCo Clement of Alexandria omit.

59. Ps. 34:11–17, 19 (LXX 33:12–18, 20), following S; ALCo omit *Many are . . . them all* (C is defective).

60. *Furthermore*: so C; S reads *and again*; ALCo omit.

61. Ps. 32 (LXX 31):10.

with singleness of mind. (2) Therefore, let us not be double-minded, nor let our soul indulge in false ideas about his excellent and glorious gifts. (3) Let this Scripture be far from us where he says, "Wretched are the double-minded, those who doubt in their soul and say, 'We heard these things even in the days of our fathers, and look, we have grown old, and none of these things have happened to us.' (4) You fools, compare yourselves to a tree, or take a vine: first it sheds its leaves, then a shoot comes, then a leaf, then a flower, and after these a sour grape, and then a full ripe bunch."[62] Notice that in a brief time the fruit of the tree reaches maturity. (5) Truly his purpose will be accomplished quickly and suddenly, just as the Scripture also testifies: "He will come quickly and not delay; and the Lord will come suddenly into his temple, even the Holy One whom you expect."[63]

24. Let us consider, dear friends, how the Master continually points out to us the coming resurrection of which he made the Lord Jesus Christ the firstfruit when he raised him from the dead. (2) Let us observe, dear friends, the resurrection that regularly occurs. (3) Day and night show us the resurrection: the night falls asleep, and day arises; the day departs, and night returns. (4) Let us take the crops: How and in what manner does the sowing take place? (5) "The sower went forth,"and cast into the earth each of the seeds.[64] These seeds, falling to the earth dry and bare, decay; but then out of their decay the majesty of the Master's providence raises them up, and from the one seed many grow and bear fruit.

25. Let us observe the remarkable sign which is seen in the regions of the East, that is, the vicinity of Arabia. (2) There is a bird, which is named the Phoenix. This bird, the only one of its species, lives for five hundred years. When the time of its dissolution and death arrives, it makes for itself a coffinlike nest of frankincense and myrrh and the other spices, into which, its time being completed, it enters and dies. (3) But as the flesh decays, a certain worm is born, which is nourished by the juices of the dead bird and eventually grows wings. Then, when

---

62. Source unknown; cf. 2 *Clem.* 11.2–3.
63. Cf. Isa. 13:22 (LXX); Mal. 3:1.
64. Cf. Mark 4:3 and parallels.

it has grown strong, it takes up that coffinlike nest containing the bones of its parent, and carrying them away, it makes its way from the country of Arabia to Egypt, to the city called Heliopolis.[65] (4) There, in broad daylight in the sight of all, it flies to the altar of the sun and deposits them there, and then it sets out on its return. (5) The priests then examine the public records of the dates, and they find that it has come at the end of the five-hundredth year.[66]

26. How, then, can we consider it to be some great and marvelous thing, if the Creator of the universe shall bring about the resurrection of those who have served him in holiness, in the assurance born of a good faith, when he shows us—by a bird, no less—the magnificence of his promise? (2) For he says somewhere: "And you will raise me up, and I will praise you";[67] and, "I lay down and slept; I rose up, for you are with me."[68] (3) And again Job says: "And you will raise this flesh of mine, which has endured all these things."[69]

27. With this hope, therefore, let our souls be bound to him who is faithful in his promises and righteous in his judgments. (2) He who commanded us not to lie all the more will not lie himself, for nothing is impossible with God, except to lie. (3) Therefore let our faith in him be rekindled within us, and let us understand that all things are near to him. (4) By his majestic word he established the universe, and by a word he can destroy it. (5) "Who will say to him, 'What have you done?' Or who will resist the might of his strength?"[70] He will do all things when he wills and as he wills, and none of those things decreed by him will fail. (6) All things are in his sight, and nothing escapes his will, (7) seeing that "the heavens declare the glory of God, and the skies proclaim the work of his hands. Day pours forth speech

---

65. *Heliopolis*: i.e., "the city of the Sun."
66. The story of the Phoenix, well known in antiquity, was widely used (with varying levels of credulity) by early Christian writers; sanction for this usage was found in Ps. 92:12 (LXX 91:13), where in the Greek LXX *phoinix* ("palm tree") was confused with *phoinix* ("phoenix bird").
67. Ps. 28 (LXX 27):7.
68. Cf. Pss. 3:5 (LXX 3:6); 23 (LXX 22):4.
69. Job 19:26.
70. Wisd. of Sol. 12:12.

to day, and night proclaims knowledge to night; and there are neither words nor speeches, whose voices are not heard."[71]

28. Since, therefore, all things are seen and heard, let us fear him and abandon the abominable lusts that spawn evil works, in order that we may be shielded by his mercy from the coming judgments. (2) For where can any of us escape from his mighty hand? And what world will receive any of those who desert him? For the Scripture[72] says somewhere: (3) "Where shall I go, and where shall I be hidden from your presence? If I ascend to heaven, you are there; if I depart to the ends of the earth, there is your right hand; if I make my bed in the depths, there is your Spirit."[73] (4) Where, then, can one go, or where can one flee from him who embraces the universe?

29. Let us, therefore, approach him in holiness of soul, lifting up to him pure and undefiled hands, loving our gentle and compassionate Father who made us his chosen portion. (2) For thus it is written: "When the Most High divided the nations, when he dispersed the sons of Adam, he fixed the boundaries of the nations according to the number of the angels of God. His people Jacob became the Lord's portion, and Israel his inherited allotment."[74] (3) And in another place he says: "Behold, the Lord takes for himself a nation out of the midst of the nations, as a man takes the firstfruits of his threshing floor; and the Holy of Holies will come forth from that nation."[75]

30. Seeing then that we are the portion of the Holy One,[76] let us do all the things that pertain to holiness, forsaking slander, disgusting and impure embraces, drunkenness and rioting and detestable lusts, abominable adultery, detestable pride. (2) "For God," he says, "resists the proud, but gives grace to the humble."[77] (3) Let us therefore join with those to whom grace

71. Ps. 19:1–3 (LXX 18:2–4).

72. *Scripture*: or perhaps *Writing*, in which case it may be a reference to the third of the three divisions of the Hebrew Bible (the first two being the Law and the Prophets).

73. Cf. Ps. 139 (LXX 138):7–10.

74. Deut. 32:8–9.

75. Cf. Deut. 4:34; 14:2; Num. 18:27; 2 Chron. 31:14; Ezek. 48:12.

76. *the portion of the Holy One*: so A; LS *a holy portion*; C *holy portions*; Co *a portion of holy ones*.

77. Prov. 3:34; James 4:6; 1 Pet. 5:5.

is given by God. Let us clothe ourselves in concord, being humble and self-controlled, keeping ourselves far from all backbiting and slander, being justified by works and not by words. (4) For he says: "He who speaks much shall hear much in reply. Or does the talkative person think that he is righteous? (5) Blessed is the one born of woman who has a short life. Do not be overly talkative."[78] (6) Let our praise be with God, and not from ourselves, for God hates those who praise themselves. (7) Let the testimony to our good deeds be given by others, as it was given to our fathers who were righteous. (8) Boldness and arrogance and audacity are for those who are cursed by God; but graciousness and humility and gentleness are with those who are blessed by God.

31. Let us therefore cling to his blessing, and let us investigate what are the ways of blessing. Let us study the records of the things that have happened from the beginning. (2) Why was our father Abraham blessed? Was it not because he attained righteousness and truth through faith? (3) Isaac with confidence, knowing the future, was willingly led to sacrifice. (4) Jacob with humility departed from his land because of his brother and went to Laban and served him, and the twelve tribes of Israel were given to him.

32. If anyone will consider them sincerely one by one, he will understand the magnificence of the gifts that are given by him. (2) For from Jacob come all the priests and Levites who minister at the altar of God; from him comes the Lord Jesus according to the flesh; from him come the kings and rulers and governors in the line of Judah; and his other tribes are held in no small honor, seeing that God promised that "your seed shall be as the stars of heaven."[79] (3) All, therefore, were glorified and magnified, not through themselves or their own works or the righteous actions which they did, but through his will. (4) And so we, having been called through his will in Christ Jesus, are not justified through ourselves or through our own wisdom or understanding or piety or works which we have done in holiness of heart, but through faith, by which

---

78. Job 11:2–3a (LXX).
79. Cf. Gen. 15:5; 22:17; 26:4.

the almighty God has justified all who have existed from the beginning; to whom be the glory for ever and ever. Amen.

33. What then shall we do, brothers? Shall we idly abstain from doing good, and forsake love? May the Master never allow this to happen, at least to us; but let us hasten with earnestness and zeal to accomplish every good work. (2) For the Creator and Master of the universe himself rejoices in his works. (3) For by his infinitely great might he established the heavens, and in his incomprehensible wisdom he set them in order. Likewise he separated the earth from the water surrounding it, and set it firmly upon the sure foundation of his own will; and the living creatures which walk upon it he called into existence by his decree. Having already created the sea and the living creatures in it, he fixed its boundaries by his own power. (4) Above all, as the most excellent and by far the greatest work of his intelligence,[80] with his holy and faultless hands he formed man as a representation of his own image. (5) For thus spoke God: "Let us make man in our image and likeness. And God created man; male and female he created them."[81] (6) So, having finished all these things, he praised them and blessed them and said, "Increase and multiply."[82] (7) We have seen[83] that all the righteous have been adorned with good works. Indeed, the Lord himself, having adorned himself with good[84] works, rejoiced. (8) So, since we have this pattern, let us unhesitatingly conform ourselves to his will; let us with all our strength do the work of righteousness.

34. The good worker receives the bread of his labor confidently, but the lazy and careless dares not look his employer in the face. (2) It is, therefore, necessary that we should be zealous to do good, for all things come from him. (3) For he forewarns us: "Behold, the Lord comes, and his reward is with him, to pay each one according to his work."[85] (4) He exhorts us, therefore, who believe in him with our whole heart, not to be idle or

---

80. *of his intelligence*: so AC; LSCo omit.

81. Gen. 1:26–27.

82. Gen. 1:28.

83. *We have seen*: so Lightfoot, adopting a previously proposed emendation (*eidomen*); ACLSCo read *Let us observe* (*idōmen*).

84. *good*: so CLSCo; A (followed by Lightfoot) omits.

85. Cf. Isa. 40:10; 62:11; Prov. 24:12; Rev. 22:12.

careless about any good work. (5) Let our boasting and our confidence be in him; let us submit ourselves to his will; let us consider the whole host of his angels, how they stand by and serve his will. (6) For Scripture says: "Ten thousand times ten thousand stood by him, and thousands of thousands served him, and they cried out, 'Holy, holy, holy is the Lord of Hosts; all creation is full of his glory.' "[86] (7) Let us also, then, being gathered together in harmony with intentness of heart, cry out to him earnestly, with one mouth, that we may come to share in his great and glorious promises. (8) For he says: "Eye has not seen and ear has not heard, and it has not entered into the heart of man, what great things he has prepared for those who patiently wait for him."[87]

35. How blessed and marvelous are the gifts of God, dear friends! (2) Life in immortality, splendor in righteousness, truth with boldness, faith with confidence, self-control with holiness! And all these things fall within our comprehension. (3) What, then, are the things being prepared for those who patiently wait for him? The Creator and Father of the ages, the all-holy One himself, knows their number and their beauty. (4) Let us therefore make every effort to be found in the number of those who patiently wait for him, so that we may share in his promised gifts. (5) But how shall this be, dear friends? If our mind is fixed on God through faith;[88] if we seek out those things which are well-pleasing and acceptable to him; if we accomplish those things which are in harmony with his faultless will, and follow the way of truth, casting off from ourselves all unrighteousness and lawlessness,[89] covetousness, strife, malice and deceit, gossip and slander, hatred of God, pride and arrogance, vanity and inhospitality. (6) For those who do these things are hateful to God; and not only those who do them, but also those who approve of them. (7) For Scripture says: "But to the sinner God said, 'Why do you recite my statutes, and take my covenant upon your lips? (8) You hated instruction and

86. Dan. 7:10; Isa. 6:3.
87. 1 Cor. 2:9; Isa. 64:4.
88. *mind . . . through faith*: so S; A reads *mind of faith is fixed on God*; CL read *mind is faithfully fixed on God*.
89. *lawlessness*: so A; CLS read *evil*.

threw away my words behind you. If you saw a thief, you joined with him, and with adulterers you threw in your lot. Your mouth produced wickedness abundantly, and your tongue wove deceit. You sat there and slandered your brother, and put a stumbling block in the way of your mother's son. (9) These things you have done, and I kept silent. You thought, you un-righteous person, that I would be like you. (10) I will convict you and set you face to face with yourself. (11) Now consider these things, you who forget God, lest he seize you like a lion, and there be no one to save you. (12) The sacrifice of praise will glorify me, and that is the way by which I will show him the salvation of God.' "[90]

36. This is the way, dear friends, in which we found our salvation, namely Jesus Christ, the High Priest of our offerings, the Guardian and Helper of our weakness. (2) Through him let us look steadily into the heights of heaven; through him we see as in a mirror his faultless and transcendent face; through him the eyes of our hearts have been opened; through him our fool-ish and darkened mind springs up into the[91] light; through him the Master has willed that we should taste immortal knowl-edge, for "he, being the radiance of his majesty, is as much superior to angels as the name he has inherited is more excel-lent."[92] (3) For so it is written: "He makes his angels winds and his ministers flames of fire."[93] (4) But of his Son the Master spoke thus: "You are my Son; today I have begotten you. Ask of me, and I will give you the Gentiles for your inheritance, and the ends of the earth for your possession."[94] (5) And again he says to him: "Sit at my right hand, until I make your enemies a footstool for your feet."[95] (6) Who, then, are these enemies? Those who are wicked and resist his will.

37. Let us, therefore, serve as soldiers, brothers, with all earnestness under his faultless orders. (2) Let us consider the soldiers who serve under our commanders, how precisely, how

90. Ps. 50 (LXX 49):16–23.
91. *the*: so LS Clement of Alexandria; C reads *the amazing*; A [Lightfoot] *his amazing* (cf. 1 Pet. 2:9).
92. Heb. 1:3–4.
93. Heb. 1:7.
94. Heb. 1:5; Ps. 2:7–8.
95. Heb. 1:13.

readily, how obediently they execute orders. (3) Not all are prefects or tribunes or centurions or captains of fifty and so forth, but each in his own rank[96] executes the orders given by the emperor and the commanders. (4) The great cannot exist without the small, nor the small without the great. There is a certain blending in everything, and therein lies the advantage. (5) Let us take our body as an example. The head without the feet is nothing; likewise, the feet without the head are nothing. Even the smallest parts of our body are necessary and useful to the whole body, yet all the members work together and unite in mutual subjection, that the whole body may be saved.

38. So in our case let the whole body be saved in Christ Jesus, and let each man be subject to his neighbor, to the degree determined by his spiritual gift. (2) The strong must not neglect[97] the weak, and the weak must respect the strong. Let the rich support the poor; and let the poor give thanks to God, because He has given him someone through whom his needs may be met. Let the wise display his wisdom not in words but in good works. The humble person should not testify to his own humility, but leave it to someone else to testify about him. Let the one who is physically pure remain so and[98] not boast, recognizing that it is someone else who grants this self-control. (3) Let us acknowledge, brothers, from what matter we were made; who and what we were, when we came into the world; from what grave and what darkness he who made and created us brought us into his world, having prepared his benefits for us before we were born. (4) Seeing, therefore, that we have all these things from him, we ought in every respect to give thanks to him, to whom be the glory for ever and ever. Amen.

39. Senseless and stupid and foolish and ignorant men jeer and mock at us, wishing to exalt themselves in their own imaginations. (2) For what can a mortal do? Or what strength does an earth-born creature have? (3) For it is written: "There was no form before my eyes; I heard only a breath and a voice. (4) What then? Shall a mortal be clean in the presence of the Lord? Or

---

96. Cf. 1 Cor. 15:23.
97. *not neglect*: so A, as restored by the editors; CLS read *care for*.
98. *remain so and*: so A, as restored; CS omit.

shall a man be blameless for his deeds, seeing that he does not trust his servants and has found some fault against his angels? (5) Not even heaven is clean in his sight: away then, you who dwell in houses of clay, the very same clay of which we ourselves are made. He crushed them like a moth, and between morning and evening they cease to exist. Because they could not help themselves, they perished. (6) He breathed upon them and they died, because they had no wisdom. (7) But call out, if someone should obey you, or if you should see one of the holy angels. For wrath kills the foolish man, and envy slays one who has gone astray. (8) And I have seen fools putting down roots, but suddenly their house was consumed. (9) May their sons be far from safety. May they be mocked at the doors of lesser men, and there will be none to deliver them. For the things prepared for them, the righteous shall eat; but they themselves will not be delivered from evil."[99]

40. Since, therefore, these things are now clear to us and we have searched into the depths of the divine knowledge, we ought to do, in order, everything that the Master has commanded us to perform at the appointed times. (2) Now he commanded the offerings and services to be performed diligently, and[100] not to be done carelessly or in disorder, but at designated times and seasons. (3) Both where and by whom he wants them to be performed, he himself has determined by his supreme will, so that all things, being done devoutly according to his good pleasure, might be acceptable to his will. (4) Those, therefore, who make their offerings at the appointed times are acceptable and blessed: for those who follow the instructions of the Master cannot go wrong. (5) For to the high priest the proper services have been given, and to the priests the proper office has been assigned, and upon the Levites the proper ministries have been imposed. The layman is bound by the layman's rules.

41. Let each of you,[101] brothers, in his proper order give

---

99. Job 4:16–18; 15:15; 4:19–5:5.

100. *to be . . . and*: so Lightfoot, emending the text (by supplying *diligently*) to relieve a grammatical difficulty. AC read *to be performed and*; LS omit.

101. *you*: so A; CS read *us*.

thanks to[102] God, maintaining a good conscience, not overstepping the designated rule of his ministry, but acting with reverence. (2) Not just anywhere, brothers, are the continual daily sacrifices offered, or the freewill offerings, or the offerings for sin and trespasses, but only in Jerusalem. And even there the offering is not made in every place, but in front of the sanctuary at the altar, the offering having been first inspected for blemishes by the high priest and the previously mentioned ministers. (3) Those, therefore, who do anything contrary to the duty imposed by his will receive death as the penalty. (4) You see, brothers, as we have been considered worthy of greater knowledge, so much the more are we exposed to danger.

42. The apostles received the gospel for us from the Lord Jesus Christ; Jesus the Christ was sent forth from God. (2) So then Christ is from God, and the apostles are from Christ. Both, therefore, came of the will of God in good order. (3) Having therefore received their orders and being fully assured by the resurrection of our Lord Jesus Christ and full of faith in the Word of God, they went forth with the firm assurance that the Holy Spirit gives,[103] preaching the good news that the kingdom of God was about to come. (4) So, preaching both in the country and in the towns, they appointed their firstfruits, when they had tested them by the Spirit, to be bishops and deacons for the future believers. (5) And this was no new thing they did, for indeed something had been written about bishops and deacons many years ago; for somewhere thus says the Scripture: "I will appoint their bishops in righteousness and their deacons in faith."[104]

43. And is it any wonder that those who in Christ were entrusted by God with such a work appointed the officials just mentioned? After all, the blessed Moses, "who was a faithful servant in all his house,"[105] recorded in the sacred books all the injunctions given to him, and the rest of the prophets followed him, bearing witness with him to the laws that he enacted. (2) For when jealousy arose concerning the priesthood, and the

102. *give thanks to*: so A; CLS read *please*.
103. *firm . . . gives*: or perhaps *fullness of the Holy Spirit*.
104. Isa. 60:17 (LXX only, which here mistranslates the Hebrew).
105. Num. 12:7; Heb. 3:5.

tribes were quarreling about which of them was to be decorated with the glorious title, he commanded the leaders of the twelve tribes to bring him rods inscribed with the name of each tribe. And taking them he tied and sealed them with the signet rings of the leaders of the tribes, and deposited them on the table of God in the tent of the testimony. (3) Then, having shut the tent, he sealed the keys as well as the doors[106] (4) and said to them, "Brothers, the tribe whose rod blossoms is the one God has chosen to be priests and to minister to him." (5) Now when morning came, he called all Israel together, all six hundred thousand men, showed the seals to the leaders of the tribes, opened the tent of testimony, and brought out the rods. And the rod of Aaron was found not only to have blossomed, but also to be bearing fruit. (6) What do you think, dear friends? Did not Moses know beforehand that this would happen? Of course he knew. But in order that disorder might not arise in Israel, he did it anyway, so that the name of the true and only God[107] might be glorified, to whom be the glory for ever and ever. Amen.

44. Our apostles likewise knew, through our Lord Jesus Christ, that there would be strife over the bishop's office. (2) For this reason, therefore, having received complete foreknowledge, they appointed the officials mentioned earlier and afterwards they gave the offices a permanent character;[108] that is, if they should die, other approved men should succeed to their ministry.[109] (3) Those, therefore, who were appointed by them

106. *doors:* so S; ACLCo read *rods.*

107. *God:* so SCo; C reads *Lord;* L *One;* A is defective.

108. *gave the offices a permanent character:* lit. (reading *epimonēn,* the emendation printed by Lightfoot) *have given permanence,* i.e., to the offices of bishop and deacon. The witnesses vary widely, with the most likely reading being that of A, *epinomēn.* But it is difficult to make sense of the word unless one either assumes the existence of a secondary meaning such as "injunction" (a meaning otherwise unattested) or gives it the same meaning as the cognate word *epinomis,* a "codicil" or "supplement." The translation would then run something like "added a codicil" or "made a decree."

109. *if they should die . . . ministry:* the translation of this sentence attempts to preserve the ambiguity of the Greek. It and the following sentence may be interpreted in at least three different ways: (1) "They" = "the apostles." If the apostles themselves die, "other approved men" succeed to the apostolic office and the right to appoint local officials, and thus are the "other reputable men" of the following sentence. (2) "They" = those first appointed by the

or, later on, by other reputable men with the consent of the whole church, and who have ministered to the flock of Christ blamelessly, humbly, peaceably, and unselfishly, and for a long time have been well spoken of by all—these men we consider to be unjustly removed from their ministry. (4) For it will be no small sin for us, if we depose from the bishop's office those who have offered the gifts blamelessly and in holiness. (5) Blessed are those presbyters who have gone on ahead, who took their departure at a mature and fruitful age, for they need no longer fear that someone might remove them from their established place. (6) For we see that you have removed certain people, their good conduct notwithstanding, from the ministry which had been held in honor by them[110] blamelessly.

45. Be contentious and zealous, brothers, but about the things that relate to salvation. (2) You have searched the Scriptures, which are true, which were given by the Holy Spirit; (3) you know that nothing unrighteous or counterfeit is written in them. You will not find that righteous people have ever been thrust out by holy men. (4) The righteous were persecuted, but it was by the lawless; they were imprisoned, but it was by the unholy. They were stoned by transgressors; they were slain by those who had conceived a detestable and unrighteous jealousy. (5) Despite suffering these things, they endured nobly. (6) For what shall we say, brothers? Was Daniel cast into the lions' den by those who feared God? (7) Or were Ananias, Azarias, and

---

apostles. If these initial appointees should die, they are to be succeeded in office by others appointed by the apostles and, later on, by the "other reputable men" with apostolic status, such as Titus or Timothy. (3) "They" = the initial appointees, and "other reputable men" = "the officials mentioned earlier." On this view, those appointed initially are responsible as a group for appointing their own successors; i.e., upon the death of one of their number, the survivors appoint an "approved man" to fill the vacancy. Lightfoot favors (3), and translates the "they" in question as "these" (*AF* 1.2.133); cf. his commentary on Philippians (*St. Paul's Epistle to the Philippians*, 8th ed. [London: Macmillan, 1888], 199–207, esp. 205. See also W. H. C. Frend, *The Rise of Christianity* (Philadelphia: Fortress, 1984), 140; and B. E. Bowe, *A Church in Crisis: Ecclesiology and Paraenesis in Clement of Rome* (Minneapolis: Fortress, 1988), 144–53, esp. 147 n. 99.

110. *had been . . . them*: so ACSCo, reading *tetimēmenēs*; but the text is thought to be corrupt by Lightfoot and Lake, who suggest *they had preserved* (*tetērēmenēs*).

Mishael shut up in the fiery furnace by those devoted to the magnificent and glorious worship of the Most High? Of course not! Who, then, were the people who did these things? Abominable men, full of all wickedness, who were stirred up to such a pitch of wrath that they tortured cruelly those who served God with a holy and blameless resolve; they did not realize that the Most High is the champion and protector of those who with a pure conscience worship his excellent name. To him be the glory for ever and ever. Amen. (8) But those who patiently endured with confidence inherited glory and honor; they were exalted, and had their names recorded by God as their memorial[111] for ever and ever. Amen.

46. Therefore we too, brothers, must follow examples such as these. (2) For it is written: "Follow the saints, for those who follow them will be sanctified."[112] (3) And again it says in another place: "With the innocent man you will be innocent, and with the elect you will be elect, and with the perverse man you will deal perversely. "[113] (4) Let us, therefore, join with the innocent and righteous, for these are the elect of God. (5) Why is there strife and angry outbursts and dissension and schisms and conflict among you? (6) Do we not have one God and one Christ and one Spirit of grace which was poured out upon us? And is there not one calling in Christ? (7) Why do we tear and rip apart the members of Christ, and rebel against our own body, and reach such a level of insanity that we forget that we are members of one another? Remember the words of Jesus our Lord, (8) for he said: "Woe to that man! It would have been good for him if he had not been born, than that he should cause one of my elect to sin. It would have been better for him to have been tied to a millstone and cast into the sea, than that he should pervert one of my elect."[114] (9) Your schism has perverted many; it has brought many to despair, plunged many into doubt, and caused all of us to sorrow. And yet your rebellion still continues!

---

111. *had their . . . memorial:* so A; CSCo read *they were inscribed by God in his memory.*

112. Source unknown.

113. Ps. 18:25–26 (LXX 17:26–27).

114. Cf. Matt. 26:24; Luke 17:1–2; and parallels.

47. Take up the epistle of the blessed Paul the apostle. (2) What did he first write to you in the "beginning of the gospel"?[115] (3) Truly he wrote to you in the Spirit about himself and Cephas and Apollos, because even then you had split into factions. Yet that splitting into factions brought less sin upon you, for you were partisans of highly reputed apostles and of a man approved by them. (5) In contrast now think about those who have perverted you and diminished the respect due your renowned love for the brotherhood. (6) It is disgraceful, dear friends, yes, utterly disgraceful and unworthy of your conduct in Christ, that it should be reported that the well-established and ancient church of the Corinthians, because of one or two persons, is rebelling against its presbyters. (7) And this report has reached not only us, but also those who differ from us, with the result that you heap blasphemies upon the name of the Lord because of your stupidity, and create danger for yourselves as well.

48. Let us therefore root this out quickly, and let us fall down before the Master and pray to him with tears, that he may be merciful and be reconciled to us, and restore us to the honorable and pure conduct which characterizes our love for the brotherhood. (2) For this is an open gate of righteousness leading to life, as it is written: "Open to me the gates of righteousness, that I may enter through them and praise the Lord. (3) This is the gate of the Lord; the righteous shall enter by it."[116] (4) Although many gates are opened, this righteous gate is the Christian gate; blessed are all those who have entered by it and direct their path in holiness and righteousness, doing everything without confusion. (5) Let a man be faithful, let him be able to expound knowledge, let him be wise in the interpretation of discourses, let him be energetic in deeds, let him be pure;[117] (6) for the greater he seems to be, the more he ought to be humble, and the more he ought to seek the common advantage of all, and not his own.

49. Let the one who has love in Christ fulfill the command-

115. Phil. 4:15.

116. Ps. 118 (LXX 117):19–20.

117. *energetic . . . pure*: so Clement of Alexandria; AC(S) read *pure in deeds*.

ments of Christ. (2) Who can describe the bond of God's love? (3) Who is able to explain the majesty of its beauty? (4) The height to which love leads is indescribable. (5) Love unites us with God; "love covers a multitude of sins";[118] love endures all things, is patient in all things. There is nothing coarse, nothing arrogant in love. Love knows nothing of schisms, love leads no rebellions, love does everything in harmony. In love all the elect of God were made perfect; without love nothing is pleasing to God. (6) In love the Master received us. Because of the love he had for us, Jesus Christ our Lord, in accordance with God's will, gave his blood for us, and his flesh for our flesh, and his life for our lives.

50. You see, dear friends, how great and wonderful love is; its perfection is beyond description. (2) Who is worthy to be found in it, except those whom God considers worthy? Let us therefore ask and petition his mercy, that we may be found blameless in love, standing apart from the factiousness of men. (3) All the generations from Adam to this day have passed away, but those who by God's grace were perfected in love have a place among[119] the godly, who will be revealed when the kingdom of Christ[120] visits[121] us. (4) For it is written: "Enter into the innermost rooms for a very little while, until my anger and wrath shall pass away, and I will remember a good day and will raise you from your graves."[122] (5) Blessed are we, dear friends, if we continue to keep God's commandments in the harmony of love, that our sins may be forgiven us through love. (6) For it is written: "Blessed are those whose iniquities are forgiven, and whose sins are covered. Blessed is the man to whom the Lord will reckon no sin, and in whose mouth there is no deceit."[123] (7) This declaration of blessedness was pronounced upon those who have been chosen by God through Jesus Christ our Lord, to whom be the glory for ever and ever. Amen.

118. 1 Pet. 4:8.

119. *have a place among*: or possibly *live in the abode of.*

120. *Christ*: so A(?)LCo Clement of Alexandria; CS (followed by Lightfoot) read *God*.

121. *visits*: or *comes to*; cf. 1 Pet. 2:12; Luke 19:44.

122. Isa. 26:20; Ezek. 37:12.

123. Ps. 32 (LXX 31):1–2; Rom. 4:7–9.

51. So, then, for whatever sins we have committed and whatever we have done through any of the tricks of the adversary, let us ask that we may be forgiven. And those, too, who set themselves up as leaders of rebellion and dissension ought to look to the common ground of hope. (2) For those who walk in fear and love prefer that they themselves, rather than their neighbors, should fall into suffering, and they would rather bring condemnation upon themselves than upon the harmony which has been so nobly and righteously handed down to us. (3) For it is good for a man to confess his transgressions rather than to harden his heart, as the heart of those who rebelled against Moses the servant of God was hardened. Their condemnation was made very clear, (4) for they went down to Hades alive,[124] and "Death will be their shepherd."[125] (5) Pharaoh and his army and all the rulers of Egypt, "the chariots and their riders,"[126] were plunged into the Red Sea and perished, for no other reason than that their foolish hearts were hardened after the signs and the wonders had been accomplished in the land of Egypt[127] by Moses, the servant of God.

52. The Master, brothers, has no need of anything at all. He requires nothing of anyone, except that he make a confession to Him. (2) For David, the chosen one, says: "I will confess to the Lord, and it will please him more than a young calf with horns and hooves. Let the poor see this and rejoice."[128] (3) And again he says: "Sacrifice to God a sacrifice of praise, and pay your vows to the Most High; call upon me in the day of your affliction, and I will deliver you, and you will glorify me. (4) For the sacrifice of God is a broken spirit."[129]

53. For you know, and know well, the sacred Scriptures, dear friends, and you have searched into the oracles of God. We write these things, therefore, merely as a reminder. (2) When Moses went up to the mountain and had spent forty days and forty nights in fasting and humiliation, God said to him: "Moses,

---

124. Cf. Num. 16:33.
125. Ps. 49:14 (LXX 48:15).
126. Exod. 14:23.
127. *the land of Egypt*: so A; CLSCo read *Egypt*.
128. Ps. 69:30–32 (LXX 68:31–33).
129. Ps. 50 (LXX 49):14–15; 51:17 (LXX 50:19).

Moses,[130] go down quickly from here, for your people, whom you led out of the land of Egypt, have broken the Law. They have quickly turned away from the path which you established for them: they have cast for themselves some idols." (3) And the Lord said to him: "I have spoken to you time and again, saying, I have seen this people, and they are stiff-necked indeed! Let me destroy them completely, and I will wipe out their name from under heaven, and I will make you into a great and wonderful nation, far more numerous than this one."[131] (4) And Moses said: "May it not be so, Lord. Forgive this people their sin, or else wipe me also out of the book of the living."[132] (5) What mighty love! What unsurpassable perfection! The servant speaks boldly with his Master: he asks forgiveness for the multitude, or demands that he himself also be wiped out with them.

54. Now, then, who among you is noble? Who is compassionate? Who is filled with love? (2) Let him say: "If it is my fault that there are rebellion and strife and schisms, I retire; I will go wherever you wish, and will do whatever is ordered by the people. Only let the flock of Christ be at peace with its duly appointed presbyters." (3) The one who does this will win for himself great fame in Christ, and every place will receive him, for "the earth is the Lord's, and all that is in it."[133] (4) These are the things that those who live as citizens of the commonwealth of God—something not to be regretted—have done and will continue to do.

55. Let us, moreover, bring forward some examples of Gentiles as well: in times of pestilence, many kings and rulers, being prompted by some oracle, have given themselves over to death, that they might rescue their subjects through their own blood. Many have left their own cities, that there might be no more rebellions. (2) We know that many among us have had themselves imprisoned, that they might ransom others. Many have sold themselves into slavery, and with the price received for themselves have fed others. (3) Many women, being strengthened by the grace of God, have performed many manly

130. *Moses, Moses*: so AC; LSCo omit.
131. Deut. 9:12–14 (Exod. 32:7–10).
132. Exod. 32:32.
133. Ps. 24 (LXX 23):1.

deeds. (4) The blessed Judith, when the city was under siege, asked the elders to permit her to go to the enemy's camp. (5) So she exposed herself to peril and went out for love of her country and of her besieged people, and the Lord delivered Holophernes into the hand of a woman. (6) To no less danger did Esther, who was perfect in faith, expose herself, in order that she might deliver the twelve tribes of Israel when they were about to be destroyed. For through her fasting and her humiliation she entreated the all-seeing Master, the God[134] of the ages, and he, seeing the humility of her soul, rescued the people for whose sake she had faced the danger.

56. Therefore let us also intercede for those who are involved in some transgression, that forbearance and humility may be given them, so that they may submit, not to us but to the will of God. For in this way the merciful remembrance of them in the presence of God and the saints will be fruitful and perfect for them.[135] (2) Let us accept correction, which no one ought to resent, dear friends. The reproof which we give one to another is good and exceedingly useful, for it unites us with the will of God. (3) For thus says the Holy Word: "The Lord has indeed disciplined me, but has not handed me over to death. (4) For whom the Lord loves he disciplines, and he punishes every son whom he accepts."[136] (5) "For the righteous," it is said, "will discipline me in mercy and shall reprove me, but let not the oil[137] of sinners anoint my head."[138] (6) And again it says: "Blessed is the man whom the Lord has reproved; do not reject the correction of the Almighty. For he causes pain, and he makes well again; (7) he has wounded, and his hands have healed. (8) Six times will he rescue you from distress, and in the seventh evil will not touch you. (9) In famine he will rescue you from death, and in war he will release you from the power of the sword. (10) From the scourge of the tongue he will hide you, and you will not be afraid when evils approach. (11) You will laugh at the unrighteous and wicked, (12) and of the wild

---

134. *Master, the God:* so A(C); LCo read *Master.*

135. *the merciful . . . for them:* or possibly *they will prove fruitful and perfect when God and the saints remember them with mercy.*

136. Prov. 3:12; Heb. 12:6.

137. *oil:* so (C)LSCo; A (and Lightfoot, rather hesitantly) reads *mercy.*

138. Ps. 141 (LXX 140):5.

beasts you will not be afraid, for wild beasts will be at peace
with you. (13) Then you will know that your house will be at
peace, and the tent in which you dwell will not fail. (14) And
you will know that your seed will be many, and your children
will be like the grass of the fields. (15) And you will come to the
grave like ripe wheat harvested at the proper time, or like a
heap on the threshing floor gathered together at the right
time."[139] (16) You see, dear friends, what great protection there
is for those who are disciplined by the Master; because he is a
kind Father, he disciplines us in order that we may obtain
mercy through his holy discipline.

57. You, therefore, who laid the foundation of the revolt,
must submit to the presbyters and accept discipline leading to
repentance, bending the knees of your heart. (2) Learn how to
subordinate yourselves, laying aside the arrogant and proud
stubbornness of your tongue. For it is better for you to be found
small but included in the flock of Christ than to have a preeminent reputation and yet be excluded from his hope. (3) For thus
says the all-virtuous Wisdom: "Listen! I will bring forth for you
a saying of my spirit, and I will teach you my word. (4) Because
I called and you did not obey, and because I held out words and
you paid no attention, but ignored my advice and disobeyed my
correction, I therefore will laugh at your destruction, and will
rejoice when ruin comes upon you, and when confusion suddenly overtakes you, and catastrophe arrives like a whirlwind,
or when tribulation and distress come upon you. (5) At that
time, when you call upon me, I will not listen to you. Evil men
will seek me but will not find me, for they hated wisdom, and
did not choose the fear of the Lord, nor did they desire to pay
attention to my advice, but mocked my correction. (6) Therefore they will eat the fruit of their own way, and will be filled
with their own ungodliness. (7) Because they wronged infants,
they will be slain, and a searching inquiry will destroy the
ungodly. But the one who hears me will dwell safely, trusting in
hope, and will live quietly, free from fear of all evil."[140]

58. Let us, therefore, obey his most holy and glorious name,
thereby escaping the threats which were spoken by Wisdom long

139. Job 5:17–26.
140. Prov. 1:23–33.

ago against those who disobey, that we may dwell safely, trusting in his most holy and majestic name. (2) Accept our advice and you will have nothing to regret. For as God lives, and as the Lord Jesus Christ lives, and the Holy Spirit (who are the faith and the hope of the elect), so surely will the one who with humility and constant gentleness has kept without regret the ordinances and commandments given by God be enrolled and included among the number of those who are saved through Jesus Christ, through whom is the glory to him for ever and ever. Amen.

59. But if certain people should disobey what has been said by him through us, let them understand that they will entangle themselves in no small sin and danger. (2) We, however, will be innocent of this sin, and will ask, with earnest prayer and supplication, that the Creator of the universe may keep intact the specified number of his elect throughout the whole world, through his beloved servant[141] Jesus Christ, through whom he called us from darkness to light, from ignorance to the knowledge of the glory of his name. (3) Grant us, Lord, to hope on your name,[142] which is the primal source of all creation, and open the eyes of our hearts, that we may know you, who alone is "Highest among the high, and remains Holy among the holy." You "humble the pride of the proud"; you "destroy the plans of nations"; you "exalt the humble" and "humble the exalted"; you "make rich and make poor"; you "kill and make alive." You alone are the Benefactor of spirits and the God of all flesh, who "looks into the depths," who scans the works of man; the Helper of those who are in peril, the "Savior of those in despair"; the Creator and Guardian of every spirit, who multiplies the nations upon the earth, and from among all of them have chosen those who love you through Jesus Christ, your beloved Servant,[143] through whom you instructed us, sanctified us, honored us. (4) We ask you, Master, to be "our Helper and Protector." Save those among us who are in distress; have mercy on

---

141. *servant*: or *child*; cf. Acts 4:27.

142. *his name . . . your name*: this switch from third to second person is quite awkward. Either a few words have dropped out of the text (*Grant us, Lord* is Lightfoot's emendation) or Clement has switched rather abruptly from talking about prayer to an actual prayer, in which case the translation might read *his name, to hope on your name.*

143. *servant*: or *child*; cf. Acts. 4:27.

the humble;[144] raise up the fallen; show yourself to those in need; heal the godless;[145] turn back those of your people who wander; feed the hungry; release our prisoners; raise up the weak; comfort the discouraged. "Let all the nations know that you are the only God," that Jesus Christ is your servant,[146] and that "we are your people and the sheep of your pasture."[147]

60. For you through your works have revealed the everlasting structure of the world. You, Lord, created the earth. You are faithful throughout all generations, righteous in your judgments, marvelous in strength and majesty, wise in creating and prudent in establishing what exists, good in all that is observed and faithful[148] to those who trust in you, merciful and compassionate: forgive us our sins and our injustices, our transgressions and our shortcomings. (2) Do not take into account every sin of your servants and slave girls, but cleanse us with the cleansing of your truth, and "direct our steps to walk in holiness and righteousness and purity[149] of heart,"[150] and "to do what is good and pleasing in your sight"[151] and in the sight of our rulers. (3) Yes, Lord, "let your face shine upon us" in peace "for our good,"that we may be sheltered "by your mighty hand" and delivered from every sin "by your uplifted arm";[152] deliver us as well from those who hate us unjustly. (4) Give harmony and peace to us and to all who dwell on the earth, just as you did to our fathers when they reverently "called upon you in faith and truth,"[153] that we may be saved,[154] while we render

144. *have . . . humble*: so C; LSCo omit.

145. *godless*: so C; LSCo read *sick*.

146. *servant*: or *child*; cf. Acts 4:27.

147. The preceding prayer is a pastiche of Old Testament quotations and allusions; sources include Num. 27; Deut. 32; 1 Sam. 2; 1 Kings 8; 2 Kings 5, 19; Job 5; Pss. 32, 79, 95, 100, 119 (LXX 31, 78, 94, 99, 118); Isa. 13; 57; Ezek. 36; Jth. 9; Sir. 16; Eph. 1. For details see Lightfoot, *AF* 1.2.172–75; Richardson, *Fathers*, 70–71.

148. *faithful*: so C; LSCo read *kind*.

149. *and righteousness and purity*: so S; CLCo omit.

150. Cf. 1 Kings 9:4; Ps. 40:2 (LXX 39:3).

151. Cf. Deut. 13:18.

152. Cf., among others, Ps. 67 (LXX 66):1; Num. 6:25–26; Jer. 21:10; Gen. 50:20; Exod. 6:1; Deut. 4:34; Jer. 32 (LXX 39:21); Ezek. 20:33–34.

153. Ps. 145 (LXX 144):18; 1 Tim. 2:7.

154. *that we may be saved*: the grammar here is very harsh, leading Lightfoot and others to conclude that some words are missing (cf. on 59.3 above); *that we might be saved* is his suggested emendation.

obedience to your almighty and most excellent[155] name, and to our rulers and governors on earth.

61. You, Master, have given them the power of sovereignty through your majestic and inexpressible might, so that we, acknowledging the glory and honor which you have given them, may be subject to them, resisting your will in nothing. Grant to them, Lord, health, peace, harmony, and stability, that they may blamelessly administer the government which you have given them. (2) For you, heavenly Master, King of the ages,[156] give to the sons of men glory and honor and authority over those upon the earth. Lord, direct their plans according to what is good and pleasing in your sight, so that by devoutly administering in peace and gentleness the authority which you have given them they may experience your mercy. (3) You, who alone are able to do these and even greater good things for us, we praise through the high priest and guardian of our souls, Jesus Christ, through whom be the glory and the majesty to you both now and for all generations and for ever and ever. Amen.

62. We have written enough to you, brothers, about the things which pertain to our religion and are particularly helpful for a virtuous life, at least for those who wish to guide their steps[157] in holiness and righteousness. (2) For we have touched upon every subject—faith, repentance, genuine love, self-control, sobriety, and patience—and have reminded you that you must reverently please almighty God in righteousness and truth and steadfastness, living in harmony without bearing malice, in love and peace with constant gentleness, just as our fathers, of whom we spoke earlier, pleased him, by being humble toward the Father and God and Creator and toward all men. (3) And we have reminded you of these things all the more gladly, since we knew quite well that we were writing to men who are faithful and distinguished and have diligently studied the oracles of the teaching of God.

63. Therefore it is right for us, having studied so many and such great examples, to bow the neck and, adopting the atti-

---

155. *excellent*: so C; LSCo read *glorious*.

156. Cf. 1 Tim. 1:17.

157. *their steps*: this represents Lightfoot's emendation (which Lake appears to accept). Otherwise it is necessary, despite the awkwardness, to take "life" as the object of the verb "to guide" (or possibly "to lead") and translate thus: *helpful to those who wish to lead a virtuous life in holiness. . . .*

tude of obedience, to submit to those who are the leaders of our souls,[158] so that by ceasing from this futile dissension we may attain the goal that is truly set before us, free from all blame. (2) For you will give us great joy and gladness, if you obey what we have written through the Holy Spirit and root out the unlawful anger of your jealousy, in accordance with the appeal for peace and harmony which we have made in this letter. (3) We have also sent trustworthy and prudent men who from youth to old age have lived blameless lives among us, who will be witnesses between you and us. (4) This we have done in order that you might know that our only concern has been, and still is, that you should attain peace without delay.

64. Finally, may the all-seeing God and Master of spirits and Lord of all flesh, who chose the Lord Jesus Christ, and us through him to be his own special people, grant to every soul that has called upon his magnificent and holy name faith, fear, peace, patience, steadfastness, self-control, purity, and sobriety, that they may be pleasing to his name through our high priest and guardian, Jesus Christ, through whom be glory and majesty, might and honor to him, both now and for ever and ever. Amen.

65. Now send back to us without delay our messengers, Claudius Ephebus and Valerius Bito, together with Fortunatus, in peace and with joy, so that they may report as soon as possible the peace and concord which we have prayed for and desire, that we too may all the more quickly rejoice over your good order.

(2) The grace of our Lord Jesus Christ be with you and with all people everywhere who have been called by God through him, through whom be glory, honor, power, majesty, and eternal dominion to him, from everlasting to everlasting. Amen.

The letter of the Romans to the Corinthians.[159]

158. *and, adopting* and *to submit . . . souls*: so S; CLCo read *and to adopt* and omit completely *to submit . . . souls*.

159. *The letter . . . Corinthians*: so reads Co, which is likely correct; ACLS all attribute it to Clement alone.

An Ancient Christian Sermon
(2 Clement)

INTRODUCTION

The so-called second letter of Clement is not a letter, nor is it by Clement. It is, in fact, a sermon or "word of exhortation" composed by an anonymous presbyter (17.3). It is the oldest complete Christian sermon that has survived. Based upon a text from Isaiah (54:1; see 2.1 below), it presents a call to repentance, purity, and steadfastness in the face of persecution. Little or nothing, however, is known about its author, date, or occasion.

Occasion and Date

In the manuscripts in which it is preserved, 2 *Clement* immediately follows 1 *Clement*, the letter addressed to the Corinthians by Clement of Rome, to whom it is attributed. This suggests that 2 *Clement* must have either been preached in Corinth or sent there for some purpose, and any attempt to reconstruct a possible setting for the document must take this into account. Among the more plausible explanations that have been put forward are the following.

W. H. C. Frend places it in Rome, perhaps around A.D. 100.[1] E. J. Goodspeed[2] has adopted the view that 2 *Clement* is really the lost letter of Bishop Soter of Rome mentioned by

---

1. W. H. C. Frend, *The Rise of Christianity* (Philadelphia: Fortress, 1984), 121, 146.

2. E. J. Goodspeed, *The Apostolic Fathers* (New York: Harper and Bros., 1950), 83. This proposal, widely attributed to Harnack (who certainly popularized it), seems to have originated with Hilgenfeld; cf. Lightfoot, *AF* 1.2.196.

Bishop Dionysius of Corinth (ca. 170),[3] but this ingenious suggestion faces the difficulty that the document in question is certainly not a letter. C. C. Richardson[4] suggests that only Alexandria "fits the temper and tone" of the sermon, particularly in light of its "semi-Gnostic phrases" and its use of the *Gospel of the Egyptians*, which Clement of Alexandria, whose very high regard for the genuine *1 Clement* is well known, also quoted. Richardson's suggestion is attractive, but the "tone" of a document is a tenuous basis upon which to erect a hypothesis, and his criticism of a major point favoring the next view is unconvincing.

Lightfoot long ago noted that the reference in 7.1 to people "coming to enter the contests," without any identification of the location, implies that the speaker was near the site of the contests, in this case Corinth, home of the well-known Isthmian games. He suggests that *2 Clement* was a sermon read to the Corinthian congregation sometime between A.D. 120 and 140 that was for some reason particularly notable and therefore preserved, along with other important documents such as the letter from Bishop Soter mentioned by Bishop Dionysius and the earlier letter from the Roman church written by Clement, whose name was eventually attached to the anonymous sermon.[5] This general hypothesis has been advanced further by K. P. Donfried, who has argued well the case that the intervention of the Roman church into the affairs of the Corinthian congregation via *1 Clement* and the mediators who conveyed it to Corinth was successful, the deposed elders were reinstated, and that *2 Clement* is nothing other than a hortatory address preached by one of these elders to the congregation on the occasion of the successful resolution of the crisis.[6] On this reading of the evidence the letter must be dated about A.D. 98–100.

More recently, Helmut Koester has suggested that *2 Clement* is an anti-Gnostic sermon from Egypt prior to the middle of

---

3. Cf. Eusebius, *Church History* 4.23.9–11.

4. Richardson, *Fathers*, 186–87.

5. Lightfoot, *AF* 1.2.194–208, esp. 197–99, 202.

6. K. P. Donfried, *The Setting of Second Clement in Early Christianity* (Leiden: E. J. Brill, 1974), 1–48.

the second century, and that it thus may be "the first tangible evidence for the existence of anti-gnostic Christianity in Egypt before the middle of II CE."[7] But he forthrightly acknowledges that his hypothesis "is by no means certain." The date and occasion of 2 *Clement*, then, remain open questions.

The Text

Only three copies of 2 *Clement* are known to exist. The manuscripts (and the symbols used to represent them) are as follows:

A = Codex Alexandrinus (fifth c.; contains 1.1–12.5a)
C = Codex Hierosolymitanus (A.D. 1056)
S = the Syriac translation (preserved in a New Testament MS dated A.D. 1169–70)

BIBLIOGRAPHY

Donfried, Karl Paul. *The Setting of Second Clement in Early Christianity.* Leiden: E. J. Brill, 1974.

Grant, Robert M., and H. H. Graham. *First and Second Clement.* The Apostolic Fathers, vol. 2. New York: Nelson, 1965.

Knopf, R. *Lehre der zwölf Apostel. Zwei Clemensbriefe.* Tübingen: Mohr, 1920.

Lightfoot, J. B. *The Apostolic Fathers, Part I: S. Clement of Rome.* 2d ed. 2 vols. London: Macmillan, 1890.

Richardson, C. C. "An Anonymous Sermon, Commonly Called Clement's Second Letter." In *Early Christian Fathers,* edited by C. C. Richardson, 183–202. Philadelphia: Westminster, 1953. Repr. Macmillan, 1970.

7. Helmut Koester, *Introduction to the New Testament.* Vol. 2, *History and Literature of Early Christianity* (Philadelphia: Fortress, 1984), 233–36.

An Ancient Christian Sermon
commonly known as Second Clement

1. Brothers, we ought to think of Jesus Christ, as we do of God, as "Judge of the living and the dead."[1] And we ought not to belittle our salvation, (2) for when we belittle him, we also hope to receive but little. And those who listen as though these are small matters do wrong, and we also do wrong, when we fail to acknowledge from where and by whom and to what place we were called, and how much suffering Jesus Christ endured for our sake. (3) What repayment, then, shall we give to him, or what fruit worthy of what he has given to us? And how many blessings do we owe him? (4) For he has given us the light; as a father he has called us sons; he saved us when we were perishing. (5) What praise, then, shall we give him, or what repayment in return for what we received? (6) Our minds were blinded, and we worshiped stones and wood and gold and silver and brass, the works of men; indeed, our whole life was nothing else but death. So while we were thus wrapped in darkness and our vision was filled with this thick mist, we recovered our sight, by his will laying aside the cloud wrapped around us. (7) For he had mercy upon us and in his compassion he saved us when we had no hope of salvation except that which comes from him, and even though he had seen in us much deception and destruction. (8) For he called us when we did not exist, and out of nothing he willed us into being.

2. "Rejoice, O barren woman, who bears no children; break forth and shout, you who have no labor pains; for the deserted woman has more children than she who has a husband."[2] Now when he said, "Rejoice, O barren woman, who bears no chil-

---

1. Acts 10:42; cf. 1 Pet. 4:5.
2. Isa. 54:1; cf. Gal. 4:27.

dren," he spoke of us, for our church was barren before children were given to it. (2) And when he said, "shout, you who have no labor pains," he means this: we should offer up our prayers to God sincerely, and not grow weary like women in labor. (3) And he said, "for the deserted woman has more children than she who has a husband," because our people seemed to be abandoned by God, but now that we have believed, we have become more numerous than those who seemed to have God. (4) And another Scripture says, "I have not come to call the righteous, but sinners."[3] (5) He means this: that it is necessary to save those who are perishing. (6) For this is a great and marvelous thing, to support not those things that are standing but those that are falling. (7) So also Christ willed to save what was perishing, and he saved many when he came and called us who were already perishing.

3. Seeing, then, that he has shown us such mercy—first of all, that we who are living do not sacrifice to dead gods, nor do we worship them, but through him have come to know the Father of truth—what else is knowledge with respect to him if it is not refusing to deny him through whom we have come to know him? (2) Indeed, he himself says, "Whoever acknowledges me before men, I will acknowledge before my Father."[4] (3) This, then, is our reward, if we acknowledge him through whom we were saved. (4) But how do we acknowledge him? By doing what he says and not disobeying his commandments, and honoring him not only with our lips but "with our whole heart and with our whole mind."[5] (5) And in Isaiah he also says, "This people honors me with their lips, but their heart is far from me."[6]

4. Let us, therefore, not just call him Lord, for this will not save us. (2) For he says, "Not everyone who says to me, 'Lord, Lord,' will be saved, but only the one who does what is right."[7] (3) So then, brothers, let us acknowledge him in our actions by loving one another, by not committing adultery or

---

3. Mark 2:17; Matt. 9:13. This appears to be the earliest instance of a New Testament passage being quoted as "Scripture."
4. Cf. Matt. 10:32.
5. Cf. Mark 12:30.
6. Isa. 29:13; cf. Matt. 15:8; Mark 7:6; *1 Clem.* 15.2.
7. Cf. Matt. 7:21.

slandering one another or being jealous, but by being self-controlled, compassionate, and kind. And we ought to have sympathy for one another, and not be avaricious. By these actions let us acknowledge him, and not by their opposites. (4) Further, we must fear more not men but God. (5) For this reason, if you do these things, the Lord said, "If you are gathered with me in my bosom, yet you do not keep my commandments, I will throw you out and will say to you: 'Get away from me; I do not know where you are from, you evildoers.' "[8]

5. Therefore, brothers, let us turn away from life as residents in this world and do the will of him who called us, and let us not be afraid to depart from this world. (2) For the Lord says, "You will be like lambs among wolves." (3) But Peter answered and said to him, "What if the wolves tear the lambs to pieces?" (4) Jesus said to Peter, "Let the lambs have no fear of the wolves after their death, and as for you, do not fear those who, though they kill you, are not able to do anything else to you, but fear him who, after you are dead, has power to cast soul and body into the flames of hell."[9] (5) Moreover you know, brothers, that our stay in this world of the flesh[10] is insignificant and transitory, but the promise of Christ is great and marvelous: rest in the coming kingdom and eternal life! (6) What, then, must we do to obtain them, except to live a holy and righteous life, and to regard these worldly things as alien to us, and not desire them? (7) For when we desire to acquire these things, we fall away from the way of righteousness.

6. Now the Lord says, "No servant can serve two masters."[11] If we wish to serve both God and money, it is harmful to us. (2) "For what good is it, if someone gains the whole world but forfeits his life?"[12] (3) This age and the one that is coming are two enemies. (4) This one talks about adultery and corruption and greed and deceit, but that one renounces these things.

---

8. Source unknown. It may be from the *Gospel of the Egyptians*; cf. the note on 12.2 below.

9. Source(s) of this series of quotations unknown; possibly from the *Gospel of the Egyptians* (cf. the note on 12.2), but for the individual sayings, cf. Luke 10:3; Matt. 10:16, 28; Luke 12:4–5.

10. *our stay . . . flesh*: or possibly *the stay of this flesh in this world*.

11. Luke 16:13; cf. Matt. 6:24.

12. Cf. Matt. 16:26; Mark 8:36; Luke 9:25.

(5) We cannot, therefore, be friends of both; we must renounce this one in order to experience that one. (6) We think that it is better to hate what is here, because they are insignificant and transitory and perishable, and to love what is there, things which are good and imperishable. (7) For if we do the will of Christ, we will find rest; but if we do not, if we disobey his commandments, then nothing will save us from eternal punishment. (8) And the Scripture also says in Ezekiel, "Even if Noah and Job and Daniel should rise up, they will not save their children"[13] in the captivity. (9) Now if even such righteous men as these are not able, by means of their own righteous deeds, to save their children, what assurance do we have of entering the kingdom of God if we fail to keep our baptism pure and undefiled? Or who will be our advocate, if we are not found to have holy and righteous works?

7. So then, my brothers, let us enter the contest, realizing that the contest is at hand, and that while many come to enter the earthly contests, not all are crowned, but only those who have trained hard and competed well. (2) Let us compete, therefore, that we may all be crowned. (3) Let us run in the straight course, the heavenly contest, and let many of us come to enter it and compete, that we may also be crowned. And if we cannot all be crowned, let us at least come close to it. (4) We must realize that if one who competes in the earthly contest is caught cheating, he is flogged, disqualified, and thrown out of the stadium. (5) What do you think? What will be done to the one who cheats in the heavenly contest? (6) For concerning those who have not kept the seal,[14] he says: "their worm will not die and their fire will not be quenched, and they will be a spectacle for all flesh."[15]

8. So, then, while we are yet on earth, let us repent. (2) For we are clay in the Craftsman's hand. For example: if while a potter is making a vessel, it becomes misshapen or breaks in his hands, he simply reshapes it; but if he has already put it into the kiln, he is no longer able to repair it. So it is with us: as long as we are in this world, let us repent with our whole heart

---

13. Ezek. 14:14–20 (abbr.).
14. *seal*: i.e., of baptism; cf. 6.9; 8.6.
15. Isa. 66:24; cf. Mark 9:48.

of the evil things which we have done in the flesh, in order that we may be saved by the Lord while we still have time for repentance. (3) For after we have departed from the world, we are no longer able there either to confess or to repent anymore. (4) So, brothers, if we have done the will of the Father and have kept the flesh pure and have observed the commandments of the Lord, we will receive eternal life. (5) For the Lord says in the Gospel: "If you did not guard something small, who will give you something great? For I say to you, whoever is faithful with very little is also faithful with much."[16] (6) Now what he means is this: keep the flesh pure and the seal unstained, in order that we may receive life.[17]

9. And let none of you say that this flesh is not judged and does not rise again. (2) Understand this: In what state were you saved? In what state did you recover your sight, if it was not while you were in this flesh? (3) We must, therefore, guard the flesh as a temple of God. (4) For just as you were called in the flesh, so you will come in the flesh. (5) If Christ, the Lord who saved us, became flesh (even though he was originally spirit) and in that state called us, so also we will receive our reward in this flesh. (6) Therefore let us love one another, that we all may enter into the kingdom of God. (7) While we still have time to be healed, let us place ourselves in the hands of God the Physician, and pay him what is due. (8) What is that? Sincere, heart-felt repentance. (9) For he is the one who knows everything beforehand, and knows what is in our heart. (10) Therefore let us give him eternal praise,[18] not from the mouth only but from the heart, in order that he may welcome us as sons. (11) For the Lord also said, "My brothers are those who do the will of my Father."[19]

10. Therefore, my brothers, let us do the will of the Father who called us, that we may live, and let us pursue virtue now more than ever; let us abandon that evil mindset, the forerunner of our sins, and flee ungodliness lest evil things overtake

16. Source uncertain; possibly the *Gospel of the Egyptians* (see the note on 12.2), but cf. also Luke 16:10–12.

17. *life*: so S; AC [Lightfoot] add *eternal* before *life* (cf. 8.4).

18. *eternal praise*: so Lightfoot's restoration; A reads only *eternal*, while CS read only *praise*.

19. Cf. Matt. 12:50; Mark 3:35; Luke 8:21.

us. (2) For if we are eager to do good, peace will pursue us. (3) This is the reason why a man is unable to find peace:[20] they[21] instill human apprehensions, preferring the pleasure of the present to the promise of the future. (4) For they do not know what great torment the pleasure of the present brings, and what delight the promise of the future brings. (5) Now if they alone were doing these things, it could be endured; but now they persist in teaching evil to innocent souls, not knowing that both they and their listeners will receive double punishment.

11. Let us therefore serve God with a pure heart, and we will be righteous. But if we do not serve him because we do not believe God's promise, we will be wretched. (2) For the prophetic word says: "Wretched are the double-minded, those who doubt in their heart and say, 'We heard all these things even in the days of our fathers, and though we have waited day after day we have seen none of them.' (3) Fools! Compare yourselves to a tree, or take a vine: first it sheds its leaves, then a shoot comes, and after these a sour grape, and then a full ripe bunch. (4) So also my people have had turmoil and tribulation, but afterward they will receive good things."[22] (5) So, my brothers, let us not be double-minded, but patiently endure in hope, that we may also receive the reward. (6) "For faithful is he who promised"[23] to pay each person the wages due his works. (7) Therefore, if we do what is right in God's sight, we will enter his kingdom and receive the promises which "ear has not heard nor eye seen nor the heart of man imagined."[24]

12. Let us wait, therefore, hour by hour for the kingdom of God in love and righteousness, since we do not know the day of God's appearing. (2) For the Lord himself, when he was asked

---

20. *to find peace*: the text is corrupt here, as ACS all read only *to find* (*heurein*). While the insertion of *peace* (*eirēnēn*) is a widely adopted emendation, its similarity to the preceding word (*heurein*) being a likely explanation of its accidental omission, Lightfoot prefers to emend *heurein* to *euēmerein* ("to prosper").

21. *they*: i.e., those who are "teaching evil" in 10.5.

22. Source unknown. The same passage (though without the final sentence) is quoted as "Scripture" in *1 Clem.* 23.3. Lightfoot speculates that it is from the lost book of Eldad and Modat mentioned by Hermas (*Vis.* 2.3.4).

23. Heb. 10:23.

24. Cf. 1 Cor. 2:9.

by someone when his kingdom was going to come, said:
"When the two shall be one, and the outside like the inside,
and the male with the female, neither male nor female."[25] (3)
Now "the two" are "one" when we speak the truth among
ourselves and there is one soul in two bodies without deception. (4) And by "the outside like the inside" he means this: the
"inside" signifies the soul, while the "outside" signifies the
body. Therefore just as your body is visible, so also let your soul
be evident in good works. (5) And by "the male with the female, neither male nor female" he means this: that when a
brother sees a sister, he should not think of her as female, nor
should she think of him as male. (6) When you do these things,
he says, the kingdom of my Father will come.

13. Therefore, brothers, let us repent immediately. Let us be
clear-headed regarding the good, for we are full of much stupidity and wickedness. Let us wipe off from ourselves our former
sins and be saved, repenting from the very souls of our being.
And let us not seek to please men. But let us not desire to
please only ourselves with our righteousness, but also those
who are outsiders, that the Name may not be blasphemed on
our account. (2) For the Lord says, "My name is continually
blasphemed among all the nations,"[26] and again, "Woe to him
on whose account my name is blasphemed."[27] Why is it blasphemed? Because you do not do what I desire. (3) For when the
pagans hear from our mouths the oracles of God, they marvel at
their beauty and greatness. But when they discover that our
actions are not worthy of the words we speak, they turn from
wonder to blasphemy, saying that it is a myth and a delusion.
(4) For when they hear from us that God says, "It is no credit to
you if you love those who love you, but it is a credit to you if
you love your enemies and those who hate you,"[28] when they
hear these things, they marvel at such extraordinary goodness.

---

25. Source unknown. A shorter version of the saying (lacking *and the outside . . . inside*) forms part of a longer dialogue cited by Clement of Alexandria
(*Stromata* 3.13.92), who attributes it to the *Gospel of the Egyptians*. Cf. also,
however, the *Gospel According to Thomas*, Saying 22, which preserves a
longer form of the saying.
26. Isa. 52:5.
27. Source unknown.
28. Cf. Luke 6:32, 35.

But when they see that we not only do not love those who hate us, but do not even love those who love us, they scornfully laugh at us and the Name is blasphemed.

14. So then, brothers, if we do the will of God our Father we will belong to the first church, the spiritual one, which was created before the sun and moon. But if we do not do the will of the Lord, we will belong to those of whom the Scripture says, "My house has become a robbers' den."[29] So let us choose, therefore, to belong to the church of life, in order that we may be saved. (2) Now I do not suppose that you are ignorant of the fact that the living church is the body of Christ, for the Scripture says, "God created man male and female."[30] The male is Christ; the female is the church. Moreover, the Books and the Apostles declare[31] that the church not only exists now, but has been in existence from the beginning. For she was spiritual, as was also our Jesus, but was revealed in the last days in order that she[32] might save us. (3) Now the church, being spiritual, was revealed in the flesh of Christ, thereby showing us that if any of us guard her in the flesh and do not corrupt her, he will receive her back again in the Holy Spirit. For this flesh is a copy of the Spirit. No one, therefore, who corrupts the copy will share in the original. This, therefore, is what he means, brothers: guard the flesh, in order that you may receive the Spirit. (4) Now if we say that the flesh is the church and the Spirit is Christ, then the one who abuses the flesh abuses the church. Consequently such a person will not receive the Spirit, which is Christ. (5) So great is the life and immortality which this flesh is able to receive, if the Holy Spirit is closely joined with it, that no one is able to proclaim or to tell "what things the Lord has prepared"[33] for his chosen ones.

15. Now I do not think that the advice I have given about self-control is unimportant; in fact, anyone who follows it will not regret it, but will save both himself and me as his advisor.

---

29. Jer. 7:11; cf. Matt. 21:13; Mark 11:17; Luke 19:46.

30. Cf. Gen. 1:27.

31. *declare*: this word has been supplied, the text being corrupt at this point.

32. *but was . . . she*: or possibly (as Lightfoot prefers) *but he was . . . he*. But the above translation is grammatically more probable.

33. Cf. 1 Cor. 2:9.

For it is no small reward to redirect an errant and perishing soul, so that it may be saved. (2) For this is the return which we are able to repay to God who created us: if the one who speaks and hears both speaks and hears with faith and love. (3) Let us, therefore, in righteousness and holiness remain true to the things we have believed, in order that we may boldly ask of God, who says, "While you are still speaking, I will say, 'Behold, I am here.' "[34] (4) For this word is the sign of a great promise, for the Lord says that he is more ready to give than the one asking is to ask. (5) So then, since we share in such great kindness, let us not begrudge each other the gaining of such great blessings. For these words bring pleasure to those who do them to the same degree that they bring condemnation to those who disobey.

16. Therefore, brothers, inasmuch as we have received no small opportunity to repent, let us, while we still have time, turn again to God who has called us, while we still have one who accepts us. (2) For if we renounce these pleasures and conquer our soul by refusing to fulfill its evil desires, we will share in Jesus' mercy. (3) But you know that "the day" of judgment is already "coming as a blazing furnace,"[35] and "some of the heavens will dissolve,"[36] and the whole earth will be like lead melting in a fire, and then the works of men, the secret and the public, will appear. (4) Charitable giving, therefore, is good, as is repentance from sin. Fasting is better than prayer, while charitable giving is better than both, and "love covers a multitude of sins,"[37] while prayer arising from a good conscience delivers one from death. Blessed is everyone who is found full of these, for charitable giving relieves the burden of sin.

17. Let us repent, therefore, with our whole heart, lest any of us should perish needlessly. For if we have orders that we should make it our business to tear men away from idols and to instruct them, how much more wrong is it that a soul which already knows God should perish? (2) Therefore let us help one another to restore those who are weak with respect to good-

34. Isa. 58:9.

35. Cf. Mal. 4:1.

36. *some*: so CS; Lightfoot (followed by Richardson) emends the text to *the powers*, as in Isa. 34:4, to which the writer is probably alluding.

37. 1 Pet. 4:8; cf. Prov. 10:12.

ness, so that we may all be saved, and let us admonish and turn back one another. (3) And let us think about paying attention and believing not only now, while we are being admonished by the elders, but also when we have returned home let us remember the Lord's commands and not allow ourselves to be dragged off the other way by worldly desires, but let us come here more frequently and strive to advance in the commandments of the Lord, in order that all of us, being of one mind, may be gathered together into life. (4) For the Lord said, "I am coming to gather together all the nations, tribes, and languages."[38] Now by this he means the day of his appearing, when he will come and redeem us, each according to his deeds. (5) And the unbelievers "will see his glory"[39] and might, and they will be astonished when they see that the kingdom of the world belongs to Jesus, saying, "Woe to us, because it was you,[40] and we did not realize it, nor did we believe; and we did not obey the elders when they spoke to us about our salvation." And "their worm will not die and their fire will not be quenched, and they will be a spectacle for all flesh."[41] (6) He means that day of judgment, when people will see those among us who lived ungodly lives and perverted the commandments of Jesus Christ. (7) But the righteous, having done good and endured torments and hated the pleasures of the soul, when they see how those who have gone astray and denied Jesus by their words or by their actions are being punished with dreadful torments in unquenchable fire, will give glory to their God as they say, "There will be hope for the one who has served God with his whole heart."

18. Therefore let us too be part of those giving thanks, that is, those who have served God, and not of the ungodly who are judged. (2) For I myself am utterly sinful and have not yet escaped from temptation; but even though I am surrounded by the tools of the devil, I make every effort to pursue righteousness, that I may succeed in at least getting close to it, because I fear the coming judgment.

19. Therefore, brothers and sisters, following the God of

---

38. Cf. Isa. 66:18.
39. Cf. Isa. 66:18.
40. *it was you* (cf. John 8:24, 28; 13:19): or possibly *you really existed.*
41. Isa. 66:24; cf. Mark 9:48.

truth[42] I am reading you an exhortation to pay attention to what is written, in order that you may save both yourselves and your reader. As compensation I ask that you repent with your whole heart, thereby giving salvation and life to yourselves. For by doing this we will set a goal for all the young people who desire to devote themselves to piety and the goodness of God. (2) Moreover, let us not be displeased or indignant, unwise as we are, when someone admonishes us and tries to turn us away from unrighteousness to righteousness. For there are times when we do evil things without realizing it because of the double-mindedness and faithlessness that exist with us, and our "understanding is darkened"[43] by empty desires. (3) Let us, therefore, practice righteousness, that we may be saved in the end. Blessed are they who obey these injunctions; though they may endure affliction for a little while in the[44] world, they will gather the immortal fruit of the resurrection. (4) So, then, the godly person should not be grieved if he is miserable at the present time; a time of blessedness awaits him. He will live again with the fathers above, and will rejoice in an eternity untouched by sorrow.

20. But do not let it trouble your mind that we see the unrighteous possessing wealth while the servants of God experience hardships. (2) Let us have faith, brothers and sisters! We are competing in the contest of a living God, and are being trained by the present life in order that we may be crowned in the life to come. (3) None of the righteous ever received his reward quickly, but waits for it. (4) For if God paid the wages of the righteous immediately, we would soon be engaged in business, not godliness; though we would appear to be righteous, we would in fact be pursuing not piety but profit. And this is why the divine judgment punishes a spirit that is not righteous, and loads it with chains.

(5) "To the only God, invisible,"[45] the Father of truth, who sent forth to us the Savior and Founder of immortality, through whom he also revealed to us the truth and the heavenly life, to him be the glory forever and ever. Amen.

42. *following . . . truth*: i.e., the Scripture lesson or reading.
43. Cf. Eph. 4:18.
44. *the*: so S; C reads *this*.
45. Cf. 1 Tim. 1:17.

The Letters of Ignatius, Bishop of Antioch

INTRODUCTION

Just as we become aware of a meteor only when, after traveling silently through space for untold millions of miles, it blazes briefly through the atmosphere before dying in a shower of fire, so it is with Ignatius, bishop of Antioch in Syria. We meet him for the first and only time for a few weeks shortly before his death as a martyr in Rome early in the second century. But during those few weeks he wrote, virtually as his "last will and testament," seven letters of extraordinary interest because of the unparalleled light they shed on the history of the church at this time and what they reveal about the remarkable personality of the author. Because of the early date of these writings and the distinctiveness of some of his ideas, particularly with regard to the nature and structure of the church, Ignatius's letters have influenced later theological reflection and continue to be a focus of scholarly contention and discussion regarding early Christian origins.

Setting and Occasion

Ignatius's letters were written under extraordinarily stressful and difficult circumstances. After his arrest (it is not known why and under what circumstances he was arrested) in Syria, which left the church in Antioch leaderless and vulnerable, Ignatius was sent to Rome in the custody of a detachment of ten soldiers (the "leopards" of *Rom* 5.1) to be executed. At a fork in the road at some point along the way through Asia Minor, probably Laodicea, the decision was made to take the northern route through Philadelphia to Smyrna, thus bypassing

79

the churches that lay along the southern route (Tralles, Magnesia, and Ephesus). It is probable that when the northern road was chosen, messengers were sent to these churches informing them of Ignatius's itinerary, and they evidently dispatched delegations to meet him in Smyrna. Ignatius responded to this show of support by sending a letter to each of the three churches, and he also sent one ahead to the church in Rome, alerting them to his impending arrival there. The guards and their prisoners next stopped at Troas, where Ignatius received the news that "peace" had been restored to the church at Antioch (*Phld.* 10.1; *Smyrn.* 11.2; *Pol.* 7.1.), about which he apparently had been quite worried, and sent letters back to the two churches he had visited, Philadelphia and Smyrna, and to his friend Polycarp, bishop of Smyrna. But before he could write any more letters the group hurried on to Neapolis and then Philippi, where he was warmly received by the church (Pol. *Phil.* 8.1; 1.1). There he disappears from view. Presumably he was taken on to Rome and thrown to the lions in the Coliseum. While it is not absolutely certain that he died a martyr's death, there is no reason to think otherwise.

It appears that three concerns were uppermost in Ignatius's mind at this time: (1) the struggle against false teachers within the churches; (2) the unity and structure of the churches; and (3) his own impending death. To Ignatius, the false teachers within posed a greater threat than the pagan society without. "Heresy" (*Eph.* 6.2; *Trall.* 6.1), whether that of the Judaizers, whose teaching tended to diminish the importance and centrality of Christ, or of the docetists who, being influenced by the common view that matter was evil, tended to deny the reality of Jesus' humanity, threatened to split the church and thereby destroy the God-given unity which for Ignatius was one of the distinguishing marks of the true faith.

In opposing the false teachers Ignatius, in addition to affirming both the divinity of Jesus and the reality of his incarnation, suffering, and resurrection, stresses the importance of the bishop in preserving the unity of the church. He does this on two levels. First, while Ignatius's ideal church may have a threefold ministry that includes deacons and presbyters, it is the bishop who is constitutive of the church: where he is, the church is.

Any activity or service that takes place without either his presence or permission has no validity. Thus those schismatics who gather separately cut themselves off from the true church. Second, the central role of the bishop organizationally has a theological rationale: the bishop is nothing less than God's representative to the congregation. Just as Christians are united with God spiritually in heaven, so it is their duty to be in communion or harmony with their bishop on earth. Conversely, one's attitude toward the bishop reflects one's attitude toward God, and thus one's behavior relative to the bishop becomes critically important. It is interesting that Ignatius provides a theological rationale for the authority and place of the bishop and does not base it, as his near contemporary Clement of Rome does, upon the concept of apostolic succession.

Ignatius's Attitude Toward Martyrdom

The vivid, almost macabre eagerness with which Ignatius apparently anticipates his death has repelled many readers, and a good deal of unwarranted criticism (e.g., labeling him "neurotic") has been directed toward him on the basis of a misunderstanding of his attitude toward martyrdom, which is quite complex. One positive factor is his sincere desire to imitate the suffering of his Lord and thereby become a true disciple; indeed, he goes so far as to claim that only since his arrest is he "beginning" to be a disciple. However off-putting his idea may be to some, it must be given due weight as a way of understanding persecution that finds parallels in both Paul and Matthew. Some of his language, particularly in his letter to the Romans, may reflect an understandable fear of failure, an effort to fortify himself and hold to the course to which he had publicly committed himself. In addition, generally the only basis for releasing a Christian condemned to death was apostasy; even if the Roman church had won his release for good reasons, rumors that he had apostasized likely would have arisen, and he no doubt wished to avoid such speculation.

Then there is the situation in Antioch, about which Ignatius is evidently quite worried. Schoedel notes Ignatius's marked tendency toward self-effacement, and that oddly enough he relates to the churches to which he writes not on the basis of his status as bishop, but as a captive about to be martyred. Schoedel then persuasively suggests that the Antiochene church was on the verge of splitting.[1] If such a split were to occur it would mean that Ignatius was a failure as a bishop because he would not have maintained the godly way of the congregation that had been entrusted to him. He may, therefore, have seen in his imminent martyrdom a means by which to reclaim the deteriorating situation in Antioch and/or to redeem his reputation as a bishop and a Christian.

Viewed in light of these factors, Ignatius's attitude toward his death is understandable and quite in line with those who died for their faith before (cf., e.g., 4 Macc.) and after him (e.g., Polycarp).

Date

There is virtually unanimous agreement that Ignatius was martyred during the reign of Trajan (A.D. 98–117), but to fix the precise year is difficult.[2] The Eusebian date of approximately 107–108 has been adopted by Frend,[3] while many place it in the second half of Trajan's reign (ca. 110–117).[4] Lightfoot himself places it "within a few years of A.D. 110, before or after."[5]

Authenticity

Everything said about Ignatius thus far rests upon the conclusion that the seven letters of the so-called middle recension are authentic. This conclusion is widely held today, but such was not always the case.

The letters exist in three basic forms. The long recension is an expanded version of the original letters created in the fourth century to which six spurious letters have been added; some of

---

1. W. R. Schoedel, *Ignatius of Antioch* (Philadelphia: Fortress, 1985), 10–14.

2. Cf. Lightfoot, *AF* 2.2.435–72.

3. W. H. C. Frend, *The Rise of Christianity* (Philadelphia: Fortress, 1984), 124.

4. Cf. Koester, *Literature*, 281.

5. Lightfoot, *AF* 2.1.30.

these came to be associated with the middle recension as well. The short recension is a Syriac abridgment of the letters to the Ephesians, the Romans, and Polycarp. The middle recension, which was known to Eusebius, preserves the original form of the letters.

During the Renaissance and Reformation, both the long and middle recensions became known in both Greek and Latin, although it was not until 1646 that the Greek text of the middle recension was published. This multiplexity of forms, together with the admixture of varying numbers of later spurious letters, created a great deal of confusion and debate about the authenticity of the letters. Progress in resolving the question was not helped by the fact that the discussion came to be heavily influenced by dogmatic concerns extraneous to the issue. Catholic scholars generally defended the authenticity of the letters because of the obvious polemical value of Ignatius's early date and emphasis on the monepiscopal form of church structure, while Protestants generally denied their authenticity for similar reasons.

A consensus of sorts in favor of the middle recension came to prevail following the publication of Pearson's *Vindiciae Ignatianae* (1672), but the question was reopened when in 1845 William Cureton published the Syriac abridgment of three of the letters (the short recension). Not until the independent work of Theodor Zahn (1873) and J. B. Lightfoot (1885) was general recognition of the authenticity of the seven letters contained in the middle recension attained. Recent challenges[6] to the current consensus have not altered the situation.[7]

The Text

The Greek text upon which the following translation is based has been reconstructed on the basis of the following witnesses:

---

6. R. Weijenborg, *Les lettres d'Ignace d'Antioche* (Leiden: E. J. Brill, 1969); J. Ruis-Camps, *The Four Authentic Letters of Ignatius, the Martyr* (Rome: Pontificium Institutum Orientalium Studiorum, 1979); R. Joly, *Le dossier d'Ignace d'Antioche* (Brussels: Éditions de l'université, 1979).

7. W. R. Schoedel, "Are the Letters of Ignatius of Antioch Authentic?" *Religious Studies Review* 6 (1980): 196–201, summarized in Schoedel, *Ignatius*, 5–7.

G   = Codex Mediceo-Laurentianus (eleventh c.; the
           only extant copy of the middle recension)
L   = the Latin version of the middle recension
P   = Berlin papyrus cod. 10581 (fifth c.; contains
           Smyrn. 3.3–12.1)
g   = the Greek manuscripts of the long recension
l   = the Latin manuscripts of the long recension
S   = the Syriac abridgment (the short recension)
S^f   = fragments of the Syriac version of the middle
           recension
A   = the Armenian version
C   = the Coptic version
Arabic   = the Arabic version

Because the letter to the Romans has a separate textual history,
the following additional symbols are necessary:

G   = Codex Parisiensis-Colbertinus (tenth–eleventh
           c.)
H   = Codex Hierosolymitanus S. Sabae (tenth c.)
K   = Codex Sinaiticus 519 (tenth c.)
T   = Codex Taurinensis (thirteenth c.)
Sm,Am   = the Syriac or Armenian versions of various narra-
           tives of Ignatius's martyrdom

The order in which the letters are presented is that of
Eusebius (*Church History* 3.36), which reflects a geographical
arrangement based upon the order of cities from which and to
which they were sent (cf. pp. 79–80 above). In G, however, they
stand in the following order:

1. Smyrnaeans	4. Magnesians
2. Polycarp	5. Philadelphians
3. Ephesians	6. Trallians
7. Romans	

This sequence is consistent with Polycarp's remark to the Philippians (Pol. *Phil.* 13.2)—"We are sending you the letters of

Ignatius that were sent to us by him [i.e., the letters to the Smyrnaeans and Polycarp] together with any others that we have in our possession [i.e., the letter to the Ephesians, etc.]"—and may well represent the order of the letters in the earliest collection made of them.

BIBLIOGRAPHY

Bammel, C. P. H. "Ignatian Problems." *Journal of Theological Studies* 33 (1982): 62–97.

Camelot, P.-Th. *Ignace d'Antioche: Lettres. Lettres et Martyre de Polycarpe de Smyrne.* 4th ed. Paris: Cerf, 1969.

Corwin, Virginia. *St. Ignatius and Christianity in Antioch.* Yale Publications in Religion 1. New Haven: Yale University Press, 1960.

Grant, R. M. *Ignatius of Antioch.* The Apostolic Fathers, vol. 4. Camden, N.J.: Nelson, 1966.

Kleist, J. A. *The Epistles of St. Clement of Rome and St. Ignatius of Antioch.* Ancient Christian Writers, vol. 1. Westminster, Md.: Newman, 1946.

Lightfoot, J. B. *The Apostolic Fathers, Part II: S. Ignatius. S. Polycarp.* 2d ed. 3 vols. London: Macmillan, 1889. Repr. Grand Rapids: Baker, 1981.

Paulsen, Henning. *Die Briefe des Ignatius von Antiochia und der Brief des Polykarp von Smyrna.* Zweite, neubearbeitete Auflage der Auslegung von Walter Bauer. Tübingen: Mohr/Siebeck, 1985.

Richardson, C. C. "The Letters of Ignatius, Bishop of Antioch." In *Early Christian Fathers,* edited by C. C. Richardson, 74–120. Philadelphia: Westminster, 1953. Repr. Macmillan, 1970.

Schoedel, W. R. "Are the Letters of Ignatius of Antioch Authentic?" *Religious Studies Review* 6 (1980): 196–201.

———. *Ignatius of Antioch. A Commentary on the Letters of Ignatius of Antioch.* Hermeneia. Philadelphia: Fortress, 1985.

Zahn, Theodor. *Ignatius von Antiochien.* Gotha: Perthes, 1873.

The Letters of Ignatius,
Bishop of Antioch

TO THE EPHESIANS

Ignatius, who is also called Theophorus,[1] to the church at Ephesus in Asia, blessed with greatness through the fullness of God the Father, predestined before the ages for lasting and unchangeable glory forever, united and elect through genuine suffering by the will of the Father and of Jesus Christ our God, a church most worthy of blessing: heartiest greetings in Jesus Christ and in blameless joy.

1. I welcome in God your well-beloved name which you possess by reason of your righteous nature,[2] which is characterized by faith in and love of Christ Jesus our Savior. Being as you are imitators of God, once you took on new life through the blood of God you completed perfectly the task so natural to you. (2) For when you heard that I was on my way from Syria in chains for the sake of our common name[3] and hope, and was hoping through your prayers to succeed in fighting with wild beasts in Rome—in order that by so succeeding I might be able to be a disciple—you hurried to visit me. (3) Since, therefore, I have received in God's name your whole congregation in the person of Onesimus, a man of inexpressible love who is also your earthly[4] bishop, I pray that you will love him in accordance with the standard set by Jesus Christ and that all of you

---

1. *Theophorus*: i.e., the "God-bearer."
2. *by reason . . . nature*: so GLg; Lightfoot adopts the longer reading of SA: *by natural right, in an upright and righteous mind.*
3. *name*: i.e., that of "Christian."
4. *earthly*: so GL [Lightfoot]; SAg, which Lightfoot is inclined to follow, omit the word. If original, as it probably is, the contrast is likely with Christ, their "heavenly" bishop.

will be like him. For blessed is he who has graciously allowed you, worthy as you are, to have such a bishop.

2. Now concerning my fellow servant Burrhus, who is by God's will your deacon, blessed in every respect, I pray that he might remain with me both for your honor and the bishop's. And Crocus also, who is worthy of God and of you, whom I received as a living example of your love, has refreshed me in every way; may the Father of Jesus Christ likewise refresh him, together with Onesimus, Burrhus, Euplus, and Fronto, in whom I saw all of you with respect to love. (2) May I always have joy in you, if, that is, I am worthy. It is proper, therefore, in every way to glorify Jesus Christ, who has glorified you, so that you, joined together in a united obedience and subject to the bishop and the presbytery, may be sanctified in every respect.

3. I am not commanding you, as though I were somebody important. For even though I am in chains for the sake of the Name, I have not yet been perfected in Jesus Christ. For now I am only beginning to be a disciple, and I speak to you as my fellow students. For I need to be trained by you in faith, instruction, endurance, and patience. (2) But since love does not allow me to be silent concerning you, I have therefore taken the initiative to encourage you, so that you may run together in harmony with the mind of God. For Jesus Christ, our inseparable life, is the mind of the Father, just as the bishops appointed throughout the world are in the mind of Christ.

4. Thus it is proper for you to act together in harmony with the mind of the bishop, as you are in fact doing. For your presbytery, which is worthy of its name and worthy of God, is attuned to the bishop as strings to a lyre. Therefore in your unanimity and harmonious love Jesus Christ is sung. (2) You must join this chorus, every one of you, so that by being harmonious in unanimity and taking your pitch from God you may sing in unison with one voice through Jesus Christ to the Father, in order that he may both hear you and, on the basis of what you do well, acknowledge that you are members of his Son. It is, therefore, advantageous for you to be in perfect unity, in order that you may always have a share in God.

5. For if I in a short time experienced such fellowship with your bishop, which was not merely human but spiritual, how much more do I congratulate you who are united with him, as the church is with Jesus Christ and as Jesus Christ is with the Father, that all things might be harmonious in unity. (2) Let no one be misled: if anyone is not within the sanctuary, he lacks the bread of God.[5] For if the prayer of one or two has such power, how much more that of the bishop together with the whole church! (3) Therefore whoever does not meet with the congregation thereby demonstrates his arrogance and has separated[6] himself, for it is written: "God opposes the arrogant."[7] Let us, therefore, be careful not to oppose the bishop, in order that we may be obedient to God.

6. Furthermore, the more anyone observes that the bishop is silent, the more one should fear him. For everyone whom the Master of the house sends to manage his own house we must welcome as we would the one who sent him. It is obvious, therefore, that we must regard the bishop as the Lord himself. (2) Now Onesimus himself highly praises your orderly conduct in God, reporting that you all live in accordance with the truth and that no heresy[8] has found a home among you. Indeed, you do not so much as listen to anyone unless he speaks truthfully about Jesus Christ.[9]

7. For there are some who maliciously and deceitfully are accustomed to carrying about the Name while doing other things unworthy of God. You must avoid them as wild beasts. For they are mad dogs that bite by stealth; you must be on your guard against them, for their bite is hard to heal. (2) There is only one physician, who is both flesh and spirit, born and unborn, God in man,[10] true life in death, both from Mary and from God, first subject to suffering and then beyond it, Jesus Christ our Lord.

8. Therefore let no one deceive you, just as you are not now deceived, seeing that you belong entirely to God. For when no

5. Cf. John 6:33.
6. *separated*: or possibly *judged*.
7. Prov. 3:34.
8. *heresy*: or perhaps here *faction*.
9. *unless . . . Christ*: so Lightfoot's widely adopted emendation of the text, following A. The reading of G is grammatically impossible; L reads *except Jesus Christ speaking in truth*.
10. *God in man*: so the early patristic quotations, followed by Lightfoot; GL read *God come in flesh* (cf. John 1:14).

dissension[11] capable of tormenting you is established among you, then you indeed live God's way. I am a humble sacrifice for you and I dedicate myself to you Ephesians, a church which is famous forever. (2) Those who are carnal cannot do spiritual things, nor can those who are spiritual do carnal things, just as faith cannot do the things of unfaithfulness, nor unfaithfulness the things of faith. Moreover, even those things which you do carnally are, in fact, spiritual, for you do everything in Jesus Christ.

9. But I have learned that certain people from there have passed your way with evil doctrine, but you did not allow them to sow it among you. You covered up your ears in order to avoid receiving the things being sown by them, because you are stones of a temple, prepared beforehand[12] for the building of God the Father, hoisted up to the heights by the crane of Jesus Christ, which is the cross, using as a rope the Holy Spirit; your faith is what lifts you up, and love is the way that leads up to God.

(2) So you are all fellow pilgrims, carrying your God and your shrine, your Christ and your holy things,[13] adorned in every respect with the commandments of Jesus Christ. I too celebrate with you, since I have been judged worthy to speak with you through this letter, and to rejoice with you because you love nothing in human life,[14] only God.

10. Pray continually for the rest of mankind as well, that they may find God, for there is in them hope for repentance. Therefore allow them to be instructed by you, at least by your deeds. (2) In response to their anger, be gentle; in response to their boasts, be humble; in response to their slander, offer prayers; in response to their errors, be "steadfast in the

---

11. *dissension*: so GL; SAg (followed by Lightfoot) read *lust*.

12. *temple, prepared beforehand*: so Lightfoot's emendation; GLA read *temple of the Father, prepared*.

13. *carrying . . . things*: here Ignatius applies to the Ephesians the image of a pagan religious procession, in which the participants carry with them their gods, idols, shrines, etc.

14. *in . . . life*: so Lightfoot's widely accepted emendation; GL(A) read *according to another life*, which may (following Schoedel, *Ignatius*, 65, 68) be translated *in your new way of life except*.

faith";[15] in response to their cruelty, be gentle; do not be eager to retaliate against them. (3) Let us show ourselves their brothers by our forbearance, and let us be eager to be imitators of the Lord, to see who can be the more wronged, who the more cheated,[16] who the more rejected, in order that no weed of the devil might be found among you, but that with complete purity and self-control you may abide in Christ Jesus physically and spiritually.

11. These are the last times. Therefore let us be reverent, let us fear the patience of God, lest it become a judgment against us. For let us either fear the wrath to come or love the grace which is present, one of the two; only let us be found in Christ Jesus, which leads to true life. (2) Let nothing appeal to you apart from him, in whom I carry around these chains (my spiritual pearls!), by which I hope, through your prayers, to rise again. May I always share in them, in order that I might be found in the company of the Christians of Ephesus who have always been in agreement with the apostles, by the power of Jesus Christ.

12. I know who I am and to whom I am writing. I am a convict, you have received mercy; I am in danger, you are secure. (2) You are the highway[17] of those who are being killed for God's sake; you are fellow initiates of Paul, who was sanctified, who was approved, who is deservedly blessed—may I be found in his footsteps when I reach God!—who in every letter remembers you in Christ Jesus.

13. Therefore make every effort to come together more frequently to give thanks and glory to[18] God. For when you meet together frequently, the powers of Satan are overthrown and his destructiveness is nullified by the unanimity of your faith. (2) There is nothing better than peace, by which all warfare among those in heaven and those on earth is abolished.

14. None of these things escapes your notice, if you have perfect faith and love toward Jesus Christ. For these are the

15. Cf. Col. 1:23.

16. Cf. 1 Cor. 6:7.

17. *highway*: Ephesus was on the route by which prisoners from the East would be taken to Rome; Ignatius seems to suggest that their spiritual position corresponds to their geographical location.

18. *to give thanks . . . to*: or possibly *for the Eucharist . . . of*.

beginning and end of life: faith is the beginning, and love is the end, and the two, when they exist in unity, are God. Everything else that contributes to excellence follows from them. (2) No one professing faith sins, nor does anyone possessing love hate. "The tree is known by its fruit";[19] thus those who profess to be Christ's will be recognized by their actions. For the Work[20] is not a matter of what one promises now, but of persevering to the end in the power of faith.

15. It is better to be silent and be real, than to talk and not be real. It is good to teach, if one does what one says. Now there is one such teacher, who "spoke and it happened";[21] indeed, even the things which he has done in silence are worthy of the Father. (2) The one who truly possesses the word of Jesus is also able to hear his silence, that he may be perfect, that he may act through what he says and be known through his silence. (3) Nothing is hidden from the Lord; even our secrets are close to him. Therefore let us do everything with the knowledge that he dwells in us, in order that we may be his temples, and he may be in us as our[22] God—as, in fact, he really is, as will be made clear in our sight by the love which we justly have for him.

16. Do not be misled, my brothers: those who adulterously corrupt households "will not inherit the kingdom of God."[23] (2) Now if those who do such things physically are put to death, how much more if by evil teaching someone corrupts faith in God, for which Jesus Christ was crucified! Such a person, having polluted himself, will go to the unquenchable fire, as will also the one who listens to him.

17. The Lord accepted the ointment upon his head[24] for this reason: that he might breathe incorruptibility upon the church. Do not be anointed with the stench of the teaching of the ruler of this age, lest he take you captive and rob you of the life set before you. (2) Why do we not all become wise by receiving God's knowledge, which is Jesus Christ? Why do we foolishly perish, ignoring the gracious gift which the Lord has truly sent?

19. Cf. Matt. 12:33.
20. *Work*: i.e., Christianity; cf. *Rom.* 3.3.
21. Ps. 33 (LXX 32):9.
22. *our*: so GL(A); S^{f}g (followed by Lightfoot) omit.
23. Cf. 1 Cor. 6:9–10.
24. Cf. Matt. 26:6–13.

18. My spirit is a humble sacrifice for the cross, which is a stumbling block to unbelievers, but salvation and eternal life to us. "Where is the wise? Where is the debater?"[25] Where is the boasting of those who are thought to be intelligent? (2) For our God, Jesus the Christ, was conceived by Mary according to God's[26] plan, both from the seed of David and of the Holy Spirit. He was born and was baptized in order that by his suffering he might cleanse the water.[27]

19. Now the virginity of Mary and her giving birth were hidden from the ruler of this age, as was also the death of the Lord—three mysteries to be loudly proclaimed, yet which were accomplished in the silence of God. (2) How, then, were they revealed to the ages? A star shone forth in heaven brighter than all the stars; its light was indescribable and its strangeness caused amazement. All the rest of the constellations, together with the sun and moon, formed a chorus around the star, yet the star itself far outshone them all, and there was perplexity about the origin of this strange phenomenon which was so unlike the others. (3) Consequently all magic and every kind of spell were dissolved, the ignorance so characteristic of wickedness vanished, and the ancient kingdom was abolished,[28] when God appeared in human form to bring the newness of eternal life; and what had been prepared by God began to take effect. As a result, all things were thrown into ferment, because the abolition of death was being carried out.

20. If Jesus Christ, in response to your prayer, should reckon me worthy, and if it is his will, in a second letter which I intend to write to you I will further explain to you the subject about which I have begun to speak, namely, the divine plan with respect to the new man Jesus Christ, involving faith in him and love for him,[29] his suffering and resurrection, (2) especially if the Lord reveals anything to me. Continue[30] to gather together,

---

25. Cf. 1 Cor. 1:20.
26. *God's*: g (followed by Lightfoot) omits.
27. *water*: i.e., of baptism.
28. *magic . . . abolished*: so Lightfoot, following SA; GL (followed by almost all other editors) read *magic was dissolved and every wicked spell vanished, ignorance was abolished, and the ancient kingdom was destroyed.*
29. *faith . . . for him*: or possibly *his faith and his love.*
30. *reveals . . . Continue*: so Lightfoot (with some hesitation) and Schoedel,

each and every one of you, collectively and individually by name, in grace, in one faith and one[31] Jesus Christ, who physically was a descendant of David, who is Son of man and Son of God, in order that you may obey the bishop and the presbytery with an undisturbed mind, breaking one bread, which is the medicine of immortality, the antidote we take in order not to die but to live forever in Jesus Christ.

21. I am devoted to you and to those whom for the honor of God you sent to Smyrna, from where I am writing to you, with thanksgiving to the Lord and love for Polycarp as well as for you. Remember me, as Jesus Christ does you. (2) Pray for the church in Syria, from where I am being led to Rome in chains, as I—the very least of the faithful there—have been judged worthy of serving the glory of God. Farewell in God the Father and in Jesus Christ, our common hope.

TO THE MAGNESIANS

Ignatius, who is also called Theophorus, to the church at Magnesia on the Maeander, which has been blessed through the grace of God the Father in Christ Jesus our Savior, in whom I greet her and wish her heartiest greetings in God the Father and in Jesus Christ.

1. When I learned how well-ordered your love toward God is, I rejoiced and resolved to address you in the faith of Jesus Christ. (2) For inasmuch as I have been judged worthy to bear a most godly name, in these chains which I bear I sing the praises of the churches, and I pray that in them there may be a union of flesh and spirit that comes from Jesus Christ, our never-failing life, and of faith and love, to which nothing is preferable, and— what is more important—of Jesus and the Father. In him we will, if we patiently endure all the abuse of the ruler of this age and escape, reach God.

2. So, then, I was permitted to see you in the persons of Damas, your godly bishop, your worthy presbyters Bassus and Apollonius, and my fellow servant, the deacon Zotion; may I

---

adopting Zahn's emendation of *hoti* ("that") to *ti* ("anything"); GL(A) read *reveals to me that you continue.*

31. *one:* so Lightfoot, following ancient citations; GLS[f] read *in.*

enjoy his company, because he is subject to the bishop as to the grace of God, and to the presbytery as to the law of Jesus Christ.

3. Indeed, it is right for you also not to take advantage of the youthfulness of your bishop, but to give him all the respect due him in accordance with the power of God the Father, just as I know that the holy presbyters likewise have not taken advantage of his youthful appearance, but yield to him as one who is[32] wise in God; yet not really to him, but to the Father of Jesus Christ, the Bishop of all. (2) For the honor, therefore, of him who loved you[33] it is right to be obedient without any hypocrisy, for it is not so much a matter of deceiving this bishop who is seen, but of cheating the One who is unseen. In such a case he must reckon not with the flesh but with God, who knows our secrets.

4. It is right, therefore, that we not just be called Christians, but that we actually be Christians, unlike some who call a man "bishop" but do everything without regard for him. Such men do not appear to me to act in good conscience, inasmuch as they do not validly meet together in accordance with the commandment.

5. Seeing then that all things have an end, two things together lie before us, death and life, and everyone will go to his own place. (2) For just as there are two coinages, the one of God and the other of the world, and each of them has its own stamp impressed upon it, so the unbelievers bear the stamp of this world, but the faithful in love bear the stamp of God the Father through Jesus Christ, whose life is not in us unless we voluntarily choose to die into his suffering.

6. Since, therefore, in the persons mentioned above I have by faith seen and loved the whole congregation, I have this advice: Be eager to do everything in godly harmony, the bishop presiding in the place of God and the presbyters in the place[34] of the council of the apostles and the deacons, who are most dear to me, having been entrusted with the service of Jesus Christ, who before the ages was with the Father and appeared

32. *one who is*: so A(g); GL read *men who are.*

33. *you*: so Ag; GL read *us.*

34. *in the place . . . in the place* (*topos*): so Glg; SA (followed by Zahn and Lightfoot) read *after the model* (*typos*).

at the end of time. (2) Let all, therefore, accept the same attitude as God and respect one another, and let no one regard his neighbor in merely human terms but in Jesus Christ love one another always. Let there be nothing among you which is capable of dividing you, but be united with the bishop and with those who lead, as an example and a lesson of incorruptibility.

7. Therefore as the Lord did nothing without the Father, either by himself or through the apostles (for he was united with him), so you must not do anything without the bishop and the presbyters. Do not attempt to convince yourselves that anything done apart from the others is right, but, gathering together, let there be one prayer, one petition, one mind, one hope, with love and blameless joy, which is Jesus Christ, than whom nothing is better. (2) Let all of you run together as to one temple of God, as to one altar, to one Jesus Christ, who came forth from one Father and remained with the One and returned to the One.

8. Do not be deceived by strange doctrines or antiquated myths, since they are worthless. For if we continue to live in accordance with Judaism, we admit that we have not received grace. (2) For the most godly prophets lived in accordance with Christ Jesus. This is why they were persecuted, being inspired as they were by his grace in order that those who are disobedient might be fully convinced that there is one God who revealed himself through Jesus Christ his Son, who is his Word which came forth from[35] silence, who in every respect pleased him who sent him.

9. If, then, those who had lived in antiquated practices came to newness of hope, no longer keeping the Sabbath but living in accordance with the Lord's day, on which our life also arose through him and his death (which some deny), the mystery through which we came to believe, and because of which we patiently endure, in order that we might be found to be disciples of Jesus Christ, our only teacher, (2) how can we possibly live without him, whom even the prophets, who were his disciples in the Spirit, were expecting as their teacher? Because of this he for whom they rightly waited raised them from the dead when he came.

---

35. *from:* so A Arabic Severus; GL read *not from.*

10. Therefore let us not be unaware of his goodness. For if he were to imitate the way we act, we are lost. Therefore, having become his disciples, let us learn to live in accordance with Christianity. For whoever is called by any other name than this one does not belong to God. (2) Throw out, therefore, the bad leaven, which has become stale and sour, and reach for the new leaven, which is Jesus Christ. Be salted with him, so that none of you become rotten, for by your odor you will be examined. (3) It is utterly absurd to profess Jesus Christ and to practice Judaism. For Christianity did not believe in Judaism, but Judaism in Christianity, in which "every tongue" believed and "was brought together"[36] to God.

11. Now I write these things, my dear friends, not because I have learned that any of you are actually like that, but, as one who is less than you, I want to forewarn you not to get snagged on the hooks of worthless opinions but instead to be fully convinced about the birth and the suffering and the resurrection, which took place during the time of the governorship of Pontius Pilate. These things were truly and most assuredly done by Jesus Christ, our hope, from which may none of you ever be turned aside.

12. May I have joy in you in every respect, if, that is, I am worthy. For even though I am in chains, I cannot be compared to one of you who are at liberty. I know that you are not conceited, for you have Jesus Christ within you. Moreover, I know that when I praise you, you feel ashamed, as it is written: "the righteous is his own accuser."[37]

13. Be eager, therefore, to be firmly grounded in the precepts of the Lord and the apostles, in order that "in whatever you do, you may prosper,"[38] physically and spiritually, in faith and love, in the Son and the Father and in the Spirit, in the beginning and at the end, together with your most distinguished bishop and that beautifully woven spiritual crown which is your presbytery and the godly deacons. (2) Be subject to the bishop and to one another, as Jesus Christ in the flesh[39] was to

36. Cf. Isa. 66:18.
37. Prov. 18:17 (LXX).
38. Cf. Ps. 1:3.
39. *in the flesh*: so GL [Lightfoot]; A Arabic omit, perhaps rightly.

the Father, and as the apostles were to Christ and to the Father,[40] that there might be unity, both physical and spiritual.

14. Knowing as I do that you are full of God, I have only briefly exhorted you. Remember me in your prayers, in order that I might reach God; remember also the church in Syria, of which I am not worthy to be called a member. For I need your united prayer and love in God, that the church in Syria might be judged worthy of being refreshed by the dew of your fervent prayers.[41]

15. The Ephesians greet you from Smyrna, from where I am writing you. They, like you, are here for the glory of God, and have refreshed me in every respect, together with Polycarp, bishop of the Smyrnaeans. All the other churches also greet you in honor of Jesus Christ. Farewell in godly harmony to you who possess an undivided spirit, which is Jesus Christ.

TO THE TRALLIANS

Ignatius, who is also called Theophorus, to the holy church at Tralles in Asia, dearly loved by God the Father of Jesus Christ, elect and worthy of God, at peace in flesh and spirit[42] through the suffering of Jesus Christ, who is our hope when we rise to be with him, which I greet in the fullness of God in the apostolic manner and offer heartiest greetings.

1. I know that you have a disposition that is blameless and unwavering in patient endurance, not from habit but by nature, inasmuch as Polybius your bishop informed me when, by the will of God and Jesus Christ, he visited me in Smyrna; so heartily did he rejoice with me, a prisoner in Christ Jesus, that in him I saw your entire congregation. (2) Having received, therefore, your godly good will through him, I praised God when I found out that you were, as I had learned, imitators of God.

2. For when you are subject to the bishop as to Jesus Christ,

---

40. *Father*: so A Arabic; GL add *and to the Spirit.*

41. *the dew . . . prayers*: so Lightfoot's emendation, on the basis of A; GL read *with dew by means of your church.* On the imagery involved, cf. Deut. 32:2; Prov. 19:12.

42. *spirit*: so g; GL(AC) read *blood.*

it is evident to me that you are living not in accordance with human standards but in accordance with Jesus Christ, who died for us in order that by believing in his death you might escape death. (2) It is essential, therefore, that you continue your current practice and do nothing without the bishop, but be subject also to the presbytery as to the apostles of Jesus Christ, our hope, in whom we shall be found, if we so live.[43] (3) Furthermore, it is necessary that those who are deacons of the "mysteries"[44] of Jesus Christ please everyone in every respect. For they are not merely "deacons"[45] of food and drink, but ministers of God's church. Therefore they must avoid criticism as though it were fire.

3. Similarly, let everyone respect the deacons as Jesus Christ, just as they should respect the bishop, who is a model of the Father, and the presbyters as God's council and as the band of the apostles. Without these no group can be called a church. (2) I am sure that you agree with me regarding these matters, for I received a living example of your love, and still have it with me in the person of your bishop, whose very demeanor is a great lesson, and whose gentleness is his power; I think that even the godless respect him. (3) Because I love you I am sparing you, though I could write more sharply on his behalf. But I did not think myself qualified[46] for this, that I, a convict, should give you orders as though I were an apostle.

4. I have many deep thoughts in union with God, but I take my own measure, lest I perish by boasting. For now I must be more careful and not pay attention to those who flatter me, for those who speak to me in this manner torture me. (2) For while I strongly desire to suffer, I do not know whether I am worthy, for the envy,[47] though not apparent to many, wages war against me all the more. Therefore I need gentleness, by which the ruler of this age is destroyed.

---

43. *live*: so GLC; Lightfoot follows gS[f], which add *in him*.

44. *mysteries*: cf. 1 Cor. 4:1.

45. *deacons*: i.e., in the sense of "servers"; cf. Acts 6:1–6.

46. *But . . . qualified*: the text is quite difficult here. GL are clearly corrupt; the translation given is based upon Lightfoot's emendation, which follows the general sense of gAC. Schoedel (*Ignatius*, 143), following A Arabic, suggests reading *I was not empowered*.

47. *envy*: i.e., of Satan.

5. Am I not able to write to you about heavenly things? But I am afraid to, lest I should cause harm to you who are mere babes. So bear with me, lest you be choked by what you are unable to swallow. (2) For I myself, though I am in chains and can comprehend heavenly things, the ranks of the angels and the hierarchy of principalities, things visible and invisible, for all this I am not yet a disciple. For we still lack many things, that we might not lack God.

6. I urge you, therefore—yet not I, but the love of Jesus Christ—partake only of Christian food, and keep away from every strange plant, which is heresy. (2) These people, while pretending to be trustworthy, mix Jesus Christ with poison[48]— like those who administer a deadly drug with honeyed wine, which the unsuspecting victim accepts without fear,[49] and so with fatal pleasure drinks down death.

7. Therefore be on your guard against such people. And you will be, provided that you are not puffed up with pride and that you cling inseparably to Jesus Christ[50] and to the bishop and to the commandments of the apostles. (2) The one who is within the sanctuary is clean, but the one who is outside the sanctuary is not clean. That is, whoever does anything without bishop and presbytery and deacons does not have a clean conscience.

8. Not that I know of any such thing among you; rather, I am guarding you in advance because you are very dear to me and I foresee the snares of the devil. You, therefore, must arm yourselves with gentleness and regain your strength[51] in faith (which is the flesh of the Lord) and in love (which is the blood of Jesus Christ). (2) Let none of you hold a grudge against his neighbor. Do not give any opportunity to the pagans, lest the godly majority be blasphemed on account of a few foolish peo-

48. *poison*: so Lightfoot's restoration of a corrupt text. Others, following SᶠA Arabic, read *themselves*, which is probably correct.

49. *without fear*: so Lightfoot's emendation (*adeōs*) of GL, which read *ēdeōs* ("gladly").

50. *Jesus Christ*: the text is uncertain; this is the reading of A Arabic, which is probably correct. GLC read *God Jesus Christ*; if, despite its awkwardness, this reading is preferred, it should be punctuated *God, Jesus Christ*. Lightfoot read [*God*] *Jesus Christ*.

51. *regain your strength*: so Lightfoot and others, following an early emendation (*anaktēsasthe*); GC read *anaktisasthe* ("renew yourselves").

ple. For "woe to him through whose folly my name is blasphemed among any."[52]

9. Be deaf, therefore, whenever anyone speaks to you apart from Jesus Christ, who was of the family of David, who was the son of Mary; who really was born, who both ate and drank; who really was persecuted under Pontius Pilate, who really was crucified and died while those in heaven and on earth and under the earth looked on; (2) who, moreover, really was raised from the dead when his Father raised him up, who—his Father, that is—in the same way will likewise also raise us up in Christ Jesus who believe in him, apart from whom we have no true life.

10. But if, as some atheists (that is, unbelievers) say, he suffered in appearance only (while they exist in appearance only!), why am I in chains? And why do I want to fight with wild beasts? If that is the case, I die for no reason; what is more, I am telling lies about the Lord.

11. Flee, therefore, from these wicked offshoots that bear deadly fruit; if anyone even tastes it, he dies on the spot. These people are not the Father's planting.[53] (2) For if they were, they would appear as branches of the cross, and their fruit would be imperishable—the same cross by which he, through his suffering, calls you who are his members. The head, therefore, cannot be born without members, since God promises unity, which he himself is.

12. I greet you from Smyrna together with the churches of God which are present with me, people who have refreshed me in every respect, physically as well as spiritually. (2) My chains, which I carry around for the sake of Jesus Christ while praying that I might reach God, exhort you: persevere in your unanimity and in prayer with one another. For it is right for each one of you, and especially the presbyters, to encourage the bishop, to the honor of the Father and to the honor[54] of Jesus Christ and of the apostles. (3) I pray that you will listen to me in love, so that I shall not, by virtue of having written to you, be a witness

---

52. Cf. Isa. 52:5.

53. Cf. Matt. 15:13.

54. *and to the honor*: so g, followed by Lightfoot; AC Arabic read *and*, while GL omit the phrase and read *Father of Jesus Christ*.

against you. But also pray for me, for I need your love in the mercy of God so that I may be reckoned worthy of the fate which I am eager[55] to obtain, in order that I not be found disqualified.[56]

13. The love of the Smyrnaeans and Ephesians greets you. Remember in your prayers the church in Syria, of which I am not worthy to be considered a member, being as I am the very least of them. (2) Farewell in Jesus Christ. Be subject to the bishop as to the commandment, and likewise to the presbytery. And love one another, each one of you, with an undivided heart. (3) My spirit is dedicated to you, not only now but also when I reach God. For I am still in danger, but the Father is faithful: he will fulfill my prayer and yours in Jesus Christ. May we[57] be found blameless in him.

TO THE ROMANS

Ignatius, who is also called Theophorus, to the church that has found mercy in the majesty of the Father Most High and Jesus Christ his only Son, beloved and enlightened through the will of him who willed all things that exist, in accordance with faith in and love for Jesus[58] Christ our God, which also presides in the place of the district of the Romans,[59] worthy of God,

55. *which I am eager*: so Lightfoot, adopting an earlier emendation; both text and meaning are uncertain.

56. Cf. 1 Cor. 9:27.

57. *we*: so gA; GLC read *you*.

58. *faith in . . . Jesus*: lit. *faith and love of Jesus* (so TAAmCg Arabic). But Jesus is the object ("faith *in* and love *for*") and not the subject ("*Jesus'* faith and love") of the two nouns. That some witnesses (GHKLSm) omit "faith and" reflects a misreading of the phrase in light of the preceding clause ("him who willed").

59. *presides . . . Romans*: this phrase, as wordy in Greek as it is in English, has been the subject of considerable discussion, primarily because of its obvious bearing on the question of the primacy of the bishop of Rome. A number of alternative ways of understanding the phrase have been proposed, most of which either strain the meaning of the vocabulary involved or require the emendation of a well-established text, and thus have little to commend them. The question itself, however, is probably anachronistic, since here it is the church (not the bishop) that is said to "preside" or "rule" (cf. *Magn.* 6), presum-

worthy of honor, worthy of blessing, worthy of praise, worthy of success, worthy of sanctification, and presiding over[60] love, observing the law of Christ,[61] bearing the name of the Father, which I also greet in the name of Jesus Christ, Son of the Father; to those who are united in flesh and spirit to every commandment of his, who have been filled with the grace of God without wavering and filtered clear of every alien color: heartiest greetings blamelessly in Jesus Christ our God.

1. Since by praying to God I have succeeded in seeing your godly faces, so that I have received more than I asked[62]—for I hope to greet you in chains for Jesus Christ, if it is his will for me to be reckoned worthy to reach the goal. (2) For the beginning is auspicious, provided that I attain the grace[63] to receive my fate without interference. For I am afraid of your love, in that it may do me wrong; for it is easy for you to do what you want, but it is difficult for me to reach God, unless you spare me.

2. For I do not want you to please men, but to please God, as you in fact are doing. For I will never again have an opportunity such as this to reach God, nor can you, if you remain silent, be credited with a greater accomplishment. For if you remain silent and leave me alone, I will be a word of God, but if you love my flesh,[64] then I will again be a mere voice.[65] (2) Grant me nothing more than to be poured out as an offering to God while

---

ably over the district in which it is located. Cf. Lightfoot, *AF* 2.2.190–91; Schoedel, *Ignatius*, 165–66.

60. *presiding over*: or perhaps *preeminent in*; the Roman church obtained at an early date a reputation for charitable acts.

61. *observing . . . Christ*: so L(SSmAAmCl), which read *christonomos*; GHKTg have *christōnumos* ("bearing the name of Christ"), likely because of the influence of the following word *patrōnumos* ("bearing the name of the Father").

62. *so that . . . asked*: so Lightfoot's emendation, which reflects the sense of Am. GHKTL(Sm)ACg read *even as I have been asking to receive yet more*; the Greek words differ by only a single letter.

63. *grace*: so GHKTLg; SA (followed by Lightfoot) read *goal*.

64. *love my flesh*: i.e., "wish to keep me alive." Ignatius's fear was that the Roman Christians, desiring to preserve his physical life, would plead his case before the magistrates and get him released, thereby frustrating his desire for martyrdom, through which he hoped to preserve his spiritual life. His concern may have been more imagined than real; cf. Schoedel, *Ignatius*, 168–69.

65. *word . . . voice*: the contrast here is between "word" as an intelligible or meaningful utterance and "voice" as an irrational cry or inarticulate sound.

there is still an altar ready, so that in love you may form a chorus and sing to the Father in Jesus Christ, because God has judged the bishop from Syria worthy to be found in the West, having summoned him from the East.[66] It is good to be setting from the world to God, in order that I may rise to him.

3. You have never envied anyone; you taught others. And my wish is that those instructions which you issue when teaching disciples will remain in force. (2) Just pray that I will have the strength both outwardly and inwardly so that I may not just talk about it but want to do it, that I might not merely be called a Christian, but actually prove to be one. For if I prove to be one, I can also be called one, and then I will be faithful when I am no longer visible to the world. (3) Nothing that is visible is good. For our God Jesus Christ is more visible now that he is in the Father. The Work[67] is not a matter of persuasive rhetoric; rather, Christianity is greatest when it is hated by the world.

4. I am writing to all the churches and am insisting to everyone that I die for God of my own free will—unless you hinder me. I implore you: do not be "unseasonably kind"[68] to me. Let me be food[69] for the wild beasts, through whom I can reach God. I am God's wheat, and I am being ground by the teeth of the wild beasts, that I might prove to be pure bread.[70] (2) Better yet, coax the wild beasts, that they may become my tomb and leave nothing of my body behind, lest I become a burden to someone once I have fallen asleep. Then I will truly be a disciple of Jesus Christ, when the world will no longer see my body. Pray to the Lord[71] on my behalf, that through these instruments I might prove to be a sacrifice to God. (3) I do not give you orders like Peter and Paul: they were apostles, I am a convict; they were free, but I am even now still a slave. But if I suffer, I will be a freedman of Jesus Christ, and will rise up free

66. *West . . . East*: lit. the *setting* and the *rising* of the sun; notice the play on these words in the next sentence.

67. *Work*: cf. *Eph.* 14.2.

68. *unseasonably kind*: apparently an allusion to an ancient proverb: "an unseasonable kindness is no different than hostility."

69. *food*: so most witnesses; SS^f Sm (followed by Lightfoot) omit.

70. *bread*: so Irenaeus, Eusebius, and Jerome; SS^f AAmCg add *of God*, while GHTLSm (followed by Lightfoot, in brackets) add *of Christ*.

71. *the Lord*: so SS^f AAmTCg; GHKLSm read *Christ*.

in him. In the meantime, as a prisoner I am learning to desire nothing.

5. From Syria all the way to Rome I am fighting with wild beasts, on land and sea, by night and day, chained amidst ten leopards (that is, a company of soldiers) who only get worse when they are well treated. Yet because of their mistreatment I am becoming more of a disciple; nevertheless "I am not thereby justified."[72] (2) May I have the pleasure of the wild beasts that have been prepared for me; and I pray that they prove to be prompt with me. I will even coax them to devour me promptly, not as they have done with some, whom they were too timid to touch. And if when I am willing and ready they are not, I will force them. (3) Bear with me—I know what is best for me. Now at last I am beginning to be a disciple. May nothing visible or invisible envy me, so that I may reach Jesus Christ. Fire and cross and battles with wild beasts, mutilation, mangling,[73] wrenching of bones, the hacking of limbs, the crushing of my whole body, cruel tortures of the devil—let these come upon me, only let me reach Jesus Christ!

6. Neither the ends of the earth nor the kingdoms of this age are of any use to me. It is better for me to die for Jesus Christ than to rule over the ends of the earth. Him I seek, who died on our behalf; him I long for, who rose again for our sake. The pains of birth are upon me. (2) Bear with me, brothers: do not keep me from living; do not desire my death. Do not give to the world one who wants to belong to God, nor tempt[74] him with material things. Let me receive the pure light, for when I arrive there I will be a man. (3) Allow me to be an imitator of the suffering of my God. If anyone has Him within himself, let him understand what I long for and sympathize with me, knowing what constrains me.

7. The ruler of this age wants to take me captive and corrupt my godly intentions. Therefore none of you who are present must help him. Instead take my side, that is, God's. Do not talk

---

72. 1 Cor. 4:4.

73. *mutilation, mangling*: so GHT(Sm)Amg [Lightfoot]; S[f] A read *mangling and*; LS Eusebius omit.

74. *tempt*: the Greek witnesses are defective here. *Tempt* is Lightfoot's restoration, following the sense of S[f] SmA; others, following L(Am), suggest *deceive*.

about Jesus Christ while you desire the world. (2) Do not let envy dwell among you. And if upon my arrival I myself should appeal to you, do not be persuaded by me; believe[75] instead these things that I am writing to you. For though I am still alive, I am passionately in love with death as I write to you. My passionate love[76] has been crucified and there is no fire of material longing within me, but only water living and speaking[77] in me, saying within me, "Come to the Father." (3) I take no pleasure in corruptible food or the pleasures of this life. I want the bread of God, which is the flesh of Christ who is of the seed of David; and for drink I want his blood, which is incorruptible love.

8. I no longer want to live according to human standards. And such will be the case, if you so desire. Do so desire, that you also may be desired! (2) With these brief lines I am making my request of you. Do believe me! And Jesus Christ, the unerring mouth by whom the Father has spoken truly, will make it clear to you that I am speaking truly. (3) Pray for me, that I may reach the goal.[78] I write to you not according to human perspective but in accordance with the mind of God. If I suffer, you will have wanted it; if I am rejected, you will have hated me.

9. Remember in your prayers the church in Syria, which has God for its shepherd in my place. Jesus Christ alone will be its bishop—as will your love. (2) But I myself am ashamed to be counted among them, for I am not worthy, since I am the very last of them and an abnormality.[79] But I have been granted the mercy to be someone, if I reach God. (3) My spirit greets you, as does the love of the churches that welcomed me in the name of Jesus Christ, rather than as a mere transient. For even churches that did not lie on my way (i.e., my physical route) went before me from city to city.

75. *believe*: so g(SmAAm); GHTLC read *be persuaded by.*

76. *love*: i.e., for the "world"; cf. Gal. 6:14.

77. *water living and speaking*: so the Greek MSS; the other witnesses vary widely. Lightfoot, suspecting here an ancient corruption, suggests that the original reading has been preserved in g: "living water welling up" (cf. John 4:10, 14). Cf. Schoedel (*Ignatius*, 185) for other parallels.

78. *goal*: so GHTLSmAmC; gA (followed, with some hesitation, by Lightfoot, who brackets the words) add *through the Holy Spirit.*

79. *abnormality*: cf. 1 Cor. 15:8.

10. I write these things to you from Smyrna via the Ephesians, who are most worthy of blessing. With me, along with many others, is Crocus, a name very dear to me. (2) Regarding those who preceded me from Syria to Rome to the glory of God, I believe that you have information. Let them know that I am near, for they are all worthy of God and of you, and it is quite proper for you to refresh them in every respect. (3) I am writing these things to you on the ninth day before the Kalends of September.[80] Farewell to the end, in the patient endurance of Jesus Christ.

TO THE PHILADELPHIANS

Ignatius, who is also called Theophorus, to the church of God the Father and of Jesus[81] Christ at Philadelphia in Asia, one that has found mercy and is firmly established in godly harmony and unwaveringly rejoices in the suffering of our Lord, fully convinced of his resurrection in all mercy, which I greet in the blood of Jesus Christ, which is eternal and lasting joy, especially if they are at one with the bishop and the presbyters and deacons who are with him, who have been appointed by the mind of Jesus Christ, whom he, in accordance with his own will, securely established by his Holy Spirit.

1. I know that the bishop obtained a ministry (which is for the whole community) not by his own efforts nor through men nor out of vanity, but in the love of God the Father and the Lord Jesus Christ. I am impressed by his forbearance; he accomplishes more through silence than others do by talking.[82] (2) For he is attuned to the commandments as a harp to its strings. Therefore my soul blesses his godly mind (well aware that it is virtuous and perfect), his steadfast character, and his lack of anger, as one living with all godly gentleness.[83]

2. Therefore as children of the light of truth flee from division and false teaching. Where the shepherd is, there follow like

---

80. *ninth . . . September*: i.e., August 24.
81. *Jesus*: so LC; Gg(A) read *Lord Jesus*.
82. *talking*: so A; GLC add *purposelessly*.
83. *as . . . gentleness*: or possibly *in all gentleness of the living God*.

sheep. (2) For many seemingly trustworthy wolves attempt, by means of wicked pleasure, to take captive the runners in God's race; but in your unity they will find no opportunity.

3. Stay away from the evil plants, which are not cultivated by Jesus Christ, because they are not the Father's planting.[84] Not that I found any division among you: instead, I found that there had been a purification. (2) For all those who belong to God and Jesus Christ are with the bishop, and all those who repent and enter into the unity of the church will belong to God, that they may be living in accordance with Jesus Christ. (3) Do not be misled, my brothers: if anyone follows a schismatic, he will not inherit the kingdom of God.[85] If anyone holds to alien views, he disassociates himself from the Passion.

4. Take care, therefore, to participate in one Eucharist (for there is one flesh of our Lord Jesus Christ, and one cup which leads to unity through his blood; there is one altar, just as there is one bishop, together with the presbytery and the deacons, my fellow servants), in order that whatever you do, you do in accordance with God.

5. My brothers, I am overflowing with love for you, and greatly rejoice as I watch out for your safety—yet not I, but Jesus Christ. Though I am in chains for his sake, I am all the more afraid, because I am still imperfect. But your prayer to God[86] will make me perfect, that I may attain the fate by which I have received mercy, since I have taken refuge in the gospel as the flesh of Jesus and in the apostles as the presbytery of the church. (2) And we also love the prophets, because they anticipated the gospel in their preaching and set their hope on him and waited for him; because they also believed in him, they were saved, since they belong to the unity centered in Jesus Christ, saints worthy of love and admiration, approved by Jesus Christ and included in the gospel of our common hope.[87]

6. But if anyone expounds Judaism to you, do not listen to him. For it is better to hear about Christianity from a man who

84. Cf. Matt. 15:13.
85. Cf. 1 Cor. 6:9.
86. *to God*: so GgC [Lightfoot]; L(A) omit.
87. Cf. 1 Tim. 1:1.

is circumcised than about Judaism from one who is not. But if
either of them fail to speak about Jesus Christ, I look on them
as tombstones and graves of the dead, upon which only the
names of men are inscribed. (2) Flee, therefore, the evil tricks
and traps of the ruler of this age, lest you be worn out by his
schemes and grow weak in love. Instead gather together, all of
you, with an undivided heart. (3) Now I give thanks to my God
that I have a clear conscience in my dealings with you, and that
no one can boast, either privately or publicly, that I was a
burden to anyone in any respect, small or great. Moreover, I
pray that all those to whom I spoke will not cause what I said
to become a witness against them.

7. For even though certain people wanted to deceive me,
humanly speaking, nevertheless the Spirit is not deceived, because it is from God; for it knows from where it comes and
where it is going,[88] and exposes the hidden things. I called out
when I was with you, I was speaking with a loud voice, God's
voice: "Pay attention to the bishop and to the presbytery and
deacons." (2) To be sure, there were those who suspected that I
said these things because I knew in advance about the division
caused by certain people. But he for whose sake I am in chains
is my witness, that I did not learn this from any human being.
No, the Spirit itself was preaching, saying these words: "Do
nothing without the bishop. Guard your bodies as the temple of
God. Love unity. Flee from divisions. Become imitators of Jesus
Christ, just as he is of his Father."

8. I was doing my part, therefore, as a man set on unity.
But God does not dwell where there is division and anger. The
Lord, however, forgives all who repent, if in repenting they
return to the unity of God and the council of the bishop. I
believe in the grace of Jesus Christ, who will free you from
every bond. (2) Moreover, I urge you to do nothing in a spirit
of contentiousness, but in accordance with the teaching of
Christ. For I heard some people say, "If I do not find it in the
archives,[89] I do not believe it in the gospel." And when I said
to them, "It is written," they answered me, "That is precisely
the question." But for me, the "archives" are Jesus Christ, the

88. Cf. John 3:8.
89. *archives*: i.e., the (what are now called Old Testament) Scriptures.

inviolable archives are his cross and death and his resurrection and the faith which comes through him; by these things I want, through your prayers, to be justified.

9. The priests, too, were good, but the High Priest,[90] entrusted with the Holy of Holies, is better; he alone has been entrusted with the hidden things of God, for he himself is the door[91] of the Father, through which Abraham and Isaac and Jacob and the prophets and the apostles and the church enter in. All these come together in the unity of God. (2) But the gospel possesses something distinctive, namely, the coming of the Savior, our Lord Jesus Christ, his suffering, and the resurrection. For the beloved prophets preached in anticipation of him,[92] but the gospel is the imperishable finished work. All these things together are good, if you believe with love.

10. Since it has been reported to me that in answer to your prayer and the compassion which you have in Christ Jesus the church at Antioch in Syria is at peace, it is appropriate for you, as a church of God, to appoint a deacon to go there on a mission as God's ambassador, to congratulate them when they have assembled together and to glorify the Name. (2) Blessed in Christ Jesus[93] is the one who will be judged worthy of such ministry, and you yourselves will be glorified. It is certainly not impossible for you to do this for the name of God, if you are willing; indeed, the neighboring churches have sent bishops, and others presbyters and deacons.

11. Now concerning Philo, the deacon from Cilicia, a man with a good reputation, who even now assists me in the word of God, along with Rhaius[94] Agathopus, a chosen man who followed me from Syria, having renounced this life: they speak well of you, and I give thanks to God on your behalf, because you received them as the Lord received you. But may those who dishonored them be redeemed by the grace of Jesus Christ.

(2) The love of the brothers in Troas greets you. I am writing you from there through Burrhus, who was sent with me by the

90. Cf. Heb. 4:14–5:10.
91. Cf. John 10:9.
92. Cf. 1 Pet. 1:10–12.
93. *Christ Jesus*: so gA; GLS*f*C read *Jesus Christ*.
94. *Rhaius*: so Lightfoot; gC read *Gaius*; GLA read *Rheus* (a name apparently otherwise unknown). Cf. *Smyrn.* 10.1.

Ephesians and Smyrnaeans as a mark of honor. The Lord Jesus Christ will honor them, on whom they set their hope in body, soul, and spirit with faith, love, and harmony. Farewell in Christ Jesus, our common hope.

TO THE SMYRNAEANS

Ignatius, who is also called Theophorus, to the church of God the Father and of the beloved Jesus Christ at Smyrna in Asia, mercifully endowed with every spiritual gift, filled with faith and love, not lacking in any spiritual gift, most worthy of God, bearing holy things: heartiest greetings in a blameless spirit and the word of God.

1. I glorify Jesus Christ, the God who made you so wise, for I observed that you are established in an unshakable faith, having been nailed, as it were, to the cross of the Lord Jesus Christ in both body and spirit, and firmly established in love by the blood of Christ, totally convinced with regard to our Lord that he is truly of the family of David with respect to human descent, Son of God with respect to the divine will and power,[95] truly born of a virgin, baptized by John in order that all righteousness might be fulfilled by him,[96] (2) truly nailed in the flesh for us under Pontius Pilate and Herod the tetrarch (from its[97] fruit we derive our existence, that is, from his divinely blessed suffering), in order that he might raise a banner for the ages through his resurrection for his saints and faithful people, whether among Jews or among Gentiles, in the one body of his church.

2. For he suffered all these things for our sakes, in order that we might be saved;[98] and he truly suffered just as he truly raised himself—not, as certain unbelievers say, that he suffered in appearance only (it is they who exist in appearance only!). Indeed, their fate will be determined by what they think: they will become disembodied and demonic.

---

95. *power*: so A Theodoret; GLC add *of God*.
96. Cf. Matt. 3:15.
97. *its*: i.e., the cross's.
98. *in order . . . saved*: so GL Severus [Lightfoot]; Cg omit.

3. For I know and believe that he was in the flesh even after the resurrection; (2) and when he came to Peter and those with him, he said to them: "Take hold of me; handle me and see that I am not a disembodied demon."[99] And immediately they touched him and believed, being closely united with his flesh and blood.[100] For this reason they too despised death; indeed, they proved to be greater than death. (3) And after his resurrection he ate and drank with them like one who is composed of flesh, although spiritually he was united with the Father.

4. Now I am advising you of these things, dear friends, knowing that you are of the same mind. But I am guarding you in advance against wild beasts in human form—men whom you must not only not welcome but, if possible, not even meet. Nevertheless, do pray for them, if somehow they might repent, difficult though it may be. But Jesus Christ, our true life, has power over this. (2) For if these things were done by our Lord in appearance only, then I am in chains in appearance only. Why, moreover, have I surrendered myself to death, to fire, to sword, to beasts? But in any case, "near the sword" means "near to God"; "with the beasts" means "with God." Only let it be in the name of Jesus Christ, that I may suffer together with him! I endure everything because he himself, who is[101] perfect man, empowers me.

5. Certain people ignorantly deny him, or rather have been denied by him, for they are advocates of death rather than the truth. Neither the prophecies nor the law of Moses have persuaded them, nor, thus far, the gospel nor our own individual suffering; (2) for they think the same thing about us.[102] For what good does it do me if someone[103] praises me but blasphemes my Lord by not confessing that he was clothed in flesh? Anyone who does not acknowledge this thereby denies him completely and is clothed in a corpse. (3) Given that they

99. Cf. Luke 24:39; the (now lost) *Gospel According to the Hebrews* and the *Teaching* [or possibly *Preaching*] *of Peter* are reported to have contained the same (or a very similar) saying.

100. *blood*: so A; GLC read *spirit*.

101. *is*: so PC Theodoret; GL read *became*.

102. I.e., they have the same opinion of Ignatius's suffering that they do of Christ's: it is all "in appearance only."

103. *it . . . someone*: so Ag Theodoret; GPLC read *someone do me if he.*

are unbelievers, it did not seem worthwhile to me to record their names. Indeed, far be it from me even to remember them, until such time as they change their mind in regard to the Passion, which is our resurrection.

6. Let no one be misled. Even the heavenly beings and the glory of angels and the rulers, both visible and invisible, are also subject to judgment, if they do not believe in the blood of Christ.[104] "The one who accepts this, let him accept it."[105] Do not let a high position make anyone proud, for faith and love are everything; nothing is preferable to them.

(2) Now note well those who hold heretical opinions about the grace of Jesus Christ which came to us; note how contrary they are to the mind of God. They have no concern for love, none for the widow, none for the orphan, none for the oppressed, none for the prisoner or the one released,[106] none for the hungry or thirsty.[107] They abstain from the Eucharist and prayer, because they refuse to acknowledge that the Eucharist is the flesh of our Savior Jesus Christ, which suffered for our sins and which the Father by his goodness raised up.

7. Therefore those who deny the good gift of God perish in their contentiousness. It would be more to their advantage to love, in order that they might also rise up. (2) It is proper, therefore, to avoid such people and not speak about them either privately or publicly. Do pay attention, however, to the prophets and especially to the gospel, in which the Passion has been made clear to us and the resurrection has been accomplished.

8. Flee from divisions, as the beginning of evils.[108] You must all follow the bishop, as Jesus Christ followed the Father, and follow the presbytery as you would the apostles; respect the deacons as the commandment of God. Let no one do anything that has to do with the church without the bishop. Only that Eucharist which is under the authority of the bishop (or whomever he himself designates) is to be considered valid. (2) Wher-

---

104. *Christ*: so GPLAC Arabic; S^f adds *who is God*, which Lightfoot prints in brackets "with very great hesitation" (*AF* 2.2.303).

105. Matt. 19:12.

106. *or the one released*: so GPL Arabic; AC(g) omit, as does Lightfoot in the translation (the phrase is in brackets in the Greek text).

107. Some editions begin sec. 7 at this point.

108. Some editions end sec. 7 at this point.

ever the bishop appears, there let the congregation be; just as wherever Jesus Christ is, there is the catholic[109] church. It is not permissible either to baptize or to hold a love feast[110] without the bishop. But whatever he approves is also pleasing to God, in order that everything you do may be trustworthy and valid.

9. Finally, it is reasonable for us to come to our senses while we still have time to repent and turn to God. It is good to acknowledge God and the bishop. The one who honors the bishop has been honored by God; the one who does anything without the bishop's knowledge serves the devil. (2) May all things, therefore, be yours in abundance in grace, for you are worthy. You refreshed me in every respect, and Jesus Christ will refresh you. In my absence and in my presence you loved me. God is your reward;[111] if you endure everything for his sake, you will reach him.

10. You did well to welcome Philo and Rhaius[112] Agathopus, who followed me for God's sake, as deacons[113] of God.[114] They too give thanks to the Lord on your behalf because you refreshed them in every way. You will certainly not lose any of this! (2) May my spirit be a ransom on your behalf, and my bonds as well, which you did not despise, nor were you ashamed of them. Nor will the perfect hope,[115] Jesus Christ, be ashamed of you.

---

109. The term *catholic* here occurs in Christian literature for the first time. In later use (by ca. A.D. 200) the word *catholic* became a technical term designating "the Catholic Church" as opposed to the heretical sects, but here the expression is used in the sense of "universal" or "general" (thus the adjective could be attached to words like "resurrection" or "salvation" as well as to "church"), or possibly "whole" (conveying the idea of organic unity or completeness); cf. Lightfoot, *AF* 2.2.310–12; Schoedel, *Ignatius*, 243–44.

110. The "love feast" (lit. *agapē*; cf. Jude 12) or "fellowship meal" was a congregational meal which (almost certainly) included the celebration of the Eucharist at some point (cf. 1 Cor. 11:17–34).

111. *God is your reward*: so P, which reads *amoibē*. The reading of G (*amoibei*) is nonsense. "God will reward you" is read by g Arabic, while Lightfoot and many others follow L and restore *ameiboi*, "may God reward you."

112. *Rhaius*: so Lightfoot; gP read *Gaius*; G(L) read *Rheus*. Cf. *Phld.* 11.1.

113. *deacons*: or possibly *ministers* or *servants*.

114. *God*: so PAC Arabic; GL read *Christ God*; Lightfoot, [*Christ God*].

115. *hope*: so PAg Arabic; GL (followed by Lightfoot) read *faith*.

11. Your prayer reached the church at Antioch in Syria; having come from there bound in the most God-pleasing chains I greet everyone, even though I am not worthy to be from there, for I am the very least of them. Nevertheless in accordance with the divine will I was judged worthy, not because of the witness of my own conscience, but by the grace of God, which I pray may be given to me in perfection, that by your prayer I may reach God. (2) Therefore, in order that your work may become perfect both on earth and in heaven, it is appropriate that your church appoint, for the honor of God, a godly ambassador to go to Syria to congratulate them, because they are at peace and have regained their proper stature and their corporate life has been restored to its proper state. (3) It seemed to me, therefore, to be a deed worthy of God[116] for you to send one of your own people with a letter, that he might join in glorifying the tranquility which by God's will has come to them, and because they have now reached, thanks to your prayers, a safe harbor. Inasmuch as you are perfect, let your intentions also be[117] perfect,[118] for if you want to do well, God is ready to help you.

12. The love of the brothers in Troas greets you. I am writing you from there through Burrhus, whom you, together with your Ephesian brothers, sent with me. He has refreshed me in every respect. Would that all were imitators of him, for he is a model of service to God. Grace will reward him in every respect. (2) I greet the bishop, so worthy of God, and the godly presbytery, and my fellow servants, the deacons, and all of you, individually and collectively, in the name of Jesus Christ and in his flesh and blood, his suffering and resurrection (which was both physical and spiritual), in unity with God and with you. Grace, mercy, peace, patience to you always.

13. I greet the households of my brothers with their wives and children, and the virgins who are called widows. I bid you farewell in the power of the Father.[119] Philo, who is with me,

---

116. *deed . . . God*: so PL(A); Gg (followed by Lightfoot) read *worthy deed*.
117. *let . . . be*: or perhaps *aim at what is*.
118. Cf. Phil. 3:15.
119. *Father*: so LA Arabic; Gg read *Spirit*.

greets you. (2) I greet the household of Gavia,[120] and pray that she may be firmly grounded in faith and love both physically and spiritually. I greet Alce, a name very dear to me, and the incomparable Daphnus, and Eutecnus and everyone else individually. Farewell in the grace of God.

TO POLYCARP

Ignatius, who is also called Theophorus, to Polycarp, bishop of the church of the Smyrnaeans, or rather who has God the Father and the Lord[121] Jesus Christ as his bishop, heartiest greetings.

1. So approving am I of your godly mind, which is grounded, as it were, upon an unmovable rock, that my praise exceeds all bounds, inasmuch as I was judged worthy of seeing your blameless face. May it bring me joy in God.

(2) I urge you, by the grace with which you are clothed, to press on in your race and to exhort all people, that they may be saved. Do justice to your office with constant care for both physical and spiritual concerns. Focus on unity, for there is nothing better. Bear with all people, even as the Lord bears with you; endure all in love, just as you now do. (3) Devote yourself to unceasing prayers; ask for greater understanding than you have. Keep on the alert with an unresting spirit. Speak to the people individually, in accordance with God's example.[122] Bear the diseases of all, as a perfect athlete. Where there is more work, there is much gain.

2. If you love good disciples, it is no credit to you; rather with gentleness bring the more troublesome ones into submission. "Not every wound is healed by the same treatment"; "relieve inflammations with cold compresses." (2) "Be as shrewd as snakes" in all circumstances, yet always "innocent as doves."[123] You are both physical and spiritual in nature for this reason, that you might treat gently whatever appears be-

120. *Gavia*: so gA; GL read *Tavia*.
121. *the Lord*: so GSA(g); L (followed by Lightfoot) omits.
122. *in . . . example*: or possibly *in a godly agreement of convictions*.
123. Matt. 10:16.

fore you; but ask, in order that the unseen things may be revealed to you, that you may be lacking in nothing and abound in every spiritual gift. (3) The time needs you (as pilots need winds and as a storm-tossed sailer needs a harbor) in order to reach God. Be sober, as God's athlete; the prize is incorruptibility and eternal life, about which you are already convinced. May I be a ransom on your behalf in every respect, and my bonds as well, which you loved.

3. Do not let those who appear to be trustworthy yet who teach strange doctrines baffle you. Stand firm, like an anvil being struck with a hammer. It is the mark of a great athlete to be bruised, yet still conquer. But especially we must, for God's sake, patiently put up with all things, that he may also put up with us. (2) Be more diligent than you are. Understand the times. Wait expectantly for him who is above time: the Eternal, the Invisible, who for our sake became visible; the Intangible, the Unsuffering, who for our sake suffered, who for our sake endured in every way.

4. Do not let the widows be neglected. After the Lord, you be their guardian. Let nothing be done without your consent, nor do anything yourself without God's consent,[124] as indeed you do not. Stand firm. (2) Let meetings be held more frequently; seek out everybody by name. (3) Do not treat slaves, whether male or female, contemptuously, but neither let them become conceited; instead, let them serve all the more faithfully to the glory of God, that they may obtain from God a better freedom. They should not have a strong desire to be set free at the church's expense, lest they be found to be slaves of lust.

5. Flee from wicked practices; better yet, preach sermons about them. Tell my sisters to love the Lord and to be content with their husbands physically and spiritually. In the same way command my brothers in the name of Jesus Christ to love their wives, as the Lord loves the church.[125] (2) If anyone is able to remain chaste to the honor of the flesh of the Lord, let him so remain without boasting. If he boasts, he is lost; and if it is made known to anyone other than the bishop, he is ruined.

---

124. *God's consent*: so SAg; GL read *God*.
125. Cf. Eph. 5:25, 29.

And it is proper for men and women who marry to be united with the consent of the bishop, that the marriage may be in accordance with the Lord and not due to lustful passions. Let all things be done for the honor of God.

6. Pay attention to the bishop, in order that God may pay attention to you. I am a ransom on behalf of those who are obedient to the bishop, presbyters, and deacons; may it be granted to me to have a place among them in the presence of[126] God! Train together with one another: struggle together, run together, suffer together, rest together, get up together, as God's managers, assistants, and servants. (2) Please him whom you serve as soldiers, from whom you receive[127] your wages. Let none of you be found a deserter. Let your baptism serve as a shield, faith as a helmet, love as a spear, endurance as armor. Let your deeds be your deposits, in order that you may eventually receive the savings that are due you.[128] Be, therefore, patient and gentle with one another, as God is with you. May I always have joy in you.

7. Since (as I have been informed) the church at Antioch in Syria is at peace through your prayer, I too have become more encouraged in a God-given freedom from anxiety—provided, of course, that through suffering I reach God, that I may prove to be a disciple by means of your prayer.[129] (2) It is certainly appropriate, Polycarp (how blessed by God you are!), to convene a council that will be most pleasing to God and to appoint someone whom you[130] consider to be especially dear and resolute, who is qualified to be called God's courier; commission him to go to Syria, that he may glorify your resolute love, to the glory of God. (3) A Christian has no authority over himself; rather he devotes his time to God. This is God's work, and will be yours, when you

126. *in the presence of*: so SS[f]Ag; GL read *in*.

127. *receive*: so GL; g (followed by Lightfoot) reads *will receive*.

128. *deposits . . . savings*: The military metaphors of the preceding three sentences are continued here. When soldiers were granted gifts of money, only half the sum due was paid to them, the balance being credited to their account. These "deposits" became the "savings" due if and when an honorable discharge was received.

129. *disciple . . . prayer* (*aitēsei*): so g(A Arabic); GL read *your disciple in the resurrection* (*anastasei*).

130. Pl., as are the following six second-person pronouns in chap. 7.

complete it. For by grace I trust that you are ready for a good work in the service of God. Knowing the intensity of your sincerity, I have exhorted you only briefly.

8. Since[131] I have not been able to write to all the churches because I am sailing at once from Troas to Neapolis, as the divine will commands, you[132] must write, as one possessing the mind of God, to the churches on this side,[133] so that they too may do likewise—those who can should send messengers, the rest letters via the people being sent by you,[134] that you[135] may be glorified by an eternal deed—for you[136] are worthy of such a thing.

(2) I greet everyone by name, including the widow of Epitropus with her whole household and those of the children. I greet Attalus, my dear friend. I greet the one who is about to be commissioned to go to Syria. Grace will be with him always, and with Polycarp, who sends him. (3) I bid you farewell always in our God Jesus Christ; may you remain in him, in the unity and care of God. I greet Alce, a name very dear to me. Farewell in the Lord.

131. *Since*: so GAC; Lg read *Therefore since*.
132. Sing.
133. *on this side*: i.e., of Antioch in Syria; Ignatius has in mind the churches between Smyrna and Antioch: Ephesus, Magnesia, and Tralles (he himself had been able to communicate with Philadelphia).
134. Sing.
135. Pl.
136. Sing.

The Letter of Polycarp
to the Philippians

INTRODUCTION

By any standard Polycarp must be reckoned as one of the more
notable figures in the early postapostolic church. Already bishop of Smyrna in Asia Minor when his friend and mentor, Ignatius of Antioch, addressed one of his letters to him (ca. A.D.
110; cf. above, p. 82), he died a martyr's death (see the *Martyrdom of Polycarp*) several decades later at age eighty-six (ca.
155–160), having served as bishop for at least forty and possibly
sixty or more years. Irenaeus (who met Polycarp as a child) and
Eusebius both considered him to be a significant link in the
chain of orthodox apostolic tradition, asserting that he had
known the apostle John. Even if one is disinclined to accept
their testimony on this last point, their general assessment of
Polycarp's importance stands, for his life and ministry spanned
the time between the end of the apostolic era and the emergence of catholic Christianity, and he was deeply involved in
the central issues and challenges of this critical era: the growing threat of persecution by the state, the emerging Gnostic
movement (he is particularly known for his opposition to one
of the movement's most charismatic and theologically innova-
tive teachers, Marcion), the development of the monepiscopal
form of ecclesiastical organization, and the formation of the
canon of the New Testament.

His letter to the Philippians, written in response to a letter
from them (3.1; 13.1), reveals, in addition to a direct and unpre-
tentious style and a sensitive pastoral manner, a deep indebtedness to the Scriptures (in the form of the Septuagint) and early
Christian writings. W. R. Schoedel suggests that it is "fairly
certain" that the letter "reflects more or less direct contact"

with the following writings: Psalms, Proverbs, Isaiah, Jeremiah, Ezekiel, Tobit; Matthew, Luke, Acts, Romans, 1–2 Corinthians, Galatians, Ephesians, Philippians, 1–2 Timothy, 1 John, 1 Peter, and *1 Clement*.[1] Polycarp seems to be particularly familiar with the last two. The way he uses these books is noteworthy: while apparently none of the New Testament books are cited as "Scripture" (the reference to Eph. 4:26 in 12.1 is a possible exception), the manner in which he refers to them clearly shows that he considered them to be authoritative documents.

H. von Campenhausen has tried to show that Polycarp was also the author of the pastoral Epistles.[2] But this hypothesis has for good reason met with little acceptance. Among other things it does not adequately take into account the way Polycarp refers in 4.1 to 1 Timothy 6:7, 10; the manner in which he cites the two verses indicates that he is dependent upon an authoritative source and not just common tradition or a document of his own composing.

Integrity and Date

Determination of the date of Polycarp's letter is dependent upon the question of its integrity. It has been suggested that the document as we now know it preserves not one but two letters written by the bishop of Smyrna.

Traditionally the letter has been dated very close to the time of the martyrdom of Ignatius (ca. 110). The references to Ignatius (1.1; 9.1) imply that he is already dead, while in 13.2 Polycarp asks for information about his fate. These references are usually understood to mean that while sufficient time has passed since Ignatius's final departure for Rome for Polycarp to assume that Ignatius has now been martyred, he has not yet received a confirmatory report.[3] Thus the letter is customarily

---

1. Schoedel, *Polycarp*, 4–5. Metzger (*Canon*, 61–62) gives the following list for the New Testament: Matthew, Luke, Romans, 1 Corinthians, Galatians, Ephesians, Philippians, 2 Thessalonians, 1–2 Timothy, Hebrews, 1 Peter, and 1 John.

2. H. von Campenhausen, "Polykarp und die Pastoralen," repr. *Aus der Frühzeit des Christentums* (Tübingen: Mohr/Siebeck, 1963), 197–252.

3. Cf. similarly H. Paulsen, *Die Apostolischen Väter*, 2d ed. (Tübingen, 1985), 112–13.

dated within a few weeks (or at most a few months) of the time of Ignatius's death.

P. N. Harrison,[4] however, has attempted to demonstrate that Polycarp's "letter" is actually two letters: a brief one (chaps. 13–14) that was written shortly after Ignatius left Philippi, and a longer one (chaps. 1–12) written several years later, about 135–137. This date is based on the reference to the "first-born of Satan" (7.1), which Harrison understands to be a reference to Marcion, whom Polycarp encountered (according to Irenaeus) shortly before Marcion arrived in Rome around 140.

Harrison's thesis is intriguing but not convincing. While Polycarp probably did refer to Marcion as the "first-born of Satan," there is nothing to indicate that Marcion was the only one Polycarp referred to in this way. Furthermore, there is nothing specifically Marcionite about the teaching refuted in chapter 7. The tensions and differences between chapters 1–12 (esp. 1.1 and 9.1) and 13–14 are not as sharp as Harrison makes them out to be. Furthermore, the traditional understanding makes a good deal of sense, particularly when one makes due allowance for the circumstances affecting travel and communication in ancient times. In any case, the remembrances of Ignatius and his companions in 1.1 and 9.1 seem too fresh and vivid to allow for the passage of two or three decades since the event being remembered.[5] Chapters 1–14 form an integral whole, and were most likely written about the time of the death of Ignatius.

The Text

The text of the letter has not been well preserved. Nine late Greek manuscripts are extant, all incomplete and all derived from the same archetype (in which 9.2 is immediately followed by the likewise incomplete text of the *Epistle of Barnabas*, beginning at 5.8). The symbol for these manuscripts is "G." Eusebius has preserved all of chapter 9 and all but the last crucial sentence of chapter 13. For the rest of the letter we are

4. P. N. Harrison, *Polycarp's Two Epistles to the Philippians* (Cambridge, 1936).

5. See further Schoedel, *Polycarp*, 4, 25–26, 29–30, 37–40; Richardson, *Fathers*, 124–25.

dependent on a Latin translation (= L) which, however, was based on a Greek text older than that represented by G and is generally reliable.

BIBLIOGRAPHY

Barnard, L. W. "The Problem of St. Polycarp's Epistle to the Philippians." In *Studies in the Apostolic Fathers and Their Background*, 31–40. Oxford: Blackwell, 1967.

Camelot, P.-Th. *Ignace d'Antioche: Lettres. Lettres et Martyre de Polycarpe de Smyrne*. 4th ed. Paris: Cerf, 1969.

Campenhausen, Hans von. "Polykarp und die Pastoralen." Reprinted in *Aus der Frühzeit des Christentums*, 197–252. Tübingen: Mohr, 1963.

Harrison, P. N. *Polycarp's Two Epistles to the Philippians*. Cambridge: Cambridge University Press, 1936.

Kleist, J. A. *The Didache. The Epistle of Barnabas. The Epistles and the Martyrdom of St. Polycarp. The Fragments of Papias. The Epistle to Diognetus*. Ancient Christian Writers, vol. 6. Westminster, Md.: Newman, 1948.

Lightfoot, J. B. *The Apostolic Fathers, Part II: S. Ignatius. S. Polycarp*. 2d ed. 3 vols. London: Macmillan, 1889. Repr. Grand Rapids: Baker, 1981.

Paulsen, Henning. *Die Briefe des Ignatius von Antiochia und der Brief des Polykarp von Smyrna*. 2., neubearbeitete Auflage der Auslegung von Walter Bauer. Tübingen: Mohr Siebeck, 1985.

Schoedel, William R. *Polycarp, Martyrdom of Polycarp, Fragments of Papias*. The Apostolic Fathers, vol. 5. Camden, N. J.: Nelson, 1967.

Shepherd, Massey H., Jr. "The Letter of Polycarp, Bishop of Smyrna, to the Philippians." In *Early Christian Fathers*, edited by C. C. Richardson, 121–37. Philadelphia: Westminster, 1953. Repr. Macmillan, 1970.

The Letter of Polycarp
to the Philippians

Polycarp and the presbyters with him to the church of God that sojourns at Philippi: may mercy and peace from God Almighty and Jesus Christ our Savior be yours in abundance.

1. I greatly rejoice with you in our Lord Jesus Christ, because you welcomed the representations of the true love[1] and, as was proper for you,[2] helped on their way those men confined by chains suitable for saints, which are the diadems of those who are truly chosen by God and our Lord; (2) and because your firmly rooted faith, renowned from the earliest times, still perseveres and bears fruit to our Lord Jesus Christ, who endured for our sins, facing even death, "whom God raised up, having loosed the pangs of Hades."[3] (3) "Though you have not seen him, you believe in him with an inexpressible and glorious joy"[4] (which many desire to experience), knowing that "by grace you have been saved, not because of works,"[5] but by the will of God through Jesus Christ.

2. "Therefore prepare for action and serve God in fear"[6] and truth, leaving behind the empty and meaningless talk and the error of the crowd, and "believing in him who raised" our Lord Jesus Christ "from the dead and gave him glory"[7] and a throne at his right hand; to whom all things in heaven and on earth were subjected,[8] whom every breathing creature serves, who is com-

---

1. I.e., Ignatius and his companions.
2. *as . . . you*: or possibly *as you had opportunity*.
3. Acts 2:24 (Western text).
4. 1 Pet. 1:8.
5. Eph. 2:5, 8–9.
6. 1 Pet. 1:13; cf. Ps. 2:11.
7. 1 Pet. 1:21.
8. Cf. 1 Cor. 15:28; Phil. 2:10; 3:21.

ing as "Judge of the living and the dead,"[9] for whose blood God will hold responsible those who disobey him.[10] (2) But "he who raised him from the dead will raise us also,"[11] if we do his will and follow his commandments and love the things he loved, while avoiding every kind of unrighteousness, greed, love of money, slander and false testimony; "not repaying evil for evil or insult for insult"[12] or blow for blow or curse for curse, (3) but instead remembering what the Lord said as he taught: "Do not judge, that you may not be judged; forgive, and you will be forgiven; show mercy, that you may be shown mercy; with the measure you use, it will be measured back to you";[13] and "blessed are the poor and those who are persecuted for righteousness' sake, for theirs is the kingdom of God."[14]

3. I am writing you these comments about righteousness, brothers, not on my own initiative but because you invited me to do so. (2) For neither I nor anyone like me can keep pace with the wisdom of the blessed and glorious Paul, who, when he was among you in the presence of the men of that time,[15] accurately and reliably taught the word concerning the truth. And when he was absent he wrote you letters;[16] if you study them carefully, you will be able to build yourselves up in the faith that has been given to you, (3) "which is the mother of us all,"[17] while hope follows and love for God and Christ and for our neighbor leads the way. For if anyone is occupied with these, he has fulfilled the commandment of righteousness, for one who has love is far from all sin.

4. "But the love of money is the beginning of all troubles."[18] Knowing, therefore, that "we brought nothing into

9. Acts 10:42.
10. Cf. Luke 11:50–51.
11. Cf. 2 Cor. 4:14.
12. 1 Pet. 3:9.
13. Matt. 7:1–2 (cf. Luke 6:36–38); *1 Clem.* 13.2.
14. Luke 6:20 and Matt. 5:10; cf. Matt. 5:3.
15. Cf. Acts 16:12.
16. *letters*: or possibly *letter*; see Lightfoot's careful discussion of the phrase (*St. Paul's Epistle to the Philippians*, 140–42), where he demonstrates that the plural can be used of a single document. Cf. also Schoedel, *Polycarp*, 14–15.
17. Gal. 4:26.
18. Cf. 1 Tim. 6:10.

the world, nor can we take anything out,"[19] let us arm ourselves with "the weapons of righteousness"[20] and let us first teach ourselves to follow the commandment of the Lord. (2) Then instruct your wives to continue in the faith delivered to them and in love and purity, cherishing their own husbands[21] in all fidelity and loving all others equally in all chastity, and to instruct the children with instruction that leads to the fear of God.[22] (3) The widows must think soberly about the faith of the Lord and pray unceasingly for everyone and stay far away from all malicious talk, slander, false testimony, love of money, and any kind of evil, knowing that they are God's altar, and that all sacrifices are carefully inspected[23] and nothing escapes him, whether thoughts or intentions[24] or "secrets of the heart."[25]

5. Knowing, therefore, that "God is not mocked,"[26] we ought to live in a manner that is worthy of his commandment and glory. (2) Similarly, deacons[27] must be blameless in the presence of his righteousness, as deacons of God and Christ and not of men: not slanderers, not insincere, not lovers of money, self-controlled in every respect, compassionate, diligent, acting in accordance with the truth of the Lord, who became "a servant of all."[28] If we please him in this present world, we will receive the world to come as well, inasmuch as he promised to raise us from the dead and that if we prove to be citizens[29] worthy of him, "we will also reign with him"[30]— if, that is, we continue to believe.

(3) Similarly, the younger men must be blameless in all things; they should be concerned about purity above all, rein-

19. Cf. 1 Tim. 6:7.
20. 2 Cor. 6:7; Rom. 6:13.
21. Cf. 1 Clem. 1.3.
22. Ibid. 21.6–8.
23. Ibid. 41.2.
24. Ibid. 21.3.
25. 1 Cor. 14:25.
26. Gal. 6:7.
27. Cf. 1 Tim. 3:8–13.
28. Cf. Mark 9:35. In Greek the word play between "deacons" (diakonoi) and "servant" (diakonos) is very clear.
29. Cf. Phil. 1:27; 1 Clem. 21.1.
30. 2 Tim. 2:12.

ing themselves away from all evil. For it is good to be cut off
from the sinful desires in the world, because every "sinful desire wages war against the spirit,"[31] and "neither fornicators
nor male prostitutes nor homosexuals will inherit the kingdom
of God,"[32] nor those who do perverse things. Therefore one
must keep away from all these things and be obedient to the
presbyters and deacons as to God and Christ. The young
women must maintain a pure and blameless conscience.

6. The presbyters, for their part, must be compassionate, merciful to all, turning back those who have gone astray, visiting all
the sick, not neglecting a widow, orphan, or poor person, but
"always aiming at what is honorable in the sight of God and of
men,"[33] avoiding all anger, partiality, unjust judgment, staying
far away from all love of money, not quick to believe things
spoken against anyone, nor harsh in judgment, knowing that we
are all in debt with respect to sin. (2) Therefore if we ask the Lord
to forgive us, then we ourselves ought to forgive, for we are in
full view of the eyes of the Lord and God, and we must "all stand
before the judgment seat of Christ," and "each one must give an
account of himself."[34] (3) So, then, let us serve him with fear and
all reverence, just as he himself has commanded, as did the
apostles, who preached the gospel to us, and the prophets, who
announced in advance the coming of our Lord.[35] Let us be eager
with regard to what is good,[36] and avoid those who tempt others
to sin[37] and false brothers and those who bear the name of the
Lord hypocritically, who lead foolish men astray.

7. For everyone "who does not confess that Jesus Christ has
come in the flesh is antichrist";[38] and whoever does not acknowledge the testimony of the cross "is of the devil";[39] and
whoever twists the sayings of the Lord to suit his own sinful
desires and claims that there is neither resurrection nor

31. 1 Pet. 2:11.
32. 1 Cor. 6:9.
33. Prov. 3:4; cf. 2 Cor. 8:21.
34. Cf. Rom. 14:10, 12; 2 Cor. 5:10.
35. Cf. Acts 7:52.
36. Cf. 1 Pet. 3:13; Titus 2:14.
37. Cf. 2 Tim. 3:5–6.
38. Cf. 1 John 4:2–3.
39. Cf. 1 John 3:8.

judgment—well, that person is the first-born of Satan. (2) Therefore let us leave behind the worthless speculation of the crowd and their false teachings, and let us return to the word delivered to us from the beginning; let us be self-controlled with respect to prayer[40] and persevere in fasting, earnestly asking the all-seeing God "to lead us not into temptation,"[41] because, as the Lord said, "the spirit is indeed willing, but the flesh is weak."[42]

8. Let us, therefore, hold steadfastly and unceasingly to our hope and the guarantee of our righteousness, who is Christ Jesus, "who bore our sins in his own body upon the tree," "who committed no sin, and no deceit was found in his mouth";[43] instead, for our sakes he endured all things, in order that we might live in him. (2) Let us, therefore, become imitators of his patient endurance, and if we should suffer for the sake of his name, let us glorify him. For this is the example he set for us in his own person,[44] and this is what we have believed.

9. I urge all of you, therefore, to obey the teaching about righteousness[45] and to exercise[46] unlimited endurance, like that which you saw with your own eyes not only in the blessed Ignatius and Zosimus and Rufus but also in others from your congregation and in Paul himself and the rest of the apostles; be assured that all these "did not run in vain"[47] but in faith and righteousness, and that they are now in the place due them with the Lord, with whom they also suffered together. For they did not "love the present world,"[48] but him who died on our behalf and was raised by God for our sakes.

10. Stand fast, therefore, in these things and follow the example of the Lord, firm and immovable in faith,[49] loving the brotherhood,[50] cherishing one another,[51] united in the truth,

---

40. Cf. 1 Pet. 4:7.
41. Matt. 6:13.
42. Matt. 26:41.
43. 1 Pet. 2:24, 22.
44. Cf. 1 Pet. 2:21.
45. Heb. 5:13.
46. *exercise*: so Eusebius; G reads *hold out with*.
47. Phil. 2:16.
48. Cf. 2 Tim. 4:10.
49. Cf. 1 Cor. 15:58.
50. Cf. 1 Pet. 2:17.
51. Cf. Rom. 12:10.

giving way to one another in the gentleness of the Lord,[52] despising no one. (2) When you are able to do good, do not put it
off,[53] because "charity delivers from death."[54] All of you be
subject to one another,[55] and maintain an irreproachable standard of conduct among the Gentiles, so that you may be praised
for your good deeds[56] and the Lord may not be blasphemed
because of you. (3) But woe to him through whom the name of
the Lord is blasphemed.[57] Therefore teach to all the self-control
by which you yourselves live.

11. I have been deeply grieved for Valens, who once was a
presbyter among you, because he so fails to understand the
office that was entrusted to him. I warn you, therefore: avoid
love of money, and be pure and truthful. "Avoid every kind of
evil."[58] (2) But how can a man who is unable to control himself
in these matters preach self-control to someone else?[59] If a man
does not avoid love of money, he will be polluted by idolatry,
and will be judged as one of the Gentiles, who are ignorant of
the Lord's judgment.[60] "Or do we not know that the saints will
judge the world,"[61] as Paul teaches? (3) But I have not observed
or heard of any such thing among you, in whose midst the
blessed Paul labored, and who were his letters of recommenda-
tion in the beginning.[62] For he boasts about you in all the
churches—those alone, that is, which at that time had come to
know the Lord,[63] for we had not yet come to know him. (4)
Therefore, brothers, I am deeply grieved for him and for his
wife; may the Lord grant them true repentance. You, therefore,

52. Cf. Rom. 12:10; 2 Cor. 10:1.
53. Cf. Prov. 3:28.
54. Tob. 4:10.
55. Cf. Eph. 5:21; 1 Pet. 5:5.
56. Cf. 1 Pet. 2:12.
57. Cf. Isa. 52:5; *Trall.* 8.2.
58. Cf. 1 Thess. 5:22.
59. Cf. 1 Tim. 3:5.
60. Cf. Jer. 5:4.
61. 1 Cor. 6:2.

62. *were . . . beginning*: or possibly *are (mentioned) in the beginning of his
letter*. For the first possibility, cf. 2 Cor. 3:2; Phil. 4:15; Lightfoot, *AF* 2.3.342–
43. For a discussion of the second (and several others), cf. Schoedel, *Polycarp*,
32–34.

63. *the Lord*: so some MSS; others read *God*.

for your part must be reasonable in this matter, "and do not regard" such people "as enemies,"[64] but, as sick and straying members, restore them, in order that you may save your body in its entirety. For by doing this you build up one another.

12. For I am convinced that you are all well trained in the sacred Scriptures and that nothing is hidden from you (something not granted to me). Only, as it is said in these Scriptures, "be angry but do not sin,"[65] and "do not let the sun set on your anger."[66] Blessed is the one who remembers this, which I believe to be the case with you.

(2) Now may the God and Father of our Lord Jesus Christ, and the eternal High Priest himself, the Son of God Jesus Christ, build you up in faith and truth and in all gentleness and in all freedom from anger and forbearance and steadfastness and patient endurance and purity, and may he give to you a share and a place among his saints, and to us with you, and to all those under heaven who will yet believe in our Lord and God[67] Jesus Christ and in his Father who raised him from the dead.[68] (3) Pray for all the saints.[69] Pray also for kings and powers and rulers, and for those who persecute and hate you,[70] and for the enemies of the cross,[71] in order that your fruit may be evident among all people, that you may be perfect in him.

13. Both you and Ignatius have written me that if anyone is traveling to Syria, he should take your letter along also. This I will do, if I get a good opportunity, either myself or the one whom I will send as a representative, on your behalf as well as ours. (2) We are sending to you the letters of Ignatius that were sent to us by him together with any others that we have in our possession, just as you requested. They are appended to this letter; you will be able to receive great benefit from them, for they deal with faith and patient endurance and every kind of spiritual growth that has to do with our Lord. As for Ignatius

64. 2 Thess. 3:15.
65. Eph. 4:26, quoting Ps. 4:5.
66. Eph. 4:26.
67. *and God*: many MSS omit these words.
68. Cf. Gal. 1:1.
69. Cf. Eph. 6:18.
70. Cf. Matt. 5:44 and Luke 6:27.
71. Cf. Phil. 3:18.

himself and those with him, if you learn anything more definite, let us know.

14. I am writing these things to you via Crescens, whom I recently commended to you and now commend again, for his conduct while with us has been blameless, and I believe that it will be likewise with you. And you will consider his sister to be commended when she comes to you. Farewell in the Lord Jesus Christ in grace, you and all those with you. Amen.

The Martyrdom of Polycarp

INTRODUCTION

The letter from the church at Smyrna to the church at Philomelium known as the *Martyrdom of Polycarp* is the oldest written account of a Christian martyrdom outside the New Testament. Apparently written by eyewitnesses (15.1) not long after the event (18.1), it records, in sometimes gruesome detail, the pursuit, arrest, trial, and execution of Polycarp, the beloved 86-year-old bishop of the church of Smyrna.

This account bears eloquent testimony to a growing challenge confronting the church around the middle of the second century. Because of its belief in one God the church found itself engaged in a struggle with the Roman state which permitted no compromise and from which eventually only one of the two parties would emerge victorious. The *Martyrdom of Polycarp* sets out quite clearly both the issue at stake—Lord Christ versus Lord Caesar—and the state's (as well as the general population's) view of Christians as disloyal atheists who threatened the well-being of the empire. In the face of this antipathy, the steadfastness of Polycarp's faith in Christ and the fearlessness with which he faced death became a model for many believers who found themselves in similar circumstances during the course of the next century and a half, until various edicts of toleration issued between A.D. 311 and 313 (including the letter of Constantine and Licinius in 313 known as the Edict of Milan) brought an end to the conflict and victory to the church.

The Date of Polycarp's Martyrdom

Chapter 21 mentions the month and day (Feb. 22, or perhaps 23), but not the year of Polycarp's death. According to Eusebius he died in A.D. 167, but in this instance the reliability of

Eusebius's information is questionable. Evidence that has come to light regarding the proconsulship of Statius Quadratus has led many to adopt a date around 156;[1] this comports well with the fact that not long before his arrest Polycarp visited Bishop Anicetus of Rome, who became bishop there no earlier than 154. In view of the various difficulties, including a possible leap year, W. R. Schoedel[2] suggests that greater precision than approximately 155 to 160 is unwarranted. If the information provided by chapter 21, which seems to be a later addition to the text (note the last sentence of chap. 20), is discounted, either the Eusebian date[3] or a date early in the reign of Marcus Aurelius (161–180) becomes possible.[4]

The Text

The sources for the text (and the symbols used to represent them) are as follows:

1. Six Greek MSS, all from the tenth to the thirteenth centuries:

> b
> p
> s   (= h in some editions)
> v
> c
> m (the "Moscow MS")
>
> G = the combined testimony of bpsvcm
> g = the combined testimony of bpsvc

Of these, m is of the most value, followed by b and p.

2. E = extracts from the letter preserved by Eusebius (*Church History* 4.15). He quotes the inscription, 1.1a, and 8.1–

---

1. Cf. R. M. Grant, *Augustus to Constantine* (New York: Harper and Row, 1970), 86–87.
2. Schoedel, *Polycarp*, 78–79; cf. T. D. Barnes, "A Note on Polycarp," *Journal of Theological Studies* 18 (1967):433–37.
3. Cf. W. H. C. Frend, *Martyrdom and Persecution in the Early Church* (Oxford: Blackwell, 1965), 268, 295 n. 1.
4. So H. Koester, *Literature*, 306: "after 160 C.E."

19.1a, and paraphrases 2.2–7.3.

3. L = the Latin version of the letter

Armenian, Syriac, and Coptic versions of the letter exist, but these are derived from Eusebius and therefore have no independent value as witnesses.

Chapters 21 and 22 may be (and the notes by Gaius, Socrates, and Pionius certainly are) later additions to the text. Moreover, differences between Eusebius's text and that preserved by the six Greek manuscripts have led scholars to ask whether some scribe, in addition to adding to the end of the text, may not have added to the story as well (the incident involving the dove in 16.1 is a key example, and the Pionius mentioned in the last paragraph a prime suspect). In particular, H. von Campenhausen[5] thinks that the story has been expanded in light of the Gospels in order to make more obvious the parallels between the sufferings of Jesus and Polycarp. One must be careful, however, not to place more weight on the differences between the various witnesses than is warranted, especially as Eusebius himself may be responsible for some of them. In any case, compared to many of the later accounts of martyrdom the story is told with a good deal of restraint, and may be judged to provide a generally reliable, and certainly very moving, account of Polycarp's martyrdom.

BIBLIOGRAPHY

Camelot, P.-Th. *Ignace d'Antioche: Lettres. Lettres et Martyre de Polycarpe de Smyrne.* 4th ed. Paris: Cerf, 1969.

Campenhausen, Hans von. "Bearbeitungen und Interpolationen des Polykarpmartyriums." *Aus der Frühzeit des Christentums,* 253–301. Tübingen: Mohr/Siebeck, 1963.

Frend, W. H. C. *Martyrdom and Persecution in the Early Church. A Study of a Conflict from the Maccabees to Donatus.* Oxford: Blackwell, 1965.

5. H. von Campenhausen, "Bearbeitungen und Interpolationen des Polykarpmartyriums," *Aus der Frühzeit des Christentums* (Tübingen: Mohr/Siebeck, 1963), 253–301.

Kleist, J. A. *The Didache. The Epistle of Barnabas. The Epistles and the Martyrdom of St. Polycarp. The Fragments of Papias. The Epistle to Diognetus.* Ancient Christian Writers, vol. 6. Westminster, Md.: Newman, 1948.

Lightfoot, J. B. *The Apostolic Fathers, Part II: S. Ignatius. S. Polycarp.* 2d ed. 3 vols. London: Macmillan, 1889. Repr. Grand Rapids: Baker, 1981.

Musurillo, Herbert, ed. *The Acts of the Christian Martyrs.* Oxford: Clarendon, 1972.

Schoedel, W. R. *Polycarp, Martyrdom of Polycarp, Fragments of Papias.* The Apostolic Fathers, vol. 5. Camden, N.J.: Nelson, 1967.

Shepherd, Massey H., Jr. "The Martyrdom of Polycarp, as Told in the Letter of the Church of Smyrna to the Church of Philomelium." In *Early Christian Fathers,* edited by C. C. Richardson, 141–158. Philadelphia: Westminster, 1953. Repr. Macmillan, 1970.

The Martyrdom of Polycarp

The church of God which sojourns at Smyrna to the church of
God which sojourns in Philomelium and to all the communities of the holy and catholic church sojourning in every place:
may mercy, peace, and love from God the Father and our Lord
Jesus Christ be multiplied.

1. We are writing to you, brothers, an account of those who
were martyred, especially the blessed Polycarp, who put an end
to the persecution as though he were setting his seal upon it by
his martyrdom. For nearly all the preceding events happened in
order that the Lord might show us once again[1] a martyrdom
which is in accord with the gospel. (2) For he waited to be
betrayed, just as the Lord did, in order that we too might be
imitators of him, "not looking only to that which concerns
ourselves, but also to that which concerns our neighbors."[2] For
it is the mark of true and steadfast love to desire not only that
oneself be saved, but all the brothers as well.

2. Blessed and noble, therefore, are all the martyrdoms that
have taken place in accordance with the will of God (for we
must reverently assign to God the power over all things). (2) For
who could fail to admire their nobility and patient endurance
and loyalty to the Master? For even when they were so torn by
whips that the internal structure of their flesh was visible as far
as the inner veins and arteries, they endured so patiently that
even the bystanders had pity and wept. But they themselves
reached such a level of bravery that not one of them uttered a
cry or a groan, thus showing to us all that at the very hour when
they were being tortured the martyrs[3] of Christ were absent
from the flesh, or rather that the Lord was standing by and

---

1. *once again*: or possibly *from above*.
2. Phil. 2:4.
3. *martyrs*: so bcv; mps read *most noble martyrs*.

conversing with them. (3) And turning their thoughts to the
grace of Christ they despised the tortures of this world, purchas-
ing at the cost of one hour an exemption from eternal punishment.[4] And the fire of their inhuman[5] torturers felt cold to
them, for they set before their eyes the escape from that eternal
fire which is never extinguished, while with the eyes of their
heart they gazed upon the good things which are reserved for
those who endure patiently, things "which neither ear has heard
nor eye has seen, nor has it entered into the heart of man,"[6] but
which were shown to them by the Lord, for they were no longer
men but already angels. (4) And in a similar manner those who
were condemned to the wild beasts endured terrible punishments: they were forced to lie on sharp shells and afflicted with
various other forms of torture in order that he[7] might, if possible, by means of the unceasing punishment compel them to
deny their faith; for the devil tried many things against them.

3. But thanks be to God, for he did not prevail against any of
them.[8] For the most noble Germanicus encouraged them, fear-
ful though they were, by his own patient endurance; he also
fought with the wild beasts in an outstanding way. For when
the proconsul wished to persuade him and asked him to consider his youthfulness, he forcibly dragged the wild beast toward himself, desiring to be released as quickly as possible
from their unrighteous and lawless life. (2) So after this all the
multitude, marvelling at the bravery of the God-loving and
God-fearing race of Christians, began shouting, "Away with
the atheists! Find Polycarp!"

4. (Now there was one man, Quintus by name, a Phrygian
recently arrived from Phrygia, who, when he saw the wild
beasts, turned coward. This was the man who had forced himself and some others to come forward voluntarily. The procon-

---

4. *an exemption . . . punishment*: m reads *eternal life.*

5. *inhuman*: so m; g reads *cruel.*

6. 1 Cor. 2:9.

7. *he* [i.e., the devil]: so m; g reads *the tyrant.*

8. *he . . . them*: so the MSS (and most translators), taking "he" to mean the
devil. But Lightfoot thinks this contradicts 4.1, and so changes *ouk* ("not") to
oun ("indeed"), thereby making God and not the devil the subject of the sentence ("he indeed prevailed against them all"). But 4.1 is likely only qualifying
3.1, rather than contradicting it; cf. Acts 4:32; 5:1.

sul, after many appeals, finally persuaded him to swear the
oath and to offer the sacrifice. For this reason therefore, brothers, we do not praise those who hand themselves over,[9] since
the gospel does not so teach.)

5. Now the most admirable Polycarp, when he first heard
the news, was not disturbed. In fact, he wanted to remain in
town, but the majority persuaded him to withdraw. So he with-
drew to a farm not far distant from the city, and there he stayed
with a few companions, doing nothing else night and day except praying for everyone and for the churches throughout the
world, for this was his constant habit. (2) And while he was
praying he fell into a trance three days before his arrest, and he
saw his pillow being consumed by fire. And he turned and said
to those who were with him: "It is necessary that I be burned
alive."

6. And as those who were searching for him persisted, he
moved to another farm. Immediately, those searching for him
arrived,[10] and not finding him, they seized two slave boys, one
of whom confessed under torture. (2) For it was really impossible for him to remain hidden, since the very persons who betrayed him were people of his own household. And the captain
of the police, who just happened to have the same name—
Herod, as he was called—was eager to bring him into the stadium, in order that he [Polycarp] might fulfill his appointed
destiny of being made a sharer with Christ, while those who
betrayed him received the punishment of Judas himself.

7. So, taking the young slave with them, on Friday about
suppertime the mounted police and horsemen set out, armed
with their usual weapons as though chasing after an armed
rebel.[11] And closing in on him late in the evening, they found
him in bed in an upstairs room in a small cottage; and though
he still could have escaped from there to another place, he
refused, saying, "May God's will be done."[12] (2) So when he
heard that they had arrived, he went and talked with them,
while those who were present marvelled at his age and his

9. *hand . . . over*: so sv(c); bmp read *come forward on their own.*
10. *arrived*: i.e., at the first farm.
11. Cf. Matt. 26:55.
12. Acts 21:14; cf. Matt. 6:10.

composure, and wondered why there was so much eagerness for the arrest of an old man like him. Then he immediately ordered that a table be set for them to eat and drink as much as they wished at that hour, and he asked them to grant him an hour so that he might pray undisturbed. (3) When they consented, he stood and prayed,[13] so full of the grace of God that for two hours he was unable to stop speaking; those who heard him were amazed, and many regretted that they had come after such a godly old man.

8. Now when at last he finished his prayer, after remembering everyone who had ever come into contact with him, both small and great, known and unknown, and all the universal church throughout the world, it was time to depart, and so they seated him on a donkey and brought him into the city on the day of a great Sabbath.[14] (2) Herod, the police captain, and his father, Nicetes, came out to meet him. After transferring him to their carriage and sitting down at his side, they tried to persuade him, saying, "Why, what harm is there in saying, 'Caesar is Lord,' and offering incense" (and other words to this effect) "and thereby saving yourself?" Now at first he gave them no answer. But when they persisted, he said, "I am not about to do what you are suggesting to me." (3) Thus failing to persuade him, they began to utter threats and made him dismount in such a hurry that he bruised his shin as he got down from the carriage. And without even turning around, he went on his way eagerly and quickly as if nothing had happened to him, and as he was led to the stadium, there was such a tumult in the stadium that no one could even be heard.

9. But as Polycarp entered the stadium, there came a voice from heaven: "Be strong, Polycarp, and act like a man." And no one saw the speaker, but those of our people who were present heard the voice. And then, as he was brought forward, there was a great tumult when they heard that Polycarp had been arrested. (2) Therefore, when he was brought before him, the proconsul asked if he were Polycarp.[15] And when he confessed that he was, the proconsul tried to persuade him to recant,

13. *prayed*: m adds *facing the East.*
14. Cf. John 19:31.
15. *Polycarp*: so gE; m (followed by Lightfoot) omits.

saying, "Have respect for your age," and other such things as they are accustomed to say: "Swear by the Genius[16] of Caesar; repent; say, 'Away with the atheists!' " So Polycarp solemnly looked at the whole crowd of lawless heathen who were in the stadium, motioned toward them with his hand, and then (groaning as he looked up to heaven) said, "Away with the atheists!" (3) But when the magistrate persisted and said, "Swear the oath, and I will release you; revile Christ," Polycarp replied, "For eighty-six years I have been his servant,[17] and he has done me no wrong. How can I blaspheme my King who saved me?"

10. But as he continued to insist, saying, "Swear by the Genius of Caesar," he answered: "If you vainly suppose that I will swear by the Genius of Caesar, as you request, and pretend not to know who I am, listen carefully: I am a Christian. Now if you want to learn the doctrine of Christianity, name a day and give me a hearing." (2) The proconsul said: "Persuade the people." But Polycarp said: "You I might have considered worthy of a reply, for we have been taught to pay proper respect to rulers and authorities appointed by God, as long as it does us no harm; but as for these, I do not think they are worthy, that I should have to defend myself before them."

11. So the proconsul said: "I have wild beasts; I will throw you to them, unless you change your mind." But he said: "Call for them! For the repentance from better to worse is a change impossible for us; but it is a noble thing to change from that which is evil to righteousness." (2) Then he said to him again: "I will have you consumed by fire, since you despise the wild beasts, unless you change your mind." But Polycarp said: "You threaten with a fire that burns only briefly and after just a little while is extinguished, for you are ignorant of the fire of the coming judgment and eternal punishment, which is reserved for the ungodly. But why do you delay? Come, do what you wish."

12. As he spoke these and many other words, he was inspired with courage and joy, and his face was filled with grace, so that not only did he not collapse in fright at the things which were said to him, but on the contrary the proconsul was aston-

---

16. *Genius*: i.e., the guardian spirit.
17. *have . . . servant*: so g; mE read *have served him*.

ished, and sent his own herald into the midst of the stadium to proclaim three times: "Polycarp has confessed that he is a Christian." (2) When this was proclaimed by the herald, the entire crowd, Gentiles as well as Jews living in Smyrna, cried out with uncontrollable anger and with a loud shout: "This is the teacher of Asia, the father of the Christians, the destroyer of our gods, who teaches many not to sacrifice or worship." Saying these things, they shouted aloud and asked Philip the Asiarch to let a lion loose upon Polycarp. But he said that it was not lawful for him to do so since he had already brought to a close the animal hunts. (3) Then it occurred to them to shout out in unison that Polycarp should be burned alive. For it was necessary that the vision which he received concerning his pillow be fulfilled, when he saw it on fire while praying, and turned and said prophetically to the faithful who were with him, "It is necessary that I be burned alive."

13. These things then happened with such swiftness, quicker than words could tell, the crowd swiftly collecting wood and kindling from the workshops and baths, the Jews being especially eager to assist in this, as is their custom. (2) When the pyre[18] was prepared, he took off all his clothes and removed his belt; he also tried to take off his shoes, though not previously in the habit of doing this, because all the faithful were always eager to be the first to touch his flesh. For he had been treated with all honor on account of his holy life even before his gray hair appeared.[19] (3) Then the materials prepared for the pyre were placed around him; and as they were also about to nail him, he said: "Leave me as I am; for he who enables me to endure the fire will also enable me to remain on the pyre without moving, even without the sense of security which you get from the nails."

14. So they did not nail him, but tied him instead. Then he, having placed his hands behind him and having been bound, like a splendid ram chosen from a great flock for a sacrifice, a burnt offering prepared and acceptable to God, looked up to heaven and said: "O Lord God Almighty, Father of your beloved and blessed Son Jesus Christ, through whom we have

---

18. *pyre*: so g; mE read *fire*.
19. *gray hair appeared*: so E; gL read *martyrdom*.

received knowledge of you, the God of angels and powers and of all creation, and of the whole race of the righteous who live in your presence, (2) I bless you because you have considered me worthy of this day and hour, that I might receive a place among the number of the martyrs in the cup of your Christ, to the resurrection to eternal life, both of soul and of body, in the incorruptibility of the Holy Spirit. May I be received among them in your presence today, as a rich and acceptable sacrifice, as you have prepared and revealed beforehand, and have now accomplished, you who are the undeceiving and true God. (3) For this reason, indeed for all things, I praise you, I bless you, I glorify you, through the eternal and heavenly High Priest, Jesus Christ, your beloved Son, through whom to you with him and the Holy Spirit be glory both now and for the ages to come. Amen."

15. When he had offered up the "Amen" and finished his prayer, the men in charge of the fire lit the fire. And as a mighty flame blazed up, we saw a miracle (we, that is, to whom it was given to see), and we have been preserved in order that we might tell the rest what happened. (2) For the fire, taking the shape of an arch, like the sail of a ship filled by the wind, completely surrounded the body of the martyr; and it was there in the middle, not like flesh burning but like bread baking or like gold and silver being refined in a furnace. For we also perceived a very fragrant odor, as if it were the scent of incense or some other precious spice.

16. When the lawless men eventually realized that his body could not be consumed by the fire, they ordered an executioner to go up to him and stab him with a dagger. And when he did this, there came out a large quantity[20] of blood, so that it extinguished the fire; and the whole crowd was amazed that there should be so great a difference between the unbelievers and the elect. (2) Among them most certainly was this man, the most remarkable[21] Polycarp, who proved to be an apostolic and pro-

---

20. *large quantity*: so E; G(L) [Lightfoot] read *dove and a large quantity*. The reference to the dove is almost certainly a later addition to the text (possibly by the Pionius mentioned in the last paragraph of the epilogue; cf. Lightfoot, *AF* 2.3.390–93).

21. *remarkable*: so mEL; g adds *martyr*. Lightfoot's Greek text omits *martyr* with mEL, while his translation includes it.

phetic teacher in our own time, bishop of the holy[22] church in
Smyrna. For every word which came from his mouth was accomplished and will be accomplished.

17. But the jealous and envious Evil One, the adversary of
the race of the righteous, when he observed the greatness of his
martyrdom and that his life was irreproachable from the beginning, and that he was now crowned with the crown of immortality and had won a prize which no one could challenge, saw
to it that not even his poor body should be taken away by us,
even though many desired to do this and to touch[23] his holy
flesh. (2) So he incited Nicetes, the father of Herod and brother
of Alce, to plead with the magistrate not to give up his body,
"or else," he said, "they may abandon the crucified one and
begin to worship this man"—all this being done at the instiga-
tion and insistence of the Jews, who even watched when we
were about to take it from the fire; they did not know that we
will never be able either to abandon the Christ who suffered for
the salvation of the whole world of those who are saved, the
blameless on behalf of sinners, or to worship anyone else. (3)
For this one, who is the Son of God, we worship, but the martyrs we love as disciples and imitators of the Lord, as they
deserve, on account of their matchless devotion to their own
King and Teacher. May we also become their partners and fellow disciples!

18. The centurion, therefore, seeing the opposition raised by
the Jews, set it in the middle and cremated it, as is their custom. (2) And so later on we took up his bones, which are more
valuable than precious stones and finer than refined gold, and
deposited them in a suitable place. (3) There gathering together,
as we are able, with joy and gladness, the Lord will permit us to
celebrate the birthday of his martyrdom in commemoration of
those who have already fought in the contest, and for the train-
ing and preparation of those who will do so in the future.

19. Such is the story of the blessed Polycarp. Although he
was martyred in Smyrna along with eleven others from Philadelphia, he alone is especially remembered by everyone, so that

22. *holy*: so mL; bspE read *catholic*.

23. *to touch*: or possibly *to receive a part of*, i.e., as a relic; the verb is
koinōnesai, usually translated "to have fellowship with."

he is spoken of everywhere, even by pagans. He proved to be not only a distinguished teacher, but also an outstanding martyr, whose martyrdom all desire to imitate, since it was in accord with the pattern of the gospel of Christ. (2) By his endurance he defeated the unrighteous magistrate and so received the crown of immortality; now he rejoices with the apostles and all the righteous, and glorifies the almighty God and Father, and blesses our Lord Jesus Christ, the Savior of our souls and Helmsman of our bodies and Shepherd of the catholic church throughout the world.

20. You did indeed request that the things which happened be reported to you in some detail, but for the present we have given a summary, as it were, through our brother Marcianus.[24] When you have informed yourselves about these things, send the letter on to the brothers who are farther away, in order that they too may glorify the Lord, who makes selection from among his own servants. (2) Now to him who is able to bring us all by his grace and bounty into his eternal kingdom, through his only begotten Son, Jesus Christ, be glory, honor, power, and majesty forever. Greet all the saints. Those who are with us greet you, as does Evarestus, who wrote this, and his whole house.

21. Now the blessed Polycarp was martyred on the second day of the first part of the month Xanthicus, seven days before the kalends of March,[25] on a great Sabbath, about two o'clock P.M. He was arrested by Herod, when Philip of Tralles was high priest during the proconsulship of Statius Quadratus, but while Jesus Christ[26] was reigning as King forever. To him be glory, honor, majesty, and the eternal throne, from generation to generation. Amen.

22. We bid you farewell, brothers, as you walk by the word of Jesus Christ which is in accord with the gospel; with whom be glory to God[27] for the salvation of the holy elect; just as the blessed Polycarp was martyred, in whose footsteps may we also be found in the kingdom of Jesus Christ.[28]

---

24. *Marcianus*: so L; m reads *Marcion*; bsp read *Mark*.
25. On the date of Polycarp's death, see above, pp. 131–32.
26. *Jesus Christ*: so bsp; m(L) read *our Lord Jesus Christ*.
27. *God*: so p; bs add *the Father and the Holy Spirit*.
28. *We bid . . . Christ*: so bps [Lightfoot]; mL omit the entire paragraph.

(2) This account Gaius transcribed from the papers of Irenaeus, a disciple of Polycarp, who also lived with Irenaeus. And I, Socrates, wrote it down in Corinth from the copies of Gaius. Grace be with everyone.

(3) And I, Pionius, wrote it down again from the previously mentioned copy, after making a search for it (for the blessed Polycarp showed it to me in a revelation, as I will explain in the sequel). I gathered it together when it was nearly worn out by age, that the Lord Jesus Christ might also gather me together with his elect into his heavenly kingdom; to whom be the glory with the Father and the Holy Spirit forever and ever. Amen.

The two preceding paragraphs as read in the Moscow MS (m):

(2) This account Gaius transcribed from the papers of Irenaeus; he also lived with Irenaeus, who had been a disciple of the holy Polycarp. For this Irenaeus, who was in Rome at the time of the martyrdom of the bishop Polycarp, instructed many; and many most excellent and orthodox writings of his are in circulation. In these he makes mention of Polycarp, saying that he had been taught by him. And he ably refuted every heresy, and handed on the ecclesiastical and catholic rule just as he had received it from the saint. He mentions this fact also, that when Marcion, after whom the Marcionites are called, once met the holy Polycarp and said, "Recognize us, Polycarp," he said in reply to Marcion, "Yes, I recognize you; I recognize the first-born of Satan!" The following statement also is made in the writings of Irenaeus, that on the very day and hour when Polycarp was martyred in Smyrna, Irenaeus, who was in the city of Rome, heard a voice like that of a trumpet saying, "Polycarp has been martyred." From these papers of Irenaeus, then, as has been stated already, Gaius transcribed a copy, and from the copy of Gaius Isocrates made another in Corinth.

(3) And I, Pionius, write it down again from the copy of Isocrates, after searching for it in obedience to a revelation of the holy Polycarp, gathering it together, when it was nearly worn out by age, that the Lord Jesus Christ might also gather me together with his elect into his heavenly kingdom; to whom be the glory with the Father and the Son and the Holy Spirit forever and ever. Amen.

The Didache
(The Teaching of the Twelve Apostles)

INTRODUCTION

The Teaching of the Lord to the Gentiles by the Twelve Apostles, or *The Teaching of the (Twelve) Apostles*, as it was known in ancient times, or simply the *Didache* ("The Teaching"), as it is usually referred to today, is one of the most fascinating yet perplexing documents to emerge from the early church. Although the title was known from references to it by ancient writers (some of whom used it as Scripture[1]), no copy was known to exist until 1873, when Bryennios discovered a manuscript that contained, among other things, the full text of the *Didache*, which he published in 1883. Since then it has been the focus of scholarly attention to an extent quite out of proportion to its modest length. Yet for all that attention such basic information as who wrote it and where and when it was written remain as much a mystery as when it was first discovered.

The document is composed of two parts: (1) instruction about the "Two Ways" (1.1–6.2), and (2) a manual of church order and practice (6.3–16.8). The "Two Ways" material appears to have been intended, in light of 7.1, as a summary of basic instruction about the Christian life to be taught to those who were preparing for baptism and church membership. In its present form it represents the Christianization of a common Jewish form of moral instruction. Similar material is found in a number of other Christian writings from the first through about the fifth centuries, including the *Epistle of Barnabas*, the *Didascalia*, the *Apostolic Church Ordinances*, the *Summary*

---

1. E.g., Clement of Alexandria, Origen, and Didymus the Blind; cf. Metzger, *Canon*, 49, 187, 214.

of Doctrine, the *Apostolic Constitutions*, the *Life of Schnudi*, and *On the Teaching of the Apostles* (or *Doctrina*), some of which are dependent on the *Didache*. The interrelationships between these various documents, however, are quite complex and much remains to be worked out. The connections between the *Didache* and the *Epistle of Barnabas* have been the focus of considerable attention. Rather than either one being directly dependent upon the other, it seems much more likely that both are dependent, perhaps indirectly, on a common source.[2]

The second part consists of instructions about food, baptism, fasting, prayer, the Eucharist, and various offices and positions of leadership. In addition to providing the earliest evidence of a mode of baptism other than immersion, it records the oldest known Christian eucharistic prayers and a form of the Lord's Prayer quite similar to that found in the Gospel of Matthew. The document closes with a brief apocalyptic section that has much in common with the so-called Synoptic Apocalypse (cf. Mark 13; Matt. 24–25; Luke 24).

Date and Place

A remarkably wide range of dates, extending from before A.D. 50 to the third century or later, has been proposed for this document. Dating the *Didache* is made difficult by a lack of hard evidence and the fact that it is a composite document. Thus the date when the anonymous author(s) stitched together this document (note the awkward transition in 6.2–3) on the basis of earlier materials must be differentiated from the time represented by the materials so utilized. The *Didache* may have been put into its present form as late as 150, though a date considerably closer to the end of the first century seems more probable. The materials from which it was composed, however, reflect the state of the church at an even earlier time. In his very thorough commentary J.-P. Audet suggests about A.D. 70, and he is not likely to be off by more than a decade in either direction.[3] The relative simplicity of the prayers, the continuing concern to

---

2. Cf. Kraft, *Barnabas and the Didache*, 4–16.
3. J.-P. Audet, *La Didachè; Instructions des Apôtres* (Paris: Gabalda, 1958), 187–206.

differentiate Christian practice from Jewish rituals (8.1), and in particular the form of church structure—note the twofold structure of bishops and deacons (cf. Phil. 1:1) and the continued existence of traveling apostles and prophets alongside a resident ministry—reflect a time closer to that of Paul (who died in the mid-60s) than Ignatius (who died sometime after 110).

Egypt or Syria are mentioned most often as possible places of origin of the *Didache*. The evidence is indirect and circumstantial, making a decision difficult. The reference to "mountains" (9.4) would appear to suggest a Syrian (or possibly Palestinian) provenance. The final editing, however, may well have occurred elsewhere.

The Text

Apart from two minuscule papyrus fragments of 1.3–4 and 2.7–3.2 (in the Oxyrhynchus Papyri, 15: 12–15), the Greek text of the *Didache* has survived in only one manuscript, the famous codex discovered by Bryennios in 1873 that also includes the *Epistle of Barnabas*, *1 Clement*, *2 Clement*, and the long form of the Ignatian letters:

C = Codex Hierosolymitanus (A.D. 1056; = "H" in some editions)

Important evidence is also provided by later translations or documents that incorporated, often with numerous changes and/or insertions, part or all of the *Didache*:

Co = the Coptic translation (only a fifth-c. fragment of 10.36–12.2a survives)
Georg = the Georgian translation
L = the Latin translation (third c. ?) of the "Two Ways" (the *Doctrina*)
ChOr = the *Apostolic Church Ordinances*
ApCon = the *Apostolic Constitutions*

In addition, the Ethiopic version of the *Apostolic Church Ordinances* preserves portions of the *Didache*.

BIBLIOGRAPHY

Audet, J.-P. *La Didachè; Instructions des Apôtres.* Études Bibliques. Paris: Gabalda, 1958.

Draper, Jonathan. "The Jesus Tradition in the Didache." In *Gospel Perspectives.* Vol. 5, *The Jesus Tradition Outside the Gospels,* edited by David Wenham, 269–87. Sheffield, England: JSOT, 1985.

Kleist, J. A. *The Didache. The Epistle of Barnabas. The Epistles and the Martyrdom of St. Polycarp. The Fragments of Papias. The Epistle to Diognetus.* Ancient Christian Writers, vol. 6. Westminster, Md.: Newman, 1948.

Knopf, R. *Die Lehre der zwölf Apostel. Die zwie Clemensbriefe.* Tübingen: Mohr, 1920.

Kraft, Robert A. *Barnabas and the Didache.* The Apostolic Fathers, vol. 3. New York: Nelson, 1965.

Richardson, C. C. "A Church Manual: The Teaching of the Twelve Apostles, Commonly Called the Didache." In *Early Christian Fathers,* edited by C. C. Richardson, 159–79. Philadelphia: Westminster, 1953. Repr. Macmillan, 1970.

Rordorf, W., and A. Tuilier. *La Doctrine des douze apôtres (Didache).* Paris: Cerf, 1978.

Vokes, F. E. "The Didache Re-Examined." *Theology* 63 (1955): 12–16.

———. "The *Didache*—Still Debated." *Church Quarterly* 3 (1970): 57–62.

———. *The Riddle of the Didache: Fact or Fiction, Heresy or Catholicism?* London: SPCK, 1938.

The Didache

or

The Teaching of the Twelve Apostles

The teaching of the Lord to the Gentiles by the twelve apostles.[1]

1. There are two ways, one of life and one of death, and there is a great difference between these two ways.

(2) Now this is the way of life: first, "you shall love God, who made you"; second, "your neighbor as yourself";[2] and "whatever you do not wish to happen to you, do not do to another."[3]

(3) The teaching of these words is this: "Bless those who curse you,"[4] and "pray for your enemies," and "fast for those who persecute you." "For what credit is it, if you love those who love you? Do not even the Gentiles do the same?" But "you must love those who hate you,"[5] and you will not have an enemy. (4) Abstain from physical and bodily cravings.[6] "If someone gives you a blow on your right cheek, turn to him the other as well,"[7] and you will be perfect.[8] If someone "forces you to go one mile, go with him two miles"; "if someone takes your cloak, give him your tunic also"; "if someone takes from you what belongs to you, do not demand it back,"[9] for you cannot do so. (5) "Give to everyone who asks you, and do

---

1. On the title, see above, p. 145.
2. Cf. Matt. 22:37, 39 (Mark 12:30–31); Luke 10:27; Deut. 6:5; Lev. 19:18.
3. Cf. Matt. 7:12; Luke 6:31.
4. Luke 6:28.
5. Cf. Matt. 5:44–47; Luke 6:27–28, 32–33, 35.
6. Cf. 1 Pet. 2:11.
7. Cf. Matt. 5:39.
8. Cf. Matt. 5:48.
9. Matt. 5:41; Luke 6:29 (Matt. 5:40); Luke 6:30.

149

not demand it back,"[10] for the Father wants something from his own gifts to be given to everyone. Blessed is the one who gives according to the command, for such a person is innocent. Woe to the one who receives: if, on the one hand, someone who is in need receives, this person is innocent, but the one who does not have need will have to explain why and for what purpose he received, and upon being imprisoned will be interrogated about what he has done, and will not be released from there until he has repaid every last cent.[11] (6) But it has also been said concerning this: "Let your gift sweat in your hands until you know to whom to give it."[12]

2. The second commandment of the teaching is: (2) "You shall not murder; you shall not commit adultery"; you shall not corrupt boys; you shall not be sexually promiscuous; "you shall not steal"; you shall not practice magic; you shall not engage in sorcery; you shall not abort a child or commit infanticide. "You shall not covet your neighbor's possessions; (3) you shall not commit perjury; you shall not give false testimony";[13] you shall not speak evil; you shall not hold a grudge. (4) You shall not be double-minded, or double-tongued, for the "double-tongue" is a deadly snare. (5) Your word must not be false or meaningless, but confirmed by action. (6) You shall not be greedy or avaricious, or a hypocrite or malicious or arrogant. You shall not hatch evil plots against your neighbor. (7) You shall not hate anyone; instead you shall reprove some, and pray for some, and some you shall love more than your own life.

3. My child, flee from evil of every kind, and from everything resembling it. (2) Do not become angry, for anger leads to murder. Do not be jealous or quarrelsome or hot-tempered, for all these things breed murders. (3) My child, do not be lustful, for lust leads to fornication. Do not be foul-mouthed or let your eyes roam, for all these things breed adultery. (4) My child, do not be an auger,[14] since it leads to idolatry. Do not be an en-

---

10. Luke 6:30.

11. Cf. Matt. 5:26; Luke 12:59.

12. Source unknown; cf. Sir. 12:1–7.

13. Cf. Exod. 20:13–17; Matt. 5:33; 19:18.

14. One who attempts to foretell the future by examining the behavior or entrails of birds or animals.

chanter or an astrologer or a magician, or even desire to see[15] them, for all these things breed idolatry. (5) My child, do not be a liar, since lying leads to theft. Do not be avaricious or conceited, for all these things breed thefts. (6) My child, do not be a grumbler, since it leads to blasphemy. Do not be arrogant or evil-minded, for all these things breed blasphemies.

(7) Instead, be humble, for "the humble shall inherit the earth."[16] (8) Be patient and merciful and innocent and quiet and good, and revere always the words which you have heard. (9) Do not exalt yourself or permit your soul to become arrogant. Your soul shall not associate with the lofty, but live with the righteous and the humble. (10) Accept as good the things that happen to you, knowing that nothing transpires apart from God.

4. My child, night and day remember the one who preaches God's word to you,[17] and honor him as though he were the Lord. For wherever the Lord's nature is preached, there the Lord is. (2) Moreover, you shall seek out daily the presence of the saints, that you may find support in their words. (3) You shall not cause division, but shall make peace between those who quarrel. You shall judge righteously; you shall not show partiality when reproving transgressions. (4) You shall not waver with regard to your decisions.[18]

(5) Do not be someone who stretches out his hands to receive, but withdraws them when it comes to giving. (6) If you earned something by working with your hands, you shall give a ransom for your sins. (7) You shall not hesitate to give, nor shall you grumble when giving, for you shall yet come to know who is the good paymaster of the reward. (8) You shall not turn away from someone in need, but shall share everything with your brother, and not claim that anything is your own.[19] For if you are sharers in what is imperishable, how much more so in perishable things!

15. *see*: so C; L ChOr add *or hear.*

16. Matt. 5:5.

17. Cf. Heb. 13:7.

18. *waver. . . . decisions*: meaning uncertain; lit. *be of two minds whether it shall be or not.*

19. Cf. Acts 4:32.

(9) You shall not withhold your hand from[20] your son or your daughter, but from their youth you shall teach them the fear of God. (10) You shall not give orders to your slave or servant girl (who hope in the same God as you) when you are angry, lest they cease to fear the God who is over you both. For he comes to call not with regard to reputation but upon those whom the Spirit has prepared. (11) And you slaves shall be submissive to your masters in respect and fear, as to a symbol of God.

(12) You shall hate all hypocrisy, and everything that is not pleasing to the Lord. (13) You must not forsake the Lord's commandments, but must guard what you have received, neither adding nor subtracting anything.[21] (14) In church you shall confess your transgressions, and you shall not approach your prayer with an evil conscience. This is the way of life.

5. But the way of death is this: first of all, it is evil and completely cursed; murders, adulteries, lusts, fornications, thefts, idolatries, magic arts, sorceries, robberies, false testimonies, hypocrisy, duplicity, deceit, arrogance, malice, stubbornness, greed, foul speech, jealousy, audacity, pride, boastfulness. (2) It is the way of persecutors of good people, of those hating truth, loving a lie, not knowing the reward of righteousness, not adhering to what is good or to righteous judgment, being on the alert not for what is good but for what is evil, from whom gentleness and patience are far away, loving worthless things, pursuing reward, having no mercy for the poor, not working on behalf of the oppressed, not knowing him who made them, murderers of children, corrupters of God's creation, turning away from someone in need, oppressing the afflicted, advocates of the wealthy, lawless judges of the poor, utterly sinful. May you be delivered, children, from all these things!

6. See that no one leads you astray from this way of the teaching, for such a person teaches you without regard for God. (2) For if you are able to bear the whole yoke of the Lord, you will be perfect. But if you are not able, then do what you can. (3) Now concerning food, bear what you are able, but in any case keep strictly away from meat sacrificed to idols, for it involves the worship of dead gods.

---

20. *withhold. . . . from*: i.e., "neglect your responsibility to."
21. Cf. Deut. 4:2; 12:32 (LXX 13:1).

7. Now concerning baptism, baptize as follows: after you have reviewed[22] all these things, baptize "in the name of the Father and of the Son and of the Holy Spirit"[23] in running[24] water. (2) But if you have no running water, then baptize in some other water; and if you are not able to baptize in cold water, then do so in warm.[25] (3) But if you have neither, then pour water on the head three times "in the name of Father and Son and Holy Spirit."[26] (4) And before the baptism, let the one baptizing and the one who is to be baptized fast, as well as any others who are able. Also, you must instruct the one who is to be baptized to fast for one or two days beforehand.

8. But do not let your fasts coincide with those of the hypocrites. They fast on Monday and Thursday, so you must fast on Wednesday and Friday.

(2) Nor should you pray like the hypocrites. Instead, "pray like this," just as the Lord commanded in his Gospel:

Our Father in heaven,
hallowed be your name,
your kingdom come,
your will be done
　　on earth as it is in heaven.
Give us today our daily bread,
and forgive us our debt,
　　as we also forgive our debtors;
and do not lead us into temptation,
but deliver us from the evil one;[27]
for yours is the power and the glory forever.[28]

(3) Pray like this three times a day.

9. Now concerning the Eucharist,[29] give thanks as follows.

---

22. *reviewed*: i.e., with those who are about to be baptized.

23. Matt. 28:19.

24. *running*: lit. *living*; so also in the next line.

25. Cf. Tertullian, *On Baptism* 4: "it makes no difference whether a man be washed in a sea or a pool, a stream or a fountain, a lake or a trough."

26. This appears to be the earliest reference to the Christian use of a mode of baptism other than immersion.

27. *the evil one*: or possibly *evil*.

28. Cf. Matt. 6:9–13.

29. *Eucharist*: i.e., "the thanksgiving." The word *eucharistia*, which in the New Testament is used in the general sense of "thankfulness" or "thanksgiv-

(2) First, concerning the cup:

> We give you thanks, our Father,
> for the holy vine of David your servant,
> which you have made known to us
> through Jesus, your servant;
> to you be the glory forever.

(3) And concerning the broken bread:

> We give you thanks, our Father,
> for the life and knowledge
> which you have made known to us
> through Jesus, your servant;
> to you be the glory forever.

(4) Just as this broken bread was scattered
> upon the mountains and then was
> gathered together and became one,
> so may your church be gathered together
> from the ends of the earth into your kingdom;
> for yours is the glory and the power
> through Jesus Christ forever.

(5) But let no one eat or drink of your Eucharist except those who have been baptized into the name of the Lord, for the Lord has also spoken concerning this: "Do not give what is holy to dogs."[30]

10. And after you have had enough, give thanks as follows:

> (2) We give you thanks, Holy Father,
> for your holy name which you
> have caused to dwell in our hearts,
> and for the knowledge and faith and immortality
> which you have made known to us
> through Jesus your servant;
> to you be the glory forever.

---

ing" (cf., e.g., Acts 24:3; Phil. 4:6; 1 Thess. 3:9), soon became a technical term for the primary act of "giving thanks," namely the Lord's Supper (cf. Ign. *Smyrn.* 6.2; Justin Martyr, *1 Apology* 65). Lightfoot, apparently in an effort to capture both the general and technical senses of the term, translates the word as "eucharistic thanksgiving."

30. Matt. 7:6.

(3) You, almighty Master, created all things for your
    name's sake,
   and gave food and drink to men to enjoy,
       that they might give you thanks;
   but to us you have graciously given
       spiritual food and drink,
   and eternal life through your servant.[31]
(4) Above all we give thanks because you are mighty;
   to you be the glory forever.
(5) Remember your church, Lord,
   to deliver it from all evil
   and to make it perfect in your love;
   and gather it, the one that has been sanctified,
   from the four winds into your kingdom,
   which you have prepared for it;
   for yours is the power and the glory forever.
(6) May grace come, and may this world pass away.
   Hosanna to the God of David.
   If anyone is holy, let him come;
   if anyone is not, let him repent.[32]
   Maranatha![33] Amen.

(7) But permit the prophets to give thanks however they wish.[34]

11. So, if anyone should come and teach you all these things that have just been mentioned above, welcome him. (2) But if the teacher himself goes astray and teaches a different teaching that undermines all this, do not listen to him. However, if his teaching contributes to righteousness and knowledge of the Lord, welcome him as you would the Lord.

(3) Now concerning the apostles and prophets, deal with them as follows in accordance with the rule of the gospel. (4) Let every apostle who comes to you be welcomed as if he were the Lord. (5) But he is not to stay for more than one day, unless there is need, in which case he may stay another. But if he stays three days, he

---

31. *servant*: so C; Co adds *Jesus*.

32. *repent*: or possibly *be converted*.

33. I.e., "Our Lord, come!"; cf. 1 Cor. 16:22.

34. Both Co and ApCon add here a section, not found in C or Georg, which reads as follows: *And concerning the ointment, give thanks as follows: We give you thanks, Father, for the fragrant ointment which you have made known to us through Jesus your servant; to you be the glory forever. Amen.* See Kraft, *Barnabas and the Didache*, 167–69, for a discussion.

is a false prophet. (6) And when the apostle leaves, he is to take nothing except bread until he finds his next night's lodging. But if he asks for money, he is a false prophet.

(7) Also, do not test or evaluate any prophet who speaks in the spirit, for every sin will be forgiven, but this sin will not be forgiven.[35] (8) However, not everyone who speaks in the spirit is a prophet, but only if he exhibits the Lord's ways. By his conduct, therefore, will the false prophet and the prophet be recognized. (9) Furthermore, any prophet who orders a meal in the spirit shall not partake of it; if he does, he is a false prophet. (10) If any prophet teaches the truth, yet does not practice what he teaches, he is a false prophet. (11) But any prophet proven to be genuine who does something with a view to portraying in a worldly manner the symbolic meaning of the church[36] (provided that he does not teach you to do all that he himself does) is not to be judged by you, for his judgment is with God. Besides, the ancient prophets also acted in a similar manner. (12) But if anyone should say in the spirit, "Give me money," or anything else, do not listen to him. But if he tells you to give on behalf of others who are in need, let no one judge him.

12. Everyone "who comes in the name of the Lord" is to be welcomed. But then examine him, and you will find out—for you will have insight—what is true and what is false.[37] (2) If the one who comes is merely passing through, assist him as much as you can. But he must not stay with you for more than two or, if necessary, three days. (3) However, if he wishes to settle among you and is a craftsman, let him work for his living. (4) But if he is not a craftsman, decide according to your own judgment how he shall live among you as a Christian, yet with-

---

35. Cf. Matt. 12:31.

36. *who does . . . church*: or possibly *who acts out in an earthly fashion the allegorical significance of the church*; lit. *who acts with a view to the earthly mystery of the church*. The phrase has never been explained satisfactorily. It may refer to the acting out of some symbolic action intended to convey spiritual truth, analogous to those performed by some of the Old Testament prophets (e.g., Hosea's marriage to Gomer), which may have seemed to some members of the community to be of doubtful propriety.

37. *find out . . . false*: lit. *know, for you will have right and left understanding*.

out being idle. (5) But if he does not wish to cooperate in this way, then he is trading on Christ. Beware of such people.

13. But every genuine prophet who wishes to settle among you "is worthy of his food." (2) Likewise, every genuine teacher is, like "the worker, worthy of his food."[38] (3) Take, therefore, all the firstfruits of the produce of the wine press and threshing floor, and of the cattle and sheep, and give these firstfruits to the prophets, for they are your high priests. (4) But if you have no prophet, give them to the poor. (5) If you make bread, take the firstfruit and give in accordance with the commandment. (6) Similarly, when you open a jar of wine or oil, take the firstfruit and give it to the prophets. (7) As for money and clothes and any other possessions, take the "firstfruit" that seems right to you and give in accordance with the commandment.

14. On the Lord's own day gather together and break bread and give thanks, having first confessed your sins so that your sacrifice may be pure. (2) But let no one who has a quarrel with a companion join you until they have been reconciled, so that your sacrifice may not be defiled. (3) For this is the sacrifice concerning which the Lord said, "In every place and time offer me a pure sacrifice, for I am a great king, says the Lord, and my name is marvelous among the nations."[39]

15. Therefore appoint for yourselves bishops and deacons worthy of the Lord, men who are humble and not avaricious and true and approved, for they too carry out for you the ministry of the prophets and teachers. (2) You must not, therefore, despise them, for they are your honored men, along with the prophets and teachers.

(3) Furthermore, correct one another, not in anger but in peace, as you find in the Gospel; and if anyone wrongs his neighbor, let no one speak to him, nor let him hear a word from you, until he repents. (4) As for your prayers and acts of charity and all your actions, do them all just as you find it in the Gospel of our Lord.

16. "Watch" over your life: "do not let your lamps go out, and do not be unprepared, but be ready, for you do not know the

38. Matt. 10:10.
39. Mal. 1:11, 14.

hour when our Lord is coming."[40] (2) Gather together frequently, seeking the things that benefit your souls, for all the
time you have believed will be of no use to you[41] if you are not
found perfect in the last time. (3) For in the last days the false
prophets and corrupters will abound, and the sheep will be
turned into wolves, and love will be turned into hate. (4) For as
lawlessness increases, they will hate and persecute and betray
one another.[42] And then the deceiver of the world will appear as
a son of God and "will perform signs and wonders,"[43] and the
earth will be delivered into his hands, and he will commit
abominations the likes of which have never happened before.
(5) Then all humankind will come to the fiery test, and "many
will fall away" and perish; but "those who endure" in their
faith "will be saved"[44] by the accursed one himself.[45] (6) And
"then there will appear the signs"[46] of the truth: first the sign
of an opening in heaven, then the sign of the sound of a trumpet,[47] and third, the resurrection of the dead—(7) but not of all;
rather, as it has been said, "The Lord will come, and all his
saints with him."[48] (8) Then the world "will see the Lord coming upon the clouds of heaven."[49]

40. Cf. Mark 13:35, 37; Matt. 24:42, 44; Luke 12:35, 40.
41. Cf. *Barn.* 4.9.
42. Cf. Matt. 24:10–12.
43. Cf. Mark 13:22.
44. Matt. 24:10, 13.
45. *by . . . himself*: or possibly *by him who was cursed* (cf. Gal. 3:13; in
either case the reference is to Christ), or *by the curse itself*. Audet (*Didachè*,
469, 472–73), following the sense of Georg., reads *from the curse*, which he
understands as the grave.
46. Cf. Matt. 24:30.
47. Cf. Matt. 24:31; 1 Cor. 15:52; 1 Thess. 4:12.
48. Zech. 14:5; cf. 1 Thess. 3:13.
49. Cf. Matt. 24:30.

The Epistle of Barnabas

INTRODUCTION

The so-called *Epistle of Barnabas* represents one of the earliest contributions outside the New Testament to the discussion of questions that have confronted the followers of Jesus since the earliest days of his ministry: How ought Christians to interpret the Jewish Scriptures? What is the nature of the relationship between Christianity and Judaism? Writing at a time when the level of antagonism between church and synagogue still ran high, the anonymous author of this "essay" deals with both of these questions as he seeks to show by means of an allegorical interpretation of Scripture that Christians are the true and intended heirs of God's covenant.

In utilizing an allegorical approach the author follows an ancient and well-respected tradition of interpretation. Developed by the Greeks, the allegorical method assumes the existence of and seeks to uncover the hidden spiritual meaning of a text, which may be quite different from (and at times, seemingly unrelated to) the apparent (and often considered to be superficial) meaning. This method of interpretation played a role in all known forms of first-century Judaism, and particularly in the writings of Philo, an Alexandrian Jew who was a contemporary of Paul. Paul himself provides an example of this approach in Galatians 4:21–31, in which Hagar and Sarah become the basis of a highly allegorical interpretation of Old Testament history. By employing this allegorical approach the author of the *Epistle of Barnabas* is able to offer a "Christian" interpretation of biblical texts that at first glance appear to have nothing to do with Jesus (e.g., 9.7–8), and to claim that only Christians understand the true meaning of the Scriptures (10.12). In short, the *Epistle of Barnabas* is a good early example of what became the dominant method of interpreting the Bible in the early and medieval church.

Date and Place of Origin

The *Epistle of Barnabas* is generally thought to have originated in Alexandria, in view of the author's fondness for the allegorical approach for which Alexandria was well known and the fact that all the earliest evidence for the existence of this document derives from there.[1] It appears to have been written after the destruction of the temple in Jerusalem in A.D. 70 (16.3–5) but before the city was rebuilt by Hadrian following the revolt of A.D. 132–135. Within these limits it is not possible to be more precise.[2]

On the relationship of the *Epistle of Barnabas* to the *Didache* and the "Two Ways", see page 146 above.

The Text

The text of the *Epistle of Barnabas* has been reconstructed on the basis of the following witnesses:

S = Codex Sinaiticus (fourth c.), the famous biblical MS discovered by Tischendorf, in which *Barnabas* is found immediately after Revelation and before the *Shepherd of Hermas*

S[c] = later correctors of S

C = Codex Hierosolymitanus (A.D. 1056; = "H" in some editions)

G = a group of nine late Greek MSS, all related, in which

---

1. Two exceptions are P. Prigent, *L'Épître de Barnabé I–XVI et Ses Sources* (Paris: Librairie Lecoffre, 1961), who suggests a Syrian milieu, and K. Wengst, *Tradition und Theologie des Barnabasbriefes* (Berlin/New York: De Gruyter, 1971), 113–18, who locates it in western Asia Minor.

2. Typical positions include those of J. A. T. Robinson (*Redating the New Testament* [Philadelphia: Westminster, 1976], 313–19), who follows Lightfoot (*AF* 1.2.505–12) in dating it to the time of Vespasian (A.D. 70–79); L. W. Barnard (*Studies in the Apostolic Fathers and Their Background* [Oxford: Blackwell, 1967], 46), who suggests Hadrian's reign (A.D. 117–138); and K. Wengst (*Tradition*, 105–13), who argues for 130–132.

the incomplete text of Polycarp's letter to the Philippians is immediately followed by *Barnabas* 5.8ff

P = a papyrus fragment containing 9.1–6[3]

L = the Latin translation (chaps. 1–17 only; chaps. 18–21 apparently never formed a part of this version)

In addition, Clement of Alexandria preserves a relatively large number of quotations. For the "Two Ways" section (chaps. 18–21), which *Barnabas* has in common with the *Didache*, see the witnesses listed in the introduction to that document (p. 147 above).

BIBLIOGRAPHY

Barnard, L. W. *Studies in the Apostolic Fathers and Their Background.* Oxford: Blackwell, 1967.

Kleist, James A. *The Didache. The Epistle of Barnabas. The Epistles and the Martyrdom of St. Polycarp. The Fragments of Papias. The Epistle to Diognetus.* Ancient Christian Writers, vol. 6. Westminster, Md.: Newman, 1948.

Kraft, Robert A. *Barnabas and the Didache.* The Apostolic Fathers, vol. 3. New York: Nelson, 1965.

Kraft, Robert A., and P. Prigent, *Epître de Barnabé.* Paris, 1971.

Prigent, P. *Les Testimonia dans le Christianisme primitif: L'Épître de Barnabé I–XVI et Ses Sources.* Paris: Libraire Lecoffre, 1961.

Wengst, K. *Tradition und Theologie des Barnabasbriefes.* Berlin/New York: De Gruyter, 1971.

Windisch, Hans. *Der Barnabasbrief.* Tübingen: Mohr, 1920.

3. R. A. Kraft, "An Unnoticed Papyrus Fragment of Barnabas," *Vigiliae Christianae* 21 (1967): 150–63.

The Epistle of Barnabas

1. Greetings, sons and daughters, in the name of the Lord who has loved us, in peace. (2) Seeing that God's righteous acts toward you are so great and rich, I rejoice with an unbounded and overflowing joy over your blessed and glorious spirits; so deeply implanted is the grace of the spiritual gift that you have received! (3) Therefore I, who also am hoping to be saved, congratulate myself all the more because among you I truly see that the Spirit has been poured out upon you from the riches of the Lord's fountain. How overwhelmed I was, on your account, by the long-desired sight of you! (4) Being convinced, therefore, of this and conscious of the fact that I said many things in your midst, I know that the Lord traveled with me in the way of righteousness, and above[1] all I too am compelled to do this: to love you more than my own soul, because great faith and love dwell in you, through the hope of his life. (5) Accordingly, since I have concluded that if I care enough about you to share something of what I have received, I will be rewarded for having ministered to such spirits, I have hastened to send you a brief note, so that along with your faith you might have perfect knowledge as well.

(6) Well then, there are three basic doctrines of the Lord: the hope of life, which is the beginning and end of our faith; and righteousness, which is the beginning and end of judgment; and love shown in gladness and rejoicing, the testimony of righteous works. (7) For the Master has made known to us through the prophets things past and things present, and has given us a foretaste of things to come. Consequently, when we see these things come to pass, one thing after the other just as he predicted, we ought to make a richer and loftier offering out

---

1. *I said . . . above*: or possibly *since I spoke among you I understand many things, because the Lord . . . righteousness, above.*

of reverence for him.[2] (8) For my part, not as a teacher but as one of you, I will point out a few things which will cheer you up in the present circumstances.

2. Inasmuch as the days are evil and the Worker[3] himself is in power, we ought to be on our guard and seek out the righteous requirements of the Lord. (2) Our faith's helpers, then, are fear and patience, and our allies are endurance and self-control. (3) When these things persist in purity in matters relating to the Lord, wisdom, understanding, insight, and knowledge rejoice with them. (4) For he has made it clear to us through all the prophets that he needs neither sacrifices nor whole burnt offerings nor general offerings, saying on one occasion: (5) " 'What is the multitude of your sacrifices to me?' says the Lord. 'I am full of whole burnt offerings, and I do not want the fat of lambs and blood of bulls and goats, not even if you come to appear before me. For who demanded these things from your hands? Do not continue to trample my court. If you bring fine flour, it is in vain; incense is detestable to me; your new moons and sabbaths I cannot stand.' "[4] (6) Therefore he has abolished these things, in order that the new law of our Lord Jesus Christ, which is free from the yoke of compulsion, might have its offering, one not made by man. (7) And again he says to them: "I did not command your fathers, when they were coming out of the land of Egypt, to bring whole burnt offerings and sacrifices, did I?[5] (8) On the contrary, this is what I commanded them: 'Let none of you bear a grudge in his heart against his neighbor, and do not love a false oath.' "[6] (9) We ought to perceive, therefore (since we are not without understanding), the gracious intention of our Father, because he is speaking to us; he wants us to seek how we may approach him, rather than go astray like they did. (10) To us, therefore, he says this: "A sacrifice to God[7] is a broken heart;[8] an aroma pleasing to the

---

2. *out of . . . him*: lit. *to his fear.*
3. *Worker*: i.e., of evil.
4. Isa. 1:11–13 (LXX).
5. Cf. Jer. 7:22–23 (LXX).
6. Cf. Zech. 8:17 (LXX).
7. *God*: so S (and LXX); CL read *the Lord.*
8. Cf. Ps. 51:17 (LXX 50:19).

Lord is a heart that glorifies its Maker."[9] So, brothers, we ought to give very careful attention to our salvation, lest the evil one should cause some error to slip into our midst and thereby hurl us away from our life.

3. Therefore he speaks again to them concerning these things: " 'Why do you fast for me,' says the Lord, 'so that today your voice is heard crying out loudly? This is not the fast I have chosen,' says the Lord, 'not a man humiliating his soul; (2) not even if you bend your neck into a circle, and put on sackcloth and lie in ashes, not even then will you call a fast that is acceptable.' "[10] (3) But to us he says: " 'Behold, this is the fast I have chosen,' says the Lord: 'Break every unjust bond, untie the knots of forced agreements, set free those who are oppressed, and tear up every unjust contract. Share your bread with the hungry, and if you see someone naked, clothe him; bring the homeless into your house, and if you see someone of lowly status, do not despise him, nor shall the members of your house or family do so. (4) Then your light will break forth early in the morning, and your healing[11] will rise quickly, and righteousness will go before you, and the glory of God will surround you. (5) Then you will cry out, and God will hear you; while you are still speaking he will say, "Here I am"—if you rid yourself of oppression and scornful gestures and words of complaint, and give your bread to the hungry from the heart, and have mercy on a downtrodden soul.' "[12] (6) So for this reason, brothers, he who is very patient, when he foresaw how the people whom he had prepared in his Beloved would believe in all purity, revealed everything to us in advance, in order that we might not shipwreck ourselves by becoming, as it were, "proselytes" to their law.

4. We must, therefore, investigate the present circumstances very carefully and seek out the things that are able to save us. Let us, therefore, avoid absolutely all the works of lawlessness lest the works of lawlessness overpower us, and let

9. Source unknown; according to a note in C, it is from the no longer extant *Apocalypse of Adam.*

10. Isa. 58:4–5 (LXX).

11. *healing* (*iamata*): so S^c (cf. LXX); CL read *garments* (*imatia*).

12. Isa. 58:6–10 (LXX).

us hate the deception of the present age, so that we may be loved in the age to come. (2) Let us give no rest to our soul that results in its being able to associate with sinners and evil men, lest we become like them. (3) The last stumbling block is at hand, concerning which the Scriptures speak, as Enoch says. For the Master has cut short the times and the days for this reason, that his beloved might make haste and come into his inheritance. (4) And so also speaks the prophet: "Ten kingdoms will reign over the earth, and after them[13] a little king will arise, who will subdue three of the kings with a single blow."[14] (5) Similarly Daniel says, concerning the same one: "And I saw the fourth beast, wicked and powerful and more dangerous than all the beasts of the earth,[15] and how ten horns sprang up from it, and from these a little offshoot of a horn, and how it subdued three of the large horns with a single blow."[16] (6) You ought, therefore, to understand. Moreover, I also ask you this, as one who is one of you and who in a special way loves all of you more than my own soul: be on your guard now, and do not be like certain people; that is, do not continue to pile up your sins while claiming that your covenant is irrevocably yours, because in fact[17] those people lost it completely in the following way, when Moses had just received it. (7) For the Scripture says: "And Moses was on the mountain fasting for forty days and forty nights, and he received the covenant from the Lord, stone tablets inscribed by the fingers of the hand of the Lord."[18] (8) But by turning to idols they lost it. For thus says the Lord: "Moses, Moses, go down quickly, because your people, whom you led out of Egypt, have broken the Law."[19] And Moses understood and hurled the two tablets from his hands, and their covenant was broken in pieces, in order that the covenant of

13. *after them*: so S (cf. LXX); CL read *afterwards*.

14. Cf. Dan. 7:24.

15. *earth*: so S; CL read *sea*.

16. Cf. Dan. 7:7–8.

17. *your covenant ... in fact*: the text is quite uncertain here. The above translation follows that of C. Many adopt the sense of L: *the covenant is both theirs and ours. Ours it is, but. . . .* Harmer suggests emending the text to read *our covenant remains to them also. Ours it is, but. . . .*

18. Cf. Exod. 34:28; 31:18.

19. Cf. Exod. 32:7; Deut. 9:12.

the beloved Jesus might be sealed in our heart, in hope inspired by faith in him. (9) (Though I would like to write a great deal more, not as a teacher but as befits one who does not like to leave out anything we possess, nevertheless I hasten to move along—your devoted servant.)

Consequently, let us be on guard in the last days, for the whole time of our faith[20] will do us no good unless now, in the age of lawlessness, we resist as well the coming stumbling blocks, as befits God's children, lest the black one find an opportunity to sneak in. (10) Let[21] us flee from every kind of vanity; let us hate completely the works of the evil way. Do not withdraw within yourselves and live alone, as though you were already justified, but gather together and seek out together the common good. (11) For the Scripture says: "Woe to those who are wise in their own opinion, and clever in their own eyes."[22] Let us become spiritual; let us become a perfect temple for God. To the best of our ability, let us cultivate the fear of God and strive to keep his commandments, that we may rejoice in his ordinances. (12) The Lord will judge the world without partiality. Each person will receive according to what he has done: if he is good, his righteousness will precede him; if he is evil, the wages of doing evil will go before him. (13) Let us never fall asleep in our sins, as if being "called" was an excuse to rest, lest the evil ruler gain power over us and thrust us out of the kingdom of the Lord. (14) Moreover, consider this as well, my brothers: when you see that after such extraordinary signs and wonders were done in Israel, even then they were abandoned, let us be on guard lest we should be found to be, as it is written, "many called, but few chosen."[23]

5. For it was for this reason that the Lord endured the deliverance of his flesh to corruption, that we might be cleansed by the forgiveness of sins, that is, by his sprinkled blood.[24] (2) For the Scripture concerning him relates partly to Israel and partly to us, and speaks as follows: "He was wounded because of our

---

20. *faith*: so S; C reads *life*; L reads *life and faith*. Cf. *Didache* 16.2.
21. *children, lest . . . Let*: so S; C reads *children. Therefore, lest . . . in, let*.
22. Isa. 5:21 (LXX).
23. Cf. Matt. 22:14.
24. *his sprinkled blood*: so S; CL read *by the sprinkling of his blood*.

transgressions, and has been afflicted because of our sins; by his wounds we were healed. Like a sheep he was led to slaughter, and like a lamb he was silent before his shearer."[25] (3) We ought, therefore, to be exceedingly thankful to the Lord, because he has both made known to us the past and given us wisdom in the present circumstance, and with regard to future events we are not without understanding. (4) Now the Scripture says, "Not unjustly are nets spread out for the birds."[26] This means that a man deserves to perish if, having knowledge of the way of righteousness, he ensnares himself in the way of darkness. (5) And furthermore, my brothers: if the Lord submitted to suffer for our souls, even though he is Lord of the whole world, to whom God said at the foundation of the world, "Let us make man according to our image and likeness,"[27] how is it, then, that he submitted to suffer at the hand of men? Learn! (6) The prophets, receiving grace from him, prophesied about him. But he himself submitted, in order that he might destroy death and demonstrate the reality of the resurrection of the dead, because it was necessary that he be manifested in the flesh. (7) Also, he submitted in order that he might redeem the promise to the fathers and—while preparing the new people for himself—prove, while he was still on earth, that after he has brought about the resurrection he will execute judgment. (8) Furthermore, by teaching Israel and performing extraordinary wonders and signs, he preached and loved them intensely. (9) And when he chose his own apostles who were destined to preach his gospel (who were sinful beyond all measure in order that he might demonstrate that "he did not come to call the righteous, but sinners"[28]), then he revealed himself to be God's Son. (10) For if he had not come in the flesh, men could in no way have been saved by looking[29] at him.[30] For when they look at merely the sun they are not able to gaze at its rays, even though it is the work of his hands and will eventu-

25. Isa. 53:5, 7.
26. Prov. 1:17 (LXX).
27. Gen. 1:26.
28. Matt. 9:13.
29. *been saved by looking*: or possibly *survived when they looked*.
30. *men . . . him*: so S(C); GL read *how could men be saved by looking at him?*

ally cease to exist. (11) Therefore the Son of God came in the flesh for this reason, that he might complete the full measure of the sins of those who persecuted his prophets to death. (12) It was for this reason, therefore, that he submitted. For God says that the wounds of his flesh came from them: "When they strike down their own shepherd, then the sheep of the flock will perish."[31] (13) But he himself desired to suffer in this manner, for it was necessary for him to suffer on a tree. For the one who prophesies says concerning him: "Spare my soul from the sword,"[32] and "Pierce my flesh with nails, for bands[33] of evil men have risen up against me."[34] (14) And again he says: "Behold, I have given my back to scourges, and my cheeks to blows, and I set my face like a solid rock."[35]

6. Therefore, when he gave the commandment, what did he say? "Who is the one who condemns me? Let him oppose me. Or who is the one who vindicates himself against me? Let him draw near to the servant of the Lord. (2) Woe to you, because you will all grow old like a garment, and a moth will devour you!"[36] And again the prophet says, since he was set in place like a mighty stone that crushes, "Behold, I will set into the foundations of Zion a precious stone, especially chosen, a cornerstone, highly valued." (3) Then what does he say? "And whoever sets his hope on[37] him will live forever."[38] Does our hope, then, rest on a rock? By no means! But he says this because the Lord has established his flesh in strength. For he says: "And he established me like a solid rock."[39] (4) And again the prophet says: "The stone which the builders rejected has become the cornerstone."[40] And again he says: "This is the great and wonderful day which the Lord has made."[41] (5) I am

---

31. Cf. Zech. 13:7; Matt. 26:31.
32. Ps. 22:20 (LXX 21:21).
33. *bands*: or perhaps *synagogues*.
34. Cf. Pss. 119 (LXX 118):120 (LXX text form only); 22:16 (LXX 21:17).
35. Isa. 50:6–7 (LXX).
36. Cf. Isa. 50:8–9 (LXX).
37. *sets his hope on*: so G; SCL read *believes in* (cf. LXX).
38. Cf. Isa. 28:16.
39. Cf. Isa. 50:7.
40. Ps. 118 (LXX 117):22; cf. 1 Pet. 2:7.
41. Cf. Ps. 118 (LXX 117):24.

writing to you very simply, so that you might understand—I, the devoted servant of your love. (6) What, then, does the prophet again say? "A band of evil men have surrounded me, they have swarmed around me like bees around a honeycomb,"[42] and "for my garments they cast lots."[43] (7) Therefore, inasmuch as he was about to be manifested and to suffer in the flesh, his suffering was revealed in advance. For the prophet says concerning Israel: "Woe to their soul, for they have plotted an evil plot against themselves by saying, 'Let us bind the righteous one, because he is troublesome to us.' "[44] (8) What does the other prophet, Moses, say to them? "Behold, thus says the Lord God: 'Enter into the good land, which the Lord promised by oath to Abraham and Isaac and Jacob, and take possession of it as an inheritance, a land flowing with milk and honey.' "[45] (9) But now learn what knowledge has to say: set your hope[46] upon Jesus, who is about to be revealed to you in the flesh. For man is earth suffering, for Adam was formed out of the face of the earth. (10) What, therefore, does "into the good land, a land flowing with milk and honey" mean? Blessed is our Lord, brothers, who endowed us with wisdom and understanding of his secrets. For the prophet speaks a parable concerning the Lord; who can understand it, except one who is wise and discerning and loves his Lord? (11) So, since he renewed us by the forgiveness of sins, he made us men of another type, so that we should have the soul of children, as if he were creating us all over again. (12) For the Scripture speaks about us when he says to the Son: "Let us make man according to our image and likeness, and let them rule over the beasts of the earth and the birds of the air and the fish of the sea." And when he saw that our creation was good, the Lord said: "Increase and multiply and fill the earth."[47] These things he said to the Son. (13) Again, I will show you how the Lord[48] speaks to us. He made a second creation in the last days. And the Lord says:

---

42. Pss. 22:16 (LXX 21:17); 118 (LXX 117):12.
43. Ps. 22:18 (LXX 21:19).
44. Isa. 3:9–10 (LXX).
45. Cf. Exod. 33:1, 3.
46. *hope*: so S^cG; SCL Clement of Alexandria read *hope, it says*.
47. Gen. 1:26, 28.
48. *the Lord*: so S [Harmer]; CL(G) read *he*.

"Behold, I make the last things as the first."[49] It was with reference to this, therefore, that the prophet proclaimed: "Enter into a land flowing with milk and honey, and rule over it."[50] (14) Observe, then, that we have been created anew, just as he says once more in another prophet: " 'Behold,' says the Lord, 'I will take away from these [that is to say, from those whom the Spirit of the Lord foresaw] their stony hearts, and put in hearts of flesh,' "[51] because he was about to be manifested in the flesh and to dwell in us. (15) For the dwelling-place of our heart, my brothers, is a holy temple dedicated to the Lord. (16) For the Lord says again: "And with what shall I appear before the Lord my God and be glorified? I[52] will confess you in the congregation of my brothers, and I will sing to you in the midst of the congregation of the saints."[53] Therefore we are the ones whom he brought into the good land. (17) So why, then, does he mention the "milk and honey"? Because the infant is first nourished with honey, and then with milk. So in a similar manner we too, being nourished by faith in the promise and by the word, will live and rule over the earth. (18) Now we have already said above: "And let them increase and multiply and rule over the fish."[54] But who is presently able to rule over beasts or fish or birds of the air? For we ought to realize that "to rule" implies that one has authority, so that the one giving orders is really in control. (19) If, however, this is not now the case, then he has told us when it will be: when we ourselves have been made perfect, and so become heirs of the Lord's covenant.

7. Understand, therefore, children of joy, that the good Lord revealed everything to us beforehand, in order that we might know to whom we ought to give thanks and praise for all things. (2) If, therefore, the Son of God, who is Lord and is destined to judge the living and the dead, suffered in order that his wounds might give us life, let us believe that the Son of God could not suffer except for our sake.

(3) But he also was given vinegar and gall to drink when he

49. Source unknown.
50. Cf. Exod. 33:3.
51. Ezek. 11:19.
52. *glorified? I*: so S; CGL read *glorified?" He says: "I.*
53. Cf. Pss. 42:2 (LXX 41:3); 22:22 (LXX 21:23).
54. Cf. 6.12 above.

was crucified. Hear how the priests of the temple have revealed something about this: when the command that "Whoever does not keep the fast shall surely die"[55] was written, the Lord commanded it because he himself was planning to offer the vessel of his spirit as a sacrifice for our sins, in order that the type established by Isaac, who was offered upon the altar, might be fulfilled. (4) What, therefore, does he say in the prophet? "And let them eat from the goat that is offered at the fast for all their sins"—pay careful attention!—"and let all the priests (but only them) eat the unwashed entrails with vinegar."[56] (5) Why? "Since you are going to give me, when I am about to offer my flesh for the sins of my new people, gall with vinegar to drink, you alone must eat, while the people fast and lament in sackcloth and ashes"—this was to show that he must suffer at their hands. (6) Pay attention to what he commanded: "Take two goats, fine and well-matched, and offer them, and let the priest take one for a whole burnt offering for sins."[57] (7) But what shall they do with the other one? "The other one," he says, "is cursed."[58] Notice how the type of Jesus is revealed! (8) "And all of you shall spit upon it and jab it, and tie scarlet wool around its head, and then let it be driven out into the wilderness."[59] And when these things have been done, the man in charge of the goat leads it into the wilderness, and he removes the wool and places it upon the bush commonly called rachia (the buds of which we are accustomed to eat when we find them in the countryside; only the fruit of the rachia is sweet).[60] (9) What is the meaning of this? Note well: "the one is for the altar, and the other is cursed," and note that the one cursed is crowned. For they will see him on that day, wearing a long scarlet robe about his body, and they will say, "Is this not the one whom we once crucified and insulted by[61] spitting upon him? Surely this was the man who said then that he was the Son of God!" (10) Now how is he like that goat? "The goats are similar, fine and

---

55. Lev. 23:29.
56. Source unknown; cf. Lev. 16.
57. Lev. 16:7, 9.
58. Cf. Lev. 16:8.
59. Source unknown.
60. Apparently some sort of blackberry bush.
61. *crucified . . . by*: so S; CGL read *crucified, insulting and piercing and.*

well-matched," for this reason: in order that when they see him coming then, they may be amazed at the similarity of the goat. Observe, therefore, the type of Jesus, who was destined to suffer. (11) And what does it mean when they place the wool in the midst of the thorns? It is a type of Jesus, set forth for the church, because whoever desires to take away the scarlet wool must suffer greatly because the thorns are so terrible, and can only gain possession of it through affliction. Likewise, he says, "those who desire to see me and to gain my kingdom must receive me through affliction and suffering."[62]

8. Now what type do you think was intended, when he commanded Israel that the men whose sins are complete should offer a heifer, and slaughter and burn it, and then the children should take the ashes and place them in containers, and tie the scarlet wool around a tree (observe again the type of the cross and the scarlet wool), and the hyssop, and then the children should sprinkle the people one by one, in order that they may be purified from their sins? (2) Grasp how plainly he is speaking to you: the calf is Jesus; the sinful men who offer it are those who brought him to the slaughter. Then the men are no more; no more is the glory of sinners.[63] (3) The children who sprinkle are those who preached to us the good news about the forgiveness of sins and the purification of the heart, those to whom he gave the authority to proclaim the gospel;[64] there were twelve of them as a witness to the tribes, because there are twelve tribes of Israel. (4) And why are there three children who sprinkle? As a witness to Abraham, Isaac, and Jacob, because these men were great in God's sight. (5) And then there is the matter of the wool on the tree: this signifies that the kingdom of Jesus is on the tree,[65] and that those who hope in him will live forever. (6) But why the wool and the hyssop together? Because in his kingdom there will be dark and evil days, in which we will be saved, because the one who suffers in body is healed by means of the dark juice of the hyssop. (7) So, that these things

62. Source unknown; cf. Acts 14:22.
63. *Then . . . sinners*: the text is quite obscure; Lightfoot and Harmer suspect that it is corrupt here.
64. *to proclaim the gospel*: lit. *of the gospel, that they should proclaim it*.
65. *tree*: i.e., the cross.

happened for this reason is obvious to us, but to them they were quite obscure, because they did not listen to the voice of the Lord.

9. Furthermore, with respect to the ears he describes how he circumcised our heart.[66] The Lord says in the prophet: "As soon as they heard, they obeyed me."[67] And again he says: "Those who are far off will hear with their ears, and they shall understand what I have done."[68] Also, "Circumcise your hearts," says the Lord.[69] (2) And again he says: "Hear, Israel, for this is what the Lord your God says."[70] And again the Spirit of the Lord prophesies:[71] "Who is the one who desires to live forever? With the ear let him hear the voice of my servant."[72] (3) And again he says: "Hear, heaven, and give ear, earth, for the Lord has spoken these things as a testimony."[73] And again he says: "Hear the word of the Lord, you rulers of this people."[74] And again he says: "Hear, children, the voice of one crying in the wilderness."[75] (4) In short, he circumcised our ears in order that when we hear the word we might believe.

But the circumcision in which they have trusted has been abolished, for he declared that circumcision was not a matter of the flesh. But they disobeyed, because an evil angel "enlightened" them. (5) He says to them: "This is what the Lord your God says [here I find a commandment]: 'Do not sow among thorns, be circumcised to your Lord.'"[76] And what does he say? "Circumcise your hardheartedness, and stop being stiff-necked."[77] Take this again:[78] "Behold, says the Lord, all the

---

66. Cf. 9.4 below.
67. Ps. 18:44 (LXX 17:45).
68. Cf. Isa. 33:13.
69. Cf. Jer. 4:4.
70. Cf. Jer. 7:2–3.
71. *And . . . prophesies*: so GLP; SC (followed by Harmer) omit.
72. Cf. Ps. 34:12 (LXX 33:13); Isa. 50:10; Exod. 15:26.
73. Cf. Isa. 1:2.
74. Cf. Isa. 1:10.
75. Cf. Isa. 40:3.
76. Jer. 4:3–4.
77. Deut. 10:16.
78. *Take . . . again*: so SC; G(P) read *Again*; L reads *And again he says*.

nations have uncircumcised foreskins, but this people has an uncircumcised heart!"[79]

(6) But you will say: "But surely the people were circumcised as a seal!"[80] But every Syrian and Arab and all the idol-worshiping priests are also circumcised; does this mean that they, too, belong to their covenant? Why, even the Egyptians practice circumcision!

(7) Learn abundantly, therefore, children of love, about everything: Abraham, who first instituted circumcision, looked forward in the spirit to Jesus when he circumcised, having received the teaching of the three letters. (8) For it says: "And Abraham circumcised ten and eight and three hundred men of his household."[81] What, then, is the knowledge that was given to him? Observe that it mentions the "ten and eight" first, and then after an interval the "three hundred." As for the "ten and eight," the I is ten and the H is eight;[82] thus you have "Jesus."[83] And because the cross, which is shaped like the T, was destined to convey grace, it mentions also the "three hundred." So he reveals Jesus in the two letters, and the cross in the other one. (9) He who placed within us the implanted gift of his covenant[84] understands. No one has ever learned from me a more reliable word, but I know that you are worthy of it.

10. Now when Moses said, "You shall not eat swine, or eagle or hawk or crow, or any fish that does not have scales,"[85] he received, according to the correct understanding, three precepts. (2) Furthermore, he says to them in Deuteronomy, "I will set forth as a covenant to this people my commandments."[86] Therefore it is not God's commandment that they should not eat; rather Moses spoke spiritually. (3) Accordingly he men-

79. Jer. 9:26 (LXX 9:25).

80. *seal*: i.e., of the covenant.

81. Cf. Gen. 14:14; 17:23.

82. In Greek (the author of *Barnabas* was obviously working with the LXX) the letters of the alphabet can have numerical value (A = 1, B = 2, Γ = 3, etc.); here H = 8, I = 10, and T = 300.

83. I.e., IH are the first two letters (and a not uncommon abbreviation) of the Greek form of "Jesus" (ΙΗΣΟΥΣ), and are understood by the author to represent the whole name.

84. *covenant*: so SC; GL read *teaching*.

85. Cf. Lev. 11:7–15; Deut. 14:8–14.

86. Cf. Deut. 4:10, 13.

tioned the swine for this reason: you must not associate, he means, with such men, men who are like swine. That is, when they are well off, they forget the Lord, but when they are in need, they acknowledge the Lord, just as the swine ignores its owner when it is feeding, but when it is hungry it starts to squeal and falls silent only after being fed again. (4) "Neither shall you eat the eagle nor the hawk nor the kite nor the crow." You must not, he means, associate with or even resemble such men, men who do not know how to provide food for themselves by labor and sweat but lawlessly plunder other people's property; indeed, though they walk about with the appearance of innocence, they are carefully watching and looking around for someone to rob in their greed, just as these birds alone do not provide food for themselves but sit idle and look for ways to eat the flesh of others—they are nothing more than pests in their wickedness. (5) "And you shall not eat," he says, "sea eel or octopus or cuttlefish."[87] You must not, he means, even resemble[88] such men, men who are utterly wicked and are already condemned to death, just as these fish alone are cursed and swim in the depths, not swimming about like the rest but living in the mud beneath the depths. (6) Furthermore, "You shall not eat the hare."[89] Why? Do not become, he means,[90] one who corrupts boys, or even resemble such people, because the hare grows another opening every year, and thus has as many orifices as it is years old. (7) Again, "Neither shall you eat the hyena."[91] Do not become, he means, an adulterer or a seducer, or even resemble such people. Why? Because this animal changes its nature from year to year, and becomes male one time and female another. (8) But he also hated the weasel, and with good reason. Do not become, he means, like those men who, we hear, with immoral intent do things with the mouth that are forbidden, nor associate with those immoral women who do things with the mouth that are forbidden. For this animal conceives through its mouth.

87. Source unknown.
88. *resemble*: so SC; GL add *by associating with*.
89. Cf. Lev. 11:5.
90. *he means*: so CL; SG (followed by Harmer) omit.
91. Source unknown.

(9) Concerning food, then, Moses received three precepts to this effect and spoke in a spiritual sense, but because of their fleshly desires the people accepted them as though they referred to actual food. (10) David also received knowledge of the same three precepts, and says: "Blessed is the man who has not followed the counsel of ungodly men"—just as the fish move about in darkness in the depths; "and has not taken the path of sinners"—just as those who pretend to fear the Lord sin like swine; "and has not sat in the seat of pestilent men"[92]—just as the birds that sit waiting for plunder. You now have the full story concerning food.

(11) Again Moses says: "Eat anything that has a divided hoof and chews the cud."[93] Why does he say this? Because when it receives food it knows the one who is feeding it and, relying upon him, appears to rejoice.[94] He spoke well with regard to the commandment. What, then, does he mean? Associate with those who fear the Lord, with those who meditate in their heart on the special significance of the word which they have received, with those who proclaim and obey the Lord's commandments, with those who know that meditation is a labor of joy and who ruminate on the word of the Lord. But why does he mention "the divided hoof"? Because the righteous person not only lives in this world but also looks forward to the holy age to come. Observe what a wise lawgiver Moses was! (12) But how could those people grasp or understand these things? But we, however, having rightly understood the commandments, explain them as the Lord intended. He circumcised our ears and hearts for this very purpose, that we might understand these things.

11. But let us inquire whether the Lord took care to foreshadow the water and the cross. Now concerning the water, it is written with reference to Israel that they would never accept the baptism that brings forgiveness of sins, but would create a substitute for themselves. (2) For the prophet says: "Be astonished, heaven, and let the earth shudder greatly at this, because

92. Ps. 1:1.
93. Cf. Lev. 11:3; Deut. 14:6.
94. *Because . . . rejoice*: or possibly *The one who receives food knows the one who gives him the food and, being refreshed, appears to rejoice in him.*

this people has done two evil things: they have abandoned me, the fountain of life, and they have dug for themselves a pit of death."⁹⁵ (3) "Is my holy mountain Sinai a desert rock? For you shall be as the fledglings of a bird which flutter about when they are taken away from the nest."⁹⁶ (4) And again the prophet says: "I will go before you and level mountains and shatter brass gates and break iron bars in pieces, and I will give you treasures that lie in darkness, hidden, unseen, in order that they may know that I am the Lord God."⁹⁷ And: "You shall dwell in a lofty cave of solid rock." (5) And: "His water will never fail; you will see the King in glory, and your soul will meditate on the fear of the Lord."⁹⁸ (6) And again in another prophet he says: "And the one who does these things will be like the tree that is planted by the streams of water, which will yield its fruit in its season and whose leaf will not wither, and whatever he does will prosper. (7) Not so are the ungodly, not so; instead they are like the dust which the wind blows from the face of the earth. Therefore the ungodly will not stand in judgment, nor sinners in the council of the righteous, because the Lord knows the way of the righteous, and the way of the ungodly will perish."⁹⁹ (8) Notice how he pointed out the water and the cross together. For this is what he means: blessed are those who, having set their hope on the cross, descended into the water, because he speaks of the reward "in its season"; at that time, he means, I will repay. But for now what does he say? "The leaves will not wither." By this he means that every word that comes forth from your mouth in faith and love will bring conversion and hope to many. (9) And again in a different prophet he says: "And the land of Jacob was praised more than any land."¹⁰⁰ This means he is glorifying the vessel of his spirit. (10) Then what does he say? "And there was a river flowing on the right hand, and beautiful trees were rising from it, and whoever eats from them will live forever."¹⁰¹ (11) By this he

---

95. Cf. Jer. 2:12–13.
96. Cf. Isa. 16:1–2.
97. Cf. Isa. 45:2–3.
98. Cf. Isa. 33:16–18.
99. Ps. 1:3–6 (LXX).
100. Cf. Zeph. 3:19 (?).
101. Source unknown; cf. Ezek. 47:1–12.

means that while we descend into the water laden with sins and dirt, we rise up bearing fruit in our heart and with fear and hope in Jesus in our spirits. "And whoever eats from these will live forever" means this: whoever, he says, hears these things spoken and believes them will live forever.

12. Similarly he once again gives an explanation about the cross in another prophet, who says: "And when shall these things be accomplished? The Lord says: 'When a tree falls over and rises again, and when blood drips from a tree.' "[102] Once again you have a reference about the cross and about him who was destined to be crucified. (2) And again he speaks to Moses,[103] when war was being waged against Israel by foreigners, and in order that he might remind those being attacked that they had been handed over to death because of their sins, the Spirit says to the heart of Moses that he should make a symbol of the cross and of him who was destined to suffer because, he is saying, unless they place their hope in him, war shall be waged against them forever. Therefore Moses piled one shield upon another in the midst of the battle, and standing high above them all he stretched out his hands, and so Israel was again victorious. But whenever he lowered them, the men began to be killed.[104] (3) Why so? So that they might learn that they cannot be saved unless they place their hope in him. (4) And again in another prophet he says: "All day long I have stretched out my hands to a disobedient people who oppose my righteous way."[105] (5) Again Moses makes a symbol of Jesus—showing that he must suffer, and that he himself whom they will think they have destroyed shall give life—in a sign given when Israel was falling. For the Lord caused all kinds of serpents to bite them, and they were perishing (since the fall[106] happened through the serpent, with the help of Eve), in order that he might convince them that they were being handed over to death because of their transgression. (6) Indeed, even though the same Moses had commanded, "You shall not have a cast or

102. Cf. 4 Ezra (2 Esd.) 4:33; 5:5.

103. *to Moses*: so SC; GL read *in Moses*, i.e., in the Pentateuch.

104. Exod. 17:8–13.

105. Cf. Isa. 65:2. The outstretched arms foreshadow, for the author, the crucifixion.

106. *fall*: lit. *transgression*.

a carved image for your God,"[107] nevertheless he himself made one in order to show them a symbol of Jesus. So Moses made a bronze serpent and set it up conspicuously, and called the people together by a proclamation. (7) When they had gathered together they begged Moses to offer a prayer for them, that they might be healed. But Moses said to them: "Whenever," he says, "one of you is bitten, let him come to the serpent that is placed upon the wooden pole[108] and let him hope and believe that though it is dead it can nonetheless give life, and he shall be saved immediately." And so they did.[109] Once again you have in these things the glory of Jesus, because all things are in him and for him.

(8) Again, what does Moses say to "Jesus"[110] the son of Nun when he gave him this name, since he was a prophet, for the sole purpose that all the people might hear that[111] the Father was revealing everything about his Son Jesus? (9) Moses said to "Jesus" the son of Nun, when he gave him this name as he sent him to spy out the land, "Take a book in your hands and write what the Lord says, that in the last days the Son of God will cut off by its roots all the house of Amalek."[112] (10) Observe again that it is Jesus, not a son of a man but the Son of God, and revealed in the flesh by a symbol.

Since, however, they were going to say that the Messiah is the son of David, David himself, fearing and understanding the error of sinners, prophesied: "The Lord said to my Lord, 'Sit at my right hand until I make your enemies a footstool for your feet.' "[113] (11) And again, Isaiah says as follows: "The Lord said to the Messiah my Lord, whose right hand I held, that the nations would obey him, and I will shatter the strength of kings."[114] Observe how David calls him "Lord," and does not call him "son."

---

107. Cf. Lev. 26:1; Deut. 27:15.
108. *wooden pole*: lit. *tree*, i.e., another symbol of the cross.
109. Cf. Num. 21:4–8; John 3:14–15.
110. "Jesus" is the Greek form of "Joshua."
111. *for . . . that*: or possibly *in order that all the people might listen to him alone, because.*
112. Cf. Exod. 17:14.
113. Ps. 110 (LXX 109): 1.
114. Cf. Isa. 45:1.

13. Now let us see whether this people or the former people is the heir, and whether the covenant is for us or for them. (2) Hear, then, what the Scripture says about "the people": "And Isaac prayed for Rebecca his wife, for she was barren; and she conceived. Then Rebecca went off to consult the Lord. And the Lord said to her: 'Two nations are in your womb, and two peoples in your belly; one people will dominate the other, and the greater will serve the lesser.' "[115] (3) You ought to understand who Isaac represents, and who Rebecca, and concerning whom he has shown that this people is greater than that one. (4) And in another prophecy Jacob speaks more clearly to Joseph, his son, saying: "Behold, the Lord has not deprived me of your presence; bring your sons to me, that I may bless them."[116] (5) And he brought Ephraim and Manasseh, intending that Manasseh, because he was the older, should be blessed, for he brought him to the right hand of his father Jacob. But Jacob saw in the Spirit a symbol of the people to come. And what does he say? "And Jacob crossed his hands and placed his right hand on the head of Ephraim, the second and younger, and blessed him. And Joseph said to Jacob, 'Transfer your right hand to the head of Manasseh, for he is my first-born son.' And Jacob said to Joseph, 'I know, my child, I know; but the greater will serve the lesser. Yet this one too shall be blessed.' "[117] (6) Observe how by these means he has ordained that this people should be first, and heir of the covenant.

(7) Now if in addition to this the same point is also made through Abraham, we add the final touch to our knowledge. What, then, does he say to Abraham, when he alone believed and was established in righteousness? "Behold, I have established you, Abraham, as the father of the nations who believe in God without being circumcised."[118]

14. Yes, indeed. But let us see if he has actually given the covenant which he swore to the fathers he would give to the people.[119] He has indeed given it; but they were not worthy to

---

115. Cf. Gen. 25:21–23.
116. Gen. 48:11, 9.
117. Cf. Gen. 48:14, 18, 19.
118. Cf. Gen. 15:6; 17:5; Rom. 4:11, 17.
119. *people*: so S; L (CG) add *Let us inquire.*

receive it because of their sins. (2) For the prophet says: "And Moses was fasting on Mount Sinai forty days and forty nights, in order to receive the Lord's covenant with the people. And Moses received from the Lord the two tablets which were inscribed by the finger of the hand of the Lord in the spirit."[120] And when Moses received them he began to carry them down to give to the people. (3) And the Lord said to Moses: "Moses, Moses, go down quickly, because your people, whom you led out of the land of Egypt, has broken the Law." And Moses realized that once again they had made cast images for themselves, and he flung the tablets from his hands, and the tablets of the Lord's covenant were shattered.[121] (4) So, Moses received it, but they were not worthy.

But how did we receive it? Learn! Moses received it as a servant, but the Lord himself gave it to us, that we might become the people of inheritance, by suffering for us. (5) And he was made manifest in order that they might fill up the measure of their sins and we might receive the covenant through the Lord Jesus who inherited it, who was prepared for this purpose, in order that by appearing in person and redeeming from darkness our hearts, which had already been paid over to death and given over to the lawlessness of error, he might establish a covenant in us by his word. (6) For it is written how the Father commands him to redeem us from darkness and to prepare a holy people for himself. (7) Therefore the prophet says: "I, the Lord your God, have called you in righteousness, and I will grasp your hand and strengthen you; and I have given you as a covenant to the people, a light to the nations, to open the eyes of the blind, and to release from their shackles those who are bound and from the prisonhouse those who sit in darkness."[122] We understand, therefore, from what we have been redeemed. (8) Again the prophet says: "Behold, I have established you as a light to the nations, that you may be the means of salvation to the ends of the earth; thus says the Lord God who redeemed you."[123] (9) Again the prophet says: "The Spirit of the Lord is

---

120. Cf. Exod. 24:18; 31:18.
121. Cf. Exod. 32:7–8, 19.
122. Isa. 42:6–7.
123. Cf. Isa. 49:6–7.

upon me, because he has anointed me to preach good news about grace to the humble,[124] he has sent me to heal the broken-hearted, to proclaim freedom for the prisoners and recovery of sight for the blind, to announce the Lord's year of favor and day of recompense, to comfort all who mourn."[125]

15. Furthermore, concerning the Sabbath it is also written, in the "Ten Words" which he spoke to Moses face to face on Mount Sinai: "And sanctify the Lord's Sabbath, with clean hands and a clean heart."[126] (2) And in another place he says: "If my sons guard the Sabbath, then I will bestow my mercy upon them."[127] (3) He speaks of the Sabbath at the beginning of the creation: "And God made the works of his hands in six days, and finished on the seventh day, and rested on it, and sanctified it."[128] (4) Observe, children, what "he finished in six days" means. It means this: that in six thousand years the Lord will bring everything to an end, for with him a day signifies a thousand years. And he himself bears me witness when he says, "Behold, the day of the Lord will be as a thousand years."[129] Therefore, children, in six days—that is, in six thousand years—everything will be brought to an end. (5) "And he rested on the seventh day." This means: when his Son comes, he will destroy the time of the lawless one[130] and will judge the ungodly and will change the sun and the moon and the stars, and then he will truly rest on the seventh day. (6) Furthermore, he says: "You shall sanctify it with clean hands and a clean heart." If, therefore, anyone now is able, by being clean of heart, to sanctify the day which God sanctified, we have been deceived in every respect. (7) But if that is not the case, accordingly then[131] we will truly rest and sanctify it only when we our-

---

124. *about . . . humble*: so G; S reads *to the poor*; L reads *to men*; C is missing several words here. Harmer emends the text to read *to the humble*.

125. Isa. 61:1–2.

126. Cf. Exod. 20:8, Deut. 5:12; Ps. 24 (LXX 23):4.

127. Cf. Exod. 31:13–17; Jer. 17:24; Isa. 56:2ff.

128. Gen. 2:2–3.

129. Cf. 2 Pet. 3:8.

130. *the lawless one*: or possibly *lawlessness*.

131. *But if . . . then*: the text is quite corrupt here. The above translation attempts to render the sense of S. Lightfoot, following ScL, reads *But if after all then and not till then. . . .* Many adopt the text of Funk–Bihlmeyer: *Observe*

selves will be able to do so, after being justified and receiving the promise; when lawlessness no longer exists, and all things have been made new by the Lord, then we will be able to sanctify it, because we ourselves will have been sanctified first. (8) Finally, he says to them: "I cannot bear your new moons and sabbaths."[132] You see what he means: it is not the present sabbaths that are acceptable to me, but the one that I have made; on that Sabbath, after I have set everything at rest, I will create the beginning of an eighth day, which is the beginning of another world. (9) This is why we spend the eighth day in celebration, the day on which Jesus both arose from the dead and, after appearing again, ascended into heaven.

16. Finally, I will also speak to you about the temple, and how those wretched men went astray and set their hope on the building, as though it were God's house, and not on their God who created them. (2) For they, almost like the heathen, consecrated him by means of the temple. But what does the Lord say in abolishing it? Learn! "Who measured heaven with the span of his hand, or the earth with his palm? Was it not I, says the Lord? Heaven is my throne, and the earth is a footstool for my feet. What kind of house will you build for me, or what place for me to rest?"[133] You now know that their hope was in vain. (3) Furthermore, again he says: "Behold, those who tore down this temple will build it themselves."[134] (4) This is happening now. For because they went to war, it was torn down by their enemies, and now the very servants of their enemies will rebuild it. (5) Again, it was revealed that the city and the temple and the people of Israel were destined to be handed over. For the Scripture says: "And it will happen in the last days that the Lord will hand over the sheep of the pasture and the sheepfold and their watchtower to destruction."[135] And it happened just as the Lord said.

(6) But let us inquire whether there is in fact a temple of God. There is—where he himself says he is building and com-

---

that then, as it appears. . . . For further details, see Kraft, *Barnabas and the Didache,* 129.

132. Isa. 1:13.

133. Cf. Isa. 40:12; 66:1.

134. Source uncertain; cf. Isa. 49:17.

135. Source uncertain; cf. *1 Enoch* 89:56–66.

pleting it! For it is written: "And it will come to pass that when the week comes to an end God's temple will be built gloriously in the name of the Lord."[136] (7) I discover, therefore, that there is in fact a temple. How, then, will it be built in the name of the Lord? Learn! Before we believed in God, our heart's dwelling-place was corrupt and weak, truly a temple built by human hands, because it was full of idolatry and was the home of demons, for we did whatever was contrary to God. (8) "But it will be built in the name of the Lord." So pay attention, in order that the Lord's temple may be built gloriously. How? Learn! By receiving the forgiveness of sins and setting our hope on the Name, we became new, created again from the beginning. Consequently God truly dwells in our dwelling-place—that is, in us.[137] (9) How? The word of his faith, the call of his promise, the wisdom of his righteous decrees, the commandments of his teaching, he himself prophesying in us, he himself dwelling in us; opening to us who had been in bondage to death the door of the temple, which is the mouth, and granting to us repentance, he leads us into the incorruptible temple. (10) For the one who longs to be saved looks not to the man[138] but to the One who dwells and speaks in him, and is amazed by the fact that he had never before heard such words from the mouth of the speaker nor for his part ever desired to hear them. This is the spiritual temple that is being built for the Lord.

17. To the extent that it is possible clearly to explain these things to you, I hope, in accordance with my desire, that I have not omitted anything of the matters relating to salvation.[139] (2) For if I should write to you about things present or things to come, you would never understand, because they are found in parables. So much, then, for these things.[140]

---

136. Source unknown; cf. Dan. 9:24.

137. *God . . . us*: lit. *in our dwelling-place truly God dwells in us*.

138. *man*: i.e., the one proclaiming the message of salvation to him.

139. *I hope* (lit. *my soul hopes*) *. . . salvation*: so (Sᶜ) (G); SCL read *I hope that I have not omitted anything*.

140. The Latin translation concludes here with this sentence: *Again you have insight concerning the majesty of Christ, how all things take place in him and through him, to whom be honor and power and glory, now and forever. Here ends the Epistle of Barnabas.*

18. But let us move on to another lesson[141] and teaching. There are two ways of teaching and power, one of light and one of darkness, and there is a great difference between these two ways. For over the one are stationed light-giving angels of God, but over the other are angels of Satan. (2) And the first is Lord from eternity to eternity, while the latter is ruler of the present era of lawlessness.

19. This, therefore, is the way of light; if anyone desires to make his way to the designated place, let him be diligent in his works. The knowledge, then, which is given to us that we may walk in it is as follows. (2) You shall love him who made you; you shall fear him who created you; you shall glorify him who redeemed you from death. You shall be sincere in heart and rich in spirit. You shall not associate with those who walk in the way of death; you shall hate everything that is not pleasing to God; you shall hate all hypocrisy; you must not forsake the Lord's commandments. (3) You shall not exalt yourself, but shall be humble-minded in every respect. You shall not claim glory for yourself. You shall not hatch evil plots against your neighbor. You shall not permit your soul to become arrogant.[142] (4) You shall not be sexually promiscuous; "you shall not commit adultery";[143] you shall not corrupt boys. The word of God shall not go forth from you among any who are unclean. You shall not show partiality when reproving someone for a transgression. Be humble; be quiet; be one who reveres the words which you have heard. You shall not bear a grudge against your brother. (5) You must not waver with regard to your decisions.[144] "You shall not take the Lord's name in vain."[145] You shall love your neighbor more than your own life. You shall not abort a child nor, again, commit infanticide. You must not withhold your hand from[146] your son or your daughter, but from their youth you shall teach them the fear of God. (6) You

---

141. *another lesson:* or perhaps *another kind of knowledge.*

142. *You . . . arrogant:* so SG; C places this after "every respect" above.

143. Exod. 20:14.

144. *waver . . . decisions:* meaning uncertain; lit. *be of two minds whether it shall be or not.*

145. *You . . . vain:* so SG; C places this after "have heard" above. On the command, cf. Exod. 20:7.

146. *withhold . . . from:* i.e. "neglect your responsibility to."

must not covet your neighbor's things; you must not become greedy. Nor be intimately associated with the lofty, but live with the humble and righteous. Accept as good the things that happen to you, knowing that nothing transpires apart from God. (7) Do not be double-minded or double-tongued.[147] Be submissive to masters in respect and fear, as to a symbol of God. You must not give orders to your slave or servant girl, who hope in the same God as you, when you are angry, lest they cease to fear the God who is over you both, because he came to call not with regard to reputation but upon those whom the Spirit has prepared. (8) You shall share everything with your neighbor, and not claim that anything is your own. For if you are sharers in what is incorruptible, how much more so in corruptible things! Do not be quick to speak, for the mouth is a deadly snare. Insofar as you are able, you shall be pure for the sake of your soul. (9) Do not be someone who stretches out his hands to receive, but withdraws them when it comes to giving. You shall love as the apple of your eye everyone who speaks the word of the Lord to you. (10) Remember the day of judgment night and day, and you shall seek out on a daily basis the presence of the saints,[148] either laboring in word and going out to encourage, and endeavoring to save a soul by the word, or with your hands, working for a ransom for your sins. (11) You shall not hesitate to give, nor shall you grumble when giving,[149] but you shall yet come to know who is the good paymaster of the reward. You shall guard what you have received, neither adding nor subtracting anything. You shall utterly hate the evil one.[150] You shall judge righteously. (12) You shall not cause division, but shall make peace between those who quarrel by bringing them together. You shall confess your sins. You shall not come to prayer with an evil conscience. This is the way of light.

20. But the way of the black one is crooked and completely cursed. For it is a way of eternal death and punishment, in

147. *double-tongued*: so SC; G adds *for the double-tongue is a deadly snare* (cf. *Didache* 2.4).

148. *the presence of the saints*: so ScG; SC omit.

149. *giving*: so SC; ScG add *give to everyone who asks you* (=*Didache* 1.5).

150. *the evil one*: or perhaps *evil*.

which lie things that destroy men's souls: idolatry, audacity, exaltation of power, hypocrisy, duplicity, adultery, murder, robbery, arrogance, transgression, deceit, malice, stubbornness, sorcery, magic art, greed, lack of fear of God. (2) It is the way of persecutors of the good,[151] of those hating truth, loving a lie, not knowing the reward of righteousness, not adhering to what is good or to righteous judgment, ignoring the widow and the orphan, being on the alert not because of fear of God but for what is evil, from whom gentleness and patience are far away and distant, loving worthless things, pursuing reward, having no mercy for the poor, not working on behalf of the oppressed, reckless with slander, not knowing him who made them, murderers of children, corrupters of God's creation, turning away from someone in need, oppressing the afflicted, advocates of the wealthy, lawless judges of the poor, utterly sinful.

21. It is good, therefore, after learning all the Lord's commandments which are written here, to walk in them. For the one who does these things will be glorified in the kingdom of God; the one who chooses their opposites will perish together with his works. This is why there is a resurrection, this is why there is recompense.

(2) I urge those in high positions, if you will accept some well-intentioned advice from me: you have among you those to whom you can do good—do not fail. (3) The day is near when everything will perish together with the evil one. "The Lord, and his reward, is near."[152] (4) Again and again I urge you: be good lawgivers to one another; continue to be faithful counselors of one another; get rid of all hypocrisy among you. (5) And may God, who rules over the whole world, give you wisdom, insight, understanding, knowledge of his commandments, and patience. (6) Be instructed by God, seeking out what the Lord seeks from you, and then do it, in order that you may be found[153] in the day of judgment. (7) And if there is any remembrance of what is good, remember me when you meditate on these things, in order that my desire and vigilance may lead to some good result; I ask you

---

151. *the good*: or possibly *good people*.
152. Cf. Isa. 40:10; Rev. 22:12.
153. *be found*: so S; G reads *be saved*; C reads *find*.

this as a favor. (8) As long as the "good vessel"[154] is still with you, do not fail in any of these things, but seek out these things constantly and fulfill every command, for they deserve it. (9) For this reason I made every effort to write as well as I could, in order to cheer you up. Farewell, children of love and peace. May the Lord of glory and all grace be with your spirit.

154. *good vessel*: i.e., the body.

The Shepherd of Hermas

INTRODUCTION

The *Shepherd of Hermas* is one of the more enigmatic documents to have survived from the postapostolic period. Relatively simple in style and widely popular in the second and third centuries, its form and theology are not very congenial to contemporary taste and perspective, and it has been misunderstood, disparged, and/or scorned by not a few modern scholars. Yet when read on its own terms, it stands as an important witness to the state of Christianity in Rome in the mid-second century. Expressing a Jewish-Christian theological perspective by means of imagery, analogies, and parallels drawn from Roman society and culture, the *Shepherd* reflects the efforts of its author(s) to deal with questions and issues—for example, postbaptismal sin and repentance, and the behavior of the rich and their relationship to the poor within the church—of great significance and concern to him and that part of the Christian community in Rome to which he belonged.

The *Shepherd* was generally well received in the early church. Irenaeus, Clement of Alexandria, and Origen (at least for a while) accepted it as Scripture, as apparently did Tertullian, although later, after he had joined the rigorous sect of the Montanists, he referred to it as the "shepherd of the adulterers" for its "lax" approach to repentance. In the fourth century, Athanasius quoted it as canonical, and even after the christology of the book proved to be congenial to his Arian opponents he continued to recommend that it be read by new converts. His Alexandrian contemporary Didymus the Blind included it in his canon of Scripture, and it stands at the end (following the Book of Revelation and the *Epistle of Barnabas*) of the important fourth-century biblical manuscript, Codex Sinaiticus.

Genre and Structure

The external structure of five visions, twelve mandates, and ten parables (or similitudes, as they are often referred to) masks the fact that on the basis of its internal structure the document falls into two parts: visions 1–4 and the *Shepherd* proper (= the mandates and parables, to which vision 5 serves as an introduction).

The genre of visions 1–4 is that of a Jewish-Christian apocalypse. A typical apocalypse (cf. Revelation) includes the following features: (1) a revelation from God, (2) usually in the form of a vision or dream, (3) often given through a mediator, (4) who provides an interpretation of the vision, (5) whose contents usually concern future events, especially the end times. Visions 1–4 neatly reflect this pattern, except for their contents: the focus is not on the end, but on the possibility of repentance because the end is not yet.

The mandates reflect the form of a typical Jewish-Hellenistic homily. The closest parallels to the parables of the *Shepherd* are found in the book of *1 Enoch*. These parables, in which typically the telling of the parable is followed by a request for and granting of an interpretation, and finally blessings and curses upon those who either do or do not heed it, are more like allegorical similes than the more familiar parables of the synoptic Gospels.[1]

There is some evidence to suggest that the two major sections, visions 1–4 and vision 5/parable 10, were written and circulated separately. Both the important Michigan Papyrus and the Sahidic Coptic version begin with vision 5, and there are some discrepancies among the different versions in the numbering of the parables and internal inconsistencies which indicate that parable 9 is a later addition. In all, it appears that two separate sections were later combined, at which time parable 9 was added to unify and link them together, creating the *Shepherd* as it is known today.

---

1. Graydon F. Snyder, *The Shepherd of Hermas* (Camden, N.J.: Nelson, 1968), 8–12.

Date and Authorship

The Hermas who wrote the *Shepherd* is certainly not Paul (a suggestion made on the basis of Acts 14:12) or the Hermas mentioned in Romans 16:14 (Origen's suggestion). According to the Muratorian Canon, the oldest (ca. A.D. 180–200) known list of New Testament and early Christian writings, Hermas was the brother of Pius, bishop of Rome (ca. 140–154). Whether or not this is so, little else is known about the author(s).

The date of the *Shepherd* is likewise difficult to establish. Reference to it by Irenaeus (ca. 175) establishes a date before which it must have been written, but on the other end dates as early as the 70s and 80s have been proposed. The evidence of the Muratorian Canon ("But Hermas wrote the Shepherd quite recently in our time in the city of Rome while his brother Pius, the bishop, was sitting on the throne of the church of the city of Rome") must be used with caution, since it appears to reflect a subtle attempt to discredit the *Shepherd*. The internal evidence is inconsistent. Data in visions 1–4, including the reference in 8.3 to "Clement," who may well be the Clement of Rome responsible for *1 Clement* (cf. above, p. 24), points to around 95–100, while the section comprising vision 5/parable 10 seems to come from a later time. If the *Shepherd* is, however, a composite document, this would resolve many of the difficulties. Visions 1–4 would represent the earliest stage of its formation, while the final editing, including the interpolation of parable 9, may well have occurred about the time suggested by the Muratorian Canon.

The Text

The text of the *Shepherd* has not been well preserved. Only three incomplete Greek manuscripts and a number of small fragments have been discovered, and no Greek text is available for nearly all of 107.3–114.5. The major extant witnesses (and their symbols) are as follows:

S = Codex Sinaiticus (fourth c.; contains 1.1–31.6)

A = Codex Athous (fourteenth–fifteenth c.; contains 1.1–107.2)

M = Papyrus Michigan 129 (third c.; contains 51.8–82.1)
L¹ = the "Old Latin" or "Vulgate" translation (the text used
for 107.3–114.5)
L² = the "Palatine" Latin translation
L = L¹ + L²
E = the Ethiopic translation

In addition, fragments of Coptic and Middle Persian translations have been discovered.

Two different reference systems exist for the text of the *Shepherd*. The older one follows the division into visions, mandates, and parables (similitudes), while the newer system employs chapter numbers. Both have been given in the translation below. The following table indicates the relation between them.

	Old		*New*			*Old*		*New*
Vis.	1	=	1–4		mand.	10	=	40–42
	2	=	5–8			11	=	43
	3	=	9–21			12	=	44–49
	4	=	22–24		Par./Sim.	1	=	50
	5	=	25			2	=	51
Mand.	1	=	26			3	=	52
	2	=	27			4	=	53
	3	=	28			5	=	54–60
	4	=	29–32			6	=	61–65
	5	=	33–34			7	=	66
	6	=	35–36			8	=	67–77
	7	=	37			9	=	78–110
	8	=	38			10	=	111–114
	9	=	39					

BIBLIOGRAPHY

Barnard, L. W. "The Shepherd of Hermas in Recent Study." *Heythrop Journal* 9 (1968): 29–36.

Dibelius, M. *Der Hirt des Hermas.* Tübingen: Mohr, 1923.

Giet, S. *Hermas et les Pasteurs: les trois auteurs du Pasteur d'Hermas.* Paris: Presses Universitaires de France, 1963.

Joly, Robert. *Hermas le Pasteur.* Paris: Cerf, 1958. Repr. with supp., 1968.

Osiek, Carolyn. *Rich and Poor in the Shepherd of Hermas. An Exegetical-Social Investigation.* Washington, D.C.: Catholic Biblical Association of America, 1983.

Snyder, Graydon F. *The Shepherd of Hermas.* The Apostolic Fathers, vol. 6. Camden, N.J.: Nelson, 1968.

The Shepherd of Hermas

VISION I

I.

1. The man who brought me up sold me to a woman named
Rhoda in Rome. Many years later I met her again and I began to
love her as a sister. (2) Some time later I saw her bathing in the
Tiber River, and I gave her my hand and helped her out of the
river. When I saw her beauty I thought to myself and said,
"How happy I would be, if I had a wife of such beauty and
character." This was the only thing I thought, nothing more. (3)
Some time later, as I was going to Cumae and glorifying God's
creatures for their greatness, splendor, and power, I fell asleep
as I walked. And a spirit took me and carried me away through
a pathless region through which a man could not make his way,
for the place was precipitous and eroded by the waters. When I
had crossed the river, I came to level ground, and I knelt down
and began to pray to the Lord and to confess my sins. (4) While I
was praying the heavens opened and I saw this woman, whom I
had desired, greeting me from heaven, saying, "Hello, Hermas." (5) And I stared at her and said, "Madam, what are you
doing here?" And she answered me, "I have been taken up in
order that I might convict you of your sins before the Lord." (6)
I said to her, "Are you now accusing me?" "No," she said, "but
listen to the words I am about to say to you. God, who dwells in
the heavens and created out of nothing the things that are, and
increased and multiplied them for the sake of his holy church,
is angry at you because you sinned against me." (7) Answering
her I said, "I sinned against you? In what way?[1] Or when have I

---

1. *In what way?*: so S^{c}AL^2 (E); SL^1 read *Where have I done so?*

ever spoken an indecent word to you? Haven't I always regarded you as a goddess? Haven't I always respected you as a sister? Why do you falsely accuse me, lady, of these evil and unclean things?" (8) She laughed at me and said, "The desire for evil rose up in your heart. Or don't you think that it is an evil thing for a righteous man if an evil desire rises up in his heart? It certainly is a sin, and a great one at that," she said, "for the righteous man aims at righteous things. So, then, as long as his aims are righteous, his reputation is secure in heaven and he finds the Lord favorably inclined in all he does. But those who aim at evil things in their hearts bring death and captivity upon themselves, especially those who lay claim to the world and pride themselves on their wealth and do not hold fast to the good things that are to come. (9) Their souls will regret it, for they have no hope; instead they have abandoned themselves and their life. But you, you pray to God, and he will heal your sins, and those of your whole house, and of all the saints."

2.

2. As soon as she had spoken these words the heavens were closed, and I was terribly shaken and upset. And I thought to myself, "If even this sin is recorded against me, how can I be saved? Or how will I propitiate God for my conscious sins? Or with what words will I ask the Lord to be gracious to me?" (2) While I was debating and discussing these things in my heart, I saw before me a great white chair made of snow-white wool, and there came an elderly woman in a shining garment with a book in her hands, and she sat down by herself and greeted me: "Hello, Hermas." And I, upset and weeping, said, "Hello, madam." (3) And she said to me, "Why are you so gloomy, Hermas? You who are patient and good-natured, the one always laughing, why do you look so depressed and unhappy?" And I said to her, "Because of a very good woman who says that I sinned against her." (4) And she said, "By no means should this thing happen to God's servant! But certainly the thought did arise in your heart concerning her. To God's servants, an intent such as this brings sin, for with respect to a devout and already approved spirit it is an evil and shocking decision if it should desire to do an evil deed, especially if it is Hermas the self-controlled, who abstains from every evil desire and is full of all sincerity and great innocence."

3.

3. "Yet this is not why God is angry at you. Rather it is in order that you may convert your family, which has sinned against the Lord and against you, their parents. But you are so fond of your children that you have not corrected your family, but have allowed it to become terribly corrupt. This is why the Lord is angry at you. But he will heal all your past evil deeds that have been done by your family, for because of their sins and transgressions you have been corrupted by the cares of this life. (2) But the great mercy of the Lord has had mercy on you and your family, and will strengthen you and establish you in his glory. Only do not be careless, but be courageous and strengthen your family. For just as the blacksmith by hammering at his work completes the task he wants to do, so also does the daily righteous word conquer all evil. Do not cease, therefore, instructing your children, for I know that if they repent with all their heart, they will be enrolled with the saints in the books of life." (3) After these words of hers ceased, she said to me, "Do you wish to hear me read?" And I said, "Yes I do, madam." She said to me, "Pay attention, and hear about the glories of God." I listened with care and amazement to things which I did not have the strength to remember, for all the words were terrifying, words which a human being cannot endure. The last words, however, I remembered, for they were beneficial to us and reassuring: (4) "Behold, the God of hosts, who by his invisible and mighty power and by his great wisdom created the world, and by his glorious purpose clothed his creation with beauty, and by his mighty word fixed the heaven and set the earth's foundations upon the waters, and by his own wisdom and providence created his holy church, which he also blessed—behold, he is removing the heavens and the mountains and the hills and the seas, and all things are becoming level for his elect, that he might keep the promise which he promised to them with great glory and joy, if they keep God's commandments, which they received with great faith."

4.

4. When she finished reading and rose from her chair, four young men came and took away the chair and went away toward the East. (2) Then she called me to her and touched my breast and said to me, "Did my reading please you?" And I said to her, "Madam, these last words please me, but the former were difficult and hard." And she responded, saying to me: "These last words are for the righteous, but the former are for the heathen and the apostate." (3) As she was speaking, two men appeared and took her by the arms and went toward the East, where the chair had also gone. And she smiled as she went away, and as she was going she said to me, "Act like a man, Hermas."

VISION 2

1.

5. When I was on the way to Cumae, about the same time as the previous year, as I walked along I remembered the vision of the previous year, and again a spirit took me and carried me away to the same place as the year before. (2) So when I reached the place, I fell to my knees and began to pray to the Lord and to glorify his name because he had considered me worthy and had made known to me my former sins. (3) And after I had risen from prayer, I saw before me the elderly woman whom I had seen the year before, walking and reading a little book. And she said to me, "Can you report these things to God's elect?" I said to her, "Madam, I cannot remember so many things, but give me the little book, so that I can copy it." "Take it," she said, "and return it to me." (4) I took it, and going away to some spot in the country I copied it all, letter by letter, for I could not make out the syllables. After I finished the letters of the little book, suddenly the little book was snatched out of my hand, but by whom I did not see.

2.

6. Fifteen days later, after I had fasted and earnestly asked the Lord, the meaning of the writing was revealed to me. And this is what was written: (2) "Your children, Hermas, have rejected God and blasphemed the Lord and by their great evil they have betrayed their parents, and are called betrayers of parents, yet they have not profited from their betrayal. But still they have added licentiousness and orgies of evil to their sins, and so the limit of their transgressions has been reached. (3) But make these words known to all your children, and to your wife, who is about to become like a sister to you, for she does not control her tongue, with which she does evil. But when she hears these words she will control it, and will find mercy. (4) After you have made known to them all these words, which the Master ordered me to reveal to you, then all the sins which they have previously committed will be forgiven them. Indeed, all the saints who have sinned up to this day will be forgiven, if they repent with all their heart and drive away double-mindedness from their heart. (5) For the Master has sworn by his own glory regarding his elect, that if sin still occurs, now that this day has been set as a limit, they will not find salvation, for repentance for the righteous is at an end; the days of repentance for all the saints are over, although for the heathen there is the possibility of repentance until the last day. (6) So speak, therefore, to the officials of the church, in order that they may direct their ways in righteousness, in order that they might receive the promises in full with much glory. (7) You, therefore, who work righteousness must be steadfast, and do not be double-minded, in order that you may gain entrance with the holy angels. Blessed are those of you who patiently endure the coming great tribulation and who will not deny their life. (8) For the Lord has sworn by his Son that those who have denied their Lord[2] have been rejected from their life, that is, those who now are about to deny him in the coming days. But to those who formerly denied him mercy has been granted because of his great mercy."

---

2. *Lord*: so S^cAL²E; S reads *Christ*; L¹ reads *son*.

3.

7. "But you, Hermas, must no longer bear a grudge against your children, nor allow your sister to have her way, in order that they might be cleansed from their former sins. For they will be disciplined with a righteous discipline if you do not bear a grudge against them. Bearing a grudge produces death. But you, Hermas, have had great tribulations of your own because of the transgressions of your family, because you did not care for them. Instead you neglected them and got mixed up in your own evil transgressions. (2) But the fact that you have not fallen away from the living God, and your sincerity and great self-control, saves you. These things have saved you, if you remain steadfast, and they save all who practice such things and walk in innocence and sincerity. These people prevail over all evil and will endure to eternal life. (3) Blessed are all those who practice righteousness; they will never be destroyed. (4) But say to Maximus: 'Behold, tribulation is coming; if it seems good to you, deny again.' 'The Lord is near to those who turn to him,' as it is written in the book of Eldad and Modat, who prophesied to the people in the wilderness."

4.

8. As I slept, brothers, a revelation was given to me by a very handsome young man, who said to me, "Who do you think the elderly woman from whom you received the little book was?" I said: "The Sibyl." "You are wrong," he said. "She is not." "Then who is she?" I said. "The Church," he replied. I said to him, "Why, then, is she elderly?" "Because," he said, "she was created before all things; therefore she is elderly, and for her sake the world was formed." (2) Afterwards I saw a vision in my house. The elderly woman came and asked me if I had already given the little book to the elders. I said that I had not given it. "You have done well," she said, "for I have words to add. So when I finish all the words, they will be made known to all the elect through you. (3) Therefore you will write two little books, and you will send one to Clement and one to Grapte. Then Clement will send it to the cities abroad, because that is his job. But Grapte will instruct the widows and orphans. But you yourself will read it to this city, along with the elders who preside over the church."

VISION 3

I.

9. The third vision I saw, brothers, was this. (2) After fasting often and begging the Lord to reveal to me the revelation which he promised to show me through the mouth of the elderly woman, that very night the elderly woman appeared to me and said, "Since you are so poorly instructed and eager to know everything, go into the field where you are farming,³ and about the fifth hour I will appear to you and show you what you must see." (3) I asked her, saying: "Madam, to what part of the field?" "Wherever you wish," she replied. I selected a beautiful secluded spot. But before I could speak to her and describe the place, she said to me: "I will go wherever you wish." (4) So I went, brothers, to the field, and I counted up the hours and went to the place where I had instructed her to come, and I saw an ivory couch placed there, and on the couch there was a linen cushion, and on it was spread out a cloth covering of flaxen linen. (5) When I saw these things sitting there and no one in the area, I was astonished and a fit of trembling seized me and my hair stood on end and I shuddered in panic, as it were, because I was alone. Then when I recovered myself and remembered the glory of God and took heart, I knelt down and once more confessed my sins to the Lord, as I had done before. (6) And she came with six young men, whom I had seen before, and she stood by me and listened attentively as I prayed and confessed my sins to the Lord. And she touched me and said, "Hermas, stop saying all these prayers for your sins. Ask also for righteousness, that you may take some part of it to your family." (7) Then she raised me by the hand and led me to the couch, and said to the young men, "Go and build." (8) And after the young men had gone and we were alone, she said to me, "Sit here." I said to her, "Madam, let the elders sit down first." "Do as I say," she said; "sit down." (9) Then when I wanted to

---

3. *are farming*: so most editors; Harmer (following ScAL²) reads *live*.

sit down on the right side, she would not let me, but indicated to me with her hand that I should sit on the left side. Then as I thought about this and was sad because she would not permit me to sit on the right side, she said to me, "Are you sad, Hermas? The place on the right side is for others, who have already pleased God and have suffered for the sake of the Name. But you fall far short of sitting with them. But persevere in your sincerity, as you are now doing, and you will sit with them, as will all who do what they have done and endure what they have endured."

2.

10. "What," I asked, "have they endured?" "Listen," she said. "Scourgings, imprisonments, severe persecutions, crosses, wild beasts, for the sake of the Name. This is why the right side of the Holiness belongs to them, and to whoever suffers because of the Name. The left side belongs to the rest. But to both, to those sitting on the right and to those sitting on the left, belong the same gifts and the same promises; the only difference is the former sit on the right and have a certain glory. (2) And you are very eager to sit on the right with them, but your shortcomings are many. Nevertheless you will be cleansed of your shortcomings; indeed, all those who are not double-minded will be cleansed of all their sins to this day." (3) Having said these things, she wished to depart. But falling at her feet I asked her by the Lord to show me the vision which she had promised. (4) So again she took me by the hand and raised me up and seated me on the couch on the left, while she herself sat on the right. And lifting up a shining rod she said to me, "Do you see something great?" I said to her, "Madam, I don't see anything." She said to me, "Look! Don't you see right in front of you a great tower being built upon the waters out of shining square stones?" (5) And the tower was being built in a square by the six young men who had come with her, and countless other men were bringing stones, some of them from the deep and some from the land, and they were giving them to the six young men. And they were taking them and were building. (6) All the stones that were dragged from the deep they placed in the building just as they were, for they had been shaped and fit at the joints with the other stones. In fact, they fit one another so closely that the joints were not visible, and the structure of the tower looked as if it were built of a single stone. (7) But of the other stones which were brought in from the dry land, some they threw away, and some they placed in the building, and others they broke in pieces and threw far away from the tower. (8) And many other stones were lying around the tower, and they were not using them for the building, for some of them were damaged and others had cracks in them, and others were too short and others were white and round, and did not fit into the building. (9) And I saw other stones thrown far from the tower and coming to the road yet not staying on the road, but rolling to the wasteland; and others were falling into the fire and burning, and others were falling near the water, yet were not able to roll into the water, even though they wanted to roll and to come to the water.

3.

11. When she had shown me these things she wished to hurry away. I said to her, "Madam, what good does it do me to have seen these things and yet not know what they mean?" Answering me, she said, "You are a crafty fellow, wanting to know all about the tower." "Yes, madam," I replied, "so that I may report to my brothers, and so that they may be cheered up, and that as a result of hearing these things[4] may know the Lord[5] in much glory." (2) Then she said, "Many will hear; but after hearing, some of them will rejoice, but others will weep. Yet even these, if they hear and repent, will also rejoice. Hear, therefore, the parables of the tower, for I will reveal everything to you. And do not bother me anymore about a revelation, for these revelations have come to an end, for they have been completed. But you will never stop asking for revelations, for you are shameless. (3) The tower which you see being built is I, the Church, which appeared to you now and previously. So ask whatever you want to about the tower, and I will reveal it to you, in order that you may rejoice with the saints." (4) I said to

---

4. *and so that . . . cheered up* and *these things*: so AL [Harmer]; SE omit.
5. *Lord*: so SLE; A reads *God*.

her, "Madam, since you once considered me worthy to reveal everything to me, reveal it." And she said to me, "Whatever can be revealed, will be revealed. Only let your heart be with God, and do not be double-minded about what you see." (5) I asked her, "Why is the tower built upon water, madam?" "As I said to you before,"[6] she said, "you do seek diligently. By seeking, therefore, you are finding the truth. Hear, then, why the tower is built upon water: it is because your life was saved and will be saved through water. But the tower has been set on a foundation by the word of the almighty and glorious Name, and is strengthened by the unseen power of the Master."

4.

12. I answered and said to her, "Madam, this thing is great and marvelous. But who are the six young men who are building, madam?" "These are the holy angels of God, who were created first of all, to whom the Lord committed all his creation to increase and to build up, and to rule over all creation. Through them, therefore, the construction of the tower will be completed." (2) "And who are the others who are bringing the stones?" "They too are holy angels of God, but these six are superior to them. The construction of the tower will be completed, and all will rejoice together around the tower and will glorify God because the construction of the tower was completed." (3) I inquired of her, saying: "Madam, I wish to know about the destination of the stones, and what kind of meaning they have." Answering me she said, "It is not because you are more worthy than all others to have it revealed to you, for others are before you and are better than you, to whom these visions ought to have been revealed. But it has been revealed to you in order that the name of God might be glorified, and it will be revealed for the sake of the double-minded, who question in their hearts whether these things are so or not. Tell them that all these things are true, and that there is nothing besides the truth, but all are powerful and reliable and firmly established."

---

6. *before*: so SL²E; AL¹ add *you are crafty concerning the Scriptures.*

5.

13. "Now hear about the stones that go into the building. The stones that are square and white and fit at their joints, these are the apostles and bishops and teachers and deacons who have walked according to the holiness of God and have ministered to the elect of God as bishops and teachers and deacons with purity and reverence; some have fallen asleep, while others are still living. And they always agreed with one another, and so they had peace with one another and listened to one another. For this reason their joints fit together in the building of the tower." (2) "But who are the ones that are dragged from the deep and placed in the building, whose joints fit together with the other stones already used in the building?" "They are those who have suffered for the name of the Lord." (3) " And I wish to know who are the other stones brought from the dry land, madam." She said, "Those going into the building without being hewn are those whom the Lord has approved because they walked in the uprightness of the Lord and rightly performed his commandments." (4) "And who are the ones who are being brought and placed in the building?" "They are young in faith, and faithful; but they are warned by the angels to do good, because wickedness was found[7] in them." (5) "Who are the ones they rejected and threw away?" "They are the ones who have sinned and wish to repent. Therefore they were not thrown far from the tower, because they will be useful for building if they repent. So, then, the ones who are about to repent, if in fact they do repent, will be strong in the faith if they repent now while the tower is being built. But if the tower is finished, they will no longer have a place, but will be rejects. The only advantage they have is this, that they lie near the tower."

6.

14. "And do you want to know who the ones that are broken in pieces and thrown far away from the tower are? These are the sons of lawlessness; they believed hypocritically, and no wicked-

---

7. *was found*: so SL²; AL¹E read *was not found*.

ness escaped them. Therefore they do not have salvation, because they are not useful for building on account of their wickedness. That is why they were broken up and thrown far away,
because of the Lord's wrath, for they angered him. (2) As for the
others that you saw lying around in great numbers and not going
into the building, the ones that are damaged are those who have
known the truth but did not abide in it, nor do they associate
with the saints. Therefore they are useless."[8] (3) "But who are
the ones with cracks?" "These are the ones who are against one
another in their hearts and are not at peace among themselves.
Instead, they have only the appearance of peace, and when they
leave one another their evil thoughts remain in their hearts.
These are the cracks which the stones have. (4) The ones that are
too short are those who have believed and live for the most part
in righteousness, but they have a certain amount of lawlessness;
that is why they are too short and not perfect." (5) "And who are
the white and round stones that do not fit into the building,
madam?" She answered and said to me, "How long will you be
foolish and stupid, asking about everything and understanding
nothing? These are the ones who have faith, but also have the
riches of this world. Whenever persecution comes, they deny
their Lord because of their riches and their business affairs." (6)
And I answered her and said, "Then when, madam, will they be
useful for the building?" "When," she replied, "their riches,
which lead their souls astray, are cut away, then they will be
useful to God. For just as the round stone cannot become square
unless it is trimmed and loses some part of itself, so also those
who are rich in this world cannot become useful to God unless
their riches are cut away. (7) Learn first from yourself: when you
were rich, you were useless, but now you are useful and beneficial to life. Be useful to God, for you yourself are to be used as one
of these stones."

7.

15. "And the other stones which you saw thrown far from
the tower and falling on the road and rolling off the road to
wastelands are those who have believed, but because of their

---

8. *nor do they . . . useless*: so AL[1]; SL[2]E omit.

double-mindedness they abandon their true road. Thinking that they can find a better way, they go astray and wander about in misery, trudging through the wastelands. (2) Those falling into the fire and burning are those who have completely rebelled against the living God, and the thought no longer enters their heart to repent on account of their licentious desires and the evil deeds they do. (3) And do you want to know who the ones that fall near the waters but are not able to roll into the water are? They are the ones who heard the word and want to be baptized in the name of the Lord. Then, when they remember the purity of the truth, they change their mind and return again to their evil desires." (4) So she finished the explanation of the tower. (5) Still unabashed, I asked her whether all these stones that were rejected and do not fit into the construction of the tower have opportunity for repentance and a place in this tower. "They have," she said, "an opportunity for repentance, but they cannot fit into this tower. (6) But they will fit into another much inferior place, but not until they have been tormented and fulfilled the days of their sins. And they will be transferred for this reason only, that they received the righteous word. And then it will happen that they will be transferred out of their torments, if the evil deeds that they have done come into their hearts; but if they do not come into their hearts, they will not be saved, because of their hard-heartedness."

8.

16. When I stopped asking her about all these things, she said to me: "Would you like to see something else?" Being very eager to see more, I was quite happy to look. (2) Looking at me she smiled and said to me, "Do you see seven women around the tower?" "I see them, madam," I said. "This tower is supported by them by the Lord's command. (3) Now hear about their functions. The first of them, the woman with the strong hands, is called Faith; through her God's elect are saved. (4) The second, who is dressed for work and acts like a man, is called Self-Control; she is the daughter of Faith. Whoever follows her will be blessed in his life, because he will refrain from all evil deeds, believing that if he refrains from every evil desire he will inherit eternal life." (5) "And who are the others, madam?" "They are daughters of one another, and they are called Sincerity, Knowledge, Innocence, Reverence, and Love. So, when you do all the works of their mother, you can live." (6) "I would like to know, madam," I said, "what power each of them has." "Listen," she said, "to the powers that they have. (7) Their powers are controlled by one another, and they follow one another, in the order in which they were born. From Faith is born Self-Control; from Self-Control, Sincerity; from Sincerity, Innocence; from Innocence, Reverence; from Reverence, Knowledge; and from Knowledge, Love. Their works, therefore, are pure and reverent and divine. (8) So whoever serves these and has the strength to master their works will have a dwelling in the tower with the saints of God." (9) Then I began to ask her about the times, in particular if the consummation had already arrived. But she cried out in a loud voice, saying: "You foolish man, can't you see that the tower is still being built? When the tower is finished being built, then the end comes. But it will be built up quickly. Do not ask me any more questions; this reminder and the renewal of your spirits is sufficient for you and for the saints. (10) But these things have not been revealed for you alone, but in order that you might show them to everyone. (11) After three days—for you must first understand it yourself—I command you first, Hermas, to speak all these words which I am about to tell you to the ears of the saints, in order that by hearing and doing them they may be cleansed from their wickedness, and you with them."

9.

17. "Listen, my children. I brought you up in much sincerity and innocence and reverence through the mercy of the Lord, who instilled righteousness in you in order that you may be justified and sanctified from all evil and from all perversity. But you don't want to cease from your wickedness. (2) Now listen to me and be at peace among yourselves, and be concerned for one another and assist one another; and do not partake of God's creation in abundance by yourselves, but also share[9] with those in need. (3) For by overeating some people bring on themselves fleshly weaknesses and injure their flesh, while the flesh of those who don't have anything to eat is injured because they don't have enough food, and their body is wasting away. (4) This lack of community spirit is harmful to those of you who have, yet do not share with those in need. (5) Look to the coming judgment. You, therefore, who have more than enough, seek out those who are hungry, until the tower is finished. For after the tower is finished, you may want to do good, but you will not have the chance. (6) Beware, therefore, you who exult in your wealth, lest those in want groan, and their groaning rise up to the Lord, and you together with your[10] good things be shut outside the door of the tower. (7) Now, therefore, I say to you officials of the church, and occupants of the seats of honor: do not be like the sorcerers. For the sorcerers carry their drugs in bottles, but you carry your drug and poison in your heart. (8) You are calloused and don't want to cleanse your hearts and mix your wisdom together in a clean heart, in order that you may have mercy from the great King. (9) Watch out, therefore, children, lest these divisions of yours deprive you of your life. (10) How is it that you desire to instruct God's elect, while you yourselves have no instruction? Instruct one another, therefore, and have peace among yourselves, in order that I too may stand joyfully before the Father and give an account on behalf of all of you to your Lord."

10.

18. So, when she stopped speaking with me, the six young men who were building came and took her to the tower, and four others picked up the couch and took it also to the tower. I did not see their faces, because they were turned away. (2) And as she went away, I asked her to give me a revelation about the three forms in which she had appeared to me. She answered me

---

9. *creation . . . share*: or perhaps *creation by yourselves, but share the abundance.*

10. *your*: so SL[1]E; A reads *your brothers'*; Harmer, perhaps following L[2], reads *your abundance of.*

and said, "Concerning these things you must ask someone else, that they may be revealed to you." (3) Now she appeared to me, brothers, in the first vision last year as a very elderly woman sitting on a chair. (4) But in the second vision she had a more youthful face, although her body and hair were old, and she spoke to me standing up, and she was more cheerful than before. (5) In the third vision, she was altogether more youthful and exceedingly beautiful, except that her hair alone was old, and she was extremely happy and seated on a couch. (6) Concerning these things I was deeply distressed; I wanted to learn about this revelation. And I saw the elderly woman in a night-time vision, saying to me: "Every request requires humility. Fast, therefore, and you will receive what you request from the Lord." (7) So I fasted one day, and there appeared to me that very night a young man, and he said to me, "Because you are continually asking for revelations in your prayers, take[11] care, lest by requesting so many things you injure your flesh. (8) These revelations are sufficient for you. Are you able to see revelations mightier than those you have seen?" (9) I answered him and said, "Sir, I ask you this one thing about the three forms of the elderly woman: that a complete revelation might be given." He answered me and said, "How long will you people lack understanding? Your double-mindedness causes you to lack understanding; indeed, you lack it because your heart is not set toward the Lord." (10) Again I answered him and said, "But from you, sir, we will learn these things more accurately."

11.

19. "Hear," he said, "about the three forms, about which you inquired. (2) In the first vision, why did she appear to you as elderly and sitting on a chair? Because your spirit was old and already withered, and you had no power because of your weaknesses and double-mindedness. (3) For just as old people, no longer having any hope of renewing their youth, look forward to nothing except their falling asleep, so also you, being weakened by the cares of this life, gave yourselves over to indifference and are not casting your concerns on the Lord.

11. *Because . . . take*: so SL²; AL¹E read *Why are you . . . prayers? Take.*

Your spirit was broken and you were aged by your sorrows."
(4) "I wish to know, sir, why she was sitting on a chair."
"Because every weak person sits on a chair because of his
weakness, in order that his bodily weakness may be supported. You now have the symbolism of the first vision."

12.

20. "In the second vision you saw her standing, and she
had a more youthful face and was more cheerful than before,
but her body and hair were old. Listen," he said, "to this
parable too. (2) Imagine an old man, who has already given up
all hope for himself because of his weakness and poverty, and
looks forward to nothing except the last day of his life. Then
an inheritance is unexpectedly left to him. Upon hearing the
news he arises and is very joyful and clothes himself with
strength; and he no longer lies down, but stands up, and his
spirit, which was already broken by his former circumstances,
is renewed, and he no longer sits, but acts like a man. So it
was with you, when you heard the revelation which the Lord
revealed to you. (3) For he had compassion on you and renewed your spirits, and you laid aside your weaknesses, and
strength returned to you, and you were made powerful in the
faith, and when the Lord saw you putting on strength he rejoiced. Therefore he has shown to you the building of the
tower, and he will show you other things, if with all your
heart you remain at peace among yourselves."

13.

21. "In the third vision you saw her more youthful, and
beautiful and cheerful, and her figure was beautiful. (2) So, just
as when some good news comes to someone who is grieving, he
immediately forgets his former sorrow and thinks about nothing except the news which he heard, and from then on is
strengthened to do good, and his spirit is renewed because of
the joy which he received, so also you have received a renewal
of your spirits by seeing these good things. (3) And because you
saw her sitting on a couch, the position is secure, because the
couch has four feet and stands securely, for even the world is
sustained by four elements. (4) Those who have fully repented,

therefore, will be young and firmly established—those who repent with all their heart. You now have the complete revelation; you shall not ask anything any more about a revelation.
But if anything is still needed, it will be revealed to you."

VISION 4

1.

22. The fourth vision that I saw, brothers, twenty days after
the previous vision occurred, was a foreshadowing of the impending persecution. (2) I was going into the country by the
Campanian Way. The place is a little over a mile from the
public road, and is easily reached. (3) So, as I was walking by
myself, I asked the Lord to complete the revelations and visions which he showed to me through his holy church, in order
that he might strengthen me and grant repentance to his servants who had stumbled, that his great and glorious name
might be glorified, because he considered me worthy to show
his wonders to me. (4) And as I was glorifying him and giving
him thanks, the sound, as it were, of a voice answered me: "Do
not be double-minded, Hermas." I began to discuss this with
myself and to say, "How can I be double-minded, when I have
been so firmly established by the Lord and have seen glorious
things?" (5) And I went on a little farther, brothers, and behold,
I saw a cloud of dust rising up, as it were, to heaven, and I began
to say to myself, "Maybe some cattle are coming and raising a
cloud of dust." And it was about two hundred yards, away from
me. (6) As the cloud of dust grew larger and larger, I began to
suspect that it was something supernatural. Then the sun
shone a little more brightly, and behold, I saw a huge beast, like
some sea monster, and from its mouth flaming locusts were
pouring out. And the beast was about one hundred feet long,
and it had a head like a ceramic jar. (7) And I began to cry and to
beg the Lord to rescue me from it. And I remembered the word
which I had heard: "Do not be double-minded, Hermas." (8) So,
brothers, having put on the faith of the Lord[12] and remembering the great things he had taught me, I took courage and faced

12. *the Lord*: so SL²E; AL¹ read *God*.

the beast. And the beast was coming on with such a rush that it could have destroyed a city. (9) I came near it, and huge though it was, the sea monster stretched itself out on the ground and merely thrust out its tongue, and did not even twitch until I had passed by it. (10) And the beast had four colors on its head: black, then the color of fire and blood, then gold, and then white.

2.

23. Now after I had passed the beast and gone on ahead about thirty feet, behold, a young lady met me dressed as if she were coming out of a bridal chamber, all in white and with white sandals, veiled up to her forehead, and her head covering was a turban, and her hair was white. (2) I knew from the previous visions that she was the Church, and I became more cheerful. She greeted me, saying, "Good morning, my man," and I greeted her in return: "Good morning, madam." (3) She answered and said to me, "Did anything meet you?" I said to her, "Madam, a beast so huge that it could destroy entire peoples, but by the power of the Lord and by his great mercy I escaped it." (4) "You deserved to escape it," she said, "because you cast your cares on God and opened your heart to the Lord, believing that you could not be saved by anything except the great and glorious Name. Therefore the Lord sent his angel who has authority over the beasts, whose name is Segri,[13] and he shut its mouth so that it might not hurt you. You have escaped a great tribulation because of your faith, and because you were not double-minded, even though you saw such a huge beast. (5) Go, therefore, and declare to the Lord's elect his mighty works, and tell them that this beast is a foreshadowing of the great tribulation that is coming. So, if you prepare yourselves in advance and turn to the Lord with all your heart, you will be able to escape it, if your heart is clean and unblemished and you serve the Lord blamelessly for the rest of the days of your life. Cast your cares upon the Lord, and he will set them straight. (6)

---

13. *Segri:* so Lightfoot and Harmer, adopting J. R. Harris's emendation based on the Aramaic word *sagar*, "to shut" (cf. Dan. 6:22). The MSS read *Thegri.*

Trust in the Lord, you who are double-minded, because he can do all things; he both turns away from you his wrath, and sends out plagues upon you who are double-minded. Woe to those who hear these words and disobey them; it would have been better for them not to have been born."

3.

24. I asked her about the four colors that the beast had on its head. And she answered me and said, "Again you are curious about such things!" "Yes, madam," I said. "Tell me what these are." (2) "Listen," she said. "The black is this world in which you live. (3) The color of fire and blood signifies that this world must be destroyed by blood and fire. (4) The gold part is you who have escaped from this world. For just as gold is tested by fire and made useful, so also you who live in them[14] are being tested. Therefore those who endure and pass through the flames will be purified by them. For just as gold casts off its dross, so also you will cast away all grief and distress, and will be purified and useful for the building of the tower. (5) The white part is the age to come, in which God's elect will live because those chosen by God for eternal life will be spotless and pure. (6) Therefore do not cease speaking to the ears of the saints. You have also the foreshadowing of the great tribulation that is coming. But if you are willing, it will be nothing. Remember what has already been written." (7) With these words she left, and I did not see where she went, for there was a noise,[15] and I turned back in fear, thinking that the beast was coming.

REVELATION 5

25. After I had prayed in my house and sat down on my bed, there came a man glorious in appearance, dressed like a shepherd, with a white skin wrapped around him and with a bag on his shoulders and a staff in his hand. He greeted me, and I

---

14. *them*: so SL, Harmer (text); AE [Harmer (trans.)] read *it*.

15. *there . . . noise*: so AL¹E; SL² read *a cloud appeared*.

greeted him in return. (2) He immediately sat down beside me and said to me, "I was sent by the most holy angel to live with you the rest of the days of your life." (3) I thought that he had come to tempt me, and I said to him, "Well, who are you? For I know," I said, "to whom I have been entrusted." He said to me, "Don't you recognize me?" "No," I replied. "I am," he said, "the shepherd to whom you were entrusted." (4) While he was still speaking, his appearance was changed, and I recognized him as the one to whom I was entrusted; and immediately I was confused, and fear seized me, and I was completely overwhelmed with sorrow, because I had answered him so wickedly and foolishly. (5) But he answered and said to me, "Don't be confused, but strengthen yourself in my commandments, which I am about to give you. For I was sent," he said, "that I might show you again everything that you saw previously, the most important points, those useful to you. First of all, write down my commandments and parables; but write down the other matters as I show them to you. This is why," he said, "I am commanding you to write down first the commandments and parables, in order that you may read them at once and be able to keep them." (6) So I wrote down the commandments and parables, just as he commanded me. (7) If, then, when you hear them you keep them and walk in them and carry them out with a clean heart, you will receive from the Lord whatever he promised you. But if after hearing them you do not repent, but continue to add to your sins, you will receive from the Lord the opposite. All these things the shepherd, the angel of repentance, commanded me to write as follows.

MANDATE I

26. "First of all, believe that God is one, who created all things and set them in order, and made out of what did not exist everything that is, and who contains all things but is himself alone uncontained. (2) Believe in him, therefore, and fear him, and fearing him, be self-controlled. Keep these things, and you will cast off all evil from yourself and will put on every virtue of righteousness and will live to God, if you keep this commandment."

MANDATE 2

27. He said to me: "Be sincere and be innocent, and you will be like little children who do not know the evil that destroys the life of man. (2) First, speak evil of no one, and do not enjoy listening to someone who does. Otherwise you, the listener, will be responsible for the sin of the one speaking evil, if you believe the slander which you have heard, for by believing it you yourself will hold a grudge against your brother. In this way you will become responsible for the sin of the one who speaks the evil. (3) Slander is evil; it is a restless demon, never at peace but always at home with dissension. So avoid it, and you will always have success with everyone. (4) Clothe yourself with reverence, in which there is no evil cause for offense, but all things are smooth and joyful. Work at that which is good, and out of your labor, which God gives you, give generously to all who are in need, not debating to whom you will give and to whom you will not. Give to all, for God wishes that from his own gifts, gifts should be given to all. (5) So, those who receive are accountable to God regarding why and for what purpose they received; for those in distress who receive will not be judged, but those who receive under false pretenses will pay the penalty. (6) Therefore the one who gives is innocent, for as he received from the Lord a ministry to carry out, he carried it out sincerely, not worrying about to whom to give or not to give. This ministry, then, when sincerely carried out, becomes glorious in God's sight. Therefore the one who serves God sincerely in this manner will live. (7) So keep this commandment, as I have told you, in order that your repentance and that of your family may prove to be sincere and your heart clean[16] and unstained."

MANDATE 3

28. Again he spoke to me: "Love truth, and allow only the truth to come from your mouth, in order that the spirit, which

---

16. *your heart clean*: so many editors; the text is corrupt. Others read *pure and innocent*.

God caused to live in this flesh, may prove to be true in the sight of all men; and thus will the Lord who lives in you be glorified. For the Lord is truthful in every word, and there is nothing false in him. (2) Therefore, those who lie reject the Lord and defraud the Lord, for they do not return to him the deposit which they received. For they received from him a spirit uncontaminated by deceit. If they return this as a lying spirit, they have polluted the Lord's commandment and become thieves." (3) When I heard these things, I wept bitterly. But when he saw me weeping, he said, "Why are you crying?" "Because, sir," I said, "I don't know if I can be saved." "How come?" he asked. "Because, sir," I replied, "never in my life have I spoken a true word; instead, I have lived[17] deceitfully with everyone, and have represented my lie as truth to all men, and no one ever contradicted me but believed my word. So how," I said, "can I live after having done these things?" (4) "Your thinking," he said, "is right and true, for you must, as God's servant, live truthfully, and an evil conscience must not live with the spirit of truth, nor bring grief to the spirit which is holy and true." "Never before, sir," I said, "have I correctly heard such words." (5) "Well," he said, "now you are hearing. Obey them, so that the previous lies you told in your business affairs may themselves prove to be credible, now that your present remarks have proved to be true; for they too can become trustworthy. If you obey these and from now on speak only the truth, you will be able to attain life for yourself. And whoever hears this commandment and has nothing to do with falsehood, that most pernicious habit, will live to God."

MANDATE 4

1.

29. "I command you," he said, "to guard purity, and let no thought enter your heart about another man's wife or about fornication, or about some such similar evil thing, for in doing

---

17. *lived*: so LE; A reads *spoken*.

this you commit a major sin. But always keep your mind on your own wife and you will never go wrong. (2) For if this desire enters your heart, you will go wrong, and if other things as evil as this enter, you commit sin. For this desire in a servant of God is a major sin, and if anyone does this evil deed, he brings death on himself. (3) So beware; have nothing to do with this desire; for where holiness lives, there lawlessness ought not to enter the heart of a righteous man." (4) I said to him, "Sir, allow me to ask you a few more questions." "Speak," he replied. "Sir," I said, "if a man has a wife who believes in the Lord, and he finds her in some adulterous situation, does the man sin if he continues to live with her?" (5) "As long as he is unaware of it," he said, "he does not sin. But if the husband knows about her sin and the wife does not repent, but persists in her immorality, and the husband continues to live with her, he becomes responsible for her sin and an accomplice in her adultery." (6) "So what, sir," I said, "should the husband do, if the wife persists in this passion?" "Let him divorce her," he said, "and let the husband live by himself. But if after divorcing his wife he should marry another, then he too commits adultery." (7) "So then, sir," I said, "if, after the wife is divorced, she repents and wants to return to her own husband, she will be taken back, won't she?" (8) "Certainly," he said. "If the husband does not take her back, he sins, and brings a major sin upon himself. In fact, the one who has sinned and repented must be taken back. But not repeatedly: for there is only one repentance for God's servants. So, because of the possibility of her repentance, the husband ought not to marry. This procedure applies to wife and husband. (9) Not only," he said, "is it adultery if a man pollutes his flesh, but whoever does anything like what the heathen do commits adultery. So, if anyone persists in actions such as these and does not repent, have nothing to do with him and do not live with him. Otherwise you too are a partner in his sin. (10) This is why you are commanded to remain single, whether husband or wife, for in such cases repentance is possible. (11) I am not," he said, "giving an excuse for this affair to end this way, but so that the sinner should sin no more. As for his previous sin, there is One who is able to give healing; it is he who has authority over everything."

2.

30. I asked him again, saying, "Since the Lord considers me worthy for you to live with me always, allow me a few more words, since I don't understand anything and my heart has been hardened by my previous deeds. Make me understand, because I am very foolish and comprehend absolutely nothing." (2) He answered me and said, "I," he said, "am in charge of repentance, and I give understanding to all who repent. Or don't you, think," he said, "that this very act of repentance is itself understanding? To repent," he continued, "is great understanding. For the man who has sinned understands that he has done evil in the Lord's presence, and the act which he committed enters his heart, and he repents and no longer does evil, but does good lavishly, and he humbles his own soul and torments it, because he sinned. You see, therefore, that repentance is great understanding." (3) "This is why, sir," I said, "that I question you so precisely about everything; first, because I am a sinner; and second, because I do not know what deeds I must do in order to live, because my sins are many and varied." (4) "You will live," he said, "if you obey my commandments and walk in them. And whoever hears these commandments and obeys them will live to God."

3.

31. "Sir," I said, "I would like to ask a further question." "Speak," he said. "Sir," I said, "I have heard from certain teachers that there is no other repentance beyond that which occurred when we descended into the water and received forgiveness of our previous sins." (2) He said to me, "You have heard correctly, for so it is. For the one who has received forgiveness of sins ought never to sin again, but to live in purity. (3) But since you inquire so precisely about everything, I will show you this also, so as to give no excuse for those who will believe at some time in the future, or those who have just now believed in the Lord. For those who have just now believed, or those who are going to believe do not have repentance for sins, but they do have forgiveness of their previous sins. (4) So, for those who were called before these days the Lord has established repentance. For since the Lord knows every heart and knows everything in advance, he knew the weakness of human beings and the cunning of the devil, and that he would do something evil to God's servants and treat them wickedly. (5) But the Lord, however, who is exceedingly merciful, had mercy on his creation and established this opportunity for repentance, and authority over this repentance was given to me. (6) But I am warning you," he said, "if, after this great and holy call, anyone is tempted by the devil and sins, he has one opportunity for repentance. But if he sins repeatedly and repents, it is of no use for such a person, for he will scarcely live." (7) I said to him, "I was restored to life again when I heard these things from you so precisely. For I now know that if I no longer add to my sins, I will be saved." "You will be saved," he said, "and so will everyone else who does these things."

4.

32. Again I asked him, saying, "Sir, since you have borne with me once, explain also this to me." "Speak," he said. "Sir, if a wife," I asked, "or for that matter a husband, dies, and the survivor marries, does the one who marries sin?" (2) "That one does not sin," he said, "but if the survivor remains single, one gains for oneself greater honor and great glory with the Lord; but even if one does remarry, one does not sin. (3) Preserve, therefore, purity and holiness, and you will live to God. All these things that I am telling you and will tell in the future, keep from this time forward, from the day you were entrusted to me, and I will live in your house. (4) But there will be forgiveness for your previous sins if you keep my commandments; in fact, there will be forgiveness for everyone, if they keep my commandments and walk in this purity."

MANDATE 5

1.

33. "Be patient and understanding," he said, "and you will overcome all evil deeds and will accomplish all righteousness.

(2) For if you are patient, the Holy Spirit who lives in you will be pure, uncontaminated by some other evil spirit; living in a spacious room, it will rejoice and be glad with the vessel in which it lives, and will serve God with much cheerfulness, for it is at peace with itself. (3) But if an angry temper approaches, immediately the Holy Spirit, which is very sensitive, is distressed because it does not have a clean place, and it seeks to leave the place. For it is choked by the evil spirit and does not have the room to serve the Lord the way it wants to, because it is polluted by the angry temper. For the Lord lives in patience, but the devil lives in an angry temper. (4) So if both spirits live together, it is unfortunate and evil for that person in whom they live. (5) For if you take a little wormwood and pour it in a jar of honey, isn't all the honey spoiled? Such a large amount of honey spoiled by such a small amount of wormwood; it spoils the sweetness, and the owner no longer cares for it, because it has become bitter and lost its usefulness. But if the wormwood is not put into the honey, the honey turns out to be sweet and is useful to its owner. (6) You see, then, that patience is very sweet, even more so than honey, and is useful to the Lord, and he lives in it. But an angry temper is bitter and useless. So, if an angry temper is mixed with patience, the patience is polluted, and the person's intercession is no longer useful to God." (7) "I would like to know, sir," I said, "how an angry temper works, in order that I can protect myself from it." "Indeed," he said, "if you do not protect yourself and your family from it, you have lost all hope. But protect yourself from it, for I am with you. And all who repent with all their heart will protect themselves from it, for I will be with them and will keep them safe, for they were all justified by the most holy angel."

2.

34. "Now hear," he said, "about how an angry temper works, how evil it is, and how it subverts God's servants by its working, and how it leads them astray from righteousness. But it does not lead astray those who are filled with faith, nor can it work on them, because the Lord's[18] power is with them. But it can lead

---

18. *the Lord's*: so L²; L¹ reads *God's*; A reads *my*.

astray those who are empty-headed and double-minded. (2) For whenever it sees such people prospering, it insinuates itself into the person's heart, and for no reason at all the man or the woman is embittered over worldly concerns, either about food or something trivial, or some friend, or about giving or receiving, or some such foolish matters. For these things are all foolish and empty and senseless and inexpedient for God's servants. (3) But patience is great and strong, and possesses a mighty and vigorous power, and prospers in a spacious area; it is joyful, exultant, free from care, glorifying the Lord at all times, having no bitterness in itself, always remaining gentle and quiet. This patience, therefore, lives with those whose faith is perfect. (4) But an angry temper is first of all foolish, fickle, and senseless. Then from foolishness comes bitterness, and from bitterness wrath, and from wrath anger, and from anger vengefulness; then vengefulness, being composed of all these evil elements, becomes a great and incurable sin. (5) For when all these spirits live in one vessel, where the Holy Spirit also lives, the vessel cannot contain them, but overflows. (6) So the sensitive Spirit, which is not used to living with an evil spirit nor with harshness, departs from a person such as this, and seeks to live with gentleness and quiet. (7) Then, when it has left that man in whom it lives, that man is emptied of the spirit of righteousness, and from then on, since he is filled with the evil spirits, he is unstable in everything he does as he is dragged about here and there by the evil spirits, totally blind with respect to good intentions. So it goes, therefore, with all those who are ill-tempered. (8) Have nothing to do, therefore, with an angry temper. Instead put on patience and resist an angry temper and bitterness, and you will be found in the company of the holiness that is loved by the Lord. So take care that you never neglect this commandment, for if you master it, you will also be able to keep the rest of the commandments that I am about to give you. Be strong in them, and empowered; indeed, let all who want to walk in them be empowered."

MANDATE 6

I.

35. "I commanded you," he said, "in the first commandment to protect faith and fear and self-control." "Yes, sir," I
said. "But now," he said, "I want to explain to you their powers, so that you may understand what the power and effect of
each of them is. For their effects are twofold; they relate to
righteousness and to unrighteousness. (2) Be sure, therefore, to
trust righteousness, but do not trust unrighteousness. For the
way of righteousness is straight, but that of unrighteousness is
crooked. But follow the straight and level way, and leave the
crooked one alone. (3) For the crooked way has no paths but
only uneven ground and many obstacles, and is rough and
thorny. Consequently, it is harmful to those who follow it. (4)
But those who follow the straight path walk smoothly and
without stumbling, for it is neither rough nor thorny. You see,
then, that it is more advantageous to follow this way." (5) "I am
pleased, sir," I said, "to follow this way." "So follow it," he
said, "and whoever turns to the Lord with all his heart will
follow it."

2.

36. "Now hear," he said, "about faith. There are two angels
with man, one of righteousness and one of wickedness." (2) "So
how, sir," I said, "will I recognize their workings, given that both
angels live with me?" (3) "Listen," he said, "and understand
them. The angel of righteousness is sensitive and modest and
gentle and tranquil. When this one enters your heart, immediately he talks with you about righteousness, about purity, about
holiness, about contentment, about every righteous deed, and
about every glorious virtue. Whenever all these things enter
your heart, you know that the angel of righteousness is with
you. These, then, are the works of the angel of righteousness. So
trust him and his works. (4) Now observe the works of the angel
of wickedness. First of all, he is ill-tempered and bitter and senseless, and his works are evil, tearing down God's servants. So
whenever this one enters your heart, recognize him by his

works." (5) "But I do not know, sir," I said, "how to recognize him." "Listen," he said. "When some angry tempermental outburst or bitterness comes over you, recognize that he is in you. Then comes the desire for much business, and extravagant kinds of foods and drink, and much drunkenness, and various kinds of unnecessary luxuries, and the desire for women, and greed and arrogance and pretentiousness, and whatever else resembles or is similar to these things. So whenever these things enter your heart, you know that the angel of wickedness is with you. (6) Recognizing, therefore, his works, shun him and do not trust him at all, because his works are evil and harmful to God's servants. You now have, then, the working of both angels; understand them and trust the angel of righteousness. (7) But shun the angel of wickedness, because his teaching is evil in every respect. For even if one is a man of faith and the thought of that angel enters one's heart, it is inevitable that that man or woman will commit some sin. (8) On the other hand, if one is an extremely sinful man or woman, and the works of the angel of righteousness enter his heart, of necessity he must do something good. (9) You see, then," he said, "that it is good to follow the angel of righteousness, but to shun the angel of wickedness. (10) This commandment explains the things about faith, in order that you may trust the works of the angel of righteousness, and that doing them, you may live to God. But believe that the works of the angel of wickedness are dangerous, so that by not doing them you will live to God."

MANDATE 7

37. "Fear the Lord," he said, "and keep his commandments. By keeping his commandments, you will be powerful in every deed, and your activity will be beyond criticism. For when you fear the Lord you will do everything well. This is the fear you must have to be saved. (2) But do not fear the devil, for if you fear the Lord you will rule over the devil, because he has no power. And where there is no power, there is no fear. But where there is glorious power, there also is fear. For everyone who has power has fear, whereas the one who has no power is despised by everyone. (3) But do fear the works of the devil, because they are evil.

When you fear the Lord you will fear the devil's works and will not do them, but will have nothing to do with them. (4) Fear, therefore, is of two kinds. If you want to do something evil, fear the Lord and you will not do it. But on the other hand, if you want to do good, fear the Lord and you will do it. So, the fear of the Lord is powerful and great and glorious. Fear the Lord, therefore, and you will live to him; and whoever fears the Lord and keeps his commandments will live to God." (5) "Why, sir," I said, "did you say about those keeping his commandments, 'they will live to God'?" "Because," he replied, "every creature fears the Lord, but not all keep his commandments. Life with God, therefore, belongs to those who fear him and keep his commandments; but those who do not keep his commandments do not have life in him, either."

MANDATE 8

38. "I mentioned to you," he said, "that the creatures of God are twofold, because self-control is also twofold. For in some things it is necessary to exercise self-control, but in some things it is not necessary." (2) "Inform me, sir," I said, "about in what things it is necessary to practice self-control, and in what things it is not necessary." "Listen," he said. "Be self-controlled regarding evil, and do not do it; but do not be self-controlled regarding good, but do it. For if you exercise self-control regarding what is good, with the result that you not do it, you commit a major sin. But if you exercise self-control regarding evil, so as not to do it, you achieve great righteousness. Exercise self-control, therefore, over all evil and do that which is good." (3) "Sir," I responded, "what are the kinds of evils over which it is necessary for us to exercise self-control?" "Listen," he said. "Adultery and fornication, lawless drunkenness, wicked luxury, many kinds of food and the extravagance of wealth and boasting and snobbery and arrogance, and lying and slander and hypocrisy, malice and all blasphemy. (4) These actions are the most wicked of all in the life of men. So, the servant of God must exercise self-control over these works, for the one who does not exercise self-control over these is not able to live to God. Listen also, therefore, to the things that follow them." (5) "Why sir," I said, "are there still other evil practices?" "Indeed, there are many," he said, "over which the servant of God must exercise self-control: theft, lying, robbery, perjury, greed, lust, deceit, vanity, pretentiousness, and whatever else is like these. (6) Don't you think that these things are evil? Indeed, to the servants of God, they are very evil," he said. "In[19] all these things the one who serves God must exercise self-control. Exercise self-control, therefore, over all these things, that you may live to God and be enrolled with those who do exercise self-control over them. These, then, are the things with respect to which you must exercise self-control."

(7) "But now listen," he said, "to those things with respect to which you must not exercise self-control, but do them. Do not exercise self-control over the good, but do it." (8) "Explain to me," I said, "the power of the good things also, so that I may walk in them and serve them, in order that by doing them I may be able to be saved." "Hear," he said, "about the works of the good things, which you must do and toward which you must not exercise self-control. (9) First of all, there is faith, fear of the Lord, love, harmony, words of righteousness, truth, patience; nothing is better than these in the life of men. If anyone keeps these things and does not exercise self-control over them, he will be blessed in his life. (10) Next hear the things that follow these: serving widows, looking after orphans and those in need, delivering God's servants from distress, being hospitable (for the practice of hospitality results in doing good, I presume), opposing no one, being quiet, becoming more needy[20] than all other men, respecting the elderly, practicing righteousness, preserving brotherhood, enduring insults, being patient, bearing no grudges, encouraging those who are sick at heart, not throwing out those who have stumbled but returning and encouraging them, admonishing sinners, not oppressing debtors and those in need, and whatever else is like these. (11) Don't you think," he said, "that these things are good?" "Why sir," I replied, "what can be better than these?" "Then walk in them," he said, "and do not exercise self-control over them,

---

19. *evil? Indeed . . . evil." he said. "In . . .* : so L²; A reads *evil?" "Indeed . . . evil,"* I said. *"In . . .* ; L¹E read *evil? Indeed . . . evil. In. . . .*

20. *needy*: or perhaps *humble*.

and you will live to God. (12) So keep this commandment; if you do good and do not exercise self-control in this respect, you will live to God; indeed, all who do so will live to God. And again, if you do not do evil and do exercise self-control over it, you will live to God; indeed, all who keep these commandments and walk in them will live to God."

MANDATE 9

39. He said to me, "Rid yourself of double-mindedness, and do not be at all double-minded about asking God for something, saying to yourself, for example, 'How can I ask for something from God and receive it, when I have sinned so often against him?' (2) Do not reason in this way, but turn to the Lord with all your heart and ask of him unhesitatingly, and you will know his extraordinary compassion, because he will never abandon you, but will fulfill your soul's request. (3) For God is not like men, who bear grudges; no, he is without malice and has compassion on his creation. (4) Do, therefore, cleanse your heart of all the vanities of this life, and of all the things mentioned to you above, and ask of the Lord, and you will receive everything, and will not fail to receive all of your requests, if you ask unhesitatingly. (5) But if you hesitate in your heart, you will certainly not receive any of your requests. For those who hesitate in their relation to God are the double-minded, and they never obtain any of their requests. (6) But those who are perfect in faith make all their requests trusting in the Lord, and they receive them, because they ask unhesitatingly, without any double-mindedness. For every double-minded man, unless he repents, will scarcely be saved. (7) So cleanse your heart of double-mindedness and put on faith, because it is strong, and trust God that you will receive all the requests you make. And whenever you ask for something from the Lord and you receive your request rather slowly, do not become double-minded just because you did not receive your soul's request quickly, for assuredly it is because of some temptation or some transgression, of which you are ignorant, that you are receiving your request rather slowly. (8) Do not, therefore, stop making your soul's request, and you will receive it. But if you become weary and double-minded as you ask, blame yourself and not the One who gives to you. (9) Beware of this double-mindedness, for it is evil and senseless, and has uprooted many from the faith, even those who are very faithful and strong. For this double-mindedness is indeed a daughter of the devil, and does much evil to God's servants. (10) So despise double-mindedness and gain mastery over it in everything by clothing yourself with faith that is strong and powerful. For faith promises all things, perfects all things; but double-mindedness, not having any confidence in itself, fails in all the works it tries to do. (11) So you see," he said, "that faith is from above, from the Lord, and has great power, but double-mindedness is an earthly spirit from the devil that has no power. (12) So serve faith, which has power, and have nothing to do with double-mindedness, which has no power, and you will live to God; indeed, all who are so minded will live to God."

MANDATE 10

1.

40. "Rid yourself," he said to me, "of grief, for it is the sister of double-mindedness and an angry temper." (2) "Sir," I asked, "how is it the sister of these? For an angry temper seems to me to be one thing, double-mindedness another, and grief another." "You are a foolish man," he said. "Don't you understand that grief is the most evil of all the spirits and very bad for God's servants, and it destroys man more than all the spirits and crushes the Holy Spirit—and again it saves." (3) "I am foolish, sir," I said, "and I do not understand these parables. For how it can both crush and save again, I do not comprehend." (4) "Listen," he said. "Those who have never searched for the truth or inquired about the Deity, but have simply believed, and have been mixed up in business affairs and wealth and pagan friendships and many other concerns of this world—well, those who are absorbed in these things do not comprehend the parables of the Deity, because they are darkened by these matters and are ruined and become barren. (5) Just as good vineyards are made barren by thorns and weeds of various kinds when they are neglected, so men who have believed and then fall into these many activities that have been mentioned above lose their understanding and do not comprehend anything at all concerning righteousness. For whenever they hear about the Deity and truth, their mind is preoccupied with their own affairs, and they understand nothing at all. (6) But those who fear God and search for the Deity and truth and direct their heart to the Lord grasp more quickly and understand everything that is said to them, because they have the fear of the Lord in themselves; for where the Lord lives, there also is much understanding. So hold fast to the Lord and you will understand and grasp everything."

2.

41. "Foolish man," he said, "hear now how grief crushes the Holy Spirit and saves again. (2) Whenever a double-minded person undertakes some action and fails at it because of his double-mindedness, this grief enters the man and grieves the Holy Spirit and crushes it. (3) Then again, when an angry temper holds fast to a man over some matter and he becomes very embittered, again grief enters the heart of the angry-tempered man, and he is grieved by what he has done, and he repents because he has done evil. (4) This grief, therefore, seems to bring salvation, because he repented after having done evil. So, both actions grieve the Spirit: the double-mindedness, because it did not succeed in its attempt, and the angry temper grieves the Spirit, because it did what was evil. So both are a cause for grief for the Holy Spirit, double-mindedness and an angry temper. (5) Rid yourself, therefore, of grief and do not oppress the Holy Spirit that lives in you, lest it intercede with God against you[21] and leave you. (6) For the Spirit of God that was given to this flesh endures neither grief nor distress."

3.

42. "Clothe yourself, therefore, with cheerfulness, which always finds favor with God and is acceptable to him, and rejoice

---

21. *against you*: so A [Harmer]; LE omit.

in it. For every cheerful man does good things and thinks good things, and despises grief. (2) But the sorrowful man always does evil; first, he does evil because he grieves the Holy Spirit, which was cheerful when given to man, and second, by grieving the Holy Spirit he acts lawlessly in that he neither prays nor confesses to God. For the intercession of a grieving man never has the power to ascend to the altar of God." (3) "Why," I asked, "does the intercession of one who is grieving not ascend to the altar?" "Because," he replied, "grief is entrenched in his heart. When the grief is mixed with the intercession, it does not permit the intercession to ascend in purity to the altar. For just as vinegar mixed together with wine in the same bottle does not have a pleasant taste, so also grief mixed with the Holy Spirit does not have the same intercession. (4) So cleanse yourself of this evil grief, and you will live to God; indeed, all will live to God who rid themselves of grief and clothe themselves with all cheerfulness."

MANDATE II

43. He showed me men seated on a bench, and another man seated on a chair. And he said to me, "Do you see those men seated on the bench?" "I see them, sir," I replied. "These," he said, "are faithful, but the one seated on the chair is a false prophet who destroys the mind of God's servants; that is, he destroys the mind of the double-minded, not of believers. (2) These double-minded ones come to him as to a fortune teller, and ask him what will happen to them. And that false prophet, not having the power of a divine spirit in himself, answers them in accordance with their questions and their wicked desires, and fills their souls just as they themselves wish. (3) For since he himself is empty, he gives empty answers to empty inquirers, for no matter what is asked, he answers according to the emptiness of the man asking. But he does speak some true words, for the devil fills him with his own spirit, to see if he will be able to break down any of the righteous. (4) So, those who are strong in the faith of the Lord, having clothed themselves with the truth, do not associate with such spirits, but have nothing to do with them. But those who are double-minded and frequently change their minds practice fortune telling like the pagans and bring greater sin upon themselves by their idolatries. For the one who consults a false prophet on any matter is an idolator and lacks the truth and is senseless. (5) For no spirit given by God needs to be consulted; instead, having the power of deity, it speaks everything on its own initiative, because it is from above, from the power of the divine Spirit. (6) But the spirit that is consulted and which answers according to the desires of the people consulting it is earthly and fickle, and has no power, and does not speak at all unless it is asked." (7) "So how, sir," I asked, "will a man know which of them is a prophet, and which is a false prophet?" "Hear," he said, "about both the prophets, and on the basis of what I am going to tell you, you can test the prophet and false prophet. Determine the man who has the divine Spirit by his life. (8) In the first place the one who has the divine[22] Spirit from above is gentle and quiet and humble, and stays away from all evil and futile desires of this age, and considers himself to be poorer than others, and gives no answer to anyone when consulted. Nor does he speak on his own (nor does the Holy Spirit speak when a man wants to speak), but he speaks when God wants him to speak. (9) So, then, when the man who has the divine Spirit comes into an assembly of righteous men who have faith in a divine Spirit, and intercession is made to God by the assembly of those men, then the angel of the prophetic spirit which is assigned to him fills the man, and being filled with the Holy Spirit the man speaks to the multitude, just as the Lord wills. (10) In this way, then, the Spirit of the Deity will be obvious. Such, therefore, is the power of discernment with respect to the divine Spirit of the Lord."

(11) "Now hear," he said, "about the earthly and worthless spirit, which has no power but is foolish. (12) In the first place, that man who thinks he has a spirit exalts himself and wants to have a seat of honor, and immediately is arrogant and shameless and talkative and well acquainted with many luxuries and with many other pleasures, and receives money for his prophesying, and if he does not receive money, he does not prophesy.

---

22. *divine*: so L²E [Harmer]; AL¹ omit.

Now, can a divine spirit receive money and still prophesy? It is impossible for a prophet of God to do this, but the spirit of such prophets who do so is earthly. (13) Next, he never comes near an assembly of righteous men; instead he avoids them, and associates with the double-minded and the empty-headed, and prophesies to them in a corner and deceives them; everything he says is in accordance with their own desires and characterized by his own empty manner, for he is answering those who are empty. For the empty vessel placed together with other empty vessels is not broken, but they match one another. (14) But when he comes to an assembly full of righteous men who have a divine Spirit, and intercession is made by them, that man is emptied and the earthly spirit flees from him in fear, and that man is rendered speechless and is completely shattered, unable to say a thing. (15) For if you store wine or oil in a storeroom and place an empty jar in among them and then later you wish to clear out the storeroom, you will find that empty jar you placed there still empty. So it is with empty prophets; whenever they encounter the spirits of the righteous, they are found to be just as they were when they arrived. (16) You now have descriptions of the life of both kinds of prophets. Therefore test by his life and his actions the man who claims that he is spirit-inspired. (17) Put your trust in the Spirit that comes from God and has power, but do not trust in any way the earthly and empty spirit, because it has no power, for it comes from the devil. (18) Listen to the parable I am about to tell you. Take a stone and throw it toward the sky; see if you can reach it. Or, for another example, take a water pump and squirt it toward the sky; see if you can penetrate it." (19) "How," I asked, "can these things be, sir? For both these things you just said are impossible." "Well then," he said, "just as these things are impossible, so also are the earthly spirits powerless and weak. (20) Now take the power that comes from above. A hailstone is a very small pellet, but when it falls on a man's head, what pain it causes! Or, for another example, take a drop that falls on the ground from the roofing tiles, and wears a hole in the rock. (21) You see, then, that even the smallest things from above falling on the earth have great power; so also the divine Spirit that comes from above is powerful. So put your trust in this Spirit, but have nothing to do with the other one."

MANDATE 12

1.

44. He said to me, "Rid yourself of all evil desire, and clothe yourself with the desire that is good and holy, for when you have clothed yourself with this desire, you will hate the evil desire and will control it as you wish. (2) For the evil desire is savage and only tamed with difficulty, for it is terrible and utterly destroys men by its savageness; in particular, if a servant of God gets entangled in it and lacks understanding, he will be terribly destroyed by it. It destroys such as do not have the garment of the good desire but are mixed up with this world. These it hands over to death." (3) "What, sir," I said, "are the works of this evil desire that hand man over to death? Tell me, so that I may avoid them." "Hear," he said, "the kind of works by which the evil desire puts to death God's servants."

2.

45. "Above all is the desire for someone else's wife or husband, and for the extravagance of wealth, and for many needless things to eat and drink, and many other foolish luxuries. For every luxury is foolish and futile for God's servants. (2) These desires, then, are evil and bring death to God's servants. For this evil desire is a daughter of the devil. You must keep away, therefore, from evil desires, in order that by keeping away from them you may live to God. (3) But those who are mastered by them and do not resist them will utterly perish, for these desires are deadly. (4) But put on the desire of righteousness and, having armed yourself with the fear of the Lord, resist them. For the fear of the Lord lives in the good desire. If the evil desire sees you armed with the fear of God and resisting it, it will flee far from you and will no longer be seen by you, because it fears your weapons. (5) So you, when you have triumphed[23] over it, come to the desire of righteousness and deliver to it the victory you have won, and serve it just as it

---

23. *triumphed*: so A; (LE) imply *gained the victory and triumphed*.

desires. If you serve the good desire and submit to it, you will be able to master the evil desire and control it as you wish."

3.

46. "I would like to know, sir," I said, "in what ways I must serve the good desire." "Listen," he said. "Practice righteousness and virtue, truth and fear of the Lord, faith and gentleness, and whatever good things are like these. By practicing these you will be an acceptable servant of God and will live to him; indeed, all who serve the good desire will live to God."

(2) So he finished the twelve commandments, and said to me: "You have the commandments; walk in them and encourage your listeners, in order that their repentance may be pure the rest of the days of their lives. (3) Carefully execute this ministry which I am giving you and you will accomplish much. For you will find favor with those who are going to repent, and they will obey your words, for I will be with you and will compel them to obey you." (4) I said to him, "Sir, these commandments are great and good and glorious, and are able to gladden the heart of the man who is able to keep them. But I do not know if these commandments can be kept by man, for they are very hard." (5) He answered and said to me, "If you propose to yourself that they can be kept, you will keep them easily and they will not be hard. But if the idea that they cannot be kept by man has already entered your heart, you will not keep them. (6) But now I say to you: if you do not keep them, but neglect them, you will not have salvation, nor will your children nor your family, since you have already decided for yourself that these commandments cannot be kept by man."

4.

47. He said these things to me very angrily, which confused me and I feared him greatly, for his appearance was so changed that a man could not endure his anger. (2) And when he saw that I was extremely agitated and confused, he began to speak to me more gently and cheerfully,[24] and said, "Foolish man,

24. *and cheerfully*: so L¹(E) [Harmer]; A omits.

lacking understanding and double-minded, don't you understand how great and mighty and marvelous God's glory is, because he created the world for the sake of man, and subjected all his creation to man, and gave him all authority to rule over everything under heaven? (3) If then," he said, "man is lord of all God's creatures and rules over everything, can't he also master these commandments? The man who has the Lord in his heart," he said, "can master everything, including[25] all these commandments. (4) But to those who have the Lord on their lips but whose heart is hardened and who are far from the Lord[26] these commandments are hard and difficult. (5) You, therefore, who are empty and fickle in the faith, put the Lord in your heart, and you will realize that nothing is easier or sweeter or more gentle than these commandments. (6) You who walk in the commandments of the devil, which are difficult and bitter and savage and licentious, be converted and do not fear the devil, for he has no power against you. (7) For I, the angel of repentance, who has mastery over him, will be with you. The devil can only cause fear, but his fear has no force. Do not fear him, therefore, and he will flee from you."

5.

48. I said to him, "Sir, listen to a few words from me." "Say what you wish," he replied. "Sir," I said, "man is eager to keep God's commandments, and there is no one who does not ask the Lord that he may be strengthened in his commandments and obey them, but the devil is hard and oppresses them." (2) "He cannot," he said, "oppress God's servants who hope in him with all their heart. The devil can wrestle with them, but he cannot throw and pin them. So, if you resist him, he will be defeated and flee from you in disgrace. But those," he said, "who are empty fear the devil, as if he had power. (3) When a man fills a large number of jars with good wine, and among these jars a few are partially empty, he does not bother to examine the full jars when he comes to the jars, for he knows that they are full. But he does examine the partially empty ones

25. *everything, including*: so AL²E [Harmer]; L¹ omits.
26. *the Lord*: so L¹; A reads *God*.

because he fears that they may have turned sour. For partially empty jars quickly turn sour, and the taste of the wine is ruined. (4) So also the devil comes to all God's servants to empty them. All those who are full in the faith resist him mightily, and he leaves them alone, because he finds no place where he can gain entrance. So then he comes to those who are partially empty, and finding a place he enters them, and then he does what he wants with them, and they become enslaved to him."

6.

49. "But I, the angel of repentance, say to you: do not fear the devil. For I was sent," he said, "to be with you who repent with all your heart, and to strengthen you in the faith. (2) So believe in God, you who because of your sins have despaired of your life, and are adding to your sins, and are making your life hard, because if you turn to the Lord with all your heart, and practice righteousness the rest of the days of your life, and serve him rightly according to his will, he will heal your previous sins, and you will have power to conquer the devil's works. But do not fear the devil's threats at all, for he is as powerless as a dead man's sinews. (3) Listen to me, therefore, and fear him who is able to do everything, to save and to destroy, and keep these commandments, and you will live to God." (4) I said to him, "Sir, now I am strengthened in all the Lord's commandments, because you are with me. I know that you will crush all the power of the devil, and we will rule over him and prevail over all his works. And I hope, sir, that I am now able to keep these commandments which you have commanded, as the Lord enables me." (5) "You will keep them," he said, "if your heart is pure toward the Lord; indeed, all who cleanse their hearts of the vain desires of this world will keep them, and will live to God."

THE PARABLES

The Parables[27] *Which He Spoke to Me*
[*Parable 1*]

50. He said to me: "You know," he said,[28] "that you who are servants of God are living in a foreign country, for your city is far from this city. If, therefore, you know," he said,[29] "your city in which you are destined to live, why do you prepare fields and expensive possessions and buildings and useless rooms here? (2) The one who prepares these things for this city, therefore, does not plan to return to his own city. (3) Foolish and double-minded and miserable man, don't you realize that all these things are foreign to you, and under someone else's authority? For the lord of this city will say, 'I don't want you to live in my city; instead, leave this city, because you do not conform to my laws.' (4) So, you who have fields and dwellings and many other possessions, what will you do with your field and your house and all the other things you have prepared for yourself when you are expelled by him? For the lord of this country has every right to say to you, 'Either conform to my laws, or get out of my country.' (5) So what are you going to do, since you are subject to the law of your own city? For the sake of your fields and the rest of your possessions, will you totally renounce your own law and live according to the law of this city? Take care; it may not be in your best interest to renounce your law, for if you should want to return to your city, you will certainly not be accepted, because you have renounced the law of your city, and will be shut out of it. (6) So take care; as one living in a foreign land, do not prepare for yourself one thing more than is necessary to be self-sufficient, and be prepared so that whenever the master of this city wants to expel you because of your opposition to his law, you can leave his city and come to your own city, and joyfully conform to your law, free from all insult. (7) Take care, therefore, that you serve God and have him in your

27. *Parables*: in Latin, *Similitudines*; consequently this part of the *Shepherd* is often referred to as the "Similitudes" (abbrev. *Sim.*).
28. *he said*: so A; LE (followed by Harmer) omit.
29. *he said*: so A; LE (followed by Harmer) omit.

heart; work God's works, remembering his commandments and the promises that he made, and trust him to keep them, if his commandments are kept. (8) So, instead of fields buy souls that are in distress, as anyone is able, and visit widows and orphans, and do not neglect them; and spend your wealth and all your possessions, which you received from God, on fields and houses of this kind. (9) For this is why the Master made you rich, so that you might perform these ministries for him. It is much better to purchase fields and possessions and houses of this kind, which you will find in your own city when you go home to it. (10) This lavish expenditure is beautiful and joyous; it does not bring grief or fear, but joy. So do not practice the extravagance of the heathen, for it is unprofitable to you, the servants of God. (11) But do practice your own extravagance, in which you can rejoice; and do not imitate or touch what belongs to another, nor covet it, for it is evil to covet someone else's things. But do your own task, and you will be saved."

Another Parable
[Parable 2]

51. As I was walking in the country I noticed an elm tree and a vine,[30] and was comparing them and their fruits, when the shepherd appeared to me and said, "What are you thinking about?" "I am thinking, sir," I said, "about the elm and the vine; specifically, that they are very well suited to one another." (2) "These two trees," he said, "are intended as a model for God's servants." "Sir," I said, "I would like to know the model represented by these trees of which you speak." "Do you see," he asked, "the elm and the vine?" "I see them, sir," I replied. (3) "This vine," he said, "bears fruit, but the elm is a fruitless tree. But unless it climbs the elm, this vine cannot bear much fruit when it is spread out on the ground, and what fruit it does bear is rotten, because it is not suspended from the elm. So, when the vine is attached to the elm it bears fruit both from itself and from the elm. (4) You see, therefore, that the elm also bears much fruit, not less than the vine, but even

---

30. *vine*: i.e., a grapevine; the use of elm trees in the cultivation of grapevines is well documented in central Italy.

more." "How, sir," I asked, "does it bear more?" "Because," he said, "the vine, when hanging on the elm, bears its fruit in abundance and in good condition; but when it is spread out on the ground, it bears little fruit, and that which it does is rotten. So this parable is applicable to God's servants, to poor and rich alike." (5) "How so, sir?" I asked. "Make this known to me." "Listen," he said. "The rich man has much wealth, but is poor in the things of the Lord, being distracted by his wealth, and he has very little confession and prayer with the Lord, and what he does have is small and weak, and has no power above.[31] So whenever a rich man goes up to a poor man and supplies him his needs, he believes that what he does for the poor man will be able to find a reward from God, because the poor man is rich in intercession and confession, and his intercession has great power with God. The rich man, therefore, unhesitatingly provides the poor man with everything. (6) And the poor man, being provided for by the rich, prays for him, thanking God for the one who shares with him. And the rich man in turn is all the more zealous on the poor man's behalf, in order that he may lack nothing in his life, for he knows that the intercession of the poor man is acceptable and rich before God. (7) They both, then, complete their work: the poor man works with prayer, in which he is rich, which he received from the Lord; this he returns to the Lord who supplies him with it. And the rich man likewise unhesitatingly shares with the poor man the wealth which he received from the Lord. And this work is great and acceptable to God, because the rich man understands about his wealth and works for the poor man by using the gifts of the Lord and correctly fulfills his ministry. (8) So, as far as men are concerned, the elm does not seem to bear fruit, and they neither know nor realize that if a drought comes the elm, which has water, nourishes the vine, and the vine, having a constant supply of water, bears double the fruit, both for itself and for the elm. So also the poor, by appealing to the Lord on behalf of the rich, complement their wealth, and again, the rich, by pro-

---

31. *power above*: so Tischendorf's conjecture, which Lightfoot and Harmer adopt; Lake suggests *other power*. L² reads *power before the Lord*; A has *human power*; LE read simply *power*.

viding for the needs of the poor, complement their souls.[32] (9)
So, then, both become partners in the righteous work. Therefore, the one who does these things will not be abandoned by
God, but will be enrolled in the books of the living. (10) Blessed
are the rich who also understand that they have been made rich
by the Lord, for the one who comprehends this will be able to
do some good work."

Another Parable
[Parable 3]

52. He showed me many trees which had no leaves, and
they appeared to me to be withered, for they were all alike. And
he said to me, "Do you see these trees?" "I see them, sir," I
said. "They are all alike, and withered." Answering me he said,
"These trees that you see are the people who live in this
world." (2) "So why, sir," I asked, "do they look like they are
withered and all alike?" "Because," he said, "neither the righteous nor sinners are distinguishable in this world, but they are
alike. For this world is winter to the righteous, and they cannot
be distinguished, because they live with the sinners. (3) For just
as in winter the trees, having shed their leaves, are all alike,
and it is not apparent which are withered and which are living,
so also in this world neither the righteous nor the sinners can
be distinguished, but all are alike."

Another Parable
[Parable 4]

53. Again he showed me many trees, some of which were
budding and some of which were withered, and he said to me,
"Do you see," he said, "these trees?" "I see them, sir," I said.
"Some are budding, but others are withered." (2) "These trees,"
he said, "that are budding are the righteous, who will live in
the age to come; for the age to come is summer to the righteous, but winter to the sinners. So when the mercy of the Lord
shines forth, then those who serve God will be revealed; in-

---

32. *souls*: so the MSS; Lake suggests *prayers*.

deed, all people will be revealed.[33] (3) For just as in summer the fruit of each one of the trees appears, and so it is known what kind they are, so also the fruit of the righteous will be revealed, and all will be known because they are flourishing in that world. (4) But the heathen and the sinners, the withered trees that you saw, such people will be found to be withered and fruitless in that world, and will be burned as firewood, and will be obvious because their conduct in their life was evil. For the sinners will be burned because they sinned and did not repent, and the heathen will be burned because they did not know the One who created them. (5) You, therefore, bear fruit, in order that in summer your fruit may be known. But avoid excessive involvement in business, and you will commit no sin. For those who are involved in business a great deal also sin a great deal, since they are distracted by their business and do not serve their own Lord in anything. (6) How, then," he said, "can such a person ask for something from the Lord and receive it, seeing that he does not serve the Lord? For those who serve him receive their requests, but those who do not serve him receive nothing. (7) But if someone is engaged in just one business, he is able to serve the Lord, for his mind will not be corrupted and turned away from the Lord, but he will serve him with a pure mind. (8) So, if you do these things, you will be able to bear fruit for the age to come; indeed, whoever does these things will bear fruit."

Another Parable
[Parable 5]
1.

54. As I was fasting while sitting on a certain mountain and giving thanks to the Lord for all that he had done for me, I saw the shepherd sitting next to me, and he said, "Why have you come here so early?" "Because, sir," I replied, "I have a station." (2) "What," he said, "is a 'station'?" "Sir," I replied, "I am fasting." "And what," he continued, "is this fast you are keeping?" "I am fasting, sir," I responded, "just as I have been accustomed to." (3) "You do not know," he said, "how to fast to

---

33. *indeed . . . revealed*: so A; ML(E) read *to all they will be revealed.*

God, and this useless fast that you are keeping for him is not a
fast." "Sir," I said, "why are you saying this?" "I am telling
you," he said, "that even though you think you are fasting, this
is not a fast. But I will teach you what a complete and acceptable fast to the Lord is." "Yes, sir," I said, "you will make me
happy if I may learn about the fast acceptable to God."[34] "Listen," he said. (4) "God does not desire such a worthless fast as
this, for by fasting to God[35] in this manner, you are accomplish-
ing nothing with respect to righteousness. But keep a fast to
God in this way: (5) Commit no evil in your life, and serve the
Lord with a clean heart; keep his commandments and walk in
his ordinances, and do not permit any evil desire to enter your
heart, and believe in God. And if you do these things and fear
him and restrain yourself from every evil deed, you will live to
God; and if you do these things, you will complete a fast that is
great and acceptable to God."

2.

55. "Listen to the parable which I am about to tell you about
fasting. (2) A certain man had a field and many slaves, and in a
part of the field he planted a vineyard. And as he was going
away on a journey,[36] he chose a certain slave who was reliable,
respected, and honest and called him over to him and said,
'Take this vineyard which I have planted and fence it in until I
return, but do not do anything else to the vineyard. Obey this
command of mine, and you will gain your freedom from me.'
Then the slave's master went away on a journey. (3) When he
had gone, the slave took and fenced in the vineyard. When he
finished fencing in the vineyard, he noticed that the vineyard
was full of weeds. (4) So he thought to himself, saying, 'This
command of the lord I have carried out. Next I will cultivate
this vineyard; indeed, it will look better after it is cultivated,
and, having no weeds, it will yield more fruit, because it will
not be choked by weeds.' So he took and cultivated the vineyard, and pulled out all the weeds that were in the vineyard,

---

34. "*Yes . . . God.*": so ML²; AL¹E (followed by Harmer) omit.
35. *to God*: so MAE; L omits
36. *as he . . . journey*: so MLE; A (followed by Harmer) omits.
40. *and the son . . . Spirit*: so L¹; AL²E (followed by Harmer) omit.

and the vineyard was very attractive and flourishing, because no weeds were choking it. (5) Some time later, the master of the slave and of the field returned, and he went to the vineyard. And when he saw the vineyard fenced in neatly, and cultivated as well, and all the weeds pulled out, and the vineyard flourishing, he rejoiced greatly at what his slave had done. (6) So he called his beloved son, who was his heir, and his friends, who were his advisors, and told them what he had commanded his servant to do and what he had found done. And they congratulated the slave on the testimony which his master gave him. (7) And he said to them, 'I promised this slave his freedom if he obeyed the command which I gave him. He has obeyed my command, and has, to my great pleasure, done a good job in the vineyard besides. Therefore, in return for this work which he has done, I wish to make him joint-heir with my son, because when the good idea occurred to him, he did not ignore it but did it.' (8) The master's son agreed with his decision that the slave should become joint-heir with the son. (9) A few days later his master gave a feast and sent him a considerable amount of food from the feast. But when the slave received the food sent to him by the master, he took enough for himself and distributed the rest to his fellow slaves. (10) And when his fellow servants received the food, they rejoiced and began to pray for him, in order that he might find even greater favor with the master, because he had treated them so well. (11) His master heard about all these things that had happened, and again he rejoiced greatly at his conduct. Calling together again his friends and son, he reported to them what the slave had done with the food which he had received, and they all the more heartily approved of the slave being made a joint-heir with his son."

3.

56. "Sir," I said, "I do not understand nor am I able to comprehend these parables, unless you explain them to me." (2) "I will explain everything to you," he said, "and will interpret for you whatever I say to you. Keep the Lord's commandments, and you will be pleasing to him[37] and will be enrolled among

---

37. *him*: so ML¹; L² (followed by Harmer) reads *God*.

the number of those who keep his commandments.[38] (3) But if you do anything good beyond God's commandment, you will gain greater glory for yourself, and will be more honored in God's sight than you otherwise would have been. So if while keeping God's commandments you also add these services, you will rejoice, if you keep them in accordance with my commandment." (4) I said to him, "Sir, whatever you command me, I will keep it, for I know that you are with me." "I will be with you," he said, "because you have such a zeal for doing good; indeed, I will be with all those," he said, "who have a zeal such as this. (5) This fasting," he said, "is very good, if you keep the Lord's commandments.[39] This, therefore, is how you must keep this fast which you are about to keep: (6) First of all, guard against every evil word and every evil desire, and cleanse your heart of all the vanities of this world. If you observe these things, this fast of yours will be perfect. (7) And this is what you must do: when you have fulfilled what has been written, you must taste nothing except bread and water on that day on which you fast. Then you must estimate the amount of the cost of the food you would have eaten on that day on which you intend to fast, and give it to a widow or an orphan or someone in need. In this way you will become humble-minded, so that as a result of your humble-mindedness the one who receives may satisfy his own soul and pray to the Lord on your behalf. (8) If, then, you complete the fast in this way, as I have commanded you, your sacrifice will be acceptable in God's sight, and this fast will be recorded, and the service performed in this way is beautiful and joyous and acceptable to the Lord. (9) This is how you must observe these things with your children and your whole household, and in observing them, you will be blessed; indeed, all those who hear and observe them will be blessed, and whatever they ask from the Lord they will receive."

---

38. *and will interpret . . . commandments*: so ML; A(E) read *including whatever I say to you. I will show you his commandments.*

39. *is very . . . commandments*: or perhaps *consisting of keeping the Lord's commandments is very good.*

4.

57. I urgently asked him to explain to me the parable of the field and the master and the vineyard and the slave who fenced in the vineyard, and the fences and the weeds which were pulled up out of the vineyard and the son and the friends who were advisors, for I understood that all these things are a parable. (2) But he answered and said to me, "You are exceedingly arrogant in asking questions. You ought not," he said, "to ask any questions at all, for if it is necessary for something to be explained to you, it will be explained." I said to him, "Sir, whatever you show me and do not explain, I will have seen in vain and will not understand what it is. In the same way, if you tell me parables and do not interpret them, I will have heard something from you in vain." (3) But again he answered and said to me: "Whoever," he said, "is a servant of God and has his own Lord in his heart asks for understanding from him and receives it, and so he interprets every parable, and the words of the Lord spoken in parables are made known to him. But those who are weak and sluggish in prayer hesitate to ask of the Lord. (4) But the Lord is extraordinarily compassionate and unceasingly gives to those who ask of him. But you, who have been strengthened by the holy angel and have received from him such power of intercession and are not sluggish, why don't you ask for understanding from the Lord, and receive it from him?" (5) I said to him, "Sir, since I have you with me, I must of necessity ask you and inquire of you, for you show me everything and speak with me; but if I had seen or heard them without you, I would have asked the Lord, that it might be explained to me."

5.

58. "I told you just now," he said, "that you are sly and arrogant in asking about the interpretation of the parables. But since you are so stubborn, I will explain to you the parable about the field and all the rest that followed it, in order that you may make them known to everyone. Now listen," he said, "and understand them. (2) The field is this world, and the lord of the field is he who created all things and perfected them and endowed them with power, and the son is the Holy Spirit,[40] and the slave is the Son of God, and the vines are this people which he himself planted. (3) The fences are the holy angels of the Lord who keep his people together, and the weeds that are pulled up out of the vineyard are the transgressions of God's servants. The foods which he sent to him from the feast are the commandments which he gave to his people through his Son, and the friends and advisors are the holy angels who were created first; and the absence of the master is the time remaining until his coming." (4) I said to him, "Sir, it is all great and marvelous, and all is glorious. Was it likely, then," I said, "that I could have understood them? Nor could any other man understand them, even if he were extremely intelligent. Furthermore, sir," I continued, "explain to me what I am about to ask you." (5) "Speak," he replied, "if you want something." "Why, sir," I said, "is the Son of God presented in the parable in the guise of a slave?"

6.

59. "Listen," he said. "The Son of God is not[41] presented in the guise of a slave, but is presented in great power and lordship." "How so, sir?" I asked. "I don't understand." (2) "Because," he said, "God planted the vineyard, that is, he created the people, and turned them over to his Son. And the Son placed the angels over them to protect them, and the Son himself cleansed their sins with great labor and enduring much toil, for no one can cultivate a vineyard without toil or labor. (3) So, when he himself had cleansed the sins of the people, he showed them the paths of life, giving them the law which he received from his Father. (4) You see," he said, "that he is Lord of the people, having received all power from his Father.[42] But hear why the Lord took his Son and the glorious angels as counselors concerning the inheritance of the slave. (5) The preexistent Holy Spirit, which created the whole creation, God caused to live in the flesh that he wished. This flesh, therefore, in which the Holy

40. *and the son . . . Spirit:* so L[1]; AL[2]E (followed by Harmer) omit.
41. *not:* so LE; A omits.
42. *You see . . . Father:* so L(M); AE omit.

Spirit lived, served the Spirit well, living in holiness and purity, without defiling the Spirit in any way. (6) So, because it had lived honorably and chastely, and had worked with the Spirit and had cooperated with it in everything, conducting itself with strength and bravery, he chose it as a partner with the Holy Spirit, for the conduct of this flesh pleased the Lord,[43] because while possessing the Holy Spirit it was not defiled upon the earth. (7) So he took the Son and the glorious angels as counselors, in order that this flesh also, having served the Spirit blamelessly, might have some place to live, and not appear to have lost the reward of its service. For all flesh in which the Holy Spirit has lived will, if it proves to be undefiled and spotless, receive a reward. (8) Now you have the explanation of this parable."

7.

60. "I am glad, sir," I said, "to hear this explanation." "Listen, now," he said. "Keep this flesh of yours clean and undefiled, in order that the Spirit that lives in it may bear witness to it, and your flesh may be justified. (2) See to it that the idea never enters your heart that this flesh of yours is mortal, lest you abuse it in some defiling way. For if you defile your flesh, you also defile the Holy Spirit; and if you defile the flesh, you will not live." (3) "But if, sir," I said, "there was any previous ignorance before these words were heard, how will the man who has defiled his flesh be saved?" "Concerning the former acts of ignorance," he said, "God alone has the power to give healing, for all authority is his. (4) But now protect yourself, and the Lord, who is exceedingly compassionate, will give healing for your previous acts of ignorance,[44] if from now on you defile neither your flesh nor the Spirit. For they belong together, and the one cannot be defiled without the other. Therefore keep both pure, and you will live to God."

---

43. *the Lord*: so L²(E) [Harmer]; L¹ reads *God*; AM read *him*.

44. *But now . . . ignorance*: so Harmer, following Gebhardt's emendation; (M) (L) (E) read *But now keep these things, and the Lord who is very compassionate will heal them.* A omits the entire phrase.

Parable 6
1.

61. As I sat in my house and glorified the Lord for all the things that I had seen, and was contemplating the commandments because they were beautiful and powerful and glorious, and able to save a man's soul, I said to myself, "I will be blessed if I walk in these commandments; indeed, whoever walks in them will be blessed." (2) As I was saying these things to myself, I suddenly saw him sitting next to me and saying these things: "Why are you double-minded about the commandments that I gave you? They are beautiful. Do not be double-minded at all, but put on the faith of the Lord, and walk in them, for I will strengthen you in them. (3) These commandments are profitable to those who are about to repent, for if they do not walk in them, their repentance is in vain. (4) You, therefore, who repent, get rid of the evil things of this world which crush you; and by putting on every virtue of righteousness you will be able to keep these commandments and no longer add to your sins. So, by adding nothing you will cut off many of your former sins. Walk, therefore, in these commandments of mine, and you will live to God. All these things have been spoken to you by me." (5) After he had said these things to me, he said to me, "Let us go into the country, and I will show you the shepherds of the sheep." "Let us go, sir," I said. And we came to a plain, and he showed me a young shepherd dressed in a suit of yellow-colored clothes. (6) He was feeding a large number of sheep, and these sheep seemed to be well fed and very frisky, and were happily skipping about here and there. And the shepherd himself was quite happy over his flock, and even the very appearance of the shepherd was exceedingly cheerful as he was running about among the sheep.[45]

2.

62. And he said to me, "Do you see this shepherd?" "I see him, sir," I replied. "This," he said, "is the angel of luxury and

---

45. *sheep*: so MALE; Pseudo-Anthanasius adds *And I saw in one place other frisky and well-fed sheep, but they were not skipping about* (cf. 62.4, 6 below).

deception.[46] He crushes the souls of God's servants and turns them away from the truth, deceiving them with evil desires in which they perish. (2) For they forget the commandments of the living God and live pleasurably in worthless luxury, and are destroyed by this angel, some to death and some to corruption." (3) I said to him, "Sir, I don't understand what 'to death' and what 'to corruption' mean." "Listen," he said. "The sheep that you saw happily skipping about are those people who have been turned away from God completely, and have handed themselves over to the lusts of this world. Among these, therefore, there is no repentance leading to life, because God's name is being blasphemed because of them. The life of people such as these is death. (4) But the sheep that you saw that were not skipping, but were feeding in one place, are those who have handed themselves over to acts of luxury and deception, but have not spoken any blasphemy against the Lord. These, therefore, have been corrupted from the truth; for them there is the hope of repentance, by which they are able to live. So corruption has some hope of renewal, but death has only eternal destruction." (5) Again we went on a little farther, and he showed me a huge shepherd who looked like a wild man, dressed in a white goatskin, and he had some kind of bag on his shoulders, and a very hard knobby staff, and a long whip. And he had such a bitter look that I was afraid of him, such a look he had. (6) This shepherd was receiving from the young shepherd those sheep who were frisky and well fed but not skipping about and was putting them in a certain precipitous place covered with thorns and briars, so that the sheep were unable to disentangle themselves from the thorns and briars, but were entangled in the thorns and briars. (7) So they were attempting to graze while entangled in the thorns and briars, and were very miserable because they were being beaten by him. And he was driving them about here and there, giving them no rest, and those sheep were not at all happy.

46. *deception*: or possibly *pleasure* (which, because it involves one in sin [as Hermas sees it], is inherently deceptive).

3.

63. When I saw them so beaten and miserable, I was sorry for them, because they were being tortured so and had no rest at all. (2) I said to the shepherd who was with me, "Sir, who is this shepherd who is so hard-hearted and mean, and has no compassion whatsoever for these sheep?" "This," he said, "is the angel of punishment; he is one of the righteous angels and presides over punishment. (3) So he receives those who have wandered away from God and walked after the desires and pleasures of this world, and punishes them, as they deserve, with various terrible punishments." (4) "I would like to know, sir," I said, "what these various punishments are." "Listen," he said. "The various tortures and punishments are tortures they experience in this life. For some are punished with losses, and others with every kind of disturbance, and others are insulted by worthless people and suffer many other things. (5) For many, vacillating in their intentions, attempt many things, but nothing ever succeeds with them. And then they say that they do not prosper in their efforts, and it never enters their hearts that they have done evil deeds; instead, they blame the Lord. (6) So, when they are afflicted with every kind of affliction, then they are handed over to me for good instruction and are strengthened in the faith of the Lord and serve the Lord with a pure heart the rest of the days of their lives. When they repent, therefore, the evil deeds which they did enter their hearts, and then they glorify God, because he is a righteous Judge and because each one rightly suffered for what he had done. And from then on they serve the Lord with pure hearts and prosper in all they do, receiving from the Lord everything they ask for. And then they glorify the Lord because they were handed over to me, and they no longer suffer any evil."

4.

64. I said to him, "Sir, explain something else to me as well." "What," he said, "do you want to know?" "Whether, sir," I said, "those who live in luxury and pleasure are tormented for the same length of time as they spend in luxury and pleasure?" He said to me, "They are tormented for the same length of time." (2) "Then they are tormented very little, sir," I said, "for those who so live in luxury and forget God ought to have been tormented seven times as long." (3) He said to me, "You are foolish and do not understand the power of torment." "True, sir," I said, "for if I had understood, I would not have asked you to explain it to me." "Hear," he said, "about the power of both.[47] (4) The time of luxury and pleasure is one hour. But an hour of torment has the power of thirty days. So if someone lives in luxury and is deceived for one day, and is tormented for one day, the day of torment is equivalent to a whole year. So, for as many days as someone lives in luxury, for that many years he is tormented. You see, therefore," he said, "that the time of luxury and deception is very short, but the time of punishment and torment is long."

5.

65. "Sir," I said, "since I don't fully understand about the time of the deception and luxury and torment, explain it to me more clearly." (2) He answered and said to me, "Your stupidity is persistent, and you do not want to cleanse your heart and serve God. Take care," he said, "lest the time be fulfilled and you are found to be still foolish. So listen," he said, "in order that you may understand the matter, just as you wish. (3) The one who lives in luxury and deception for one day and does what he wants has clothed himself in much foolishness and does not understand what he is doing, for on the next day he forgets what he did the day before. For luxury and deception have no memories, because of the foolishness with which they are clothed. But when punishment and torment cling to a man for a single day, he is punished and tormented for a year, for punishment and torment have long memories. (4) So, being punished and tormented for a whole year, he then remembers the luxury and deceit and realizes that he is suffering these evils because of them. Every man, therefore, who lives in luxury and deception is tormented in this way, because even though they have life, they have handed themselves over to death." (5) "Sir," I said, "what kinds of luxuries are harmful?"

47. *both*: Pseudo-Athanasius [Harmer] add *luxury and torment*.

"Everything a man enjoys doing," he said, "is a luxury for him. For even the ill-tempered man indulges himself when he gives free rein to his passion. And the adulterer and the drunkard and the slanderer and the liar and the anxious and the robber and the one who does things such as these each gives free rein to his own sickness; he indulges himself, therefore, by his action. (6) All these luxuries are harmful to God's servants; because of these pleasures, therefore, those who are punished and tormented suffer. (7) But there are also luxuries which save men, for many indulge themselves in doing good, being carried away by the pleasure it gives them. This luxury, therefore, is profitable for God's servants and brings life to such a man. But the harmful luxuries mentioned above bring torments and punishments to them; and if they persist and do not repent, they bring death upon themselves."

Parable 7

66. A few days later I saw him on the same plain where I had also seen the shepherds, and he said to me, "What are you looking for?" "I am here, sir," I said, "to have you order the punishing shepherd to leave my house, because he is afflicting me greatly." "It is necessary," he said, "for you to be afflicted. For this," he said, "is what the glorious angel ordered concerning you, for he wants you to be tested." "Why, sir?" I said; "What evil thing have I done, that I should be handed over to this angel?" (2) "Listen," he said. "Your sins are numerous, but not so numerous that you should be handed over to this angel. But your family has committed great sins and iniquities, and the glorious angel was incensed by their deeds, and for this reason he ordered that you should be afflicted for a while, in order that they too might repent and cleanse themselves from every desire of this world. So when they repent and are cleansed, then the angel of punishment will leave." (3) I said to him, "Sir, even if they have perpetrated such deeds that the glorious angel is incensed, what have I done?" "They cannot otherwise be afflicted," he said, "unless you, the head of the family, are afflicted. For if you are afflicted, they, too, will necessarily be afflicted; but if you are prosperous, they cannot experience any affliction." (4) "But look, sir," I said, "they have repented with all their heart." "I am quite aware," he said, "that they have repented with all their heart. So, do you think that the sins of those who repent are forgiven immediately? Certainly not! But the one who repents must torment his own soul and be extremely humble in everything he does and be afflicted with a variety of afflictions; and if he endures the afflictions that come upon him, then assuredly the one who created all things and endowed them with power will be moved with compassion and will give some healing. (5) And this will certainly be the case, if[48] he sees that the heart of the one who repents is free of every evil thing. But it is beneficial for you and your family to be afflicted now. But why am I telling you so much? It is necessary for you to be afflicted, just as that angel of the Lord who handed you over to me ordered. And give thanks to the Lord for this, that he considered you worthy to reveal the affliction to you in advance, so that by knowing about it in advance, you might endure it with fortitude." (6) I said to him, "Sir, be with me, and I will be able to endure my affliction." "I will be with you," he said, "and I will ask the punishing angel to afflict you more lightly. But you will be afflicted for a short time, and you will be restored again to your family.[49] Only continue to be humble and to serve the Lord with a clean heart, with your children and your household, and walk in my commandments which I give you, and it will be possible for your repentance to be strong and pure. (7) And if you, with your family, keep these commandments, all affliction will leave you; indeed," he said, "affliction will leave all who walk in these commandments of mine."

Parable 8

1.

67. He showed me a great[50] willow tree that overshadowed plains and mountains, and all who are called by the name of the Lord came under the shade of the willow. (2) And by the willow there stood an angel of the Lord, glorious and very tall, with a

---

48. *will . . . if:* Harmer suggests (on the basis of LE) *God will do, when.*

49. *family:* so A; MLE read *place.*

50. *great:* so AE [Harmer]; ML omit.

huge pruning hook, and he was lopping off branches from the willow and giving them to the people who were in the shade of the willow; he gave them small sticks, about eighteen inches long. (3) After they all had received the sticks, the angel laid down the pruning hook, and the tree was sound, just as I had initially seen it. (4) And I was amazed, and said to myself, "How can the tree be sound after so many branches were lopped off?" The shepherd said to me, "Do not be amazed that the tree remained sound after so many branches were lopped off. Wait," he said, "until you see everything, and what this means will be explained to you." (5) The angel who had given the sticks to the people asked for them back again, and they were summoned to him in the same order as they had received them, and each of them returned the sticks. And the angel of the Lord took them and examined them. (6) From some he received the sticks withered and eaten, apparently by grubs; the angel ordered those who returned sticks in this condition to stand off by themselves. (7) And others returned them withered but not eaten by grubs, and these too he ordered to stand off by themselves. (8) And others returned them half-withered; these also stood off by themselves. (9) And others returned their sticks half-withered and cracked; these also stood off by themselves. (10) And others returned their sticks green and cracked, and they stood off by themselves. (11) And others returned the sticks half-withered and half-green, and they stood off by themselves. (12) Others presented their sticks two-thirds green and one-third withered, and they stood off by themselves. (13) And others returned them two-thirds dry and one-third green, and these stood off by themselves. (14) And others returned their sticks nearly all green, but with just a little bit of their sticks withered, just the end, but they did have cracks in them; these also stood off by themselves. (15) Those of the others had only a very small part green, and the rest of each stick was withered; and these stood off by themselves. (16) Others came presenting their sticks green, just as they received them from the angel. Most of the multitude returned their sticks in this condition, and the angel rejoiced greatly over them, and these stood off by themselves. (17) Others returned their sticks green and with buds; these too stood off by themselves, and the angel rejoiced greatly over them. (18) And others returned their sticks green and with buds, and their buds seemed to have some fruit. And those people whose sticks were found in this condition were extremely happy, and the angel rejoiced over them, and the shepherd was very glad for them.

2.

68. And the angel of the Lord ordered that crowns be brought. And crowns were brought, apparently made of palm leaves, and he crowned the people who had returned the sticks which had the buds and some fruit, and sent them off to the tower. (2) And he also sent to the tower the others who had returned their sticks green and with buds, but with no fruit on the buds; and he gave them a seal. (3) And all those who went to the tower had the same clothes, as white as snow. (4) And he sent off those who had returned their sticks green as they had received them, giving them white clothes and seals. (5) After the angel had finished these things he said to the shepherd, "I am going away, but you must send these people inside the walls, insofar as any deserve to live there. Examine their sticks carefully, and send them off accordingly. But be careful in examining them. See to it that no one escapes you," he said. "But if anyone does escape you, I will test them upon the altar." After he had said this to the shepherd, he left. (6) And, after the angel had left, the shepherd said to me, "Let us take everyone's sticks and plant them, to see whether any of them can live." I said to him, "Sir, how can these withered things live?" (7) He answered and said to me, "This tree is a willow, and this species of tree is very hardy. So, if the sticks are planted and get a little moisture, many of them will live. And then let us try to pour some water on them also. If any of them can live, I will rejoice with them; but if none live, at least I will not be found negligent." (8) So the shepherd ordered me to call them, in the order in which each of them stood. And they came row by row, and returned the sticks to the shepherd. And the shepherd took the sticks and planted them in rows, and after he planted them he poured so much water on them that the sticks could not be seen because of the water. (9) And after he had watered the sticks he said to me, "Let us go now, and in a few days let us return and inspect all the sticks, for the one who created this tree wants all those who have received sticks from this tree to live. And I too hope that most of these sticks, now that they have received some moisture and have been watered, will live."

3.

69. I said to him, "Sir, tell me what this tree means, for I am perplexed about it, because even though so many branches were lopped off, the tree is sound, and nothing appears to have been lopped off from it; consequently, I am perplexed." (2) "Listen," he said. "This great tree, which overshadows plains and mountains and all the earth, is the law of God, which is given to the whole world, and this law is the Son of God, who has been proclaimed to the ends of the earth. And the people who are under the shadow are those who have heard the preaching and believed in him. (3) And the great and glorious angel is Michael, who has authority over this people and guides them, for he is the one who puts the law into the hearts of those who believe. He, therefore, examines those to whom he gave it, to see if they have kept it. (4) Now observe the sticks of each one, for the sticks are the law. When you see that many sticks have been made useless, you will know that they are all those who have not kept the law, and you will see each one's dwelling." (5) I said to him, "Sir, why did he send some off to the tower, but leave others for you?" "All those," he said, "who transgressed the law which they received from him he left under my authority for repentance; but all those who have already satisfied the law and kept it he retains under his own authority." (6) "So who, sir," I asked, "are those who have been crowned and are going into the tower?" He answered and said to me, "Those who are crowned are the ones who have wrestled with the devil and conquered him. These are the ones who have suffered for the law. (7) And the others who also returned their sticks green and with buds, though not with fruit, are those who were persecuted for the law, but did not suffer, nor did they deny their law. (8) Those who returned them green, just as they received them, are reverent and righteous people who have walked with an

extraordinarily clean heart and have kept the Lord's commandments. But the rest you will learn when I examine these sticks
that have been planted and watered."

4.

70. After a few days we came to the spot, and the shepherd
sat down in the place of the great angel, while I stood beside
him. And he said to me, "Tie a towel around your waist and
assist me." So I tied a clean towel made of sackcloth around my
waist. (2) And when he saw me with the towel around my waist
ready to assist him, he said: "Call the people whose sticks have
been planted, according to the order in which they returned
their sticks." And I went to the plain and called them all, and
they all stood in rows. (3) He said to them, "Let each person
pull out his own stick and bring it to me." (4) The first to return
them were those who had had the withered and chewed-up
sticks, and when they were found to be still withered and
chewed-up, he ordered them to stand off by themselves. (5)
Then those whose sticks were withered but not chewed-up
returned them, and some of them returned the sticks green, but
some returned them withered and chewed-up, as though by
grubs. So those who returned them green he ordered to stand
off by themselves, but those who returned them withered and
chewed-up he ordered to stand with the first group. (6) Then
those whose sticks were half-withered and cracked returned
them; many returned them green and without cracks, and
some returned them green and budded, with fruit on the buds,
like those who were crowned and went into the tower had had,
but some returned them withered and eaten, and some withered but not eaten, and some were as before, half-withered and
cracked. He ordered each one of them to stand off by themselves, some with their own group and others by themselves.

5.

71. Then those whose sticks were green and cracked returned them. These all returned them green, and stood in their
own group. And the shepherd rejoiced over these, because they
were all changed and had gotten rid of their cracks. (2) And

those whose sticks were half-green and half-withered also returned them. The sticks of some were found to be completely green, of some half-withered, of some withered and eaten, and of some green and with buds. These were all sent away, each to his own group. (3) Then those whose sticks were two-thirds green and one-third withered returned them; many of them returned them green, but many half-withered, and others withered and eaten. These all stood in their own group. (4) Then others returned their sticks, which had been two-thirds dry and one-third green. Many of them returned them half-withered, and some withered and eaten, and some half-withered and cracked; but a few returned them green. These all stood in their own group. (5) And those whose sticks were green, but with a small part withered and cracked, returned them. Of these some returned them green, and some green and with buds. They too went off to their own group. (6) Then those whose sticks were just a little bit green and the rest withered returned them. The sticks of these were, for the most part, found to be green and budded, with fruit on the buds, and others completely green. The shepherd rejoiced greatly over these sticks, because they were found in this condition. And these went off, each to his own group.

6.

72. After the shepherd had examined the sticks of them all, he said to me, "I told you that this tree is very hardy. Do you see," he said, "how many repented and were saved?" "I see, sir," I said. "In order that you might see," he said, "that the abundant compassion of the Lord is great and glorious, he has also given the Spirit to those who are worthy of repentance." (2) "Then why, sir," I said, "don't they all repent?" "To those," he said, "whose hearts he saw were about to become pure, and who were about to serve him with all their heart, he gave repentance; but to those whose deceit and wickedness he saw, who were about to repent hypocritically, he did not give repentance, lest they should somehow again profane his name." (3) I said to him, "Sir, now explain to me about those who have returned their sticks, that is, what kind of person each of them is, and where they live, in order that when those who

have believed and have received the seal and have broken it
and have not kept it sound hear this, they may recognize what
they are doing, and repent and thereby receive a seal from you,
and glorify the Lord because he has had mercy on them and
sent you to renew their spirits." (4) "Listen," he said. "Those
whose sticks were found withered and eaten by grubs are the
apostates and traitors to the church, who by their sins have
blasphemed the Lord, and in addition were ashamed of the
Lord's name by which they were called. These, therefore, utterly perished to God. And you see that not one of them repented, even though they heard the words which you spoke to
them, which I commanded you. From men of this sort life has
departed. (5) But those who returned the withered and uneaten
sticks are very close to them, for they were hypocrites and
brought in strange doctrines, and perverted God's servants,
especially the ones who had sinned, by not allowing them to
repent, but dissuading them instead with their moronic doctrines. These, then, have the hope of repentance. (6) And you
see that many of them have indeed repented, ever since you
spoke my commandments to them, and still more will repent.
But those who will not repent have lost their life; those of
them who have repented, on the other hand, became good,
and have found their home within the first walls, and some
have even ascended into the tower. So you see," he said, "that
repentance from sin brings life, but failure to repent means
death."

7.

73. "As for those who returned their sticks half-withered
and with cracks in them, hear about them as well. Those
whose sticks were half-withered are the double-minded, for
they are neither alive nor dead. (2) But those whose sticks were
half-withered and had cracks in them are both double-minded
and slanderers, and are never at peace among themselves, but
are always causing dissensions. Yet even for these," he said,
"repentance is possible. You see," he said, "that some of them
have already repented, and there is still hope of repentance in
them. (3) So those of them," he said, "who have repented have

their home within the tower, but those of them who have repented more slowly will live within the walls; and those who do not repent, but persist in what they are doing, will surely die. (4) But those who returned their sticks green and cracked were faithful and good at all times, but they had a certain jealousy of one another over questions of preeminence and about some kind of distinction. But they are all fools to be jealous of one another regarding preeminence. (5) But these also, because they are good, cleansed themselves and quickly repented when they heard my commandments. Their home, therefore, is in the tower. But if anyone again turns to dissension, he will be thrown out of the tower and will lose his life. (6) Life is for all those who keep the Lord's commandments, but in the commandments there is nothing about preeminence or any kind of distinction, but patient endurance and a man's humility. In such men, therefore, is the life of the Lord, but in dissentious and lawless men there is death."

8.

74. "The ones who returned their sticks half-green and half-withered are those who are absorbed in business and do not associate with the saints; this is why one-half of them lives, but the other half is dead. (2) Many, then, repented when they heard my commandments. Those who have repented have their home within the tower. But some of them fell away completely. These, therefore, have no repentance, for on account of their business affairs they blasphemed the Lord and denied him. So they lost their life because of the evil they did. (3) But many of them were double-minded. These still have an opportunity to repent, if they repent quickly, and their home will be within the tower; but if they repent more slowly, they will live within the walls. But if they do not repent at all, they too have lost their lives. (4) And the ones who returned the sticks two-thirds green and one-third withered are those who have denied the Lord repeatedly. (5) Many have repented and gone off to live inside the tower, but many fell away from God completely; these ultimately lost their lives. And some of them were double-minded and caused dissensions. For these, then, there is repentance, if they repent quickly and do not persist in their pleasures. But if they persist in their actions, they too produce death for themselves."

9.

75. "The ones who returned their sticks two-thirds withered and one-third green are those who had been faithful, but became rich and acquired a reputation among the pagans. They clothed themselves with great pride and became arrogant and abandoned the truth and did not associate with the righteous, but lived with and according to the standards of pagans, and this life-style was more pleasant to them. Yet they did not fall away from God, but continued in the faith, though they did not do the works of faith. (2) Many of them, therefore, repented, and their home was within the tower. (3) But others, living entirely among the heathen and being corrupted by the worthless opinions of the heathen, fell away from God and behaved like the heathen. These, therefore, were counted with the heathen. (4) But others of them were double-minded, no longer hoping to be saved because of the deeds that they had done; and others were double-minded and caused divisions among themselves. For these, then, who became double-minded because of their deeds, there is still repentance; but their repentance ought to be swift, in order that their home may be within the tower. But for those who do not repent, but persist in their pleasures, death is near."

10.

76. "Those who returned their sticks green, but with the tips withered and cracked, were always good and faithful and glorious in God's sight, but they sinned just a little because of small desires and petty matters which they held against one another. But when they heard my words, the majority quickly repented, and their home was in the tower. (2) But some of them were double-minded, and some, being double-minded, caused a greater dissension. In these, then, there is still hope of repentance, because they were always good, and scarcely one of them will die. (3) But the ones who returned their sticks withered, yet with a very small part green, are those who believed but practiced the works of lawlessness. Still, they never fell away from God, but bore the name gladly, and gladly welcomed God's servants into their houses. So when they heard of this repentance, they repented unhesitatingly and are practicing every virtue and righteousness. (4) And some of them are even suffering, and are bearing their distress gladly,[51] knowing the deeds that they did. The home of all of these, therefore, will be in the tower."

11.

77. And after he had finished the explanations of all the sticks, he said to me, "Go and speak to all people, in order that they may repent and live to God, for the Lord in his compassion sent me to give repentance to all, though some, because of their deeds, do not deserve to be saved.[52] But being patient, the Lord wants those who were called through his Son to be saved." (2) I said to him, "Sir, I hope that all who hear them will repent. For I am convinced that each one, when he realizes what he has done and fears God, will repent." (3) He answered and said to me, "Those who repent," he said, "with all their heart and cleanse themselves from all their evil deeds just described, and no longer add anything more to their sins, will receive healing from the Lord for their previous sins, unless they are double-minded about these commandments, and they will live to God. But those," he said, "who add to their sins and walk in the desires of this world will condemn themselves to death. (4) But as for you, walk in my commandments, and you will live to God; indeed, whoever walks in them and acts rightly will live to God." (5) Having shown me all these things and told me everything, he said to me, "The rest I will show you in a few days."

51. *even suffering . . . gladly*: so M; A reads *also afraid*; Harmer emends the text to read *even suffering persecution willingly*.
52. *to be saved*: so ML; A (followed by Harmer) omits.

Parable 9
1.

78. After I had written down the commandments and parables of the shepherd, the angel of repentance, he came to me
and said to me, "I want to explain to you what the Holy Spirit,
which spoke with you in the form of the Church, showed you;
for that Spirit is the Son of God. (2) For since you were too weak
in the flesh, it was not explained to you by an angel; but when
you were given power by the Spirit, and grew strong in your
strength, so that you could even see an angel, then the building
of the tower was revealed to you through the Church. You saw
all things well and reverently, as from a young girl; but now
you see it from an angel, though by the same spirit. (3) Yet you
must learn everything more accurately from me. For it was for
this purpose that I was assigned by the glorious angel to live in
your house, in order that you might see everything as clearly as
possible, with none of the fear you formerly had." (4) And he
led me away to Arcadia, to a certain rounded mountain, and
seated me on top of the mountain, and showed me a great plain,
and around the plain twelve mountains, and each mountain
had a different appearance. (5) The first was black as soot, and
the second was bare, without any vegetation, and the third was
full of thorns and briars. (6) The fourth had half-withered vegetation; the tops of the plants were green, but the part by the
roots was dry. And some of the plants were withering when the
sun scorched them. (7) The fifth mountain had green grass and
was very rugged, and the sixth mountain was all full of ravines,
some small and some large, and the ravines had vegetation, but
the vegetation was not very flourishing, but looked rather withered. (8) The seventh mountain had blooming[53] vegetation, and
the whole mountain was thriving, and cattle and birds of every
kind were feeding on the mountain; and the more the cattle
and the birds ate, the more and more the vegetation of that
mountain flourished. The eighth mountain was full of springs,
and every species of the Lord's creation drank from the springs
on that mountain. (9) The ninth mountain had no water at all,
and was entirely desert; it had wild beasts and deadly reptiles

53. *blooming*: lit. *cheerful*.

that destroyed men. The tenth mountain had very large trees and was completely shaded, and beneath the shade sheep lay resting and chewing their cud. (10) The eleventh mountain was thickly wooded all over, and these trees were very productive, each adorned with various kinds of fruit, so that anyone who saw them wanted to eat of their fruit. And the twelfth mountain was completely white, and its appearance was very bright, and the mountain in and of itself was extraordinarily beautiful.

2.

79. And in the middle of the plain he pointed out to me a great white rock rising up from the plain. And the rock was higher than the mountains and square, so that it could hold the whole world. (2) And that rock was old, and a door had been hewn out of it; but the door seemed to me to have been hewn quite recently. And the door was so much more radiant than the sun that I marveled at the brightness of the door. (3) Around the door stood twelve virgins. The four who stood at the corners seemed to me to be more glorious (though the others were also glorious), and they stood at the four sides of the door, with a pair of virgins between each of them. (4) And they were dressed in linen tunics which were becomingly belted around them, their right shoulders bare, as though they were about to carry some load. Thus were they ready, for they were very cheerful and eager. (5) After seeing these things I wondered to myself, because I was seeing great and glorious things. And again I was perplexed by the virgins, because though they were delicate, they stood bravely, as if they intended to carry the whole heaven. (6) And the shepherd said to me, "Why are you debating with yourself and becoming perplexed, and troubling yourself? Do not attempt, as though you were intelligent, to understand things you cannot comprehend, but ask the Lord that you may receive the intelligence to understand them. (7) You are not able to see things behind you, but you do see what is in front of you. Let what you cannot see alone, and do not trouble yourself about it; but master those things that you do see, and do not concern yourself about the rest. But I will explain to you everything that I show to you. So, carefully watch the rest."

3.

80. I saw that six men had come, tall and glorious and alike in appearance, and they called a multitude of men. And those who came were also tall men, handsome and powerful. And the six men ordered them to build a tower above the rock.[54] And there arose a great noise from those men who had come to build the tower as they ran here and there around the door. (2) And the virgins standing around the door were telling the men to hurry to build the tower, and the virgins had spread out their hands as though they were about to receive something from the men. (3) And the six men ordered stones to come up from some deep place and to go into the structure of the tower. And ten square stones, polished and unhewn, came up. (4) And the six men called the virgins and ordered them to pick up all the stones which were to go into the structure of the tower and to pass through the door and hand them to the men who were about to build the tower. (5) And the virgins put the first ten stones that arose from the deep on one another, and they carried them together, stone by stone.

4.

81. In the same order in which they stood together around the door, those who seemed to be the strongest picked up the stone and got under its corners, while the others got under the sides of the stone, and thus they carried all the stones. They carried them through the door, just as they were ordered, and handed them to the men for the tower, and they took them and built. (2) The tower was built upon the great rock and above the door. So those ten stones were fitted together, and they covered the whole rock. And these formed the foundation for the construction of the tower. (3) And after the ten stones, twenty-five[55] other stones came up from the deep, and these were fitted into the structure of the tower, having been carried in by the virgins like the previous ones. And after these thirty-

---

54. *rock*: so AE; L reads *upon the rock and above the door*; Harmer emends the text to read *above the door*.

55. *twenty-five*: so L; A reads *twenty*; E reads *fifteen*.

five came up, and these were likewise fitted into the tower. After these, forty other stones came up, and these were all put into the structure of the tower. So four tiers were laid in the foundations of the tower. (4) And the stones stopped coming up from the deep, and the builders also stopped for a little while. And next the six men ordered the multitude of the people to bring in stones from the mountains for the construction of the tower. (5) So stones of various colors were brought in from all the mountains, having been quarried by the men, and handed to the virgins, and the virgins carried them through the door and handed them over for the construction of the tower. And when the various stones were set into the building, they all alike became white and lost their various colors. (6) But some stones were delivered by the men for the building which did not become bright, but were found to be the same color as when they were put in; for they were not handed along by the virgins, nor had they been carried through the gate. These stones, therefore, were unsuitable for the building of the tower. (7) When the six men saw the unsuitable stones in the building, they ordered them to be removed and taken down to their own place, from where they had been brought. (8) And they said to the men who were bringing in the stones, "You must not bring any stones at all into the building, but only place them by the tower, so that the virgins can carry them through the door and hand them over for the building. For if," they said, "they are not carried through the gate by the hands of these virgins, they cannot change their colors. So do not labor," they said, "in vain."

5.

82. And the construction was finished for that day, though the tower was not yet completed, for it was to be built up further, and there was a pause in the construction. And the six men ordered all the builders to take a break for a little while and rest, but they ordered the virgins not to take a break from the tower. And it seemed to me that the virgins were to guard the tower. (2) After they had all taken a break and were resting, I said to the shepherd, "Why sir," I said, "was the building of the tower not completed?" "The tower," he said, "cannot yet be completed until its master comes and tests this building, so that if any stones are found to be defective he may replace them, for the tower is being built according to his will." (3) "I would like to know, sir," I said, "what the construction of this tower means, and about the rock and door, and the mountains and the virgins, and the stones that came up from the deep and were unhewn, but went into the building just as they were; (4) and why first ten stones were placed on the foundation, then twenty-five, then thirty-five, then forty; and about the stones that had gone into the building and were then removed and put back into their own place. Put my soul at rest regarding all these things, sir, and explain them to me." (5) "If," he said, "your interest proves to be more than idle curiosity, you will know everything. For in a few days we will come here, and you will see the rest of the things that will happen to this tower, and will understand all the parables accurately." (6) And after a few days we came to the place where we had been seated, and he said to me, "Let us go to the tower, for the owner of the tower is coming to inspect it." So we went to the tower, and there was no one near it at all, except for the virgins only. (7) And the shepherd asked the virgins whether the master of the tower had arrived. And they said that he was just about to come to inspect the tower.

6.

83. And behold, a little later I saw an array of many men coming, and in the midst a man of such lofty stature that he stood taller than the tower. (2) And the six men who had supervised the building were walking with him on his right and on his left, and with him were all those who worked on the building, and many other glorious beings were around him, and began to walk around the tower beside him. (3) And that man inspected the building so carefully that he felt every single stone. And he held a rod in his hand, and struck every stone that had been put into the building. (4) And when he struck the stones, some of them became black as soot, and some rough, and some cracked, and some too short, and some neither white nor black, and some became uneven and did not fit in with the other stones, and some badly spotted; these were the various kinds of defective stones found in the building. (5) So he ordered all these to be removed from the tower and placed by the side of the tower, and other stones brought and put in their place. (6) And the builders asked him from what mountain he wanted stones to be brought and put in their place. But he did not order them to be brought from the mountains; instead he ordered them to be brought from a certain plain that was nearby. (7) And the plain was excavated, and brilliant square stones were found there, but some were round. And all the stones that were found in that plain were brought in and were carried through the door by the virgins. (8) And the square stones were trimmed and set in the place of those that had been removed, but the round ones were not placed in the building, because they were too hard to shape and it took too long. So they were placed beside the tower, as though they were going to be shaped and put into the building, for they were extraordinarily brilliant.

7.

84. So, when the glorious man who was lord of the whole tower had finished these things, he called the shepherd to him and handed over to him all the stones that had been removed from the building which were lying beside the tower, and said to him, (2) "Clean these stones carefully, and use those that can fit with the others in the construction of the tower, but throw those that do not fit far away from the tower." (3) After giving these orders to the shepherd, he left the tower, together with all those with whom he had come. And the virgins stood around the tower watching it. (4) I said to the shepherd, "How can these stones go back into the structure of the tower after they have been rejected?" He answered me and said, "Do you see," he said, "these stones?" "I see them, sir," I said. "I myself," he said, "will trim the majority of these stones and put them into the building, and they will fit with the rest of the stones." (5) "How, sir," I said, "can they still fill the same space after they have been trimmed?" He answered and said to me, "those that are found to be small will be placed in the middle of the building, but those that are larger will be set on the outside and will hold them together." (6) Having spoken these things to me, he said to me, "Let us go, and after two days let us return and clean these stones and put them into the building, for everything around the tower must be cleaned up, lest the master should come unexpectedly and find things around the tower dirty and become incensed, in which case these stones will not go into the construction of the tower, and I will appear to be careless in my master's sight." (7) And after two days we came to the tower, and he said to me, "Let us inspect all the stones, and see which ones can go into the building." I said to him, "Sir, let us inspect them."

8.

85. So we inspected the stones, beginning first with the black ones. They were found to be in the same condition as when they were taken from the building, and the shepherd ordered them removed from the tower and taken away. (2) Then he inspected the rough ones, and took and trimmed many of them, and ordered the virgins to take them and place them in the building, in the middle of the tower. But the rest he ordered to be placed with the black ones, for these were also found to be black. (3) Then he inspected the cracked ones, and of these he trimmed many, and ordered them to be carried by the virgins to the building. And they were put on the exterior, because they were found to be stronger. But the rest could not be trimmed because of the large number of cracks and for this reason they were rejected for the construction of the tower. (4) Then he inspected the ones that were too short, and many black ones were found among them, and some had developed huge cracks, and he ordered these also to be placed with those that had been discarded. But he cleaned and trimmed the ones that were left, and ordered them to be placed in the building. So the virgins picked them up and fitted them into the middle of the tower's structure, for they were rather weak. (5) Then he inspected those that were half-white and half-black. Many of them were now found to be black, and he ordered these also to be taken away with those that had been discarded. But all the rest[56] were

---

56. *rest:* so A; L¹(L²E) [Harmer] add *were found to be white and.*

taken by the virgins themselves. And they were placed on the exterior because they proved to be sound and thus could support the ones put in the middle, for not one of them was too short. (6) Then he inspected the hard, uneven ones, and a few of them were thrown away because they could not be trimmed, for they proved to be very hard. But the rest of them were trimmed and taken by the virgins and fitted into the middle of the tower's structure, for they were rather weak. (7) Then he inspected the spotted ones, and of these a few had turned black and were thrown away with the rest. But the remainder were found to be bright and sound, and those were fitted into the building by the virgins; and they were placed toward the exterior, owing to their strength.

9.

86. Finally he came to inspect the round white stones, and he said to me, "What should we do with these stones?" "How do I know, sir?" I said. "Then you don't notice anything about them?" (2) "Sir," I said, "I do not possess this skill, nor am I a stonecutter, nor can I understand." "Don't you see," he said, "that they are very round, and that if I want to make them square, a great deal must be cut off them? Yet some of them must of necessity be placed in the building." (3) "So if it is necessary, sir," I said, "why do you torment yourself? Why not just choose the ones you want for the building, and fit them into it?" He chose the largest and brightest of them, and trimmed them; and the virgins took them and fitted them into the exterior portion of the building. (4) But the rest that were left were taken and put back in the plain from which they had been brought; they were not, however, thrown away "because," he said, "there still remains a little of the tower to be built. And the master of the tower is most anxious to have these stones fitted into the building, because they are very bright." (5) And twelve women were called, whose appearance was extraordinarily beautiful, dressed in black, belted, with their shoulders bare and hair hanging loose. And these women seemed to me to be savage. And the shepherd ordered them to take the stones discarded from the building and carry them back to the mountains from which they had been brought. (6)

And they cheerfully picked up and carried away all the stones and put them back where they had been taken from. And after all the stones had been taken back, and not a stone still lay around the tower, the shepherd said to me, "Let us go around the tower and see if there is any defect in it." So I went around the tower with him. (7) And when the shepherd saw that the tower's structure was beautiful, he was extremely happy; for the tower was so well built that I envied its construction when I saw it, for it was built as if it were from a single stone, without one joint in it. And the stone looked as if it had been hewn out of the rock, for it seemed to me to be all one stone.

10.

87. And as I walked with him I was glad to see so beautiful a sight. And the shepherd said to me, "Go and bring some plaster and a thin piece of broken pottery, that I may fill in the imprints on the stones that have been taken up and put into the building, for it must be smooth all around the tower." (2) And I did as he ordered, and brought them to him. "Assist me," he said, "and the work will be finished soon." So he filled in the imprints on the stones that had gone into the building, and ordered the area around the tower swept and cleaned. (3) And the virgins took brooms and swept, and they removed all the rubbish from the tower, and sprinkled some water, and the site of the tower became cheerful and attractive. (4) The shepherd said to me, "Everything," he said, "has now been cleaned. If the Lord comes to look over the tower, he will have nothing for which to blame us." Having said these things he wished to leave. (5) But I grabbed hold of his shoulder bag and began to implore him by the Lord to explain to me what he had showed me. He said to me, "I am busy for a little while, but then I will explain everything to you. Wait here for me until I come." (6) I said to him, "Sir, what will I do while I am here alone?" "You are not alone," he said, "for these virgins are with you." "Then commend me to them," I said. The shepherd called them and said to them, "I am entrusting this man to you until I return," and he left. (7) And I was alone with the virgins, and they were most cheerful and gracious to me, especially the four of them who were more glorious in appearance.

II.

88. The virgins said to me, "The shepherd is not coming here today." "So what," I said, "should I do?" "Wait for him until evening," they said, "and if he comes, he will speak with you; but if he does not come, stay with us until he does." (2) I said to them, "I will wait for him until evening, and if he does not come, I will go home and come back in the morning." But they answered and said to me, "You were entrusted to us; you cannot leave us." (3) "Where, then," I said, "will I stay?" "You will sleep with us," they said, "as a brother and not as a husband, for you are our brother, and from now on we are going to live with you, for we love you very much." But I was ashamed to stay with them. (4) And the one who seemed to be their leader began to kiss me and embrace me, and the others, seeing her embrace me, began to kiss me themselves, and to lead me around the tower and play with me. (5) And I seemed to have become younger, and I began to play with them myself; for some were doing choral dancing, and some were dancing, and others were singing. But I remained silent as I was walking around the tower with them, and was happy with them. (6) When evening came, I wanted to go home, but they would not let me go, but detained me. And I spent the night with them and slept beside the tower. (7) For the virgins spread out their linen tunics on the ground, and made me lie down in the midst of them, and they did nothing at all except pray; and I prayed with them without ceasing, and not less than they. And the virgins rejoiced that I prayed like that. And I stayed there with the virgins until about eight o'clock the next morning. (8) Then the shepherd came, and he said to the virgins, "Have you done him any harm?" "Ask him," they said. I said to him, "Sir, I enjoyed staying with them." "What," he asked, "did you have for dinner?" "Sir," I said, "I dined on the words of the Lord the whole night." "Did they treat you well?" he asked. "Yes, sir," I said. (9) "Now," he said, "what do you want to hear first?" "Just as you showed me from the beginning, sir," I said. "I am asking you, sir, to explain them to me just as I ask you." "Just as you wish," he said, "so I will explain them to you, and I will not hide anything whatsoever from you."

12.

89. "First of all, sir," I said, "explain this to me: Who is the rock and the door?" "This rock," he said, "and the door are the Son of God." "How is it, sir," I said, "that the rock is old, but the door is new?" "Listen," he said, "and understand, foolish man. (2) The Son of God is far older than all his creation, with the result that he was the Father's counselor in his creation. This is why the rock is old." "But why is the door new, sir?" I said. (3) "Because," he said, "he was revealed in the last days of the consummation; that is why the door is new, in order that those who are going to be saved may enter the kingdom of God through it. (4) Did you notice," he said, "that the stones which came through the door have gone into the construction of the tower, but those which did not come through it were returned to their own place?" "I noticed, sir," I said. "In the same way," he said, "no one will enter the kingdom of God unless he receives the name of his Son. (5) For if you want to enter some city, and that city is walled all around and has only one gate, can you enter that city except by the gate it has?" "How, sir," I said, "could it be otherwise?" "If, therefore, you cannot enter the city except through its gate," he said, "so too a man cannot enter the kingdom of God except by the name of his Son, who was loved by him. (6) Did you see," he said, "the multitude that was building the tower?" "I saw them, sir," I said. "Those," he said, "are all glorious angels. By them the Lord is walled about. But the door is the Son of God; there is only this one entrance to the Lord. No one, therefore, will enter into him in any other way than through his Son. (7) Did you see," he said, "the six men, and the glorious and mighty man in their midst, who walked around the tower and rejected the stones from the building?" "I saw him, sir," I said. (8) "The glorious man," he said, "is the Son of God, and those six are the glorious angels who surround him on his right and on his left. Not one of these glorious angels," he said, "enters God's presence without him; whoever does not receive his name will not enter the kingdom of God."

13.

90. "And who," I asked, "is the tower?" "This tower," he said, "is the Church." (2) "And who are these virgins?" "They," he said, "are holy spirits; and there is no other way a man can be found in the kingdom of God other than that they clothe him with their clothes. For if you receive only the Name, but do not receive clothing from them, it does not benefit you. For these virgins are powers of the Son of God. If you bear the Name but do not bear his power, you will bear his name in vain. (3) And the stones," he said, "which you saw rejected are the ones who bore the Name, but did not clothe themselves with the virgins' clothing." "What kind of clothing do they have, sir?" I asked. "The names themselves," he said, "are their clothing. Whoever bears the name of the Son of God ought also to bear their names, for even the Son of God himself bears the names of these virgins. (4) All the stones," he said, "which you saw go into the structure of the tower, delivered by their hands and remaining in the building, are clothed with the power of these virgins. (5) This is why you see that the tower has become a single stone with the rock. So also those who have believed in the Lord through his Son and clothe themselves with these spirits will become one spirit and one body, and their clothes will be one color. And the home of such people as bear the names of the virgins is in the tower." (6) "Now, sir," I said, "about the rejected stones—why were they rejected? For they passed through the door and were placed in the structure of the tower by the hands of the virgins." "Since everything interests you," he said, "and you are inquiring carefully, listen regarding the rejected stones. (7) All these," he said, "received the name of the Son of God, and also received the power of these virgins. Having received, therefore, these spirits, they were strengthened and were with God's servants, and they had one spirit and one body and one garment; for they had the same mind and did what was right. (8) Then after a while they were seduced by the women whom you saw dressed in black garments, with the bare shoulders and loosened hair and attractive figures. When they saw them they desired them and put on their power, and laid aside the clothes and[57] the power of the virgins. (9) These, therefore, have been thrown out of God's house and handed over to those women. But those who were not deceived by the beauty of these women remained in God's house. Now you have," he said, "the explanation of the rejected stones."

14.

91. "So what will happen, sir," I asked, "if these men, being what they are, repent and cast aside their desire for these women and return to the virgins and walk in their power and in their works? Will they not enter God's house?" (2) "They will enter," he said, "if they cast aside the works of these women and take up again the power of the virgins and walk in their works. For this is why there was a pause in the construction, so that if these repent, they may go back into the structure of the tower. But if they do not repent, then others will go in, and these will be cast out in the end." (3) I gave thanks to the Lord for all these things, because he had mercy on all those who called upon his name, and sent forth the angel of repentance to us who had sinned against him and renewed our spirit and, when we were already ruined and had no hope of life, restored our life. (4) "Now, sir," I said, "explain to me why the tower is not built on the ground but upon the rock and the door." "Are you still," he said, "stupid and senseless?" "I am obliged, sir," I said, "to ask you about everything, for I am absolutely unable to comprehend anything at all; for all these matters are awesome and glorious, and difficult for men to understand." (5) "Listen," he said. "The name of the Son of God is great and incomprehensible, and sustains the whole world. If, therefore, all creation is sustained by the Son of God, what do you think of those who are called by him and bear the name of the Son of God and walk in his commandments? (6) Do you see, then, what kind of people he sustains? Those who bear his name with their whole heart. So he himself has become their foundation and gladly sustains them because they are not ashamed to bear his name."

---

57. *the clothes and*: so L[1]E; AL[2] (followed by Harmer) omit.

15.

92. "Tell me, sir," I said, "the names of the virgins and of the women who dressed in the black garments." "Hear," he said, "the names of the stronger virgins who are stationed at the corners. (2) The first is Faith, and the second, Self-Control, and the third, Power, and the fourth, Patience. And the others standing between them have these names: Sincerity, Innocence, Purity, Cheerfulness, Truth, Understanding, Harmony, and Love. The one who bears these names and the name of the Son of God will be able to enter the kingdom of God. (3) Hear also," he said, "the names of the women with the black clothes. Of these also four are more powerful. The first is Unbelief, the second, Self-Indulgence, the third, Disobedience, and the fourth, Deceit. And the ones who follow them are called Grief, Evil, Licentiousness, Ill-Temper, Falsehood, Foolishness, Slander, and Hatred. The servant of God who bears these names will see the kingdom of God but will not enter it." (4) "And who are the stones, sir," I said, "that came from the deep and were fitted into the building?" "The first ones," he said, "the ten that were placed on the foundations, are the first generation, and the twenty-five[58] are the second generation of righteous men. The thirty-five are God's prophets and his ministers, and the forty are apostles and teachers of the proclamation of the Son of God." (5) "So why, sir," I said, "did the virgins also deliver these stones for the construction of the tower, after carrying them through the door?" (6) "Because," he said, "these were the first to bear these spirits, and they never separated from one another at all, neither the spirits from the men, nor the men from the spirits, but the spirits remained with them until they fell asleep; and if they had not had these spirits with them, they would not have been useful for the construction of this tower."

16.

93. "Sir, explain something else to me," I said. "What else do you want to know?" he said. "Why, sir," I said, "did the

---

58. *twenty-five:* so AL; E reads *fifteen* (cf. 81.3).

stones come up from the deep, and why were they put into the building, even though[59] they had borne these spirits?" (2) "It was necessary," he said, "for them to come up through water in order to be made alive, for otherwise they could not enter the kingdom of God, unless they laid aside the deadness of their former life. (3) So even those who had fallen asleep received the seal of the Son of God and entered the kingdom of God. For before a man," he said, "bears the name of the Son of God, he is dead, but when he receives the seal, he lays aside his deadness and receives life. (4) The seal, therefore, is the water; so they go down into the water dead and they come up alive. Thus this seal was proclaimed to them as well, and they made use of it in order that they might enter the kingdom of God." (5) "Why, sir," I said, "did the forty stones also come up with them from the deep, when they had already received the seal?" "Because," he said, "when these apostles and teachers who preached the name of the Son of God fell asleep in the power and faith of the Son of God, they preached also to those who had previously fallen asleep, and they themselves gave to them the seal of the preaching. (6) Therefore they went down with them into the water, and came up again. But these went down alive and came up alive, whereas those who had previously fallen asleep went down dead and came up alive. (7) So they were made alive through them, and came to full knowledge of the name of the Son of God. This is why they also came up with them and were fitted together with them into the structure of the tower, and were joined together without being hewn, for they fell asleep in righteousness and in great purity, only they did not have this seal. You now have the explanation of these things as well." "I do, sir," I said.

17.

94. "Now then, sir, explain to me about the mountains: Why is their appearance different from one another, and so diverse?" "Listen," he said. "These twelve mountains are the twelve tribes that inhabit the whole world. To them, therefore, the Son of God was proclaimed by the apostles." (2) "But ex-

---

59. *even though*: or possibly *since*.

plain to me, sir, why the mountains are so diverse, and different from one another in appearance." "Listen," he said. "These twelve tribes which inhabit the whole world are twelve nations, and they are diverse in thought and mind. So just as you observed that the mountains are diverse, so also there are diversities of mind and thought among the nations. And I will explain to you the operation of each one." (3) "Sir," I said, "first tell me this: given that the mountains are so diverse, why is it that when their stones were set into the building, they became bright and all one color, just like the stones that had come up from the deep?" (4) "Because," he said, "all the nations that dwell under heaven, when they heard and believed, were called by the name of the Son of God. So when they received the seal, they had one thought and one mind, and one faith and one love became theirs, and they bore the spirits of the virgins along with the Name. This is why the construction of the tower shone with one color, as bright as the sun. (5) But after they went in together and became one body, some of them polluted themselves and were cast out of the society of the righteous, and again became as they were before, or rather even worse."

18.

95. "How, sir," I said, "did they become worse, after they had come to know God?" "The one who does not know God," he said, "and does evil receives some punishment for his evil, but the one who has come to know God ought no longer to do evil, but to do good. (2) If, then, the one who ought to do good does evil, doesn't that one appear to do greater evil than the one who does not know God? This is why those who have not known God and do evil are condemned to death, whereas those who have known God and have seen his mighty works and yet do evil will be doubly punished and will die forever. In this way, therefore, the church of God will be purified. (3) And just as you saw the stones removed from the tower and handed over to the evil spirits and thrown away from there, so there will be one body of those who have been purified; just as the tower became as though made of one stone after it had been purified, so also will the church of God be after it has been purified, and the wicked and hypocrites and blasphemers and double-minded and those who do various kinds of evil have been cast out. (4) When these have been cast out, the church of God will be one body, one thought, one mind, one faith, one love; and then the Son of God will rejoice and be glad in them, because he has received back his people pure." "All these things are great and glorious, sir," I said. (5) "Tell me more, sir," I said, "about the power and the functions of each one of the mountains, in order that every soul that trusts in the Lord may glorify his great and marvelous and glorious name when he hears about them." "Listen," he said, "to the variety of the mountains and of the twelve nations."

19.

96. "From the first mountain, the black one, are believers such as these: apostates and blasphemers against the Lord, and betrayers of God's servants. For these there is no repentance, but there is death, and this is why they are black, for their kind is lawless. (2) And from the second mountain, the bare one, are believers such as these: hypocrites and teachers of evil. These, then, are like the first in not having the fruit of righteousness. For as their mountain is without fruit, so also men such as these have the Name, but are devoid of faith, and there is no fruit of truth in them. To these, then, repentance is offered, if they repent quickly; but if they delay, their death will be with the first group." (3) "Why, sir," I said, "is there repentance for them but not for the first group? For their actions are almost the same." "This is why," he said, "repentance is offered to them: they have not blasphemed their Lord, nor become betrayers of God's servants. Yet because of the desire for gain they acted hypocritically, and each one taught to suit the desires of sinful men. But they will pay a penalty; yet repentance is offered to them, because they did not become blasphemers or betrayers."

20.

97. "And from the third mountain, the one with thorns and briars, are believers such as these: some of them are rich, and some are entangled in many business affairs. The briars are the rich, and the thorns are those who are entangled in various business affairs. (2) So these who are entangled in many and various business affairs do not associate with God's servants, but being choked by their affairs they go astray. Meanwhile the rich associate with God's servants only with difficulty, for they are afraid that they may be asked for something by them. Such people, therefore, will enter the kingdom of God only with difficulty. (3) For just as it is difficult to walk on briars with bare feet, so it is difficult for such people to enter the kingdom of God. (4) But for all these repentance is possible, but it must be quick, so that they may now retrace the days when in former times they failed to do anything, and do something good. So, if they repent and do something good, they will live to God; but if they persist in their actions, they will be handed over to those women, who will put them to death."

21.

98. "And from the fourth mountain, the one with much vegetation, which was green at the top and withered at the roots, and some of which was dried up by the sun, are believers such as these: the double-minded and those who have the Lord on their lips but do not have him in their hearts. (2) That is why their foundations are dry and have no power, and only their words are alive, but their works are dead. Such people are neither alive nor dead. They are, therefore, like the double-minded, for the double-minded are neither green nor withered, for they are neither alive nor dead. (3) For just as these plants were dried up when they saw the sun, so the double-minded worship idols because of their cowardice and are ashamed of the name of their Lord whenever they hear about a persecution. (4) Such people are, therefore, neither alive nor dead. Yet these, too, if they repent quickly, will be able to live. But if they do not repent, they have already been handed over to the women who take away their lives."

22.

99. "And from the fifth mountain, the rugged one with the green grass, are believers such as these: they are faithful, but slow to learn, arrogant, and self-satisfied; though they want to know everything, they know nothing at all. (2) Because of this arrogance of theirs, understanding has left them and a foolish stupidity has taken possession of them. Yet they praise themselves for having wisdom and want to be volunteer teachers, foolish though they are. (3) So, because of this pride many people, while attempting to exalt themselves, have been ruined, for arrogance and overconfidence are a mighty demon. Many of these, therefore, were rejected, but some, comprehending their own foolishness, repented and believed, and submitted themselves to those with understanding. (4) And of the rest of these people repentance remains a possibility, for they were not really evil but rather stupid and short on understanding. So these will, if they repent, live for God, but if they do not repent they will dwell with the women who do harm to them."

23.

100. "And from the sixth mountain, the one with large and small ravines and withered plants in the ravines, are believers such as these: (2) the ones with small ravines are those who have something against one another; because of their backbiting they are withered in the faith. But many of these have repented, and the rest will repent when they hear my commandments, for their backbiting is relatively minor, and they will quickly repent. (3) But the ones with the large ravines are those who persist in their backbiting and hold grudges in their rage toward one another. These, therefore, were thrown away from the tower and rejected from its construction. Such people will find it difficult to live. (4) If our God and Lord, who rules over all things and has authority over all his creation, holds no grudge against those who confess their sins and is merciful, can a human being, who is mortal and full of sin, hold a grudge against someone, as though he could destroy or save him? (5) But I, the angel of repentance, am telling you, whoever holds this view must lay it aside and repent, and the Lord will heal your previous sins, if you cleanse yourselves of this demon. But if you do not, you will be handed over to him to be put to death."

24.

101. "And from the seventh mountain, where the vegetation was green and blooming and the whole mountain was thriving and cattle of every kind and birds of the sky were feeding on the vegetation on that mountain, and the vegetation on which they fed became all the more luxuriant, are believers such as these: (2) they were always sincere and innocent and blessed, holding nothing against one another but always rejoicing in God's servants and clothed in the holy spirit of these virgins, and always having compassion for every person, and from their labors they supplied every person's needs without reproach and without hesitation. (3) The Lord, therefore, seeing their sincerity and utter childlikeness prospered them in the labors of their hands and favored them in all that they did. (4) And I, the angel of repentance, declare to you who are such people: continue to be such, and your descendants will never be blotted out. For the Lord has tested you and has enrolled you among our number, and all your descendants will live with the Son of God, for you have partaken of his Spirit."

25.

102. "And from the eighth mountain, where there were many springs and all the Lord's creation drank from the springs, are believers such as these: (2) apostles and teachers who preached to the whole world and who reverently and purely taught the word of the Lord, and who misappropriated nothing for evil desire, but always walked in righteousness and truth, just as they had also received the Holy Spirit. Such people, therefore, will enter in with the angels."

26.

103. "And from the ninth mountain, which was desert, which had on it reptiles and wild beasts that destroy men, are believers such as these: (2) the ones with the spots are deacons who carried out their ministry badly and plundered the livelihood of widows and orphans, and profited themselves from the ministry which they received to carry out. If, therefore, they persist in the same evil desire, they are dead and there is no hope of life for them. But if they turn about and fulfill their ministry purely, they will be able to live. (3) And the ones who are rough are those who have denied and have not returned to their Lord, but have become barren and desertlike; because they do not associate with God's servants but remain alone, they destroy their own souls. (4) For just as a vine left alone along the fence and neglected is ruined and stunted by weeds and eventually becomes wild and is no longer useful to its owner, so also men such as these have despaired of themselves and become useless to their Lord, since they are growing wild. (5) For these, then, there is repentance, unless they are found to have denied from the heart. But if someone is found to have denied from the heart, I do not know if it is possible for him to live. (6) And I do not say this regarding these days, so that someone who denies may receive repentance, for it is impossible for one who denies his Lord from now on to be saved; but for those who denied him long ago repentance seems to be a possibility. If, however, anyone is about to repent, let him do so quickly, before the tower is completed, or else he will be destroyed by the women and put to death. (7) And the short ones are treacherous backbiters; these are the snakes you saw on the mountain. For just as snakes poison and kill a person with their venom, so also the words of such men poison and kill a person. (8) These, therefore, are short in their faith because of their conduct toward one another, but some repented and were saved. And the rest of those who are like this can be saved, if they repent; but if they do not repent, they will meet their death at the hands of those women whose power they have."

27.

104. "And from the tenth mountain, where trees were sheltering some sheep, are believers such as these: (2) bishops,[60] hospitable men, who were always glad to welcome God's servants into their homes without hypocrisy. And the bishops always sheltered the needy and the widows by their ministry without ceasing, and conducted themselves in purity always.

---

60. bishops: so Harmer, following L²E; A reads bishops and.

(3) All these, then, will be sheltered by the Lord forever. The ones, therefore, who have done these things are glorious in God's sight, and their place is already with the angels, if they continue serving the Lord to the end."

28.

105. "And from the eleventh mountain, where trees were full of fruit, each adorned with various kinds of fruit, are believers such as these: (2) those who suffered for the name of the Son of God, who suffered willingly with all their heart, and gave up their lives." (3) "Why then, sir," I said, "do all the trees have fruit, but the fruit of some is more beautiful than others?" "Hear," he said. "All who have ever suffered for the Name are glorious in God's sight, and the sins of all of these have been taken away, because they suffered for the name of the Son of God. But hear why their fruits are varied, and some are superior to others. (4) As many," he said, "as were questioned with torture when brought before the authorities and did not deny, but suffered willingly, these are the more glorious in the Lord's sight; theirs is the superior fruit. But as many as were cowardly and hesitated, and debated in their hearts whether they should deny or confess, and yet suffered, their fruit is of lesser excellence, because this thought arose in their heart; for this thought—that a servant should deny his own lord—is evil. (5) Take care, therefore, you who entertain these ideas, lest this thought persist in your hearts and you die to God. But you who suffer for the sake of the Name ought to glorify God, because God has considered you worthy that you should bear this name and that all your sins be healed. (6) So consider yourselves blessed; indeed, think that you have done a great work if any of you suffers for God's sake. The Lord is granting you life, but you do not realize it; for your sins weighed you down, and if you had not suffered for the sake of the Lord's name, you would have died to God. (7) I say these things to you who are hesitating about denial or confession. Confess that you have the Lord, lest by denying you get thrown in prison. (8) For if the heathen punish their slaves, if one of them denies his master, what do you think the Lord, who has authority over everything, will do to you? Rid your hearts of these thoughts, so that you may live to God forever."

29

106. "And from the twelfth mountain, the white one, are believers such as these: they are as veritable infants, into whose heart nothing evil enters, nor do they even know what wickedness is, but they have remained childlike forever. (2) People such as these, therefore, undoubtedly dwell[61] in the kingdom of God, because they in no way defiled God's commandments, but have continued in innocence all the days of their lives in the same state of mind. (3) All of you, therefore, who continue," he said, "and will be as infants, with no wickedness, will be more glorious than all those who have been mentioned previously, for all infants are glorious in God's sight and stand foremost with him. Blessed are you, therefore, who have cast aside evil from yourselves and clothed yourselves in innocence; you will live to God first of all."

(4) After he finished the parables of the mountains, I said to him: "Sir, now explain to me about the stones that were taken from the plain and put into the building in place of the stones that were taken from the tower, and about the round stones which were placed in the building, and about those that are still round."

30

107. "Hear also," he said, "about all these things. The stones which were taken from the plain and put into the structure of the tower in place of the ones that were rejected are the roots of this white mountain. (2) So since those who believed from the white[62] mountain were all found innocent, the lord of the tower ordered these from the roots of this mountain to be put into the structure[63] of the tower. For he knew that if these

61. *dwell*: so AL²; L¹ reads *will dwell.*

62. *the white*: so ALE; Harmer emends to *this.*

63. *from the roots . . . structure*: or perhaps *to be taken from the roots of this mountain for the construction.*

stones went into the structure of the tower, they would remain bright and not one of them would turn black. (3) But if he had put in stones from the other mountains, he would have had to visit the tower again and cleanse it. But all those who have believed and who will believe have been found to be white, for they are of the same kind. Blessed is this kind, for it is innocent. (4) Hear now also about the stones that are round and bright. All these are also from this white mountain. Now hear why they were found round. Their riches have obscured them a little from the truth and darkened them, yet they never departed from God, nor did any evil word come out of their mouth, but only all justice and true virtue. (5) When, therefore, the Lord discerned that their minds could favor the truth and remain good, he ordered their wealth to be cut away, yet not to be taken away completely, so that they might be able to do some good with that which was left to them, and they will live to God, because they are of the good kind. Therefore they were cut down a little, and placed in the structure of this tower."

31.

108. "But the others, which still remained round and had not been fitted into the structure, because they had not yet received the seal, were returned to their place, for they were found very round. (2) For this world and the vanities of their possessions must be cut away from them, and then they will be fit for the kingdom of God. For it is necessary for them to enter the kingdom of God, because the Lord has blessed this innocent kind. So not one of this kind will perish. Indeed, even though one of them, being tempted by the most wicked devil, does something wrong, he will quickly return to his Lord. (3) I, the angel of repentance, pronounce all of you who are as innocent as infants blessed, because your part is good and honorable in God's sight. (4) So I say to all of you who have received this seal: maintain your sincerity and bear no grudge, and do not persist in your wickedness or the memory of bitter offenses, but become of one spirit and heal these evil divisions and get rid of them from among you, so that the owner of the flocks may rejoice in them. (5) For he will rejoice, if all are found safe and none of them are scattered.[64] But if any of them are found scattered, woe be to the shepherds. (6) But if the shepherds themselves are found scattered, what will they say to the owner of the flock? That they were scattered by the sheep?[65] They will not be believed, for it is an unbelievable thing for the shepherd to be injured by the sheep; instead they will be punished for their lie. And I, too, am a shepherd, and most certainly have to give an account for you."

32.

109. "Mend your ways, therefore, while the tower is still being built. (2) The Lord lives among people who love peace, for peace is truly dear to him, but he keeps his distance from the quarrelsome and those destroyed by wickedness. So return, therefore, your spirit to him whole, just as you received it. (3) Suppose you gave a cleaner a new undamaged garment, wanting to receive it back undamaged, but the cleaner returned it to you torn; would you accept it? Wouldn't you immediately flare up and attack him with insults, saying, 'The garment I gave you was undamaged; why did you tear it and make it useless? Because of the rip you made in it, it can't be used!' Wouldn't you say all this to a cleaner just for a rip he made in your garment? (4) If, therefore, you get so worked up about your garment and complain because you did not get it back undamaged, what do you think the Lord, who gave you the spirit undamaged, will do to you when you return it completely useless, so that it cannot be of any use at all to its Lord? For its use began to be useless when it was corrupted by you. Will not the Lord of this spirit punish you with death because of this deed of yours?" (5) "Certainly," I said, "he will punish all those whom he finds continuing to bear malice." "Do not trample on his mercy," he said, "but rather honor him, because he is so patient

---

64. *and none . . . scattered*: so reads the text as quoted by Antiochus; L (followed by Harmer) omits.

65. *what will . . . the sheep*: so Antiochus; L (followed by Harmer) reads *how will they answer for their flocks? Will they say they were harassed by the sheep?*

with your sins, and is not like you. Repent, therefore, in a way that is beneficial to you."

33.

110. "All these things that are written above I, the shepherd, the angel of repentance, have declared and spoken to God's servants. If, therefore, you believe and hear my words, and walk in them and mend your ways, you will be able to live. But if you persist in wickedness and bearing malice, no one of this kind will live to God. All these things that I had to say to you have now been said." (2) The shepherd himself said to me, "Have you asked me everything?" "Yes, sir," I said. "Then why didn't you ask me about the marks on the stones that were put into the building, why we filled in the marks?" And I said, "I forgot, sir." (3) "Hear now," he said, "about them. They are those who have now heard my commandments and repented with all their hearts. And when the Lord saw that their repentance was good and pure, and that they could continue in it, he ordered their former sins to be wiped out. These marks, then, were their former sins, and they were smoothed over so that they would not show."

Parable 10
1.

111. After I had written this book, the angel who had turned me over to the shepherd came to the house where I was and sat on the couch, and the shepherd stood at his right hand. Then he called me and said to me, (2) "I have turned you and your household," he said, "over to this shepherd, so that you may be protected by him." "Yes, sir," I said. "So if," he said, "you want to be protected from all trouble and cruelty, to be successful in every good deed and word, and to have every virtue of righteousness, walk in his commandments which I have given you, and you will be able to overcome all wickedness. (3) For if you keep his commandments, every evil desire and delight of this world will be subject to you, and success will accompany you in every good undertaking. Embrace his maturity and self-restraint, and tell all people that he is held in great honor and esteem with the Lord and is a ruler of great power and authority in his office. To him alone in the whole world has authority over repentance been given. Does he not seem powerful to you? Yet you despise his maturity and moderation which he demonstrates toward you."

2.

112. I said to him, "Ask him himself, sir, whether I have done anything contrary to his command by which I have offended him since he has been in my house." (2) "I know," he said, "that you have done nothing out of order, and are not about to do so. And so I am saying these things to you so that you may persevere. For he has given me a good report about you. You, therefore, must tell these things to others, that they, too, who have repented or are going to repent may share your attitude, so that he can give a good report about them to me, and I to the Lord." (3) "I myself, sir," I said, "proclaim to everyone the mighty acts of the Lord, for I hope that all who have sinned in the past will gladly repent and regain life if they hear these things." (4) "Then continue in this service and complete it. All who fulfill his commandments will have life, and the one who does so will have great honor with the Lord. But all who do not keep his commandments are running away from their own life and oppose him;[66] they do not follow his commandments, but hand themselves over to death, and every one of them is guilty of his own blood. But I am telling you to obey these commandments, and you will have a cure for your sins."

3.

113. "Moreover, I have sent these virgins to you to live with you, for I saw that they were friendly to you. You have them, therefore, as helpers, so that you may be better able to keep his commandments, for it is impossible for these commandments to be kept without the help of these virgins. I also see that they are glad to be with you; nevertheless I will instruct them not to

---

66. *him*: some MSS add here *such people, however, have their own 'honor' before God. So they oppose him* . . . .

leave your house at all. (2) Only you must keep your house clean, for they will gladly live in a clean house, for they are clean and chaste and industrious, and all have favor with the Lord. If, therefore, they find your house pure, they will remain with you. But if the slightest impurity turns up, they will leave your house at once, for these virgins do not love impurity in any form." (3) I said to him, "I hope, sir, that I will please them, so that they will gladly live in my house always. And just as he to whom you turned me over finds no fault in me, neither will they find any fault in me." (4) He said to the shepherd, "I know that the servant of God wants to live, and will keep these commandments, and will support these virgins in purity." (5) Having said these things he again turned me over to the shepherd, and calling the virgins he said to them,[67] "Since I see that you are glad to live in this man's house, I entrust him and his house to you; do not leave his house at all." And they were glad to hear these words.

4.

114. Then he said to me, "Carry out your ministry manfully; declare the Lord's mighty acts to every person, and you will find favor in this ministry. Whoever, therefore, walks in these commandments will live and will be happy in his life; but whoever neglects them will not live and will be unhappy in his life. (2) Tell everyone who is able to do right not to stop; to work at good works is beneficial to them. Moreover, I say that every person ought to be rescued from distress, for one who is in need and suffers distress in daily life is in great anguish and hardship. (3) So whoever rescues such a person from misery wins great joy for himself. For the one who is harassed by distress of this sort is afflicted with the same anguish as one who is in chains. For many people, because of afflictions of this kind, commit suicide[68] when they can no longer endure them. Therefore the one who knows the misery of such a person and does not rescue him commits a great sin and becomes guilty of

---

67. *And just as he to whom . . . to them*: so reads a fragment of a Greek text (Oxyrhynchus Papyrus 404); the Latin reads somewhat differently.

68. *commit suicide*: lit. *bring death upon themselves*.

that person's blood. (4) Do good works, therefore, you who have received from the Lord, lest while you put off doing them the building of the tower is completed. For it is on your account that the work of building has been interrupted. So unless you act quickly to do right, the tower will be completed, and you will be excluded."

Now when he had finished speaking to me, he rose from the couch and departed, taking the shepherd and the virgins with him, telling me, however, that he would send the shepherd and the virgins back to my house.

The Epistle to Diognetus

INTRODUCTION

The *Epistle to Diognetus*, which Lightfoot, echoing widely shared sentiments, called "the noblest of early Christian writings," is unique among the apostolic fathers in that it is addressed not to "insiders," or fellow believers, as are the rest of the documents in the collection, but to "outsiders." The inclusion of this "epistle" (really more a "tract" or apology in epistolary form) among the apostolic fathers is more a matter of tradition than logic; in terms of both purpose and genre, it may more fittingly be placed among the Christian apologists.

The Christian Apologists

For most of the first century A.D. Christianity was, in the larger world of the Roman Empire, scarcely noticed or noticeable. But in the second century, as Christianity continued to expand rapidly, the Roman state and pagan culture became increasingly aware of what the Roman historian Tacitus called a "pernicious superstition." Because Christian beliefs and practices often ran counter to Greco-Roman values and customs, the church found itself in the midst of an increasingly hostile environment. Rumors that Christians practiced incest, cannibalism, and infant sacrifice were widespread among the general population; the state regarded these "atheists" (for Christians did not believe in the traditional Greek or Roman gods) as a threat to its own well-being and guilty of a capital crime; and educated intellectuals like the satirist Lucian of Samosata, Fronto, the tutor of Marcus Aurelius, and especially Celsus attacked Christian doctrines as a recent and perverse corruption of sound ancient traditions.

In the face of such attacks the Christian apologists (ca. 130–200) sought to defend the faith to which they had committed themselves. They attempted, for example, to dispel the rumors arising out of half-truths and ignorance by describing in general terms Christian beliefs and rituals, to win for the faith a fair hearing from the authorities by asserting their loyalty and value to the government, and to counter the charge of newness by asserting that Christianity was, by virtue of its Jewish heritage, more ancient than Greek philosophy. Writers whose works have survived are Justin Martyr (d. 165), Athenagoras (ca. 170–180), Aristides (ca. 145), Theophilus of Antioch (ca. 180–185), and Tatian (d. 180?). Only fragments have been preserved of the works of Quadratus (ca. 125–130), Melito of Sardis (ca. 170–180?), and Apollinaris of Hierapolis (ca. 170–180), while those of Aristo of Pella (ca. 140?) and Miltiades (ca. 160–180?) have been lost. These, together with the *Epistle to Diognetus*, comprise the Greek Christian apologists.

Authorship and Date

The author of the *Epistle to Diognetus* writes with skill and perception, and is as concerned with style as content. The purpose and plan of the work are fairly clear: the author seeks to answer three specific inquiries regarding the nature and significance of the Christian faith (cf. sec. 1). The answers given betray the author's deep indebtedness to both Hellenism and Judaism, but everything that has been borrowed has been put to use within a distinctly Christian perspective and for a clear missionary purpose. In many respects the author anticipates later Alexandrian writers.

Beyond this, much about this document remains a mystery. The author is anonymous, the identity of the recipient is uncertain, the date is unknown, the ending is missing, and, rather surprisingly, no ancient or medieval writer is known to have mentioned it.

The fact notwithstanding that no adequate means of determining the authorship of this document exists, numerous suggestions have been made; the names of Hippolytus of Rome, Theophilus of Antioch, and Pantaenus of Alexandria are among the less improbable of those proposed. More intriguing, however, is the suggestion that this document is the lost apology by

Quadratus.[1] Eusebius (*Church History* 4.3.1–2) preserves all that is known about him:

> When Trajan had reigned for nineteen and a half years, Aelius Hadrian succeeded to the imperial authority. To him Quadratus addressed a treatise, composing an apology for our religion because some evil men were trying to trouble the Christians. It is still extant among many of the brothers, and we ourselves have a copy. From it can be seen the clear proof of his intellect and apostolic orthodoxy. He reveals his early date by what he says in his own words as follows:
> "But the works of our Savior were always present, for they were true; those who were healed and those who rose from the dead were seen not only when they were healed and when they were raised, but were constantly present, and not only while the Savior was living, but even after he had gone they were alive for a long time, so that some of them survived to our own time."

While it is true that this sentence does not occur in the *Epistle to Diognetus*, there is a gap between verses 6 and 7 of section 7 into which it would fit very well. The evidence supporting this hypothesis, however, is all circumstantial, and the question must be left open.

Nothing is known about the addressee. If Quadratus is the author, then the recipient is to be identified with Hadrian; others suggest he was one of the teachers of Marcus Aurelius. It may be, however, that "Diognetus" is only a fictional character, created to ask the questions that the anonymous author wished to address.

The date of the document is a matter of conjecture as well. Reasonable suggestions range from 117 to after 313. Between 150 and 225 seems the most likely; Lightfoot, Meecham, and Frend favor the earlier of these dates,[2] while R. M. Grant places it somewhat later.[3]

1. P. Andriessen, "The Authorship of the Epistula ad Diognetum," *Vigiliae Christianae* 1 (1947): 129–36.

2. Lightfoot, *Apostolic Fathers*, 248; H. G. Meecham, *The Epistle to Diognetus* (Manchester: University of Manchester Press, 1949), 19; Frend, *Rise of Christianity*, 236, 261 n. 24 (the evidence suggests "a relatively early date, not later than A.D. 150").

3. R. M. Grant, *Greek Apologists of the Second Century* (Philadelphia: Westminster, 1988), 178–79.

What has been said thus far about authorship and date applies only to sections 1–10, for there is a major break in the text at that point (see below, pp. 292–93), and the two sections that follow almost certainly belong to some other work. Apparently the manuscript from which the scribe was copying was missing the leaves containing the end of the *Epistle to Diognetus* and the beginning of this other document. It is not likely, however, that much of the epistle is missing, for the author has essentially covered the points raised in the opening lines.

Even more than in the case of the *Epistle to Diognetus*, the authorship and date of this second document is entirely a matter of conjecture. Hippolytus of Rome (ca. 170–236) is frequently suggested; Lightfoot hazards the conjecture that it was Pantaenus (d. ca. 190), who preceded Clement of Alexandria as head of the catechetical school in that city.[4]

The Text

The text of the *Epistle to Diognetus* was preserved in a single manuscript dating from the thirteenth or fourteenth century, Codex Argentoratensis Graec. ix (= A), which ultimately found a home in Strasbourg. But even this manuscript is no longer extant, for it was lost to fire in 1870 when Strasbourg was shelled during the Franco-German War. Fortunately, competent scholars had made a number of copies and issued printed editions of the manuscript prior to its destruction, so the text of this unique document has been preserved.

Unfortunately, the exemplar from which Codex Argentoratensis was copied appears to have been defective at a number of points, and so scholars have had to resort to conjecture more often than usual in order to attempt to make sense of the text. The notes accompanying the following translation reflect this state of affairs.

---

4. Lightfoot, *Apostolic Fathers*, 248–49.

BIBLIOGRAPHY

Brändle, R. *Die Ethik der "Schrift An Diognet": Eine Wiederaufnahme paulinischer und johanneischer Theologie am Ausgang des zweiten Jahrhunderts.* Zürich, 1975.

Fairweather, Eugene R. "The So-called Letter to Diognetus." In *Early Christian Fathers*, edited by C. C. Richardson, 205–24. Philadelphia: Westminster, 1953. Repr. Macmillan, 1970.

Grant, Robert M. *Greek Apologists of the Second Century.* Philadelphia: Westminster, 1988.

Kleist, James A. *The Didache. The Epistle of Barnabas. The Epistles and the Martyrdom of St. Polycarp. The Fragments of Papias. The Epistle to Diognetus.* Ancient Christian Writers, vol. 6. Westminster, Md.: Newman, 1948.

Marrou, H. I. *À Diognète.* [2d ed.] repr. avec supplement. Paris: Cerf, 1965.

Meecham, Henry G. *The Epistle to Diognetus. The Greek Text with Introduction, Translation and Notes.* Manchester: University of Manchester Press, 1949.

The Epistle to Diognetus

1. Since I see, most excellent Diognetus, that you are extremely interested in learning about the religion of the Christians and are asking very clear and careful questions about them—specifically, what God do they believe in and how do they worship him, so that they all disregard the world and despise death, neither recognizing those who are considered to be gods by the Greeks nor observing the superstition of the Jews; what is the nature of the heartfelt love they have for one another; and why has this new race of men or way of life come into the world we live in now and not before?—I gladly welcome this interest of yours, and I ask God, who empowers us both to speak and to listen, that I may be enabled to speak in such a way that you will derive the greatest possible benefit from listening, and that you may listen in such a way that the speaker will have no regrets.

2. Come, then, clear your mind of all its prejudices and cast aside the custom that deceives you, and become a new man, as it were, from the beginning, as if you were about to hear a new message, even as you yourself admit. See not only with your eyes but also with your intellect what substance or what form those whom you call and regard as gods happen to have. (2) Is not one of them stone, like that which we walk upon, and another bronze, no better than the utensils that have been forged for our use, and another wood, already rotted away, and another silver, which needs a watchman to guard it lest it be stolen, and another iron, corroded by rust, and another pottery, not a bit more attractive than that made for the most unmentionable use? (3) Are not all these made of perishable matter? Are they not forged by iron and fire? Did not the sculptor make one of them, and the coppersmith another, the silversmith another, and the potter yet another? Before they were shaped by the skills of these craftsmen into the form they have,[1] was it not possible—indeed, is it not even now possible—for each of them to have been given a different form?[2] Might not the ordinary utensils now formed out of the same material be made similar to such images as these, if the same craftsmen were available? (4) Again, could not these things which are now worshiped by you be made by men into utensils like the rest? Are they not all deaf and blind, without souls, without feelings, without movement? Do they not all rot, do they not all decay? (5) These are the things you call gods; you serve them, you worship them, and in the end you become like them. (6) This is why you hate the Christians: because they do not consider these objects to be gods. (7) For do not you yourselves, who now regard and worship them as gods,[3] in fact much more despise them? Are you not mocking and insulting them much more when you leave unguarded the stone or pottery gods you worship but lock up the silver and gold ones at night and post guards by them during the day, lest they be stolen? (8) And as for the honors that you think you are offering them: if they are aware of them, then you are in fact insulting them; but if they are not aware, then you are showing them up by worshiping them with the blood and fat of victims. (9) Let one of you undergo this treatment, let someone allow these things to be done to him! Why, there is not a single individual who would willingly submit to such punishment, for a human being has feelings and reason; but the stone does submit, for it has no feeling. Therefore you disprove its ability to feel.[4] (10) Well, I could say many other things about the fact that Christians are not enslaved to such gods, but if these arguments should seem insufficient to anyone, then I think it is useless to say more.

3. And next I suppose that you are especially anxious to hear why Christians do not worship in the same way as the

---

1. *the form they have*: so A; Harmer (following Böhl) emends to *this form*.

2. *possible . . . form*: so A and most editors; Harmer (following Lachmann) reads *possible for each of them to have been changed in form to represent something else.*

3. *who . . . gods*: so Harmer (following Lachmann's emendation). Others, adopting a different emendation, read *who think and suppose that you are praising them.*

4. *Therefore . . . feel*: or possibly *Do you not, therefore, disprove its ability to feel?*

Jews. (2) The Jews indeed, insofar as they abstain from the kind of worship described above, rightly claim to worship the one God of the universe and to think of him as Master; but insofar as they offer this worship to him in the same way as those already described, they are altogether mistaken. (3) For whereas the Greeks provide an example of their stupidity by offering things to senseless and deaf images, the Jews, thinking that they are offering these things to God as if he were in need of them, could rightly consider it folly rather than worship. (4) For he who made the heaven and the earth and all that is in them, and provides us all with what we need, cannot himself need any of the things that he himself provides to those who imagine that they are giving to him. (5) In any case, those who imagine that they are offering sacrifices to him by means of blood and fat and whole burnt offerings and are honoring him with these tokens of respect do not seem to me to be the least bit different from those who show the same respect to deaf images: the latter make offerings to things unable to receive the honor, while the former think they offer it to the One who is in need of nothing.

4. But with regard to their qualms about meats, and superstition concerning the Sabbath, and pride in circumcision, and hypocrisy about fasting and new moons, I doubt that you need to learn from me that they are ridiculous and not worth discussing. (2) For is it not unlawful to accept some of the things created by God for human use as created good but to refuse others as useless and superfluous? (3) And is it not impious to slander God, as though he forbids us to do any good thing on the Sabbath day? (4) And is it not also ridiculous to take pride in the mutilation of the flesh as a sign of election, as though they were especially beloved by God because of this? (5) And as for the way they watch the stars and the moon, so as to observe months and days, and to make distinctions between the changing seasons ordained by God, making some into feasts and others into times of mourning according to their own inclinations, who would regard this as an example of godliness and not much more of a lack of understanding? (6) So then, I think you have been sufficiently instructed to realize that the Christians are right to keep their distance from the thoughtlessness and deception common to both groups and from the fussiness and pride of the Jews. But as for the mystery of the Christian's own religion, do not expect to be able to learn this from man.

5. For Christians are not distinguished from the rest of humanity by country, language, or custom. (2) For nowhere do they live in cities of their own, nor do they speak some unusual dialect, nor do they practice an eccentric life-style. (3) This teaching of theirs has not been discovered by the thought and reflection of ingenious men, nor do they promote any human doctrine, as some do. (4) But while they live in both Greek and barbarian cities, as each one's lot was cast, and follow the local customs in dress and food and other aspects of life, at the same time they demonstrate the remarkable and admittedly unusual character of their own citizenship. (5) They live in their own countries, but only as aliens; they participate in everything as citizens, and endure everything as foreigners. Every foreign country is their fatherland, and every fatherland is foreign. (6) They marry like everyone else, and have children, but they do not expose their offspring. (7) They share their food but not their wives. (8) They are "in the flesh," but they do not live "according to the flesh." (9) They live on earth, but their citizenship is in heaven. (10) They obey the established laws; indeed in their private lives they transcend the laws. (11) They love everyone, and by everyone they are persecuted. (12) They are unknown, yet they are condemned; they are put to death, yet they are brought to life. (13) They are poor, yet they make many rich; they are in need of everything, yet they abound in everything. (14) They are dishonored, yet they are glorified in their dishonor; they are slandered, yet they are vindicated. (15) They are cursed, yet they bless; they are insulted, yet they offer respect. (16) When they do good, they are punished as evildoers; when they are punished, they rejoice as though brought to life. (17) By the Jews they are assaulted as foreigners, and by the Greeks they are persecuted, yet those who hate them are unable to give a reason for their hostility.

6. In a word, what the soul is to the body, Christians are to the world. (2) The soul is dispersed through all the members of the body, and Christians throughout the cities of the world. (3) The soul dwells in the body, but is not of the body; likewise Christians dwell in the world, but are not of the world. (4) The soul, which is invisible, is confined in the body, which is visible; in the same way, Christians are recognized as being in the world, and yet their religion remains invisible. (5) The flesh hates the soul and wages war against it, even though it has suffered no wrong, because it is hindered from indulging in its pleasures; so also the world hates the Christians, even though it has suffered no wrong, because they set themselves against its pleasures. (6) The soul loves the flesh that hates it, and its members, and Christians love those who hate them. (7) The soul is enclosed in the body, but it holds the body together; and though Christians are detained in the world as if in a prison, they in fact hold the world together. (8) The soul, which is immortal, lives in a mortal dwelling; similarly Christians live as strangers amidst perishable things, while waiting for the imperishable in heaven. (9) The soul, when poorly treated with respect to food and drink, becomes all the better; and so Christians when punished daily increase more and more. (10) Such is the important position to which God has appointed them, and it is not right for them to decline it.

7. For this is, as I said, no earthly discovery that was committed to them, nor some mortal idea that they consider to be worth guarding so carefully, nor have they been entrusted with the administration of merely human mysteries. (2) On the contrary, the omnipotent Creator of all, the invisible God himself, established among men the truth and the holy, incomprehensible word from heaven and fixed it firmly in their hearts, not, as one might imagine, by sending to men some subordinate, or angel or ruler or one of those who manage earthly matters, or one of those entrusted with the administration of things in heaven, but the Designer and Creator of the universe himself, by whom he created the heavens, by whom he enclosed the sea within its proper bounds, whose mysteries all the elements faithfully observe, from whom the sun has received the measure of the daily courses to keep, whom the moon obeys as he commands it to shine by night, whom the stars obey as they follow the course of the moon, by whom all things have been ordered and determined and placed in subjection, including the heavens and the things in the heavens, the earth and the things in the earth, the sea and the things in the sea, fire, air, abyss, the things in the heights, the things in the depths, the things in between—this one he sent to them! (3) But perhaps he sent

him, as a man might suppose, to rule by tyranny, fear, and terror? (4) Certainly not! On the contrary, he sent him in gentleness and meekness, as a king might send his son who is a king; he sent him as God; he sent him as a man to men. When he sent him, he did so as one who saves by persuasion, not compulsion, for compulsion is no attribute of God. (5) When he sent him, he did so as one calling, not pursuing; when he sent him, he did so as one loving, not judging. (6) For he will send him as Judge, and who will endure his coming? . . . [5] (7) [Do you not see] how they are thrown to wild beasts to make them deny the Lord, and yet are not conquered? (8) Do you not see that as more of them are punished, the more others increase? (9) These things do not look like the works of man; they are the power of God, they are proofs of his presence.

8. For what man had any knowledge at all of what God was, before he came? (2) Or do you accept the empty and nonsensical statements of those pretentious philosophers, some of whom said that God was fire (the very thing they are headed for, they call God!), and others, water, and still others some other one of the elements created by God. (3) And yet, if any of these statements is worthy of acceptance, then every one of the other created things might just as well be declared to be God. (4) No, these things are merely the illusions and deceit of the magicians. (5) No one has either seen or recognized him, but he has revealed himself. (6) And he revealed himself through faith, which is the only means by which it is permitted to see God. (7) For God, the Master and Creator of the universe, who made all things and arranged them in order, was not only tender-hearted but also very patient. (8) Indeed, so he always was and is and will be, kind, good, without anger, and true, and he alone is good. (9) And after conceiving a great and marvelous plan, he communicated it to his Child alone. (10) Now as long as he kept it a secret and guarded his wise design, he seemed to neglect and be unconcerned about us, (11) but when he revealed it through his beloved Child and made known the things pre-

---

5. There is an obvious break in the text at this point. According to a marginal note added by the copyist, the break already existed in the document from which he was copying. The following words in brackets were supplied by Henri Estienne (Stephanus), the first editor of the MS.

pared from the beginning, he gave us everything at once, both to share in his benefits and to see and understand things which none of us ever would have expected.

9. So then, having already planned everything in his mind together with his Child, he permitted us during the former time to be carried away by undisciplined impulses as we desired, led astray by pleasures and lusts, not at all because he took delight in our sins, but because he was patient; not because he approved of that former season of unrighteousness, but because he was creating the present season of righteousness, in order that we who in the former time were convicted by our own deeds as unworthy of life might now by the goodness of God be made worthy, and, having clearly demonstrated our inability to enter the kingdom of God on our own, might be enabled to do so by God's power. (2) But when our unrighteousness was fulfilled, and it had been made perfectly clear that its wages—punishment and death—were to be expected, then the season arrived during which God had decided to reveal at last his goodness and power (oh, the surpassing kindness and love of God!). He did not hate us, or reject us, or bear a grudge against us; instead he was patient and forbearing; in his mercy he took upon himself our sins; he himself gave up his own Son as a ransom for us, the holy one for the lawless, the guiltless for the guilty, "the just for the unjust,"[6] the incorruptible for the corruptible, the immortal for the mortal. (3) For what else but his righteousness could have covered our sins? (4) In whom was it possible for us, the lawless and ungodly, to be justified, except in the Son of God alone? (5) O the sweet exchange, O the incomprehensible work of God, O the unexpected blessings, that the sinfulness of many should be hidden in one righteous man, while the righteousness of one should justify many sinners! (6) Having demonstrated, therefore, in the former time the powerlessness of our nature to obtain life, and having now revealed the Savior's power to save even the powerless, he willed that for both these reasons we should believe in his goodness and regard him as nurse, father, teacher, counselor,

6. Cf. 1 Pet. 3:18.

healer, mind, light, honor, glory, strength, life, and not be anxious about food and clothing.[7]

10. If this faith is what you too long for, then first of all you must acquire[8] full knowledge of the Father. (2) For God loved men, for whose sake he made the world, to whom he subjected everything on earth, to whom he gave reason, to whom he gave mind; them alone he permitted to look up to heaven,[9] them he created in his own image, to them he sent his one and only Son, to them he promised the kingdom in heaven, which he will give to those who have loved him. (3) And when you have acquired this knowledge, with what joy do you think you will be filled, or how will you love him who so loved you first? (4) By loving him you will be an imitator of his goodness. And do not be surprised that a person can become an imitator of God; he can, if God is willing. (5) For happiness is not a matter of lording it over one's neighbors, or desiring to have more than weaker men, or possessing wealth and using force against one's inferiors. No one is able to imitate God in these matters; on the contrary, these things are alien to his greatness. (6) But whoever takes upon himself his neighbor's burden, whoever wishes to benefit another who is worse off in something in which he himself is better off, whoever provides to those in need things that he has received from God, and thus becomes a god to those who receive them, this one is an imitator of God. (7) Then you will see that though your lot is on earth, God lives[10] in heaven, then you will begin to declare the mysteries of God, then you will both love and admire those who are punished because they refuse to deny God, then you will condemn the deceit and the error of the world, when you realize what the true life in heaven is, when you despise the apparent death here on earth, when you fear the real death, which is reserved for those who will be condemned to the eternal fire which will punish to the very end those delivered to it. (8) Then you will admire those

7. *and not be . . . clothing*: Harmer and Meecham drop this phrase from the text, regarding it as a later insertion based on Matt. 6:25, 28, 31.

8. *then . . . acquire*: so Harmer and others, following Gebhardt's conjecture (*katalabe*). If the reading of the MS (*kai labes*, "and if you first acquire") is adopted, then apparently there would be another gap in the text at this point.

9. *heaven*: so Harmer (following Lachmann); the MS reads *him*.

10. *lives*: or possibly *rules*.

who for righteousness' sake endure the transitory fire, and you
will consider them blessed, when you comprehend that other
fire. . . .[11]

11 I am not talking about strange things, nor am I engaged in
irrational speculation, but having been a disciple of apostles, I
am now becoming a teacher of the Gentiles. To those who are
becoming disciples of the truth I try to minister in a worthy
manner the teachings that have been handed down. (2) Indeed,
does anyone who has been rightly taught and has come to love
the Word not seek to learn exactly the things openly made
known by the Word to disciples? To them the Word appeared and
revealed these things, speaking quite plainly as he did so;
though not understood by unbelievers, he explained them to
disciples who, being regarded as faithful by him, learned the
mysteries of the Father. (3) This is why he sent the Word,
namely, that he might appear to the world; though dishonored
by the chosen people, he was preached by apostles and believed
in by Gentiles. (4) This is he who was from the beginning, who
appeared as new yet proved to be old, and is always young as he is
born in the hearts of saints. (5) This is the Eternal One, who
today is accounted a Son, through whom the church is enriched
and grace is unfolded and multiplied among the saints, grace
which gives understanding, reveals mysteries, announces seasons, rejoices over the faithful, is given to those who seek—
those, that is, by whom the pledges of faith are not broken nor
the boundaries set by the fathers transgressed. (6) Then the reverence of the law is praised in song, and the grace of the prophets is
recognized, and the faith of the Gospels is established, and the
tradition of the apostles is preserved, and the joy[12] of the church
exults. (7) If you do not grieve this grace, you will understand
what the Word has to say, through whomever he chooses, whenever he wishes. (8) For we are simply sharing with you whatever
we have been prompted to speak with such difficulty by the will

11. The text breaks off here, as a marginal note in the MS indicates. The
missing portion, however, was probably not very long, inasmuch as the author
has essentially answered the questions raised in the opening lines of the epistle. Cf. p. 294 above.

12. *joy*: so Harmer, following Lachmann's emendation (*chara*). The MS
(followed by many editors) reads *grace* (*charis*).

of the commanding Word, being motivated as well by a love for the things that have been revealed to us.

12. When you have read these truths and listened[13] attentively to them, you will know what God bestows on those who love him as they should, who become a paradise of delight, raising up in themselves a flourishing tree bearing all kinds of fruit, who are adorned[14] with various fruits. (2) For in this garden a tree of knowledge and a tree of life have been planted. But the tree of knowledge does not kill; on the contrary, disobedience kills. (3) For it is not without significance that the Scriptures record that God in the beginning planted a tree of knowledge and a tree of life in the midst of Paradise, thereby revealing that life is through knowledge. Because our first parents did not use it purely, they were left naked[15] by the deceit of the serpent. (4) For there is neither life without knowledge, nor sound knowledge without true life; therefore each tree stands planted near the other. (5) Discerning the significance of this, the apostle blamed the knowledge which is exercised apart from the truth of the commandment which leads to life and said, "knowledge puffs up, but love builds up."[16] (6) For the one who thinks he knows anything without the true knowledge that is confirmed by the life knows nothing; he is deceived by the serpent, because he did not love life. But the one who reverently has gained knowledge and seeks life plants in hope, anticipating fruit. (7) Let your heart be knowledge, and your life the true teaching,[17] fully comprehended. (8) If this is the tree you cultivate, and whose fruit you pick, then you will always be harvesting the things that God desires, things that the serpent cannot touch and deceit cannot infect. Nor is Eve corrupted; instead, a virgin is trusted.[18] (9) Furthermore, salvation is made

---

13. *read . . . listened*: in antiquity it was apparently the custom to read aloud, even when alone; cf. Acts 8:30; 2 Macc. 15:39: "the style of the story delights the ears of those who read the work."

14. *raising up . . . adorned*: or alternatively with Lightfoot *a flourishing tree bearing all kinds of fruit, growing up in themselves and adorned.*

15. *left naked*: or perhaps *stripped of it.*

16. 1 Cor. 8:1.

17. *teaching*: or possibly *reason* or *word.*

18. *a virgin is trusted*: or possibly (with Lightfoot and others) *she is believed on as a virgin.*

known, and apostles are instructed,[19] and the Passover of the
Lord goes forward, and the congregations are gathered together,
and all things are arranged in order,[20] and the Word rejoices as
he teaches the saints, the Word through whom the Father is
glorified. To him be glory forever. Amen.

19. *instructed*: or given *understanding*, or perhaps *interpreted*.

20. *congregations . . . order*: Both text and meaning are uncertain. The MS
reads "candles (*kēroi*) are gathered together and is arranged in order (*meta
kosmou*)." The problem is that the second verb is singular and does not agree
with the plural subject, *candles*. Some translators and editors simply change
the singular verb ending (*-etai*) to plural (*-ontai*), "are arranged." Others make
the same change to the verb and also change the subject to "seasons"(*kairoi*).
Goodspeed and Lake make these same two changes but give a different sense to
the last phrase in the sentence: instead of "arranged in order," they translate
meta kosmou as "harmonized with the world." The translation given above
reflects Lightfoot's adoption of two suggestions by Bunsen: (1) he changes *kēroi*
to *klēroi* which Lightfoot rendered as "congregations"; and (2) rather than
making the second verb plural, he supplies a second subject (*panta*, "all
things") that is grammatically suitable for the verb as it is found in the MS.

The Fragments of Papias

INTRODUCTION

Papias, bishop of Hierapolis in Asia Minor, who probably is best known as the author of the five-volume work entitled *Expositions of the Sayings of the Lord*, appears to have been well respected and widely quoted during the early centuries of the church. Yet today only scattered fragments of his work survive, and then only as quotations embedded in later writings. Furthermore, next to nothing is known about this man who by all appearances was one of the leading figures of the postapostolic era.

It is not known when Papias was born or when he died. He appears to have been a contemporary of Polycarp, whose dates (ca. A.D. 70 to 155–160; cf. above, pp. 119, 131–32 provide a general indication of when Papias lived. Circumstantial evidence (such as his name and his rhetorical style) suggests that he was a native of the area where he served as bishop. He probably published his magnum opus within a decade or so of A.D. 130.

Papias provides some of the very earliest testimony about the early church's stance on the millennium and the authorship of Matthew, Mark, John, and Revelation. For this reason a great deal of interest and attention has been focused on what he has to say. But many of his statements (e.g., that Matthew "composed" the "oracles" in the "Hebrew language") are more baffling than helpful, and have sparked a great deal of discussion about their meaning and significance, neither of which is obvious or clear.

For all the confusion and uncertainty he engenders, Papias does nevertheless clearly and forcibly remind us that (1) the written Gospels represent only a fraction of the material by and about Jesus in circulation in the last half of the first and first half of the second centuries (cf. John 20:30; 21:25); (2) even

307

after the Gospels were written, oral traditions continued to circulate and to influence the written text; and (3) oral tradition was often more highly valued than written materials in a cultural setting that relied upon and trusted memory far more than is customary today. These points, rather than his comments about authorship, may in fact be Papias's most valuable contribution toward a reconstruction of the early history of the transmission and reception of the Gospel narratives.

The Fragments

The various collections of fragments that have been published differ with respect to size, numbering and sequence,[1] and principles of selection. The Funk–Bihlmeyer edition,[2] for example, limits itself to quotations from and references to Papias's lost work, whereas Lightfoot's more inclusive collection includes any reports about his life and theological opinions that have been preserved. To his collection there have been added for this edition some additional fragments (nos. 21–26) that have subsequently come to light. Thus the following collection of fragments contains virtually everything by or about Papias that has survived and that identifies him by name.

Fragment 4 is unique to Lightfoot's collection and calls for special comment. Lightfoot included the story of Jesus and the woman taken in adultery (= John 7:53–8:11, a later addition to the Gospel[3]) among the items attributed to Papias. He did so on the strength of the similarity of the wording in fragment 3 (a "woman accused of many sins") and the unusual form of the story as found in certain manuscripts of the New Testament, especially Codex Bezae Cantabrigiensis, the earliest (fifth c.) New Testament manuscript to contain the account.

It is unlikely, however, that Papias knew the story in precisely this form, inasmuch as it now appears that there were at

1. A concordance of several of the numbering systems is given below, p. 312.

2. Karl Bihlmeyer, *Die apostolischen Väter. Neubearbeitung der Funkschen Ausgabe*, 3d ed., revised by W. Schneemelcher (Tübingen: Mohr/Siebeck, 1970), 133–40; translation in Schoedel, *Polycarp*, 94–123.

3. See any major commentary on the Gospel of John for a discussion of this point.

least two independent stories about Jesus and a sinful woman in circulation among Christians in the first two centuries of the church, and that the traditional form found in many New Testament manuscripts may well represent a conflation of two independent shorter, earlier versions of the incident.[4] One form, apparently found in the *Gospel According to the Hebrews*, was also known to Didymus the Blind, a late fourth-century Alexandrian biblical scholar, who provides the following account:

> We find, therefore, in certain gospels [the following story]. A woman, it says, was condemned by the Jews for a sin and was being sent to be stoned in the place where that was customary to happen. The saviour, it says, when he saw her and observed that they were ready to stone her, said to those who were about to cast stones, "He who has not sinned, let him take a stone and cast it." If anyone is conscious in himself not to have sinned, let him take up a stone and smite her. And no one dared. Since they knew in themselves and perceived that they themselves were guilty in some things, they did not dare to strike her.[5]

Notice the most distinctive elements: (1) the woman was already condemned; (2) Jesus is the one who takes the initiative to intervene; and (3) there is no conversation between Jesus and the woman.

Another form is paraphrased in the *Didascalia Apostolorum*, a Greek document written in Syria, probably near the beginning of the third century.[6] In the course of encouraging bishops to receive repentant sinners back into the congregation, the author writes:

> But if you do not receive him who repents, because you are without mercy, you shall sin against the Lord God. For you do not obey our Saviour and our God, to do as even He did with her who had sinned, whom the elders placed before Him, leaving the judgement in His hands, and departed. But He, the searcher of

4. Bart D. Ehrman, "Jesus and the Adulteress," *New Testament Studies* 34 (1988): 24–44.

5. Ibid., 25.

6. J. Quasten, *Patrology*, 3 vols. (Westminster, Md.: Newman, 1951–1960), 2:147–52.

hearts, asked her and said to her: "Have the elders condemned you, my daughter?" She says to him: "Nay, Lord." And he said unto her: "Go, neither do I condemn you." (VIII, ii 24)[7]

Again note the distinctive elements: (1) "elders" bring the woman to Jesus; (2) she had not yet been condemned; and (3) Jesus speaks only to the woman.[8]

Which of these forms of the story did Papias know? According to Eusebius (see fragment 3), Papias relates an account about a "woman accused of many sins before the Lord." That is, the woman was brought to Jesus but was not yet condemned. This suggests that Papias knew the *Didascalia* form of the story. In fragment 23, however, Papias is credited with a story in which an uncondemned woman is led to Jesus (corroborating Eusebius), but in which Jesus also converses with the Jewish leaders. This combination of features (trial scene, conversation with Jewish leaders) occurs only in the traditional form of the story. Thus the evidence is mixed. With regard to fragment 23 it may be that the author simply assumed that Papias knew the same (and probably only) form of the story that he himself knew, namely the traditional one.[9] In this case his testimony would be of no value. In short, it seems more likely that Papias knew the *Didascalia* form of the story, but it is not possible to be certain.

In view of this uncertainty regarding which of the various forms of the story Papias knew (or, according to fragment 26, wrote!) it seems best to view fragment 4 as the traditional form of the story, and not necessarily the form known to Papias. The translation of the story given below follows the text of Codex Bezae, inasmuch as it preserves the earliest extant text of the traditional form and agrees with Papias in mentioning a woman caught in "sin" rather than adultery. Within this story, however, the elements that are parallel to the *Didascalia* form that Papias may have known have been placed in italics, and the elements that appear to be derived from the form known to

7. Ehrman, "Jesus and the Adulteress," 33.

8. Against the suggestion that the author paraphrases the traditional form, see Ehrman, "Jesus and the Adulteress," 33–34, esp. nn. 42, 44.

9. Note that Eusebius in fragment 3 made exactly the same mistake with respect to the *Gospel According to the Hebrews*.

Didymus and the *Gospel According to the Hebrews* have been placed inside brackets.

The "Traditions of the Elders"

In his edition Lightfoot included a collection of the "reliques of the elders." These are traditions preserved in Irenaeus which he variously attributes to "the divine elder," "one better than we are," "one of the ancients," "a certain elder," "one who was before us," and so on. Strictly speaking, these fragments belong to the study of Irenaeus rather than the apostolic fathers.

Reasons have been advanced, however, for thinking that some of these "traditions of the elders" were mediated to Irenaeus through Papias.[10] These have been extracted from Lightfoot's larger collection and are presented below. They remain, however, anonymous fragments whose present wording owes an undeterminable debt to Irenaeus, and must be used with caution.

BIBLIOGRAPHY

Körtner, Ulrich H. J. *Papias von Hierapolis. Ein Beitrag zur Geschichte des frühen Christentums.* Göttingen: Vandenhoeck and Ruprecht, 1983.

Kürzinger, Josef. *Papias von Hierapolis und die Evangelien des Neuen Testaments.* Regensburg: Verlag Friedrich Pustet, 1983.

Schoedel, W. R. *Polycarp, Martyrdom of Polycarp, Fragments of Papias.* The Apostolic Fathers, vol 5. Camden, N.J.: Nelson, 1967.

Walls, A. F. "Papais and Oral Tradition." *Vigiliae Christianae* 21 (1967): 137–40.

10. F. Loofs, *Theophilus von Antiochien Adversus Marcionem und die anderen theologischen Quellen bei Irenaeus* (*Texte und Untersuchungen* 46; Leipzig: Hinrichs, 1930), 311–12; earlier Lightfoot, *Essays*, 194–202. Cf. Schoedel, *Polycarp*, 124. Against connecting them with Papias, see T. Zahn, *Forschungen zur Geschichte des neutestamentlichen Kanons.* Vol. 6, *I. Apostel und Apostelschüler in der Provinz Asien. II. Brüder und Vettern Jesu* (Leipzig: A. Deichert'sche Verlagsbuchhandlung, 1900), 88–94.

A CONCORDANCE OF FRAGMENTS
IN VARIOUS COLLECTIONS

1. The Fragments of Papias

Lightfoot/Holmes	Funk/Bihlmeyer (Schoedel)	Preuschen[11]	Kürzinger	Körtner
1	—	1	cf. 6	2
2	—	2	2	4
3	2	3	4	5
4	—	—	—	—
5	11	5	16	10
6	12	6	17	17
7	—	7a	7	7
8	—	7b	8	8
9	—	7c	9	9
10	5	8	12	11
11	4	9	13	12
12	6	10	14	15
13	7	11	15	16
14	1	12	1	1
15	8	4	10	13
16	9	13	11	14
17	10	14	18	18
18	3	16	5	6
19	13	17	21	20
20	—	18	20	21
21	—	—	—	3
22	—	15	19	19
23	—	—	22	—
24	—	—	23	—
25	—	cf. 20	24	—
26	—	—	25	—

2. The "Traditions of the Elders"

Lightfoot/Holmes	Lightfoot	Schoedel
1	4	1
2	13	2
3	15	3
4	16	4
5	17	5+6

11. E. Preuschen, *Antilegomena. Die Reste der ausserkanonischen Evangelien und urchristlichen Überlieferungen herausgegeben und übersetzt.* 2d ed. (Giessen: Töpelmann, 1905), 91–99, 195–202.

The Fragments of Papias

1

Irenaeus and others record that John, the theologian and apostle, survived until the time of Trajan. After this Papias of Hierapolis and Polycarp, bishop of Smyrna, both of whom had heard him, became well known.

Eusebius (ca. 260–340), Chronicle[1]

2

At this time there flourished in Asia Polycarp, the disciple of the apostles, who had been appointed to the bishopric of the church in Smyrna by the eyewitnesses and ministers of the Lord. At this time Papias, who was himself bishop of the diocese of Hierapolis, became well known.

Eusebius, Church History 3.36.1–2

3

Five books of Papias are in circulation, which are entitled "Expositions of the Sayings of the Lord." Irenaeus also mentions these as the only works written by him, saying something like this: "Papias, a man of the early period, who was a hearer of John and a companion of Polycarp, bears witness to these things in writing in the fourth of his books. For there are five books composed by him." (2) So says Irenaeus. Yet Papias himself, in the preface to his discourses, indicates that he was by no means a hearer or eyewitness of the holy apostles, but shows by the language he uses that he received the matters of the faith from those who had known them:

---

1. Edited by A. Schoene, 2 vols. (1866–1875), 2:162; also edited by R. Helm (2d ed., 1956; *GCS* vol. 47) and J. K. Fotheringham (London, 1923).

(3) I will not hesitate to set down for you, along with my interpretations, everything I carefully learned then from the elders and carefully remembered, guaranteeing their truth. For unlike most people I did not enjoy those who have a great deal to say, but those who teach the truth. Nor did I enjoy those who recall someone else's commandments, but those who remember the commandments given by the Lord to the faith and proceeding from the truth itself. (4) And if by chance someone who had been a follower of the elders should come my way, I inquired about the words of the elders—what Andrew or Peter said, or Philip, or Thomas or James, or John or Matthew or any other of the Lord's disciples, and whatever Aristion and the elder John, the Lord's disciples, were saying.[2] For I did not think that information from books would profit me as much as information from a living and abiding[3] voice.

(5) Here it is worth noting that he lists the name of John twice. The first he mentions in connection with Peter and James and Matthew and the rest of the apostles, clearly meaning the Evangelist, but he classes the other John with others outside the number of the apostles by changing the wording and putting Aristion before him, and he distinctly calls him "elder." (6) Moreover, by these remarks he confirms the truth of the story told by those who have said that there were two men in Asia who had the same name, and that there are two tombs in Ephesus, each of which even today is said to be John's. It is important to notice this, for it is probably the second, unless one prefers the first, who saw the Revelation that circulates under the name of John. (7) And Papias, of whom we are now speaking, acknowledges that he had received the words of the apostles from those who had followed them, but he says that he was himself a hearer of Aristion and John the Elder. In any event he frequently mentions them by name and includes their traditions in his writings as well. Let these statements of ours not be wasted on the reader.

(8) It is worthwhile to add to the statements of Papias given

2. *were saying*: lit. *says*, in contrast to the preceding *said*. Lightfoot (*Essays*, 150 n. 3) thinks the difference is only a stylistic one. The entire section is much debated; Schoedel (*Polycarp*, 97–100) has a good discussion of the key issues.

3. *abiding*: or possibly *surviving*.

above other sayings of his, in which he records some other remarkable things as well, which came down to him, as it were, from tradition. (9) That Philip the Apostle resided in Hierapolis with his daughters has already been stated,[4] but now it must be pointed out that Papias, their contemporary, recalls that he heard an amazing story from Philip's daughters. For he reports that in his day a man rose from the dead, and again another amazing story involving Justus, who was surnamed Barsabbas: he drank a deadly poison and yet by the grace of the Lord suffered nothing unpleasant. (10) The Book of Acts records that after the ascension of the Savior the holy apostles put forward this Justus with Matthias and prayed for the choice by lot to fill out their number in place of the traitor Judas; the passage runs as follows: "And they put forward two, Joseph, called Barsabbas, who was surnamed Justus, and Matthias; and they prayed and said. . . . "[5] (11) The same writer has recorded other accounts as having come to him from unwritten tradition, certain strange parables of the Lord and teachings of his and some other statements of a more mythical character. (12) Among other things he says that there will be a period of a thousand years after the resurrection of the dead when the kingdom of Christ will be set up in material form on this earth. These ideas, I suppose, he got through a misunderstanding of the apostolic accounts, not realizing that the things recorded in figurative language were spoken by them mystically.[6] (13) For he certainly appears to be a man of very little intelligence, as one may say judging from his own words. Yet he was the reason that so many ecclesiastical writers after him held the same opinion, on the grounds that he was a man of the early period— like Irenaeus, for example, and anyone else who has expressed similar ideas.

(14) In his writing he also hands on other accounts of the sayings of the Lord belonging to Aristion, who has been mentioned above, and the traditions of John the Elder, to which we refer those interested. For our present purpose we must add to

---

4. Cf. Eusebius, *Church History* 3.31.3.

5. Acts 1:23.

6. *realizing . . . mystically*: or perhaps *understanding the things spoken by them mystically in figurative language*.

his statements already quoted above a tradition concerning Mark, who wrote the Gospel, which has been set forth in these words:

> (15) And the Elder used to say this: "Mark, having become Peter's interpreter, wrote down accurately everything he remembered, though not in order, of the things either said or done by Christ.[7] For he neither heard the Lord nor followed him, but afterward, as I said, followed Peter, who adapted his teachings as needed but had no intention of giving an ordered account of the Lord's sayings. Consequently Mark did nothing wrong in writing down some things as he remembered them, for he made it his one concern not to omit anything which he heard or to make any false statement in them."[8]

Such, then, is the account given by Papias with respect to Mark. (16) But with respect to Matthew the following was said:

> So Matthew composed the oracles in the Hebrew language and each person interpreted them as best he could.[9]

(17) The same writer utilized testimonies from the first letter of John and, likewise, from that of Peter. And he has related another account about a woman accused of many sins before the Lord, which the Gospel According to the Hebrews contains. And these things we must take into account, in addition to what has already been stated.

Eusebius, *Church History* 3.39

---

7. *Christ*: so some MSS and editors, including Lightfoot; other MSS and editors read *the Lord*.

8. For discussions of this much debated passage, see Schoedel, *Polycarp*, 105–19; R. P. Martin, *Mark: Evangelist and Theologian* (Grand Rapids: Zondervan, 1973), 80–83; and M. Hengel, *Studies in the Gospel of Mark* (Philadelphia: Fortress, 1985), 47–50, 69–70.

9. For discussions of this text, see Schoedel, *Polycarp*, 109–10; R. H. Gundry, *Matthew: A Commentary on His Literary and Theological Art* (Grand Rapids: Eerdmans, 1982), 609–20.

4

They went each to his own house, but Jesus went to the Mount of Olives. Early in the morning he came again to the temple and all the people came to him. The scribes and Pharisees *brought a woman who had been taken in sin, and standing her in the midst they spoke to him, the priests putting him to the test in order that they might have some accusation to bring against him: "Teacher, this woman has been caught in the act of adultery. Moses in the law ordered us to stone such women. But now what do you say?"* But Jesus bent down and with his finger wrote on the ground. And as they kept on questioning, [he stood up and said to them: "Let the one who is without sin among you be the first to throw a stone at her."] And again he bent down and with his finger wrote on the ground. [And each one of the Jews went away, beginning with the oldest, with the result that all went away, and he was left alone,] with the woman still in front of him. *Standing up, Jesus said to the woman:* "Where are they? *Has anyone condemned you?" And she said to him:* "No one, sir." *And he said:* "Then neither do I condemn you. You may go; from now on, do not sin again."

The Story of the Woman Caught in Adultery
(John 7:53–8:11), According to Codex Bezae[10]

5

Papias, bishop of Hierapolis, who was a disciple of John the Theologian and a companion of Polycarp, wrote five books on the sayings of the Lord. In them he made a list of apostles, and after Peter and John, Philip and Thomas and Matthew, he included among disciples of the Lord Aristion and another John, whom he also called "the Elder." So, some think that this John is the author of the two short catholic epistles which circulate under the name of John, because the men of the earliest period accept only the first epistle. And some have mistakenly thought that the Apocalypse was also his.

---

10. Only the words in italics likely represent the form of the story known to Papias; see above, pp. 308–9.

And Papias is also in error regarding the millennium, and so is Irenaeus, who follows him.

Papias says in his second book that John the Theologian and James his brother were killed by the Jews. The aforesaid Papias recorded, on the authority of the daughters of Philip, that Barsabbas, who was also called Justus, drank the poison of a snake in the name of Christ when put to the test by the unbelievers and was protected from all harm. He also records other amazing things, in particular one about Manaim's mother, who was raised from the dead. As for those who were raised from the dead by Christ, he states that they survived until the time of Hadrian.

Philip of Side (fifth c.),
Church History[11]

6

After Domitian, Nerva reigned one year. He re-called John from the island[12] and allowed him to live in Ephesus. At that time he was the sole survivor of the twelve disciples, and after writing the Gospel that bears his name was honored with martyrdom. For Papias, the bishop of Hierapolis, who had seen him with his own eyes, claims in the second book of the *Sayings of the Lord* that he was killed by the Jews, thus clearly fulfilling, together with his brother, Christ's prophecy concerning them and their own confession and agreement about this.

For when the Lord said to them, "Are you able to drink the cup that I drink?" and they eagerly assented and agreed, he said: "You will drink my cup and will be baptized with the baptism with which I am baptized."[13] And this is to be expected, for it is impossible for God to lie. Moreover the encyclopedic Origen also affirms in his interpretation of the Gospel According to Matthew that John was martyred, indicating that he had learned this from the successors of the apostles. In addition, the well-informed Eusebius says in his *Ecclesiastical His-*

---

11. C. de Boor, *Texte and Untersuchungen*, vol. 2 (Leipzig, 1888), 170.
12. *island*: i.e., Patmos; cf. Rev. 1:9.
13. Cf. Mark 10:38–39.

tory:[14] "Thomas was alloted Parthia, while John received Asia, where he made his residence and died in Ephesus."

George the Sinner (ninth c.),
Chronicle[15]

7

Papias, a hearer of John and bishop of Hierapolis, wrote only five books, which he entitled *An Exposition of the Discourses of the Lord*. In them, when he asserts in his preface that he is not following diverse conjectures but has the apostles as his authorities, he says:

I used to inquire about what Andrew or Peter had said, or Philip or Thomas or James or John or Matthew, or any other of the Lord's disciples, and what Aristion and John the Elder, disciples of the Lord, were saying. For books to read are not as useful to me as the living voice sounding out clearly up to the present day in the persons of their authors.

From this it is clear that in the list of names itself there is one John who is placed among the apostles, and another, John the Elder, whom he lists after Aristion. We have mentioned this fact because of the statement made above, which we have recorded on the authority of a considerable number of people, that the two later epistles of John are not the work of the Apostle but of the Elder. He is the one who is said to have promulgated the Jewish tradition of a millennium, and he is followed by Irenaeus, Apollinarius, and others, who say that after the resurrection the Lord will reign in the flesh with the saints.

Jerome (ca. 342–420),
Famous Men 18[16]

---

14. *Church History* 3.1.

15. H. Nolte, *Theologische Quartalschrift* 44 (1862): 466–67.

16. *De viris illustribus* 18; edited by E. C. Richardson (*Texte und Untersuchungen* 14,1 [1896]: 19).

8

Moreover, the rumor reaching you—that the books of Josephus and the writings of saints Papias and Polycarp have been
translated by me—is false; I have neither the leisure nor the
strength to translate works such as those into another language
with corresponding elegance.

Jerome, *To Lucinus*
(Letter 71.5)[17]

9

Irenaeus . . . a disciple of Papias (who was a hearer of John
the Evangelist) . . . relates. . . .

Jerome, *To Theodora* (Letter 75.3)[18]

10

Regarding, however, the divine inspiration of the book [i.e.,
the Revelation of John] we think it superfluous to speak at
length, since the blessed Gregory (I mean the Theologian) and
Cyril, and men of an older generation as well, namely Papias,
Irenaeus, Methodius, and Hippolytus, bear witness to its genu-
ineness.

Andrew of Caesarea (563–637),
Preface to the Apocalypse[19]

11

But Papias says, word for word:
"Some of them"—obviously meaning those which once were
holy—"he assigned to rule over the orderly arrangement of the
earth, and commissioned them to rule well." And next he says:
"But as it turned out, their administration came to nothing. And
the great dragon, the ancient serpent, who is called the Devil and

---

17. I. Hilberg, ed., *Sancti Eusebii Hieronymi Epistulae* (CSEL vol. 55;
Vienna/Leipzig, 1912), 6; Eng. trans.: W. H. Fremantle, in *Nicene and Post-
Nicene Fathers*, 2d ser., vol. 6 (New York: Christian Literature, 1893), 153.

18. Hilberg, *Epistulae*, 32; Fremantle, 156.

19. J. Schmid, *Studien zur Geschichte des griechischen Apokalypse-
Textes*, 3 vols. (Munich, 1955/1956), 1:10.

Satan, was cast out; the deceiver of the whole world was cast down to the earth along with his angels."

Andrew of Caesarea, *On the Apocalypse,*
chap. 34, serm. 12[20]

12

. . . taking their cue from the great Papias of Hierapolis, who was a disciple of the Bosom-Friend,[21] and Clement, from Pantaenus, the priest of the Alexandrians, and Ammonius, the most learned scholar, those ancient and earliest interpreters who agree with each other in understanding[22] the whole "six days"[23] to refer to Christ and the church.

Anastasius of Sinai (d. ca. 700),
Considerations on the Hexaemeron 1[24]

13

So then, the more ancient interpreters of the churches—I mean Philo, the philosopher and contemporary of the apostles, and the famous Papias of Hierapolis, the disciple of John the Evangelist, Irenaeus of Lyons and Justin the martyr and philosopher, Pantaenus the Alexandrian and Clement the Stromateus, and their associates—interpreted the sayings about Paradise spiritually, and referred them to the church of Christ.

Anastasius of Sinai,
Considerations on the Hexaemeron 7[25]

14

The blessing thus foretold undoubtedly belongs to the times of the kingdom, when the righteous will rise from the dead and reign, when creation, too, renewed and freed from bondage, will produce an abundance of food of all kinds "from the dew of

20. Ibid., 1:129–30.
21. *Bosom-Friend*: i.e., John the Evangelist; cf. John 13:23, 25; 21:20.
22. *and earliest . . . in understanding*: so some editors; others suggest *interpreters before the councils who understood.*
23. *"six days"*: lit. *hexaemeron*, i.e., the six days of creation in Gen. 1.
24. J. B. Pitra, *Analecta Sacra* 2 (1844): 160–61.
25. H. Nolte, *Theologische Quartalschrift* 49 (1867):55–56.

heaven and from the fertility of the earth,"[26] just as the elders, who saw John the disciple of the Lord, recalled having heard from him how the Lord used to teach about those times and say:

> The days will come when vines will grow, each having ten thousand shoots, and on each shoot ten thousand branches, and on each branch ten thousand twigs, and on each twig ten thousand clusters, and in each cluster ten thousand grapes, and each grape when crushed will yield twenty-five measures of wine. And when one of the saints takes hold of a cluster, another cluster will cry out, "I am better, take me, bless the Lord through me." Similarly a grain of wheat will produce ten thousand heads, and every head will have ten thousand grains, and every grain ten pounds of fine flour, white and clean. And the other fruits, seeds, and grass will produce in similar proportions, and all the animals feeding on these fruits produced by the soil will in turn become peaceful and harmonious toward one another, and fully subject to man.

Papias, a man of the early period, who was a hearer of John and a companion of Polycarp, bears witness to these things in writing in the fourth of his books, for there are five books composed by him. And he goes on to say: "These things are believable to those who believe." "And," he says, "when Judas the traitor did not believe and asked, 'How, then, will such growth be accomplished by the Lord?' ", the Lord said, 'Those who live until those times will see.' "

Irenaeus of Lyons,
Against Heresies 5.33.3–4 (written ca. 180–185)

15

They used to call those who practiced a godly innocence "children," as Papias shows in the first book of the *Expositions of the Lord*, and also Clement of Alexandria in his *Pedagogue*.

Maximus the Confessor (ca. 580–662),
Scholia on Dionysius the Areopagite,
On the Ecclesiastical Hierarchy, chap. 2[27]

26. Cf. Gen. 27:28.
27. J. P. Migne, *Patrologia Graeca*, 4:48.

16

When he says these things he is hinting, I think, at Papias, who was then bishop of Hierapolis in Asia and flourished in the days of the holy Evangelist John. For this Papias, in the fourth book of his *Expositions of the Lord*, mentioned food among the sources of enjoyment in the resurrection. Later on Apollinarius believed this doctrine, which some refer to as the millennium. . . . and Irenaeus of Lyons says the same thing in the fifth book of his *Against Heresies* and cites in support of his statements the above-mentioned Papias.

Maximus the Confessor,
Scholia on Dionysius the Areopagite,
On the Ecclesiastical Hierarchy, chap. 7[28]

17

Indeed, [Stephen Gobarus follows] neither Papias, the bishop and martyr of Hierapolis, nor Irenaeus, the holy bishop of Lyons, when they say that the kingdom of heaven is the enjoyment of certain material foods.

Photius (ninth c.),
Bibliotheca 232[29]

18

From Apollinarius: Judas did not die by hanging but lived on, having been cut down before he choked to death. Indeed, the Acts of the Apostles makes this clear: "Falling headlong, he burst open in the middle and his intestines spilled out."[30] Papias, the disciple of John, recounts this more clearly in the fourth book of the *Exposition of the Sayings of the Lord*, as follows:

> Judas was a terrible, walking example of ungodliness in this world, his flesh so bloated that he was not able to pass through a place where a wagon passes easily, not even his bloated head by itself. For his eyelids, they say, were so swollen that he could not

---

28. Ibid., 4:176.
29. R. Henry, ed., *Photius, Bibliothèque* (Paris, 1967), 5:77.
30. Acts 1:18.

see the light at all, and his eyes could not be seen, even by a doctor using an optical instrument, so far had they sunk below the outer surface. His genitals appeared more loathsome and larger than anyone else's, and when he relieved himself there passed through it pus and worms from every part of his body, much to his shame. After much agony and punishment, they say, he finally died in his own place, and because of the stench the area is deserted and uninhabitable even now; in fact, to this day no one can pass that place unless they hold their nose, so great was the discharge from his body and so far did it spread over the ground.

Apollinaris of Laodicaea (fourth c.);
reconstructed from fragments compiled by various editors[31]

19

Here begins the summary of the Gospel According to John: The Gospel of John was made known and given to the churches by John while he was still in the flesh, as a man of Hierapolis by the name of Papias, a beloved disciple of John, has related in the exoteric[32] —that is, the last—part of his five books. Indeed, he wrote down the Gospel correctly as John dictated.

Codex Vaticanus Alexandrinus 14 (ninth c.)[33]

20

For the last of these, John, surnamed "the Son of Thunder," when he was a very old man (as Irenaeus and Eusebius and a succession of other trustworthy historians have handed it down to us) and about the time when terrible heresies had cropped up, dictated the Gospel to his own disciple, the virtuous Papias of Hierapolis, to complete the message of those before him who had preached[34] to the peoples of the whole world.

Anonymous comment from a commentary[35] on the Gospel
of John consisting of comments drawn
from the writings of various Greek fathers

31. Cf. E. Preuschen, *Antilegomena* (Giessen: Töpelmann, 1905), 97–99.

32. *exoteric*: probably an error for "exegetical"; cf. Schoedel, *Polycarp*, 123.

33. J. B. Pitra, *Analecta Sacra*, 2:160; cf. Lightfoot, *Essays*, 210.

34. *to complete . . . preached*: or possibly *to fill out what was lacking in those before him who had preached the Word.*

35. *Catena patrum Graecorum in sanctum Ioannem*, first published by B. Corder (Antwerp, 1630).

21

But so great a light of godliness shone upon the minds of Peter's listeners that they were not satisfied with a single hearing or with the oral teaching of the divine proclamation. So, with all kinds of exhortations they begged Mark (whose Gospel is extant), since he was Peter's follower, to leave behind a written record of the teaching given to them verbally, and did not quit until they had persuaded the man, and thus they became the immediate cause of the Scripture called "The Gospel According to Mark." And they say that the apostle, aware of what had occurred because the Spirit had revealed it to him, was pleased with their zeal and sanctioned the writing for study in the churches. Clement quotes the story in the sixth book of the *Hypotyposes,* and the bishop of Hierapolis, named Papias, corroborates him. He also says that Peter mentions Mark in his first epistle which, they say, he composed in Rome itself, as he himself indicates, referring to the city metaphorically as Babylon in these words: "She who is in Babylon, who is likewise chosen, sends you greetings, as does Mark, my son."[36]

Eusebius, *Church History* 2.15

22

. . . and the great Methodius . . . and also Irenaeus, bishop of Lyons, and Papias, bishop of Hierapolis; the first won the crown of martyrdom, while the latter two were men of apostolic character. But we do not follow them whenever they treated the truth too lightly and were led to speak against the generally accepted ecclesiastical teaching. We do not at all, however, take anything away from their patristic honor and glory.

Photius, *Letter to Archbishop and Metropolitan Aquileias*[37]

36. 1 Pet. 5:13.

37. J. N. Baletta, *Photii epistolae* (London, 1864; repr. Hildesheim, 1978), letter 1:5, 10 (pp. 196–97); cf. J. Kürzinger, *Papias von Hierapolis und die Evangelien des Neuen Testaments* (Regensburg: Verlag Friedrich Pustet, 1983), 120–21.

23

At this time there lived in Hierapolis a prominent teacher and author of many treatises; he wrote five treatises about the Gospel. In one of these treatises, which he wrote concerning the Gospel of John, he relates that in the book of John the Evangelist there is a report about a woman who was an adulteress. When the people led her before Christ our Lord, he spoke to the Jews who had brought her to him: "Whoever among you is himself certain that he is innocent of that of which she is accused, let him now bear witness against her." After he had said this, they gave him no answer and went away.

Agapius of Hierapolis
(tenth c.), *World History*[38]

24

And Papias spoke in the following manner in his treatises: "Never does heaven receive his terrestrial thanks, because it is impossible for light to participate in darkness. He fell to earth, here to live; and when mankind came here, where he was, he did not permit them to live in natural passions; on the contrary, he enticed them into much evil. But Michael and his legions, who are guardians of the world, help mankind, as Daniel learned; they gave laws and made the prophets wise. And all this was war against the dragon, who sets stumbling blocks for men. Then the war extended into heaven, even to Christ himself. Therefore Christ came; and the law, which was impossible for anyone else, he fulfilled in his body, according to the apostle. He rejected sin and condemned Satan, and spread abroad his righteousness through his death for all. As this occurred, the victory of Michael and his legions, the guardians of mankind, became complete, and the dragon could resist no more. Because the death of Christ destroyed him and threw him to the earth, accordingly Christ said: 'I saw Satan fall from heaven like a lightning bolt.' "

In this sense the teacher understood not his first fall, but the

---

38. Josef Linder, "Papias und die Perikope von der Ehebrecherin (Joh 7,53–8,11) bei Agapius von Manbiğ," *Zeitschrift für Katholische Theologie* 40 (1916): 191–99; cf. Kürzinger, *Papias*, 126–27.

second, which was through the cross; and this did not consist of a spatial fall, as at first, but rather judgment and expectation of a mighty punishment. . . .

Andrew of Caesarea,
On the Apocalypse, on Rev. 12:7–9[39]

25

But concerning the aloe which people brought [to Jesus' tomb; cf. John 19:39], some say that it was a mixture of oil and honey, but aloe is certainly a kind of incense. The Geographer and Papias report that there are fifteen kinds of aloe in India. . . .

Vardan Vardapet (thirteenth c.),
Explanations of Holy Scripture[40]

26

That story of the adulterous woman, which the other Christians have written in their gospel, was written by a certain Papias, a disciple of John, who was declared and condemned as a heretic. Eusebius said this.

Vardan Vardapet,
Explanations of Holy Scripture[41]

THE TRADITIONS OF THE ELDERS

1

But that the age of thirty years is the prime of a young man's ability, and that this extends even to the fortieth year, everyone will admit; but after the fortieth and fiftieth years, it begins to verge toward advanced age. This was our Lord's age when he taught, inasmuch as the Gospel and all the elders who lived with John, the Lord's disciple, in Asia testify that John deliv-

---

39. From the Armenian translation of Constantine of Hierapolis, published by F. Siegert, "Unbeachtete Papiaszitate bei armenischen Schriftstellern," *New Testament Studies* 27 (1981): 605–14; cf. Kürzinger, *Papias*, 128–33.

40. Siegert, "Papiaszitate"; cf. Kürzinger, *Papias*, 132–35.

41. Siegert, "Papiaszitate"; cf. Kürzinger, *Papias*, 134–37.

ered this tradition to them. For he remained with them until the time of Trajan. And some of them saw not only John, but other apostles as well, and heard this same account from them and testify concerning the previously mentioned account.

Irenaeus, *Against Heresies* 2.22.5

2

Where then was the first man placed? In Paradise, obviously, as it is written: "And God planted Paradise eastward in Eden, and there he placed the man whom he had formed." And from there he was expelled into this world, because of his disobedience. Therefore the elders, disciples of the apostles, also say that those who were translated were translated there (for Paradise was prepared for righteous and inspired men; the apostle Paul also was carried there, and "heard words unspeakable,"[42] to us at least in this present life), and that those who are translated will remain there until the end of all things, as a prelude to immortality.

Against Heresies 5.5.1

3

Now such being the state of the case, and since this number is found in all the good and old copies, and the very men who had seen John with their own eyes testify to it, and reason teaches us that the number of the name of the Beast, according to the reckoning of the Greeks (i.e., by the letters contained therein), is 666 . . . some, though I do not know how, have erred, following a particular reading, and have taken liberties with the middle number of the name, subtracting the value of fifty and choosing to have only one ten instead of six.[43]

Against Heresies 5.30.1

42. Cf. 2 Cor. 12:4.
43. I.e., 616; cf. Rev. 13:18.

4

The blessing thus foretold undoubtedly belongs to the times of the kingdom . . . just as the elders, who saw John the disciple of the Lord, recalled having heard from him. . . .

Against Heresies 5.33.3 (see fragment 14 above)

5

As the elders say, then[44] will those who have been deemed worthy of an abode in heaven go there, while others will enjoy the delight of Paradise, and still others will possess the brightness of the city; for in every place the Savior will be seen, to the degree that those who see him are worthy. They say, moreover, that this is the distinction between the dwelling of those who bring forth a hundredfold, and those who bring forth sixtyfold, and those who bring forth thirtyfold: the first will be taken up into the heavens, and the second will dwell in Paradise, and the third will inhabit the city. For this reason, therefore, our Lord has said, "In my Father's house there are many rooms";[45] for all things are of God, who gives to all their appropriate dwelling. . . . The elders, the disciples of the apostles, say that this is the order and arrangement of those who are being saved, and that they advance by such steps, and ascend through the Spirit to the Son, and through the Son to the Father, the Son finally yielding his work to the Father, as it is also said by the apostle: "For he must reign until he puts all enemies under his feet."[46]

Against Heresies 5.36.1–2.

44. *then*: i.e., after the appearance of the new heaven and new earth.
45. John 14:2.
46. Cf. 1 Cor. 15:25.

Index of Subjects and Authors

Index of Scripture
and Extrabiblical Literature

OLD TESTAMENT

NEW TESTAMENT

SEPTUAGINT

JEWISH PSEUDEPIGRAPHA

OLD TESTAMENT APOCRYPHA

APOSTOLIC FATHERS

EARLY CHRISTIAN AND GNOSTIC WRITINGS

PAPYRI

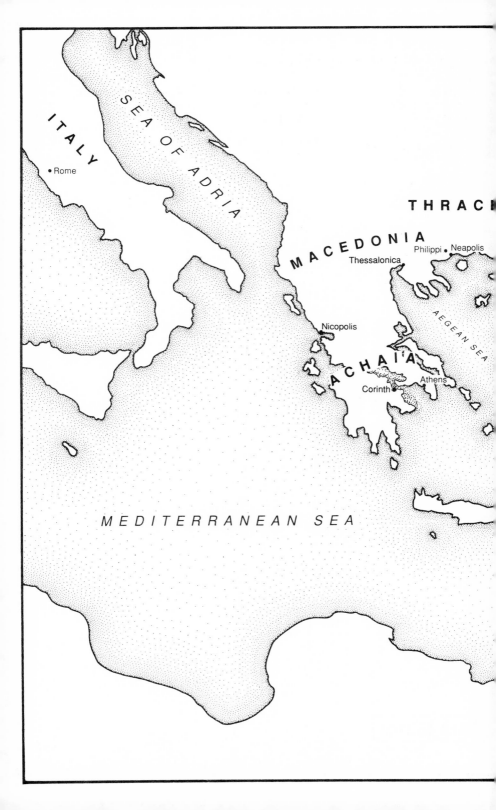

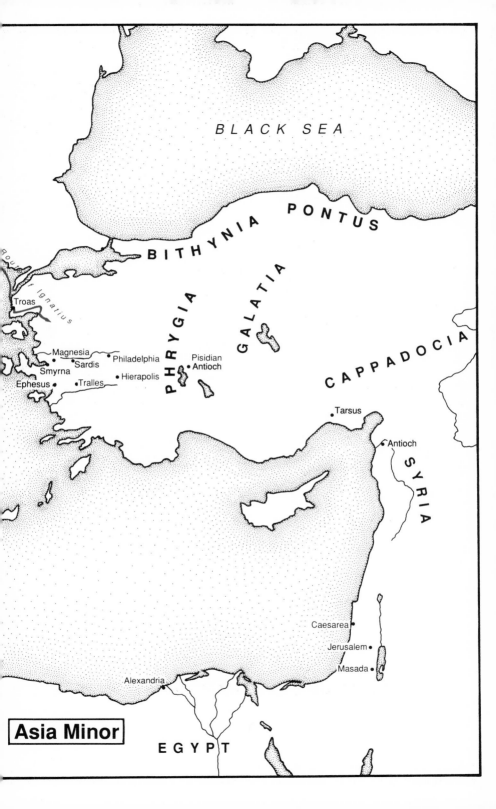

BLACK SEA

BITHYNIA PONTUS

PHRYGIA

GALATIA

CAPPADOCIA

SYRIA

EGYPT

Route of Ignatius

Troas

Magnesia
Sardis
Smyrna
Ephesus
Tralles
Philadelphia
Hierapolis
Pisidian
Antioch

Tarsus

Antioch

Caesarea

Jerusalem

Masada

Alexandria

Asia Minor

The Spread of Christianity